# DOLLS AND PUPPETS

BY
MAX VON BOEHN

TRANSLATED BY
JOSEPHINE NICOLL

WITH A NOTE ON PUPPETS BY
GEORGE BERNARD SHAW

*With Thirty Plates in Colour and
464 other Illustrations*

WOMAN HOLDING A MALE DOLL
Sessai Tsu Kioka. About 1800

# NOTE ON PUPPETS

## *By* GEORGE BERNARD SHAW

[IN the original German a translation of a letter sent by Mr Shaw to Vittorio Podrecca appears in the text after the quotation from Eleonora Duse (p. 395). Feeling that in its passage through two or three languages back to English the ideas might have suffered, I sent my literal rendering together with the German translation to Mr Shaw, who, declaring that he could not now " recapture the original wording " of the letter, very generously sent me a modified version, with a comment to say that he had originally written to Podrecca giving it as his view that " flesh-and-blood actors can learn a great deal about their art from puppets, and that a good puppet-show should form part of the equipment of every academy of stage art." Since the passage printed here has not the form and wording of the letter once sent to Podrecca, and in view of its great importance, I thought it best to abstract it from the position it occupied in Herr von Boehn's book and print it in this place, although strictly it applies to the section on the marionettes.—*Translator.*]

I ALWAYS hold up the wooden actors as instructive object-lessons to our flesh-and-blood players. The wooden ones, though stiff and continually glaring at you with the same overcharged expression, yet move you as only the most experienced living actors can. What really affects us in the theatre is not the muscular activities of the performers, but the feelings they awaken in us by their aspect; for the imagination of the spectator plays a far greater part there than the exertions of the actors.. The puppet is the actor in his primitive form. Its symbolic costume, from which all realistic and historically correct impertinences are banished, its unchanging stare petrified (or rather lignified) in a grimace expressive to the highest degree attainable by the carver's art, the mimicry by which it suggests human gesture in unearthly caricature—these give to its performance an intensity to which few actors can pretend, an intensity which imposes on our imagination like those images in immovable hieratic attitudes on the stained glass of Chartres Cathedral, in which the gaping tourists seem like little lifeless dolls moving jerkily in the draughts from the doors, reduced to sawdusty insignificance by the contrast with the gigantic vitality in the windows overhead.

G. B. S.

# ACKNOWLEDGMENT

THE author and the publishers wish to thank those in charge of various public and private collections who have given help in the preparation of this book. They feel that they are specially indebted to the following: the Department of Prints at the Staatliche Kunstbibliothek, the Kunstgewerbe Museum, and the Propyläen-Verlag, Berlin; Herr Georg Zink, the town librarian at Heidelberg; Privatdozent Dr Carl Niessen, of Cologne; the Victoria and Albert Museum and the Bethnal Green Museum, London; the Bayerische National-Museum, the Museum für Völkerkunde, the Theater-Museum (Clara-Ziegler Foundation), and the Armee-Museum, Munich; the Germanische National-Museum, the Bayerische Landesgewerbe Anstalt, Nürnberg; the Staatliche Porzellanmanufaktur, Nymphenburg; M. Henri d'Allemagne, of Paris; the Spielzeug-Museum, Sonneberg; the Kunstgewerbe Museum, Zürich.

Herr Dr Lutz Weltmann, of Berlin, was good enough to allow the use of his literary material for a history of the puppet theatre; for this both the author and the publishers welcome the opportunity of offering him their particular thanks. Dr Weltmann's studies were directed principally toward the literary significance of the puppet theatre, and that subject could not have been introduced into this book without making it inordinately lengthy. It is sincerely to be hoped that Dr Weltmann may have the opportunity of bringing before the public his valuable researches.

Grateful acknowledgment is also due to Herr Direktor Dr Glaser, of Berlin, and Herr Geheimrat Dr Schnorr von Carolsfeld, of Munich, for their courtesy and assistance in providing access to the collections under their care.

YOUNG GIRL WITH DOLL AND DOLL'S CRADLE
Woodcut by the artist using the monogram I.R.
About 1540

# CONTENTS

## PART I: DOLLS

## PART II: PUPPETS

# DOLLS AND PUPPETS

# ILLUSTRATIONS

## PLATES IN COLOUR

11

# DOLLS AND PUPPETS

## ILLUSTRATIONS IN THE TEXT

# ILLUSTRATIONS

13

# DOLLS AND PUPPETS

# ILLUSTRATIONS

15

# DOLLS AND PUPPETS

16

# ILLUSTRATIONS

# DOLLS AND PUPPETS

# ILLUSTRATIONS

19

# DOLLS AND PUPPETS

20

# ILLUSTRATIONS

21

# DOLLS AND PUPPETS

# DOLLS AND PUPPETS

## PART I: DOLLS

I

### PREHISTORIC IDOLS

THE doll is the three-dimensional representation of a human figure, a plastic creation, which, however, is far removed from the sphere of the fine arts. It has about as much in common with art as the ape has with *homo sapiens*. Both enjoy a complete freedom from dependence on material: in all three realms of nature there is no substance out of which a doll or a work of art cannot be made. In their dimensions also they are so far alike that each may fluctuate in size from a few millimetres to a considerable number of metres. Apart from that it is easier to feel the difference between them than to frame an indisputable definition. This is due to the fact that they proceed from the same source. In the doll we have before us the beginnings of fine art; and to-day, following the precedent of Alois Riegl, these beginnings are recognized to lie in the field of sculpture. Sculpture has the power of reproducing directly corporeal forms. Its subject not only can be appreciated through the eye,

FIG. I. MARBLE IDOL FROM TROY (THIRD BURNED CITY)

like drawing and painting, but, since it can be touched and handled on all sides, appeals to all the senses. Plastic art can be grasped even by primitive man without special training, for it remains within the sphere of all living things familiar with the three dimensions of matter. Painting and drawing presuppose a cultural development which, whether in the creative process or in the appreciation, must abstract from the reality and mentally translate the object on to a flat plane.

The first, still tentative, attempt at formative plastic modelling is the doll, but when this plastic modelling develops into art the

23

doll does not disappear; one might say that while the doll was not permitted to enter into art's holy of holies it was allowed to remain in the courtyard of the temple. Art, in rejecting the non-essential and the fortuitous, has striven to present a reflection of the soul; the doll has renounced this psychological motive in order to accentuate and intensify the shallow and the external. The creations of art have to take the spectator's imagination into account; the doll does not allow the slightest scope for the play of the imagination. The sculptor of the present day works

according to the same rules and with the same methods as his predecessor thousands of years ago. He directs his attention to the emotions and reaches the same result as they. The doll, on the contrary, has forced into its service all the refinements of a progressive technique, not striving toward an æsthetic impression, but aiming at ever completer illusion. It can come surprisingly close to nature, but the nearer it approaches its goal the farther is it removed from art; it can create an illusion, but the true essence of artistic enjoyment—the raising of the soul to a higher plane—is denied to it.

Properly speaking, the doll is regarded now only as a child's toy, but, if its historical development be examined, it will be found that the toy doll appears at a comparatively late stage. The doll form, the more or less complete representation of man, existed for thousands of years before the first child took possession of it. For adults it possessed

FIG. 2. LEAD
IDOL FROM TROY

an occult significance with mystical-magical associations which in an inexplicable way united the present and the past and reached deep into the world of the unseen.

If the genesis of the doll is sought for it will be found, according to the views of Ernst Vatter and of other scholars, in a quality, which is shared alike by primitive races and by children—namely, the ability to discern human and animal forms in all sorts of freaks of nature. Natural and fortuitously developed forms, recognizable in rocks, horns, bones, branches, and roots, must have stimulated the imagination of primitive men, and must have been the point of departure for the shaping, often with but trifling modifications, of figures which were at least something like human beings. In this connexion mention must be made of the so-called *Lösskindel* (loess dolls)—concretions of loam which are occasionally found at Löss and by chance often assume human form. The museum at Strasbourg possesses several examples from Achenheim. Among Palæolithic sculptures it is often to be recognized that the original shape of the material has evidently suggested the object finally represented by the artist. These 'figure stones,' natural fragments of rock in which the more or less striking resemblance to human or animal forms seems to have been still further accentuated by the work of the artist, stand at the very beginning of plastic statuary, and H. Klaatsch would associate them with the otherwise entirely inartistic Neanderthal man. In these he sees the first attempts made to depict natural objects. This tendency to let natural forms which resemble certain objects influence the modelling of figures has remained until the present day peculiar to the spirit of the folk, and forms a striking characteristic in the wood-carving technique of the Alpine pastoral art.

FIG. 3. FLAT BONE IDOLS FROM TROY

For long the sculpture which was concerned with the representation of human beings remained stationary at this stage of strict dependence on the forms offered directly by nature itself. Hörnes draws attention to the fact that periods of incalculable length, whole thousands of years of primitive culture, are filled with precisely the same sort of art products, and that this runs completely counter to our expectation of finding progress and development everywhere or to our theories cast in terms of decadence and decay.

FIG. 4. AMBER IDOL FROM SCHWARZORT

To the sophisticated modern eye the small plastic figures of prehistoric times will hardly seem like images of men at all. They are blocklike, body, head, and limbs of one piece, with the distribution of the limbs indicated by mere scratches. Originally perhaps the features were accentuated by colours which have been obliterated by their long lying in the ground. The art of representation among the prehistoric peoples in this respect runs parallel with that of the nature peoples. There too are figures lacking completely arms and legs; a step forward is marked when two independent legs can be traced; the insertion

25

of arms usually came last. The correspondence between the art of the polar races and that of the Palæolithic is so great that Hildebrand assumes a direct descent of the Arctic peoples from the Palæolithic, regarding the Eskimos as the Aurignac race of to-day. He makes this assertion on the basis of the small statuettes which are by them produced skilfully with the same materials and with the same tools as were at the command of the Palæolithic peoples.

FIG. 5. RED CLAY IDOL
About 3000 B.C.

The discoveries made by Schliemann in the most ancient strata of Troy permit us to follow the development from the formless stone to the human figure. First come the small coniform stones, which only gradually assume human shapes, and do so only if the observer brings with him a lively imagination and a keen desire to recognize this metamorphosis. In the most ancient specimens the head is wanting; a pointed piece of stone to indicate a head marks a higher stage; then a long developed neck appears; and finally small indentations are to be noted as characteristic features, a great advance being made when scratched lines indicate hair, eyes, nose, frontal arches, and necklace. So far as arms are concerned, this type of art does not go beyond the barest suggestion. These sculptures of the Neolithic Age, also called 'board idols,' because of their excessively flat-shaped bodies, give the impression of having originated from plain flat pebbles which could be adapted to human shape by a simple process of cutting and boring. ·

Closely allied in form to these are the little amber figures, likewise belonging to the Stone Age, which have been dredged up in the Kurisches Haff, East Prussia. For long men adhered to this board-like type. When, however, the artists proved themselves no longer dependent on stones they had found, but had learned to model in clay, there appeared at Cyprus idols of baked clay which just indicated the features, hair, and ornaments by means of white, indented, decorative lines. Only in the upper part of the body can modelling in a true sense be spoken of; the lower part becomes a rectangular 'cake,' which, according to

FIG. 6. CAKE-FORMED IMAGES IN TERRA-COTTA
Cyprus

the highly plausible suggestion of Hörnes, was probably covered with pieces of cloth. Among the bronzes of the Hallstatt and of the first Iron Age these flat idols are again met with; worked in

| FIG. 7. PHŒNICIAN TERRA-COTTA IDOL Sidon | FIG. 8. FEMALE TERRA-COTTA IDOL FROM NIPPUR, CHALDÆA | FIG. 9 EARLY TERRA-COTTA IDOL FROM TANAGRA |

metal, they give the impression of sawed-out or stamped-out tin. A whole depot of such little dolls, which might be regarded as the ancestors of our tin soldiers, was brought to light at Todi, near Perugia.

27

The 'board idols' of Hissarlik are undoubtedly the most. primitive examples of prehistoric sculpture, but they are by no means the most ancient. Indeed, the attempts to produce representations of the human form might be traced back to the beginnings of the human race itself, even back to the Ice Age. They begin in the Quaternary period with the Aurignacian civilization in the first half of the fourth Ice Age, and continue through the Solutrian down to the Magdalenian, a period which,

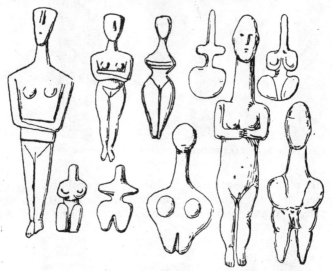

FIG. 10. PRE-MYCENÆAN STONE SCULPTURE
Idols from Amorgos, Naxos

according to Penck, covers about 30,000 to 50,000 years. In the Palæolithic caves of France, at Brassempouy, in the Grimaldi grottoes near Mentone, in Switzerland, and in Moravia figurines have been found which, although they are made of a material—steatite—easy to manipulate, are executed in a very rough and ready manner. The artist's aim has not once gone beyond mere suggestion of features, although, on the other hand, there is a highly abnormal development of breasts and hips. The best-known example of the whole of this group is the so-called 'Willendorf Venus,' which comes from the Aurignacian culture of Willendorf, near Krems, on the Danube. This little figure, only 11 cm. high, is made of limestone and was originally painted red.

Female obesity, which leads to exaggerated development of the lower part of the body, must have dominated men's tastes completely for centuries; it is found spread over the whole of Europe in the relics of primitive statuary, extending to the Mediterranean islands and as far as Egypt. The Hottentots still

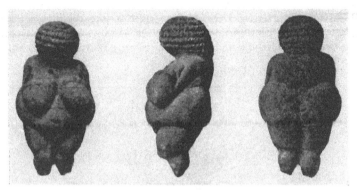

FIG. 11. THE SO-CALLED 'WILLENDORF VENUS'
Palæolithic limestone idol

adhere to this ideal, as Schweinfurth discovered during his explorations in Africa. In art it was dominant up to the later Stone Age, with especial persistence in the Balkans. In excavations in Serbia, Rumania, Bulgaria, East Rumelia, and Thessaly,

FIG. 12. PRIMITIVE BRONZE DOLLS OF PREHISTORIC TIMES

alongside others of a stick-like shape, these exaggeratedly obese figurines are frequently met with. Nowadays the original forms are sought for in the sculpture of early African negro art. From such figures with steatopygous bodies the violin-shaped idols,

29

belonging to a culture which extends beyond that of Mycenæ, no doubt originated. During the Copper-Bronze Age these so-called 'violin idols' were disseminated across the Cyclades as far as Troy.

Prehistoric statuettes were at first represented as completely naked, then with diadems, while in the final stage attempts were made to delineate the dress. The artists were conventional, and

FIG. 13. CLAY DOLL FROM
MYCENÆ
1000–800 B.C.

FIG. 14. MARBLE
DOLL FROM DELOS

lost themselves in stylization which, as, for example, in the clay figurines discovered on the Greek mainland in the late Mycenæan strata, departed far from nature. The 'Rhakmany idols' of Thessaly too belong to the group of statuettes in which only the merest outline of human form is rendered. These are bipartite, consisting of a cone-formed peg stuck into a wide socket. The peg represents the head, the socket the body, while two wing-like appendages indicate arms; eyes and nose are supplied by painting.

In Europe during the later Stone Age two centres of the so-called idol statuary were established, the common model of which probably derives from the East. One was situated in

30

Southern Russia, and extended from the Pontine coast across East Galicia and Transylvania as far as Southern Moravia and Silesia. This statuary is traceable through Rumania, Serbia,

FIG. 15
TERRA-COTTA
IDOL FROM
TIRYNS

FIG. 16. FEMALE CLAY
IDOL FROM KNOSSOS,
CRETE
1800–1600 B.C.

Bosnia, and Bulgaria. The figurines, almost always female, are made of clay; they stand naked, in an upright position, with closed legs; the arms are mere stumps. The face is indicated only

FIG. 17. CLAY IMAGES, WITH INDICATION OF TATTOOING, FOUND IN
CUCUTENI, NEAR JASSY, RUMANIA
Late neolithic

in crude outline; the eyes are represented by points and holes; the nose sticks out from the mass like a beak. Several examples, especially those originating in the Balkans, are ornamented with indented or painted spirals, which, it is conjectured, must represent

31

tattooing. The second group is that of the so-called 'island figures,' little images from 15 to 40 cm. high, carved very

FIG. 18. NEOLITHIC 'ISLAND FIGURES'
Greece

crudely and roughly from limestone and marble. These are found on the Greek islands as far as the coast of Egypt. Hörnes

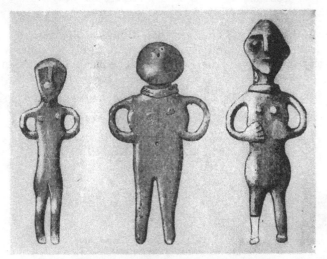

FIG. 19. BRONZE DOLLS FROM KÄLLEBORG AND SCHONEN
About 700 B.C.

is inclined to trace their origin to the Babylonian goddess Istar, while Reinach attributes to them a European origin. The farther north from Egypt are the localities where these pieces have been

PREHISTORIC IDOLS

unearthed the more primitive is the execution, because, as
Robert Forrer suggests, of the rustic treatment of the work of the
better southern artists.

The productions of prehistoric statuary, thanks to their small
size, were disseminated over the whole world of European culture. Late Neolithic Iberian idols of limestone, alabaster, slate,
or bone are so similar to the Trojan figures and 'island figures'
of the Ægean Sea as easily to be mistaken for these. It is uncertain whether this similarity results from the lack of ability in the
primitive modellers or only from a scrupulous retention of early
tradition; at any rate, the imaginative quality which they displayed must have been understood by all races.

As we have observed in connexion with the Trojan figurines,
all these images pass through diverse stages or planes of perfection.
At one end are coarse little blocks of stone or clay difficult of
identification, and at the other images which at least resemble
natural form. The treatment may be rough or it may be excessively painstaking. Hörnes has proved that the technique and
decoration of the clay figures correspond in all details to the then
predominating styles in ceramic art, and that these figures have
obviously come from the hands of potters. To whichever periods
they may belong, however, to whichever region and whichever
style, one characteristic is common to the prehistoric figures—
their subjects are confined almost exclusively to women. The
features may be neglected, the limbs may be treated carelessly,
but the sexual features of women are accentuated and brought
into undue prominence. The strong preponderance of feminine
forms prevails in the doll world even now; in a hundred modern
dolls twelve at the most of the masculine gender can be counted.
The explanation of these two facts—that the plastic representation of woman precedes by a long time that of man, and that it
is to be found so much more abundantly among extant remains
—must be sought for in the communal standard of centuries
based on the mother-right. Man's prehistoric cultural life
comes very close to the cultureless existence of the animal world;
the mother occupies the higher rôle in the social order; the conception of the father's importance has not yet developed.

Male figurines of the early period are so rare that they can
well-nigh be counted separately, and they do not become com-
moner before the first Iron Age. While the female figurines
display only the sexual features, without any recognizable association with the world around them, the figures of men, representing
warriors, have a special importance, owing to the accessories
assigned to them. Probably the earliest of these are the *schardana*

c

33

figures, abundantly unearthed in Sardinia and Italy, so called
because this (*schardana*) was the name used by the Phœnicians
and the Egyptians for the Sardinian mercenaries who, about the
year 1000 B.C., were serving in the Egyptian battalions. The
little bronze figures, of Phœnician style, bear tall helmets, small
shields, and short swords. The Hallstatt and La Tène periods
are relatively richer in metal figurines of warriors. Such have
been found in Istria bearing Etruscan helmets, with movable
rings on the arms and the legs, and with a third ring passing
between the legs through the barely suggested clothing. In the

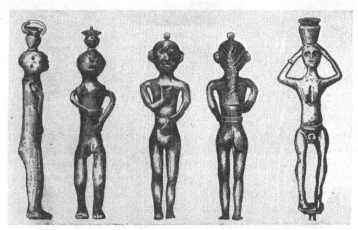

FIG. 20.  ETRUSCAN BRONZE DOLLS FOUND IN NOVILARA AND VERONA
Eighth century B.C.

deepest layer of the Altis (the sacred grove of Jove) at Olympia
was discovered a similar bronze statuette, an archaic Greek
warrior with face-helmet, breastplate, and greaves. To the prehistoric Egyptians belong the 'stake figures,' which consist of
sticks at the top of which are faces, generally scratched out in a
rough manner, and made lifelike only occasionally, not always,
by means of inserted eyes. A thickening represents the body;
the arms and legs are not delineated at all. There are also
female 'stake figures,' which indicate their sex by a drawing in of
the waist, an expansion of the hips, and an arching of the breast.
In Africa these figures still hold their ground, for Carl Hagemann,
who travelled there for several years, discovered that the Was-
seramo tribe, in East Africa, fenced in their dancing place with
fantastically arrayed stick images of the same kind.
    The prehistoric period provides an immense wealth of

statuettes, which we must call 'dolls,' difficult of classification. No documentary tradition accompanies them. The question naturally arises: What do they represent? A former generation of scholars gave an unhesitating reply; without further consideration they regarded as idols everything that could not be explained. Thus, Schliemann at once thought of the numerous dolls which were found at Troy as representations of the 'owl-headed' Athena. Since then Schuchhardt has discredited "the layman's

FIG. 21. ETRUSCAN BRONZE
FIGURE OF A WOMAN
700–600 B.C.

FIG. 22. PRIMITIVE
BRONZE DOLL

tendency to relate everything unexpected in the relics of prehistoric times to sacrifice and adoration," and consequently other explanations have been sought.

Was it only that the primitive play of imagination was here at work, the creative instinct of man, the endeavour to establish the imaginative pictures which arose in his mind, an instinct in which Conze descries the first motive for the art of sculpture? Must one not suppose that these naïve creations were designed to express fully defined ideas, and that they present not only the first still childish examples of sculpture, but the earliest evidence for the awakening of intellect among the primitive peoples? No animal, not even the most intelligent, can, consciously and voluntarily, create images of itself. Since man had advanced

35

sufficiently to make such images he must have left far behind him that primitive condition when his only cares were for nourishment and reproduction. Without absolute certainty, but with some justifications from analogy, we may draw a parallel between the condition of the nature peoples of to-day (or, at least, of those who were so before they had the misfortune to come into contact with Europeans) and of the primitive races.

The whole of nature is regarded by children and savages as animated; they believe in the power of material objects, in their ability and will to bring benefits or injuries. Hence primitive man feels himself always and everywhere menaced, subject to unknown powers which encircle him at every step, a terrifying emanation of his animistic conception of the world. So the image which he himself had created was regarded by him not as a dead object. We know further, from a very much later time, that classic antiquity did not consider its sculpture as a dead thing, but assumed that it was inspired with divine life. From this belief originated the legends concerning statues which moved of their own accord, raised their hands, and shut their eyes. The myths of the Christian Church took over these conceptions, and had to tell of more than one crucifix which spoke, wept, shed blood, and so forth. In Semitic thought too a demonic element is not to be separated from the representation of man. The Koran has appropriated this notion, for according to its teaching every image made in idle folly will demand a soul from its maker at doomsday. Woe to him! For, since he cannot give it, he will be damned. When some travellers once presented Baghdad women with dolls for their children, these women looked on the gifts as spirits, and retained them in order to keep their children from harm. The doll is put into the sphere of that great mystery which lies in the other world, and is associated with those thoughts which cannot grasp the supernatural, but seek to draw it nearer by means of signs and symbols.

# II
## ANCESTOR IMAGES

THE mere existence of all these figures testifies to the fact that their makers had arrived at a high stage of knowledge. They must have possessed a religion, and must have been able to formulate conceptions of the unknown powers on which they felt themselves dependent. This feeling expressed itself in awe and terror, a spiritual condition which of itself was bound to lead· to the desire of finding protection against inimical influences and of seeking for means of defence. The helplessness of man in face of death must have passed most directly into his consciousness. Not unjustly has Feuerbach called the grave the birthplace of the gods.

To the nature peoples the death of a relation does not signify his complete annihilation, but merely a change in existence. The dead man continues to belong to the family, for it is believed that, although he is invisible, he is near to the living and has the power of returning. Since it is robbed of all pleasures the soul is regarded as full of envy and vindictiveness, and for this reason the Indians of South America consider the dead to be tormenting spirits. From this conviction regarding the insoluble connexion between the present and the past originates that ancestor-worship which is one of the most important elements in primitive culture. The belief in the immortality of the spirit life which is thus manifested truly settled the trend of religious thought among primitive races. To this spirit-complex they have given a material being by transferring it to sculpture. The ancestor images represent the dead and form a substitute for the dead, since all the spiritual qualities of the deceased have passed into them. It is the dead man himself who, in sculptured form, continues to participate in the life of the community.

Ancestor-worship has led to still further developments; for, since the image constitutes an object of veneration and adoration, it soon becomes an idol. So long as all the sculptured images of man in the art of the nature peoples were regarded as idols, all the prehistoric figures were designated as idols also. Since it has come to be recognized that the majority of these figures

37

among the nature peoples are really ancestor images, a change has taken place in the attitude toward the extant prehistoric examples. The decision has therefore been reached that the idol theory must be abandoned and that the majority of these primitive figures are to be regarded as ancestor images.

However, the assurance is hardly required that in this mystical sphere, where we move doubtfully on unsure ground in almost complete darkness, no sharply defined boundaries are to be determined. Everything is in a state of flux, and no one can say with certainty at what point the ancestor image becomes an idol, or when and where it develops into the fetish, the amulet, the talisman, but it is safe to assume that the ancestor figure formed the starting-point of all the attempts to gain an influence over the dominating principle in the unseen and other world. The living look to the ancestor image for protection from harm: hence the veneration with which it is regarded—a veneration which is manifested among the negroes by the smearing of the image with oil and blood. Among the Golds (or Tunguses) and Gilyaks of Amur meat and drink are set before the *panja*, a figure which represents the dead—even pipes for smoking are provided. During the great fast held after the death of a member of the Chevsuri tribe, in the Caucasus, an image clothed in the dress of the dead man is placed on his grave; relatives and friends make offerings of drink and grain to this figure and hold a night watch over it. On the death of a distinguished Mongolian the corpse is burned. Then the ashes are gathered together, mixed with clay, and formed into a human-shaped figure, which is set up on the site of the pyre. These figures are held to be holy. It is but a step to the offering before an idol.

The early stages of the ancestor cult can be traced back to the middle of the Palæolithic period. Even then men must often have been afraid of the return of the dead; through this conception alone can be explained the peculiar method of burial whereby the corpse was set in its grave in a crouching position with the limbs tightly bound—a practice designed to prevent the dead from returning. The continued worship of the dead resulted from the practice of burying bodies first in dwelling caves and later in houses. "Among our forefathers," writes Servius, "all the dead were buried in the houses; this is the origin of the worship of the *lares*." From the coexistence of dead and living in one room arose the Roman conception of ancestors as house gods, which assumed visible form in the *di penates* and the *lar familiaris*. These ancestor spirits, as patron gods of the Roman house, were responsible for the family's prosperity. Their little images, made of wood, polished and shining with wax, were set up on the hearth in the *atrium* and were allowed to participate in the family meals, small dishes of food being placed before them. They were represented in the high-girdled, short-sleeved Doric *chiton*, with a piece of cloth as a belt. On their feet they wore short boots. In their right hands they held drinking-horns and in their left shells for offerings.

The *atrium* of many a better-class house had even a special cupboard in which the *imagines* of the ancestors were kept. At first only the death-mask was taken, and with its help was made a realistically painted and equipped bust, with glass eyes, real hair, and draped in cloth—a custom which was followed up to the fourth century B.C. Later life-size images were produced to represent the entire figure of the dead man. One of these, having the body of wood and the head, hands, and feet of wax, was dressed in the festival garments of the deceased and took his place. At some special obsequies of those related to patrician houses these *imagines* were carried in processions.

The primitive Trojan figurines which Schliemann had regarded as idols are now considered to be similar ancestor images, which were looked upon as the seat of the souls of the departed, and were preserved in the house. At Butmir, in Bosnia, and at Jablanica, in Serbia, so many Neolithic clay figurines have been brought to light that it is impossible to believe that these were not ancestor images. At Butmir seventy-two human figurines were found, the largest 20 cm. high. They were formed like little blocks, the heads on long necks, the features barely indicated. Some were naked, others clothed; among the latter even ornaments and headdress were represented. At Jablanica there were eighty-three figures, exclusively of women. Very similar images have been discovered in Bulgaria; the latter bear a strong resemblance to ordinary chess-men.

The course of development of the ancestor image among the nature peoples of to-day has been clearly sketched out by Eckart von Sydow in his entertaining studies. The mere preservation of the dead man's skull marks the lowest stage. The second stage is reached when this skull is fitted to a wooden frame, whereby the figure is rendered complete. A nose and ears of wood are added, and eyes are supplied from fruit kernels or glass beads. In the New Hebrides a reproduction of the entire body is attempted. On the dead man's skull itself is modelled a face made of coco fibre, clay, and adhesive tissue. Over the surface a resinous stuff is spread and then painted. A stick is added for a nose, round snails' shells for eyes; the deceased's own hair is

39

used, and a plume stuck on the top; the body is built up of
bamboo, straw, and bark fibre, and then is covered with resin;

FIG. 23. TUB OF ANCESTORS' SKULLS OF THE NGUMBA (CAMEROONS),
WITH MALE AND FEMALE ANCESTOR FIGURES

painting emphasizes details such as navel, nipples, knees,
toes, and fingers. The whole figure is then provided with

clothing, feathered ornaments, and armlets; in its right hand it is given a shell horn and in the left the jaw-bone of a pig; and at great festivals food is set before it. Such images, however, in tropical climates were liable to swift decay, and the third stage is marked by the making of the entire figure out of carved wood hung round with cloth and rags. A striving toward lifelikeness is often obvious here; among the Maoris even the tattooing of the face is closely imitated.

Africa and Oceania are the chief centres of this ancestor-image

FIG. 24. ANCESTOR FIGURE OF THE BANGWA (CAMEROONS)

FIG. 25. ANCESTOR FIGURE OF THE BALUBA (BELGIAN CONGO)

FIG. 26. FEMALE AN-CESTOR IMAGE OF THE BALUBA (BELGIAN CONGO)

cult. In Neu Mecklenburg, Polynesia, the ancestor images are made to commission by hand-workers as an ordinary article of trade. These exceedingly primitive objects, made of chalk, have cylindrical bodies, with arms marked out in relief. They are painted a red-brown and are of two types, male and female, the sexual features being strongly emphasized. On the Solomon Islands and throughout Melanesia are to be found similar wooden figures, 8 to 11 cm. high, on which the marks of tattooing on face and body are duly indicated. Hair and beard are represented by small bristly heads of corn, the eyes by lozenge-shaped pieces of mother-of-pearl. These figures are supposed to symbolize the ancestors. The *korwars* of Papuan negroes of West New Guinea are very similar in form and have the same purpose. They are made of dark wood, and at their manufacture by the medicine-men the relatives of the deceased have to be present. The *korwar*, designed to catch the spirit of the dead man, is carefully preserved. At Sumatra, Celebes, and the neighbouring islands ancestor images, 24 to 27 cm. high, are roughly carved from wood, special prominence being given to the sexual features.

FIG. 27. WOODEN IDOLS FROM SUMATRA

These figures, clothed with small patches of cloth and orna-mented with feathers, represent deceased relatives and are hung up in the houses; it is the custom to give them once a year a sacrificial offering in the shape of an egg, a hen, or a pig. The New Zealand natives also preserve in their houses small carved-wood figures, in each of which dwells an ancestor's spirit. In India small hollow clay figures, in which the souls of Brahmins reside after death, are manufactured by the thousand. The Pangwe, an African tribe, set up male and female figures as tokens on the barrels in which the skulls of their forefathers are collected together. In course of time the images are separated from the receptacle on which they served only as a kind of epitaph, and so become independent.

This interesting tribe both makes use of its ancestor images at those high festivals which are concerned with the worship of the dead and employs them as marionettes, much as the figures in European puppet-shows. The images have feather crests on their heads, and the lower part of their bodies is covered with cloth. They are taken in the hand and made to dance in front of a curtain; they turn and shake, climb up the curtain, and finally, as if tired out by their exertions, hang downward. Whether this play is native to them or influenced by Europeans seemingly cannot now be determined.

FIG. 28. WOODEN ANCESTOR IMAGES FROM SUMATRA

Not only among the southern peoples is ancestor-worship common. On the south-western coast of Alaska are to be found monuments to the dead which consist of figures roughly worked out and dressed with cloth. The Cheremis, a Finnish tribe, until a short time ago were in the habit of placing in a corner of their houses ancestor images in the form of roughly carved wooden male figures dressed up in cloth. Often the ancestor images of the African negroes do not exceed the size of small ivory dolls, and are worn by the living on neck or arm; this indicates the passage of the ancestor image into the amulet and talisman. The æsthetic value of these tiny figures is almost negligible. It is to be noted that in these statuettes the head is rendered extraordinarily large in relation to the body and the body in relation to the limbs—a peculiarity which gives the clue to the estimation in which these parts of the body are held, since, by analogy with the living, it is presumed that in the head the soul of the departed establishes itself. When the inhabitants of the New Hebrides desire to converse with the spirits of their forefathers they put their ancestor images in the bushes, sit down near them in the dusk, and entice the souls by playing on bamboo flutes. The spirits proclaim their presence by the rustling of the foliage, and are welcomed with passionate outbursts of joy and grief by their descendants.

From the point of view of technique we are concerned mainly with wooden figures, especially among the negroes. Wood,

43

which is so much easier to handle than the essentially hard stone, answers to the touch of the unskilled hand as well as to that of the skilled, and permits of a freer expression of feeling. Attempts have been made to prove that the hunting tribes in primitive times possessed greater talent than the agricultural peasants for naturalistic sculpturing, due to the cultivation of their powers of observation, but this seems to be an erroneous idea, for the

FIG. 29. ANCESTOR IMAGE
FROM THE FIJI ISLANDS
*Museum für Völkerkunde, Berlin*

FIG. 30
ANCESTOR IMAGES FROM
THE FIJI ISLANDS

agricultural peasant, as a cattle-raiser, has just as much opportunity as the other of observing nature. Apart from that, settled habitation must be regarded as the preliminary condition for the development of artistic skill. The wooden figures made by the nature peoples consist of one model, in which little attention is paid to the arms. The dependence on the material used is again obvious; thus Vatter traces to the shape of the tree-trunk selected by the carvers the decadent, graceful type of ancestor image in Malekula, with arms tightly pressed to the body. Where wood was lacking, as among the Siberian Tschuktschi, little figures, 8 cm. high, were made of the teeth of walruses, while in New Zealand the natives have taken the hard nephrite and, with arduous labour, using only their primitive implements of bone and stone, have shaped from it their small *tiki* images.

44

# ANCESTOR IMAGES

Figures which their makers and possessors held to be inhabited by spirits, and which were supposed to be the embodiment of their dead relatives, necessarily gathered around them a dense atmosphere of superstition. From the ancestor image radiate

FIG. 31. ANCESTOR IMAGE FROM THE CAROLINE ISLANDS

mystical aspirations of the most diverse kinds; thus, when elements of demonic power are regarded as truly bound up with the image of man in doll form, these images entice the soul along strange labyrinths in nature's kingdom of night. In these figures a tendency of man's spirit has taken shape—the tendency which leads him, ever inquisitive and searching for secrets, to

45

# DOLLS AND PUPPETS

desire to subjugate powers which, because they are intangible, can only dimly be felt, but the existence of which has never been doubted. Never has the belief in magic died. Prehistoric man, primitive man of to-day, and civilized European, separated

though they may be by chasms so far as thought and practice are concerned, accept the belief in occult powers—the one openly, the other secretly. The more the modern age departs from faith, the more deeply does it sink into superstitions, and where this tendency is put into practice it cannot—to-day as thousands of years ago—do without images. "They laugh and don't know that they are laughing at themselves."

The change of ancestor image into idol must have come quite automatically. The ancestor images, piously preserved and acquiring a certain cult through the ceremony of anointing with oil, in which were supposed to reside secret powers, from which help and protection were looked for, must soon have come to be regarded as idols, revered for themselves. For that reason Sydow calls the conception on which the art of ancestor imagery is based deification. The ancestor becomes an idol, the symbol of divinity. Thus, the Mesopotamian culture possessed nail-goddesses, which depended on the custom of laying down nails on the foundation stone of a temple as a kind of documentary attestation. These little figures, made of copper, with thick hair on the head and clasped hands, were preserved in brick cases and placed on the foundation stone. It was thought that this attestation, by aid of the divinity, would thus be bound to the earth. The extant pieces belong to the time of Ur-Ninā of Lagash, about the year 3200 B.C.

FIG. 32 ANCESTOR IMAGE FROM THE NEW HEBRIDES

FIG. 33. PROTECTIVE FIGURE FROM THE NICOBAR ISLANDS

In the New World the Spaniards found idolatry common among the natives, especially those of the West Indies. The small idols of human type were meant to reproduce the forms in which the spirits had manifested themselves. Several of these carvings bore in remembrance the names of deceased relatives—an observance which indicates that even here idol-worship had originated from an ancestor cult.

46

# ANCESTOR IMAGES

Thousands of examples were discovered, and on an island near Haiti, where resided a tribe of idol-makers who confined their activities to making figurines of night spirits, there was a kind of wholesale production of these things. Idolatry must have flourished in Peru also.

Perhaps idol-worship has lost ground in the course of centuries, but it has not completely disappeared, being found among both

FIG. 34. SPIRIT OF A DEAD SHAMANIST (IN WOOD)
Golds and Gilyaks in Amur, Siberia

FIG. 35. WOODEN IDOLS
Golds and Gilyaks in Amur, Siberia

nature peoples and civilized races, even among those who profess Christianity. On the Australian islands prayers are made to the god Tangarva, who is worshipped with human sacrifice. His wooden image is hollow and is filled with smaller wooden images which represent the offerings. At Bali and Lombok, in the Malay Archipelago, there appear the god Sakti Kumulan and the goddess Dalem Kamenuh, the images of which are made of Chinese copper coins gilded at the edges, with faces of coloured sandal-wood. These figures are dressed in white-and-red pieces of cloth, and are borne in procession to the sea temple. In Siberia F. R. Martin came across house idols of pine-wood dressed in costumes of motley cotton material and caps of blue

47

wool. The natives got these made by the Russified Ostiaks in Surgut. Every family possessed at least one such piece, which it kept, carefully hidden, but by no means forgotten, to take on journeys. The Shamanist priests of Amur, whose chief activities

FIG. 36. WOOD-CARVED IDOLS OF THE TSCHUKTSCHI, SIBERIA

are concerned with assisting the souls of the dead in the other world, are aided in their ceremonies by spirits, who are represented by small, roughly carved idols. The Museum für

FIG. 37. HOUSE IDOLS OF THE OSTIAKS IN JUGAN

Völkerkunde in Berlin possesses about twenty such figures, all different from one another.

The cult ceremonies of the Hopi Indians of North America have developed along very peculiar lines. They conduct their worship with dolls, which are set up at altars in subterranean

48

DOLLS OF THE TUSAYAN INDIANS
Hopi dolls representing Kā-tci-nās (intercessory spirits
between the dead and the gods)

rooms, and which personify the masked dancers who, at the great feasts in July and August, have to represent gods and demons. These motley-coloured wooden dolls, dressed in leather and adorned with feathers, are called *ti'hus*, and create an extraordinarily fantastic impression because of their strange costume, which is said to symbolize storm-clouds. Here are to be found the star-god, the snake-god, the war-god, besides female demons and goddesses. All these figures are modern, and J. Walter Fewkes, who has lived among the Tusayan Indians, is certain that although they may quite probably be images of gods once revered, they are no longer worshipped as idols. They are sprinkled with flour and employed for the ceremonial rites, but when the ceremonies are over they are left to the children to be used as toys: this rapid and surprising transition from idol to playing doll makes us think. It is to be assumed that this is done in order to give the children a living conception of the most important aspects of religion. They are said also to serve as ornaments in the living rooms, and are freely used as articles of commerce. Of these the Museum für Völkerkunde in Berlin possesses a very rich collection. Among the same Indians a serious *rôle* is played by stone house idols, which, although lacking arms and legs, have indications of eyes, and are finished off with feather ornaments round the neck. From time to time they are sprinkled with flour, and, as it seems, are still revered as idols. The holy war-club bundle of the Winnebagos (a tribe of Prairie Indians), in Nebraska, also serves in the practice of a cult. Besides many other objects it includes a richly ornamented cloth warrior-doll with tall leather boots and long plaits.

Among the Chinese, one of the most ancient civilized peoples in the world, no house lacks its little altar, with tutelary deities of divers kinds, to which is rendered a peculiarly personal and intimately coloured worship. The small images are made of steatite and agalmatolite (soapstone or talc), materials which are soft and plastic and so easy to work with. It is the custom to give presents to these luck-bearing figurines, the best examples of which belong to the period from the sixteenth to the eighteenth century, in order to bring blessing to the presenter and to protect him from sickness—a custom showing the transition of the idol into the amulet.

Even among Christian peoples themselves tendencies of a heathen ancestry were retained until late in the nineteenth century, and are possibly to be noticed even to-day, in the shape of a belief in idols. In various peasant farms of Norway worship was devoted to the *fakse* and *hernos*, house idols to which, until a

D                                                                              49 few decades ago, it was customary to offer sacrifice. These were half-life-size human figures carved in wood, with long hair and beard. The feet were only suggested, the figures being finished below in a snake-like form. On Christmas Eve the figure was taken to a high position, and some beer was poured into the hollow of its head; at the time of the winter solstice others were smeared with fat; in summer they were given offerings of whey on the mountain pasturelands. These Norwegian figures find parallels in the Polish and Czech *dziady* ('old men'), likewise intermediate between ancestor images and idols.

The Catholic Church quickly turned to its own advantage the belief in idols which is deeply rooted in the instinct of the folk, skilfully transforming these into figures of mercy. The miracle-working images of Mary and of the saints, arrayed like dolls and covered with rich ornaments, were once to be numbered by the thousand. Several of the famous divine images possessed, and still possess, a rich and costly wardrobe. In the church of the Holy Cross at Augsburg Friedrich Nicolai in 1780 saw a statue of the Blessed Virgin with real hair, powdered and dressed *à la mode* in a silk *adrienne*, with wrist-frills of pointed Brabant. During the same period Gretser saw at the high altar of St Emmeran's in Regensburg a crucifix clad in the full vestments of a priest celebrating Mass. In 1751 in Austria it was forbidden to set wigs on the statues of the saints. A Spanish synod held at Orihuela in 1660 took exception to these fooleries, and decreed that the figures of the Madonna and of the saints should be no longer dressed with real hair, arrayed in silk, and hung with ornaments, but the childishly naïve worship of the folk did not permit of much sympathy for these orders. Many idle nuns, in the seclusion of their cloisters, continued to find a pastime in toying with an infant Christ dressed up as richly as possible.

## III

## FETISHES, AMULETS, AND TALISMANS

EVEN in ancient times it is to be noted that the smaller images of gods change into fetishes, so that the artistically formed figurines act as substitutes for that which they represent. By the term fetish is understood a natural object or an object of art with which a cult is associated and to which its possessor ascribes supernatural powers. Like the ancestor image and the idol from which it has sprung, it is one of the earliest religious possessions of mankind, and has preserved over thousands of years down to our own day a belief in the power of material objects. This is no mere chance, for it finds its firm basis in the fact that belief in the fetish arouses the power of suggestion which may often bring the desired object to fulfilment. Should the protecting or healing result be long in coming, the fetish or the amulet is not at fault, but want of true belief on the part of its possessor. The fetish to-day is still omnipresent, and does not rely on primitive ideas alone. Its possessor is accustomed to devote to it a wholly personal cult; for the fetish is usually the idol of one man, who, it is true, is wont to abandon it if the protecting or healing power which he attributes to it denies him anything. Any object can become a fetish, but generally human forms are preferred. For this purpose images of gods obviously were eminently suitable. The skald Hallfred was reproached for having taken into his own possession an image of Thor as a fetish.

One of the chief centres of the fetish cult is to be found among the negro tribes of West and Central Africa, where the demand for protective and aiding figures is extraordinarily great. Indeed, there is among these fetishes a regular division of labour. As Pechuel-Loesche records:

> Among these some bring to the merchants good profits, others to travellers comfortable lodgings, others to the fishermen and hunters rich booty, others to childless couples issue. There are others which assist the secreting of mother-milk, the birth and teething of children, the faithfulness of wives and of husbands, the egg-laying of hens, the increase of goats and sheep, the prospering of crops, the

51

good result of a courtship or of a lawsuit, success in war, the recovery of an invalid. Others are expected to loosen fetters, to attract bondsmen, to alleviate the weight of burdens, to strengthen limbs, to make eyes keener, to open up trade, to give glimpses into the future, to pass judgment on doubtful cases, to divert rain-clouds from the camp, to destroy vermin, to provide food, to prevent external trouble and suffering, especially bodily hurt, to avert witches, ghosts, and wild animals. The timid are not satisfied with

FIG. 38. FETISH OF THE
BASSONGE (CONGO)

FIG. 39. NAIL FETISH
FROM THE LOANGO COAST

a general fetish against the dangers of war—they must have one fetish which protects them against arrows, a second against a blow with a naked weapon, a third against a blow from a club. Maybe they will take still more which preserve them from falling into an ambush, from being caught in a snare, or from being captured, and so forth. A person undertaking a commercial expedition can make use of various fetishes for the purchase of palm-kernels, of palm-oil, or of caoutchouc, for the hiring of reliable porters, for strength in marching, against sand-storms, losing of the way, bad roads, and swollen rivers, against attacks of all sorts, against thieves, and against avaricious landowners. A person about to marry requires a good few fetishes, such as are necessary to keep his wife faithful, to display himself from the very beginning as a strong master, to avert the slipping in of evil spirits on the marriage night.

Most of these fetishes, generally of human shape, are described by Sydow as "frightful phantoms, both repulsive and fascinating," and when we look at them in the museums we realize that he is right. Very important for an understanding of the nature of the fetish are the wooden 'nail fetishes,' which are often stuck all over with nails and bits of glass. This is done in order to entice and incite them to use their power; there are recipes, of a very mechanical sort, for the ceremony. They are

FIG. 40. WOODEN NAIL FETISH OF THE BAWILI, LOANGO COAST (FRENCH EQUATORIAL AFRICA)

FIG. 41. WOODEN DOLL "HAMPATONG" Amulet for head-hunters, Borneo

FIG. 42. FETISH OF THE BATEKA (FRENCH EQUATORIAL AFRICA)

strewn with cola-nut, smeared with blood and oil, caressed, shaken, patted, and warmed. If they delay too long in giving their aid they are beaten, and if the result still fails to appear they are pitched into the fire.

If the fetish is an animated object possessing its own power or an image forming a connecting-link between soul, god, and demon, amulets and talismans are charms which bear no value in themselves, but receive a power imparted to them from without. In contrast to the actively working fetish they are quite passive, merely giving defence, for the most part, against evil spirits. Idols or little images of gods have been from of old chosen for this purpose. In Egypt there has been found a great number of bronze, silver, and lead figurines representing all the

53·

gods, some from the New Kingdom, the majority from the later periods and the epoch of the Ptolemies. Apparently even large specimens among them were worn on the neck suspended on chains, thus serving as talismans. Attached to small amulets in the shape of pigs, they proved a protection against the evil eye.

The small dolls which the Eskimos carve out of bone are hung on their kayaks to prevent the capsizing of the boat. Old Japan had its rag dolls, made over a wooden foundation, called *amakatsu* or *otagiboko*, which had an original significance as

FIG. 43. LEATHER DOLLS FROM SOUTH-WEST AFRICA
The first and last are supposed to represent Herero, the other three Hottentots.
Perhaps used for cult purposes
*Staatliches Museum für Völkerkunde, Munich*

amulets for easy confinement; in later times, however, they descended to the *rôle* of children's playthings. Another kind of painted wooden doll, originating from various Japanese provinces, is shaped very peculiarly, like a cone or a roll, with head often barely suggested and painted face; this represented at first a protective amulet against illness, but later was changed into a fertility charm. In the Batak lands in Sumatra the medicine-men make use of a doll-formed jar with a head made of brown wood covered with tin. This is about 19 cm. high, and is handled so dexterously that the figure seems to be alive. It is called Perminak, and forms a talisman against the bite of poisonous snakes, besides rendering its possessor shot-proof. The Tschuktschi in the Bering Strait carve wooden male and female dolls, with eyes of tin or ivory, some of which serve as protective amulets against ghosts, while to others is assigned the task of

54

enticing seals. The Golds and Gilyaks in Amur carve from bone little human figures which serve them as amulets against the evil spirits who, they think, are the cause of the back-ache, phthisis, consumption, and epilepsy from which they suffer so much.

But it is not necessary to roam far afield in order to learn of the customs which depend upon the unshakable basis of superstition. Superstition is to be encountered in the very midst of civilization, on the asphalt of the great cities. Looking round, one finds the *de luxe* motor-cars of the rich equipped with little dolls which often have the significance of a talisman. These dolls are manufactured out of soft cloth for sportsmen of all kinds; it is said that in Paris the *bébés porte-bonheur* have achieved great popularity since the Armistice and that they are eagerly sought after.

Psychologists and criminologists speak of 'doll fetishism' as a special form of nervous mental disorder. "The love of dolls," says Féré, "can intrude so far as to eliminate entirely any affection for a living issue." Women among whom the love of dolls persists even in advanced age are not rare. Vinchon knew an hysterical French woman who from infancy was so passionately devoted to dolls that she stole silk in order to clothe them smartly; they assumed for her the position of a fetish.

· History has to tell of various examples among adults of this love of dolls. According to Indian mythology the goddess Parwati made so lovely a doll for herself that she hid it from her husband Siwa. He saw it, however, and fell so deeply in love with it that he gave it life and made it his mistress. When Cortés met Montezuma he found that emperor and his Court playing with dolls. Queen Catharine de' Medici, when she became a widow, amused herself in the seclusion of her chamber with dolls which had to be clothed, like herself, in mourning. Tallement des Réaux relates that the Duchesse d' Enghien (*née* de Brézé), a niece of Cardinal Richelieu, continued to play with dolls even after her marriage, treating them like children, dressing and undressing them, giving them food and medicine, etc. Henrietta, Duchess of Marlborough, a daughter of the first Duke of Marlborough, was very friendly with the author Congreve, and when he died, in 1729, she caused a life-size image of him to be made; this was so exact that it even showed an open sore on his leg from which he had suffered during his lifetime. She paid a doctor to dress this wound, and went about with the figure as if it were a living being. When a certain Count Harcourt died, in 1769, his grief-stricken widow ordered a large wax image of her husband to be made, got it clad in his dressing-gown, and set it in an easy chair by her bedside. Margravine Sibylle von Baden-Baden caused a hermitage to be built in her favourite park, in the dining-room of which the Holy Family sat at table. The Blessed Virgin, Joseph, and the child Christ were wooden dolls, with heads and hands of wax, dressed in real clothes. Between them stood a little chair for the Margravine when she condescended to eat with the carpenter couple. Countess Augusta Dorothea von Schwarzburg, a princess of the house of Brunswick, consoled herself during her widowhood by playing with dolls. She ordered twenty cupboards to be made in the form of dolls' rooms, in which she herself and her Court were represented naturalistically. Skilled monks of Erfurt modelled the heads of wax, while the Countess herself made the clothes. From 1716 to 1720 this collection was exhibited in Schloss Monplaisir, at Arnstadt, and in 1820 Vulpius saw it at Schloss Augustenburg. Princess Augusta of Saxe-Gotha, the wife of Frederick Prince of Wales (the son of King George II), preferred to pay more attention to her dolls than to her husband. So unceremoniously did she play with these that her sisters-in-law had to beg her to desist in order to prevent the common people from becoming aware of her propensities.

Ancestor image, idol, fetish, talisman, amulet, depend in their general conception upon the idea that the representation of a god or a demon or a man confers upon the person who makes the image and who calls by name the thing represented the power to make use of its strength or to influence it. On these grounds the law of Moses forbade, as idolatry, the making of images. With the image are associated ideas of a magic dwelling within it, a magic powerful enough to make use of the image. Thus it is that the doll, both among ancient and among modern peoples, plays an important part in magical practice. Generally the image is utilized for the purpose of doing harm to some one; seldom does one hear of images employed in order to do a good turn. The active agent undertaking a thing of this nature uses a symbolic magic which is in itself a copy or pantomimic suggestion of the result to be brought about by these means. The belief is that whatever one desires can be carried out in actuality.

# IV

## IMAGE MAGIC

THIS conviction, that one's desire can be accomplished by proxy, finds expression in the 'fertility magic' of some folk customs. With a certain tenacity superstition associates dolls with the whole sexual life of woman. On the Santa Cruz islands is found the male spirit-doll Menata, the duty of which, in general, is to take care of the women's health. Among the Suaheli a girl during menstruation has always to carry a wooden doll in her hand or on her back. E. von Weber noted that the Fingo girl in the Orange Free State carries about a doll from the time she is marriageable until she has had a child. This doll is then laid aside and a new one provided until the birth of the next child. These dolls are treasured and regarded as sacred. Magic is regularly resorted to in connexion with childlessness among married couples. Some negro tribes of South Africa have dolls which are borne on the back like children, nursed and suckled, and even given names. This use of what scientists call 'imitative magic' is widespread, and is to be found in Africa on the Ivory Coast, in Senegal, and in the Sudan. Among the negroes of the Wapogoro and Wagindo tribes women who desire children get dolls made out of gourds. The sphere of this magic, however, goes far beyond Africa, extending to America, the South Sea Islands, and even to Australia. The last-mentioned fact, according to W. Foy, proves that the magic belongs to a very ancient cultural level, for the Australian natives, both in their physical structure and in their manners and customs, stand at the lowest grade of civilization. The Bataks in Sumatra and the natives of New Zealand often carry about dolls as a protection against sterility. A sterile woman of the Nischinam tribe in California is presented by her friends with a grass doll, which she carries around like a living child. If a pregnancy results other dolls are called into use. In the Torres Strait the expectant mother busies herself with a male doll in the hope of bringing a boy into the world. The Dayak women of Borneo sacrifice a little house filled with their own dolls for the purpose of averting some illness threatening an expectant mother.

57

When there is fear of an approaching abortion among the tribe of Annamites the magic-man makes two straw dolls for mother and child and carries through his ceremonies with these.

One need not, however, go out of Europe to discover examples of such customs. Russian peasant women who were childless and wished for children used to make a pilgrimage to a famous nunnery at Smolensk which possessed a wonder-working baby doll—apparently an image of the child Christ. This they rocked in their arms, while at their side a nun prayed that they might be freed from their unfortunate sterility. Among the wandering Perchten of Tal von Gastein it was the custom to fasten a baby doll on to a long cord and to throw it to the young women, who kept it or threw it back according as they desired the blessing of children or not. Not long ago in Brunswick the peasant women kept as a dowry a wedding spinning-wheel finely carved of red wood, especially plum-tree wood, and adorned with ribbons and artificial flowers.

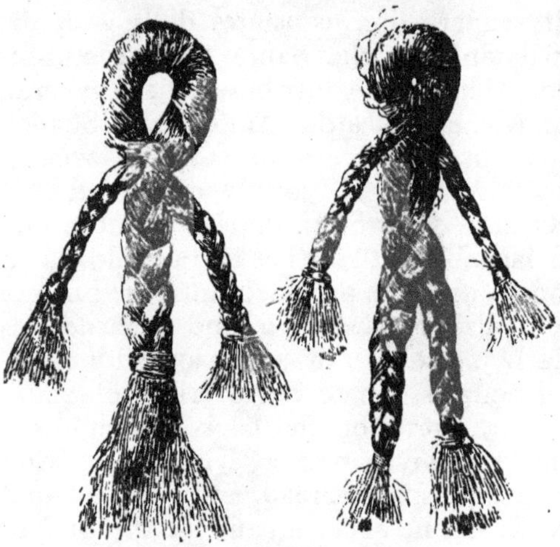

FIG. 44. YOUTH AND MAIDEN
Flax dolls for a bridal spinning-wheel, Brunswick

This was often hung with six to eight small male and female dolls made of twisted flax, with recognizable head, arms, legs, and dress. These dolls formed a talisman supposed to make the marriage fruitful. Sometimes, too, they were used as a cure for ague, in which case they were burned to ashes and swallowed. The doll could be utilized also for the successful issue of a confinement. At Klingnau, in Switzerland, during Shrovetide a masked fool used to stroll round with a large doll. He visited the houses of the newly married couples and showed the doll to the young wives, for which he was rewarded with a gratuity.

Image magic proper necessitates the making of a figure of the man whose hurt is secretly sought; this figure is pierced with holes, lacerated, and burned, on the assumption that all that is done to it is transferred to the living original. The belief in the

# IMAGE MAGIC

efficacy of this magic goes back to dimmest antiquity. Hentze holds that the figurines found in the Magdalenean and Solutrian culture strata are naught but magic images, made in order to gain power over those they represent. On the Chaldean bricks of the time of Assur-nazir-pal II (883–858 B.C.) incantations are spoken of. "They have created effigies conformable with my image and similar to my form." "With an ointment of hurtful herbs have they rubbed me; to my death they have led me." In these texts mention is made, too, of protective measures in which likewise an image has to play its magical part: "Repeat the incantation in a whispering voice and let an image of clay be by." "The incantation of those who have made effigies conformable with my image, similar to my form, who have taken away my breath, pulled out my hair, torn my garments, prevented my feet from moving by means of dust—may the fire-god disperse their charms!" An Egyptian papyrus of the time of Rameses III records the trial of a conspirator who made little wax figures and uttered incantations over them for the purpose of insinuating himself into the Pharaoh's harem. Another man was sentenced for making wax images in order to harm his enemies.

This conception of the possibility and efficacy of image magic was carried to the West from the Orient. Plato is fully cognizant of the practice of wizardry by means of wax figures. In an ode of Anacreon the poet advises the throwing of a wax figure of Amor into the fire that love itself may thereby be consumed. Lucian of Samosata relates that when he was a schoolboy his ears were boxed for his having made some wax figures; this in itself indicates that even such childish play was regarded as dangerous. Among the Greeks and Romans image magic was freely employed in love affairs. In Theocritus's idylls Samaitha puts a charm on her faithless lover:

> The Spirit aids, the mammet melts above;
> And so may he,
> Delphis the Myndian, melt in grids of love,
> As utterly. [1]

Proof of the existence of this love magic in Rome is provided by Horace and Ovid, cloth-dressed dolls being utilized in their day for this purpose. These wooden magic images, representing both sexes, were called *ipsullices*. In the country they were made of bark and hung on the branches of trees.

In the Middle Ages similar love magic is said to have been

[1] Translation by Jack Lindsay (*Theocritos*, Fanfrolico Press, 1929).

practised with the use of little images of wax. These were baptized and melted, and thus the person in question was supposed to be inflamed with love. Jakob Grimm records a poem relating to this written by one of the wandering scholars:

> With wondrous magic art
> I shall teach you how to mould
> Of wax a human counterpart—
> If its magic you would hold,
> Baptise it in the well; that done,
> Let it stand i' th' heat o' th' sun.

When a girl of the Transylvanian gipsy tribe wants to capture the affections of a lad she makes a doll of dough mixed with his hair, blood, spittle, and nails, and baptizes it in the name of the beloved person. This she then buries at a cross-road under the light of the new moon, defiles it, and says, "N.N., I love you. When your little image is rotted you must, as the dog after the bitch, run after me, your sweetheart." The girls of the Chippeway Indians also employ a love magic, in which they make an image of the loved one and sprinkle it in the region of the heart with a certain powder.

The belief in the power of image magic had a remarkably tenacious life. King Louis X of France ordered Enguerrand de Marigny to be executed for having sought after his life by this means; the Duchess of Gloucester in 1445 was accused of a similar crime against King Henry VI of England; for this she was imprisoned, while her three accomplices were sent to the scaffold. Charles IX of France made de la Mole pay with his head for the same offence. When Urban VIII occupied the papal chair it was prophesied to Cardinal Ascoli that he would be his successor. Meanwhile, as affairs moved on and the Pope did not die, the Cardinal's nephew lost patience and decided to accelerate Urban's decease. He made a wax image of the Pope, and by melting this slowly to the accompaniment of various incantations he intended to free St Peter's chair for his uncle. Urban VIII did not die from this procedure, which, on the contrary, cost the over-zealous nephew and his accomplices their lives. Even at the beginning of the eighteenth century at Turin there was executed a man against whom no other charge was brought than that he had aimed at the Duke's life by means of image magic.

It is a well-attested fact that to-day, in the East, in America, and in France, there exist coteries devoted to Satanism where these magical practices are still pursued. A little image of the person whose destruction is desired is made of red wax. This is pierced with needles or melted, thus, it is supposed, causing the person in question to become ill or to die.

In China the same ideas prevail. In the year 100 B.C. a certain prince was charged with having injured the Emperor by means of wooden, paper-clad dolls which a wizard had animated with evil spirits. In the year 602 a prince whose father lived too long made a doll in his likeness, pierced it in the heart, and buried it, with the idea of shortening the days of his old lord. When vengeance is desired on an enemy a straw doll is made, with a head of cotton and clad in blood-stained paper. To the accompaniment of divers incantations it is then pierced through with needles. In the Temple of Unfortunate Women at Canton there formerly hung upside down many paper figures of men, made by wives for the reforming of their evil husbands—"so that thereby his heart might be changed." The revenge doll is known also in Japan. A Japanese woman who finds herself betrayed makes a straw doll intended to represent the faithless man, bores it through with nails, and buries it in the place where he sleeps. Whether this is intended to draw him back or is conceived only as a punishment remains uncertain. If one is robbed, a paper doll is made, hung upside down on the wall, and pierced with needles. This doll represents the god of riches, whose business it is to discover the thief, and since he is fastened by the feet he cannot escape before he has fulfilled his duty.

Belief in the revenge image dwells not less strongly in Europe. The Scottish Highlanders are convinced that the death of one they hate may be attained by means of a *corp creadh*—an image of white clay with black glass-bead eyes and teeth made of splinters of wood, which is supposed to represent the person in question. If death only is desired this image is placed in a stream running eastward, and so is washed away. If the enemy is to die slowly and of a painful illness it is pierced with needles, or stuck through with rusty nails, and then placed in slowly flowing water. Formerly similar figures were carried through the villages in election time, the nails with which they were pierced showing contempt for the candidate whose election was not desired. Belief in this revenge image in Britain, however, is by no means confined to the Scottish Highlanders. At a charity bazaar held at London in 1901 there was exhibited an image of the Boer President Kruger which visitors were allowed to pierce thrice on payment of sixpence.

Among the Walachians a revenge image is employed which shows love magic used in the interests of a betrayed girl. The figure has to be made by a witch, who must carry out a tripartite

61

magical ceremony, consisting of baptism, incantation, and curse. The girl sticks a needle into the heart of the figure, spits on it, defiles it, and finally buries it under an elder-bush in the name of all the evil spirits. In India, too, wooden figures pierced with nails are made use of to bring injury to enemies. The Aymara Indians of Bolivia make small clay images of their enemies and stick thorns into them; so long as these thorns are allowed to remain in position the adversary is supposed to suffer. The Chippeway Indians of North America make wooden images of those to whom they desire harm; these they pierce in the head and breast so as to cause their enemies pain, or bury them when they desire to take their opponents' lives.

Among the Parivara, a Hindu tribe, a faithless wife was in the past punished by death; nowadays this punishment is carried out symbolically, a clay doll of the adultress being made, pierced with thorns in the eyes, and cast aside.

Opposed to these are the healing dolls, which to a certain extent have to act as an antidote to black magic. In the Middle Ages when it was thought that an illness had been caused by witchcraft, a little doll was made of wax and a priest bidden to read three Masses over it on a fast day. The figure was then pricked in the place where the invalid felt pain, the witch thus being forced to retract the spell. In China, under similar circumstances, a paper image of the sick man is cut out, and this has to be burned with some accompanying ceremonies in order to remove the disease. In Amoy, indeed, paper images of this kind are made for all the inmates of a house, loaded (as images) with every illness which could afflict the living persons, and then cast into the fire. Similar customs are known in Japan. Twice during the year, at the symbolic purification festivals in the Shinto temples, paper dolls representing the faithful are laid before the altar of *kami* in order to act as a protection against all possible evil. When a member of the Orang tribe, in the Malay Archipelago, falls ill a wooden image is made into which the evil spirits are driven by means of incantations; afterward this is thrown from the shore into the sea, which carries it away along with the illness. At Celebes in such cases male figures are worked out of fibre bound round with strips of bast; as soon as the priest has charmed the disease into them these substitutes for the patients are removed, sometimes being placed on coco-nuts filled with rice, and cast, along with their evil spirits, into the sea. A similar magic is practised in the Balkans and in the Caucasus for the purpose of calling down rain as necessity arises. The maidens of the village make a female doll, carry it round on an ass, and eventually place it on a raft made of straw and branches which is set alight and thrust into the current of the river.

In Borneo there are luck images manufactured from wood gathered in certain peculiar circumstances—*e.g.*, in moonlight on some lonely and hardly accessible spot. These bring all possible benefits to their possessors and are hung up over the hearth. At each festival season they are conse-crated anew, being smeared with the blood of sacrifice—often enough that of a man. In the islands near Sumatra are dolls which guard the owners from being de-voured by evil spirits. These dolls are hung up over the money chest to increase its contents, or are employed to bring success on head-hunting expeditions, and so on.

FIG. 45. MAGIC DOLL
Celebes

Dolls are used for many other matters connected with magical rites; these have always to be images of men, for to such is ascribed the greatest effi-cacy. The Baluba tribe of the Southern Belgian Congo maintain that the great spirit Nkulu gave a thumb-sized model to one of their medicine-men so that the necessary magi-cal figures could be made from it. In Africa are to be found magical figures, such as the *nomori* of Sierra Leone, the mean-ing of which the negroes themselves no longer know, and which they do not even manufacture any more; these, however, they regard as possessing magical powers, and when they find them they bury them in their fields. The number of African magical figures is exceptionally large, since each has only one possible application. Their power is bound up with magical matters with which they are, so to say, laden. They are em-ployed even in legal affairs, use being made of them in order to reveal the unknown perpetrator of a crime, usually a theft,

63

by the thrusting of a red-hot iron nail into a wooden figure. Through this the guilty one is made ill, and can become well again only when he has made restitution and the nail is removed. Although plastic images are rare among the Akikuyu of East Africa, that tribe possesses a kind of magical clay doll which serves in the celebration of dances at the maize-harvesting. These figures may be of either sex and are carefully preserved. The Luiseño Indians of Southern California make life-size

FIG. 46. THE GOD SAKTI KUMULAN AND
THE GODDESS DALEM KAMENUH
Made of gilded Chinese copper coins. Bali

figures of elder-wood, with fringed coats, which are used for the image dances performed at their puberty festival. These are carried about, symbolically presented with gifts, and burned at the close of the ceremony.

A special magic seems to rule over the birth and growth of children. Greek mothers, after the birth of their first child, were wont to consecrate a little image in the temple of Eileithyia, and similar customs are to be found among the nature peoples. Catlin relates that when a child of the Odschibbewa Indians (of Lake Superior) dies, the mother makes a feather doll as a substitute, and carries this about with her tied up in a bundle along with the clothes and toys of the dead child. The Indians call the whole thing a 'doll of misfortune.' According to Richard Andree, an animistic idea lies at the root of this custom: since the child is still too small to be able to fend for itself in the other world, the mother must support it until its spirit has sufficiently developed.

The doll is employed too for the purpose of getting in touch with the other world. When a Chinaman wishes to learn something from the dead he makes a doll into which a witch, the doll's 'aunt,' has charmed the soul of a child, and which is then burned so that the information sought may be gathered on the other side of the grave. At Bali and Lombok when a special supplication is to be made to the gods, female wooden figures with painted white face, black hair, and yellow breast and arms, and having an inscription on their backs telling of the desires which the gods are bidden to fulfil, are sacrificed on the altars of the temple.

Very common is the use of dolls possessing magical power in order to obtain rich harvests. On the Santa Cruz islands bottle-shaped dolls with real hair and decorated with ornaments are carried by the women on their backs like children, and borne with them to the plantations in the expectation that they will secure a good harvest. There, too, the *tapa* doll—husband and wife represented in intimate embrace—is employed as a kind of fertility magic in the cocoa plantations. Up to a short time ago the primitive tribes in Central India indulged in human sacrifice during their fertility rites; now they make use of monkeys or, more commonly, dolls of wood or straw. It was the custom formerly in India, in order to increase the harvest, to stick an iron hook into the back of a living man, to draw him upward and swing him round; nowadays this magical practice is carried out only symbolically, by means of a doll, *sidi viranna*.

Image magic has maintained itself most strongly among the wandering gipsies of Hungary—the so-called tent gipsies. For this purpose they make use of anything which has to do with the dead. From gum removed from the trees in a churchyard, from the hair and nails, burned to powder, of a dead child or virgin girl, and from the ashes of the burned clothes of a dead man they make little figures—the so-called 'dead men' (*manush mulengré*). These are human images supposed to bring to the possessor the favour of demons. They are also ground down to powder and mixed with forage as a protection against witchcraft; for this paste the rotten wood of old coffins and grave crosses is also used. Those gipsies who work as broom-makers or tree-fellers make the image of an earth spirit, *phuwusch* or *maschurdalo*, which they cast into the bushes; fishermen and seamen make a similar figure, called *nivaschi*, which they throw into the water; both serve as a protection against devils. In these images the features are rendered in a very rough and ready manner.

The belief in the animation of the doll reaches a culmination, vital yet half devilish, in the mandrake, or 'gallowsman.' The mandrake, which is mentioned even in the Bible, bears a name which itself signifies a living idol. It is in reality the root of the white bryony, which closely resembles the human form, or of the mandragora (called also *Allermannskraut*), which grows in the Southern Alps. Pliny knows of it and speaks of its peculiarities. In the Middle Ages it was believed that it originated from the last seminal effusion of a man hanged on the gallows, and that when uprooted it uttered a moaning cry. Since he who digs it up must die, it is tied to the tail of a black dog, which is then made to drag it from the earth. It must be washed with wine, bathed, nursed, and suitably clothed. Its demonic character is revealed by the fact that it will not leave its possessor; of itself, if it is carried away, it returns to him. Should anyone desire to get rid of the root he must sell it more cheaply than he has

FIG. 47. MALE AND FEMALE MANDRAKES
From the *Hortus Sanitatis*, Mainz, 1491

bought it, and the last purchaser has to keep it. It brings luck to its possessor, makes him rich, opens up secrets to him, and many professional thieves to-day still hold to the conviction that with its help the doors of any castle can be unlocked. The former Court library in Vienna possesses the mandrakes, of both sexes, which belonged to Emperor Rudolph II, each wrapped in a little dark velvet mantle. Perger tells a story of how a peasant, whom a gipsy girl initiated into the secret, pulled up a bryony root on a Monday morning under the favourable conjunction of the moon with Venus and Jupiter. He planted it in the grave of a man, and for a whole month watered it each evening before sunset with whey in which he had drowned three bats. Then he pulled it up; by this time it looked much more like a man in shape than before. After heating his oven with verbena he dried the root and covered it with a little bag made of a piece

66

of linen. So long as the peasant possessed this root he was lucky in whatsoever he did—he won at play, he found various objects of value, and daily increased in wealth.

Throughout the entire Orient the mandrake is regarded as a valuable talisman, for it is believed that it makes its possessor proof against cut, thrust, and bullet; it is esteemed as an aphrodisiac; since, too, the conviction is held that it can cure its possessor's illnesses and transfer them to others, it is a highly coveted article. Luschan records that at Mersina and Antioch skilful artisans are employed in the trade of working these mandrakes into human shape. By wrapping up the root of the growing plant, and so training it to assume the desired form, surprising results, it is said, are produced, the mandrakes thus grown revealing a most naturalistic resemblance to men. In Mariazell mandrakes were used by the priests at high festivals and sold to pilgrims as 'lucky mannequins.'

A similar image appears in the Habsburg art collection in the Vienna museum: a little black glass figure inserted in a prism of imitation topaz. It was regarded as a *"spiritus familiaris,* which was cast out of one possessed and imprisoned in this glass." Visitors to the imperial treasury at the beginning of the eighteenth century always found this curiosity "touching to look upon." As the greatest rarities could be produced so easily clever forgers devoted themselves to providing examples of the Baphomet for a sensation-seeking public. In the eighteenth century, when secret societies flourished and Freemasonry sprang into fame, historic interest in the Knights Templars awoke, and artists readily seized their opportunity by manufacturing forged antiquities, offering to the public the Baphomet, which was said to have been the idol of the unfortunate Knights and to have been used by them in ceremonies both mysterious and obscene. They made coarse, grotesque figures, fantastic abortions of an imagination rioting in misunderstood symbols. The result was, as always, advantageous to the impudent swindlers. Scholars and laymen alike fell victims to the importunity of active dealers, and an Orientalist such as Joseph von Hammer-Purgstall, widely versed in Eastern studies, was actually persuaded to occupy himself with these alleged idols and their meaning.

## V

## VOTIVE IMAGES

THE mystery inherent in the primitive belief regarding man's image has produced also the votive image, or *ex voto*. The man who strives to catch in idol, fetish, amulet, or talisman something of divine power, in order to make use of it for his own protection, has likewise endeavoured at all times to persuade the divinity he worships to be gracious and propitious to him. For this purpose sacrifices serve—especially sacrifices of highly esteemed objects (with Richard Andree we recall here the ring of Polykrates!) and, in an ideal sense, images of the persons making sacrifice, who thereby symbolically present themselves as offerings to the god. This use of the *ex voto* figure is extremely old. In Samuel v and vi a description is given of how the Philistines carried off the Jewish Ark of the Covenant, and of how they were punished therefore by "emerods in their secret parts." They were forced not only to restore the ark, but to provide golden replicas of the affected parts of their bodies—which Luther euphemistically calls "thumbs." Hörnes is inclined to regard as votive in origin the many figures preserved from the Hallstatt and La Tène periods; among them, certainly, there is no lack of unquestionable votive figures. In the sanctuary of the snake-goddess at Knossos, in

FIG. 48. FAIENCE FIGURE OF A PRIESTESS OF THE SNAKE-GODDESS IN KNOSSOS, CRETE
About 1800–1600 B.C.

Crete, great numbers of plastic female votive images of glazed clay were unearthed. They belong to a time which lies some two thousand years before the Christian era, and show the women in a very peculiar national dress which anticipated the hoop petticoat of the rococo period by some four thousand years.

A female figure found at Kličevač, in Serbia, wears a curious dress so similar to that worn by the Knossos dolls that Hörnes suspects that there is a connexion between the two. Dress and ornament on this image of the Bronze Age are carefully indicated by engraving; possibly it also was a votive figure. A whole depot of votive dolls, belonging to the early Mycenæan period, was unearthed in 1913 on the road between Mycenæ and Nemea; among these female board-shaped figures with long dress and the *stephane*, or high headdress, predominated. Bell-shaped figures too have frequently been discovered in Bœotia. In the deepest strata of the Altis of Olympia primitive images of bronze and terra-cotta have been unearthed by the hundred; these are regarded by Furtwängler as *ex voto* figures, since they were found on the altars of Zeus and Hera. Identical figures, childishly clumsy in form, have been discovered in the

FIG. 49. CLAY DOLL FROM A GRAVE OF THE BRONZE AGE NEAR KLIČEVAČ, SERBIA

sanctuary of Asklepios in Epidaurus, in the Temple of Isis at Pompeii, at Vulci, Calvi, Cervetri, and elsewhere. In 1836 the Alpine lake at Monte Falcone yielded nearly seven hundred small bronze votive figures, all male images, with arms outstretched in the ancient gesture of prayer.

Only those votive figures made of clay or metal have been preserved, but the characteristic material for this purpose was wax. According to Macrobius, the gift of a wax image formed a symbolic substitute for the expiatory sacrifice of the whole man, but such images are no longer extant. In earliest times the living man was sacrificed, and this offering was later replaced by the little *ex voto* doll. At the close of the ancient Roman festival of the Saturnalia the citizens were accustomed to give each other presents of these wax and clay figures. Such *sigilla*, at any rate those of clay, have been plentifully preserved; the Louvre and

69

other archæological collections have got dozens of examples. The Roman legend ran that Hercules it was who, after his victory over Geryon, abolished human sacrifice, substituting for it the *argei*, small dolls which, as substitutes for the living persons,

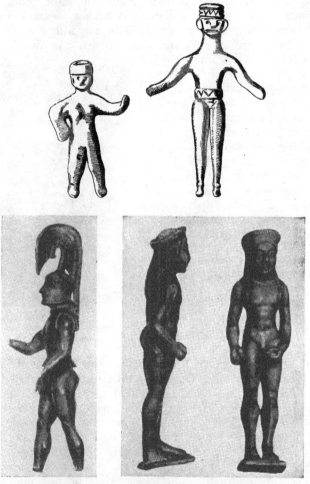

FIGS. 50–52. VOTIVE BRONZES FROM OLYMPIA

were thrown, during the month of May, at full moon, into the Tiber from the Pons Sublicius by the vestals.

The wax offering subsisted throughout the whole of the Middle Ages; so far as Germany is concerned there is documentary proof of it as early as the eleventh century. Just as in the saint-worship of the Christian Church ancient polytheistic images lingered on, the heathen gods merely assuming new masks, so also the tendencies toward sacrifice and self-offering remained alive. The faithful Christian made an image in some precious material of his own body weight, wax, too, because of its costliness, being used for this purpose. The idea repeatedly alluded to of image-power, of the superstitions associated with the human figure, led also, by the material sacrifice, to the preservation of the gift as an efficacious thing since it had taken the form of the human body. To this connexion of ideas the votive doll owed its origin, and the desire to make the image as true and lifelike as possible imparted a naturalistic style to wax sculpture. Portraiture in wax, as I. von Schlosser has emphasized, moved in a peculiar *milieu*, conditioned by its association with the Church, in which ancient demonic conceptions are strangely bound up with ecclesiastical and secular pomp. Superstition, seizing its opportunity, here clad itself in its richest raiment.

FIG. 53. VOTIVE FIGURE, MIDDLE OF SEVENTEENTH CENTURY
Upper Bavarian. Modern wax casting from the original mould
*Photo Delia*

The miracle books mention· wax offerings taking the form of human figures—men, women, and children —some as heavy as twelve pounds. Commonplace gifts of pure wax were remelted and made into candles, but the presentations of princes, in their armour or rich dress, were often carefully preserved. When in 1398 the son of Philip the Bold, Duke of Burgundy, was bitten by a mad dog the distracted father, in order to avert ill consequences, set up an image of his son's weight in the church at Vienne. At Paris in 1389 King Charles VI of France ordered Dino Raspondi to make a life-size wax image in his likeness to be placed on the grave of the blessed Petrus of Luxembourg at Avignon. The artist received 360 gold francs for his work, a sum that would represent a small fortune in our times. In 1466 Queen Anne caused wax figures of herself and her daughter to be set up before the gracious image of the Lady of Cléry. When in 1478

71

# DOLLS AND PUPPETS

Lorenzo de' Medici luckily escaped a conspirator's dagger he got life-size wax images of himself, each different from the other, but all magnificently dressed, placed in three separate Florentine churches.

The erecting of magnificent votive figures became literally a mania in the later Middle Ages—not only Popes, emperors, and kings, but ordinary citizens and peasants set up their life-size plastic replicas in those churches and chapels with which they were connected. In 1518 Ottheinrich, Count Palatine of the Rhine, presented a life-size wax figure of himself to the church of St Wolfgang on the Obersee. The church, however, which won greatest fame in this regard was the church of the Servites—SS. Annunziata—in Florence. The churches of Orsanmichele and the Madonna delle Grazie also possessed numerous *boti*, as these figures were called in the Florentine dialect, but they could not vie with SS. Annunziata. The oldest examples there went back to the thirteenth century; even in the fourteenth century the church was so overstocked that further additions had to be prohibited. The cloth-clad figures, some of them on horseback, hung on cords attached to the roof or stood on pedestals and consoles. Covered with dust and decayed, eaten by moths and mice, they must have presented a miserable spectacle.

The flourishing of this art came in the fifteenth and sixteenth centuries, when the figures were made of canes over a wooden frame, with wax face and hands. These were dressed in cloth and painted. Orsino de Benintendi, whom Vasari praises as a modeller in wax, received for each one of his figures twenty-five gold ducats. The sculptor Montorsoli, a pupil of Michelangelo, and Benvenuto Cellini, who made a wax figure for the Cardinal of Ravenna in 1548, gained great fame in this style. Pietro Tacca made an image of the Grand Duke Cosimo II, who died in 1621, in so lifelike a manner, with crystal eyes, real hair, beard, and eyebrows, that his mother could not bear to look on it.

At the beginning of the seventeenth century the Florentine church of the Servites possessed 600 life-size *boti* and countless smaller ones. Since these seriously impaired the appearance of the church and formed a menace to visitors, for the rotting cords could no longer bear the weight of the figures, which came crashing down and caused much damage, they were then removed, but the custom did not disappear. The church of S. Maria delle Grazie in Mantua still possesses a similar collection, but its figures are of *papier mâché* and make no claim to artistic perfection.

Life-size clothed wax figures were still being offered a short time ago at the church of the Fourteen Saints at Lichtenfels. Special attention there is devoted to lifelikeness in appearance, the illusion being increased by the dress. These figures are preserved in glass cases. The offering of smaller votive figures has not yet ceased, but they are no longer moulded solidly as before, but are hollow, and the material used contains more tallow than wax. Some moulds for such wax figures are very ancient; in spite of their antiquated modes, they have out-lived the centuries. Richard Andree and his wife discovered in the stock of the Court wax-moulder Ebenböck, in Munich, moulds which belonged to the seventeenth century and were still in general use. While wax was certainly the commonest material employed for the making of these votive figures it was not the only substance used; pious souls have also utilized gold and silver for this purpose. The Elector Charles Albert of Bavaria—who later became Emperor Charles VII—set up in 1736 a silver statue of his first-born prince at Alt-Ötting. Its weight corresponded to that of the body of the boy, who was then eight years old. Children are often to be found among these votive figures, either because children were desired or because it was thought that living children would be protected by means of this 'betrothal' to a sacred spot. In earliest times these children were always represented as babies in swaddling clothes, or, as they are called in Southern Germany, *Falschkind*. Except for the head every vestige of human shape

FIG. 54. THE IRON MAN OF BUTTEN-WIESEN
*Augsburg Museum*

has vanished; the poor little creature is done up in a parcel, body, arms, and legs strapped tightly and condemned to complete immobility. An ancient votive figure of this kind is the famous *Santissimo Bambino* of the church of Ara Cœli in Rome, an object greatly reverenced by Catholics and possessing its own little cart on which it is borne to invalids who desire its aid.

Costly *ex voto* figures were, of course, unobtainable by less opulent folk, who had to make use of simpler materials. In Bavarian villages iron, which was itself of greater value than it is now, was much used for this purpose. These votive figures, of both men and animals, are, with a few exceptions, always forged; sometimes they are cut from sheet-iron, but are hardly ever moulded. When the village blacksmith was called on to

73

prepare them they were worked out pretty roughly, with the lineaments of the body barely suggested. Men are naked, women are recognizable by their long clothes, and sometimes the sexual features are heavily accentuated, no doubt because it was believed that the *ex voto* figures could alleviate 'secret' pain. So far as the models are concerned the tradition has remained stationary, the more so because the primitive technique

| | | | |
|---|---|---|---|
| FIG. 55 SACRIFICIAL IRON MAN<br>Found near St Leonhard, in Lavanttale, Austria | FIG. 56. SACRIFI-CIAL IRON FIGURE OF A WOMAN<br>Found near St Leonhard, in Lavanttale, Austria | FIG. 57 SACRIFICIAL IRON FIGURE (LOWER BAVARIA)<br>'Captive of St Leonard' | FIG. 58. SACRIFICIAL WOODEN FIGURE OF A MAN<br>Drei Åhren |

permits hardly any thought of progress. Thus a number of the extant examples appear certainly to be antiques, and there are coarsely fashioned specimens, such as the great iron man of Buttenwiesen, in Augsburg, which have been accepted by antiquarians as prehistoric house gods. As a matter of fact, as Richard Andree has shown, the oldest of these iron figures belong to the later Middle Ages. In no respect, as their appearance leads us to conjecture, do they reach back to the beginnings of art; it is only that the creative process, which remains the same over long centuries, has produced identical results. A decline is first marked when the figures are no longer forged, but are cut, silhouette-fashion, out of sheet-iron. To-day it often happens that such an image is borrowed at a price for the ordination, and then is returned to the sexton after the festival.

The most interesting pieces of this kind are the so-called 'Captives of St Leonard,' male figures with forged rings and chains, representing a peculiarly close fettering to that saint who had been revered since the twelfth century. The average size is from 10 to 12 cm., but there existed larger ones of 40 to 50 cm. high. These large and coarse *ex voto* figures became in time connected with all kinds of superstitions. They are called 'Leonard's louts' or else *Würdinger*, after an Aigen family of that name who possessed a remarkable example, a knight in armour and helmet, 145 kg. in weight and 78 cm. high. When Richard Andree wrote his book in 1904 there were still at Aigen six such 'Leonard's louts,' rough-bodied figures, 40 to 50 cm. high and 30 to 50 kg. in weight. They served then as tests of strength and conscience for the country lads. He who desired to be protected from illness during the following year had, at St Leonard's festival, to lift one such 'lout' up to his shoulders and then throw it backward to the ground. For this there was required not only a great muscular strength, but also an innocence of all the deadly sins, for only the pure could pass the test.

# VI

## FUNERAL AND OTHER IMAGES

THE ancestor image, as we saw, is rightly to be regarded as the oldest doll form; this leads logically to the idol, and from that on to the fetish, the amulet, the talisman, and the votive figure. It all started at the grave regarded as a guide to the unknown world beyond. The grave, however, has produced still another creation likewise connected with death—the grave image. The idea of dualism of body and soul developed late among primitive peoples, who refused to see in death merely the final cessation of life. Primitive man was unable to rise to the conception that after death all is done with; instead, in face of his helplessness, he set up an ideal philosophy which granted to the soul a wandering and a future life. He considered those who had passed away as still living, and as a result the earliest cult of the dead is nothing but a continuation of social duties across the great barrier. The beginnings of the ritualistic cult of the dead reach back in Europe to the Palæolithic Age; in the East it is a later development. Up to the present day this cult has been maintained in some districts in its original form of the sacrifice, which was determined by wholly concrete, earthly ideas. The soul of the departed in its wanderings through the other world, it was thought, could not do without that which in the widest sense was necessary for its nourishment and existence here. Because of this there was presented to it clothing, weapons, and ornament—and not only these, but women, servants, slaves, and horses, which followed the corpse to the grave. In the Assyria of pre-Babylonian times we know that at the burial of kings rich sacrifices of men and animals were offered up. In prehistoric Germany slaves were killed at the obsequies of nobles and rich men so that they might serve their masters in the other world; thus many of his servants were burned with Sigurd's body. The dying Brunhild commanded five girls and eight noble boys, their foster-brothers, to escort her to the other world. In 1314, at the funeral rites of a Lithuanian grand duke, his horse, his favourite servant, and three captive German knights were burned alive on the pyre which consumed his corpse. The same custom was known in the Greek heroic period. Homer describes how at the burial of Patroclus twelve Trojans were slain so that they might accompany the hero's soul in the other world as attendant spirits. The Vikings, too, set their dead sea-kings in burning ships, together with followers, horses, and hounds. Herodotus, writing about 450 B.C., declares that even the Scythians beyond the Pontus followed this custom. At the burial of one of their princes the dead man's concubines, his cup-bearer, his equerry, and fifty of his best servants together with their horses were strangled and appointed as a retinue for the dead man.

This gruesome custom ruled throughout the whole world. Wives and servants in crowds followed the Peruvian Incas to their death; it is alleged that about a thousand dependents of his family and house were slain on the demise of Huayna Capac. In many provinces of Peru not only were weapons and treasures buried with prominent persons, but their wives were buried alive or else hanged themselves by their own hair. At the death of Atahuallpa his wives and servants refused to allow the privilege of following their lord voluntarily to the other world to be taken from them. In the Congo, according to Kund, no man of importance could die without the slaughter of wives and slaves to serve him in the other world. Often enough the number of these unfortunate persons is said to have reached a hundred or more.

In China the voluntary or, if that could not be secured, the enforced death offering of living persons endured till late in historic times. Probably introduced by the Tartars, it was practised first, according to Chinese records, about the year 768 B.C. in the Tsin district. Prince Ts'in Ou-Kong, who died in 678 B.C., ordered sixty-six of his household to follow him to the other world. At the death of his son and successor Mou-Kong the number of sacrificed persons amounted to 174 of the retinue, besides three heroes of noble birth chosen by lot. The songs in which the folk bewailed the cruel fate of these victims still survive. Emperor Chin Shih Huang Ti, who reigned from 246 to 210 B.C., commanded all who belonged to his Court to be killed after his death and laid in his grave. People of high rank ordered at least their favourite concubines to be buried alive with them. It is reported that at the death of very prominent persons hundreds to thousands of living people had to share their fate. The two travellers Huc and Gabet in their wanderings through Mongolia noted that at the burial of princes or chieftains a great crowd of their relations had to be ready to serve them in

77

the other world. The prettiest children were selected and made to swallow quicksilver until they died, preference being given to this kind of death because the miserable human sacrifice retained

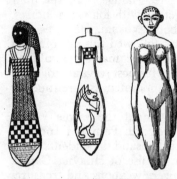

thus its fresh colours. Their bodies, equipped with fans, pipes, and other articles of their service, were placed round the body of the dead prince.

Without going further it is evident that suchlike customs must be fatal to all social life. When on each occasion of death a large part of the movable possessions of the deceased was rendered useless by being placed in the grave, and so many ser-

FIG. 59. ANCIENT EGYPTIAN GRAVE DOLLS

vants were killed outright (in such low estimation was held the value of human life), the very existence of civilization was imperilled. Very soon, therefore, a means was sought of substituting a symbolic for a real death sacrifice. No longer was genuine money placed in the grave, but in its stead coins of pressed tin, such as are still to be found in Greek graves. In place of the massive offerings of gold, such as Schliemann, for example, dug up in Mycenæ, recourse was had to gilded paper or clay, and in place of slaughtered women, slaves, or even free-born persons the graves were filled with dolls.

The soil of ancient Egypt, being dry enough to preserve such objects unimpaired through centuries, has yielded the richest treasure-trove of these grave images. From the Vth Dynasty images of servants, generally in considerable numbers, are to be found in the Egyptian graves. During the period of the New Kingdom

FIG. 60. EGYPTIAN WOODEN DOLL FROM A MUMMY'S COFFIN

FIG. 61 EGYPTIAN IVORY DOLL

(1600 to 1100 B.C.) these figures were produced in the mass. They are stamped in clay, carved in wood, covered with stucco and painted, made of limestone and alabaster, often inlaid

78

with pieces of coloured glass, embossed in copper, produced in diverse materials and of every quality. The shape is cursorily defined, the resemblance to human forms being just suggested; indeed it seems that no real attempt is made to imitate it. The little female figures, supposed to represent the concubines of the deceased, are made generally of flat wooden

FIG. 62. EGYPTIAN WOODEN STATUETTES—PRIEST AND PRINCESS
End of XVIIIth Dynasty
*Cairo Museum*

boards painted conventionally with wood beads for hair and no legs, "so as not to be able to run away." In the grave, unearthed in 1919 at Thebes, of Mehenkwetre, a landed proprietor and chancellor of Pharaoh, belonging to the XIth Dynasty, about 2000 B.C., were found many dozens of these dolls. There were small ships with crews for fishing, passenger boats, a carpenter's workshop, a stall for cattle, a slaughter-house, shepherds, and other representations of what had been the dead man's property on earth, and which now accompanied him to the kingdom of the dead as substitutes for the riches left behind—all giving the illusory impression of toys, yet not created for that purpose.

79

The *ushabti* figure served as a substitute for the soul of the dead. In the Middle Kingdom this is usually a portrait image of the deceased, taking the form of the enshrouded mummy. Only the head and hands, which hold whip and staff, are free. The *ushabti* figure may be of gold or bronze, but usually it is made of glazed clay. These images have a magical significance. In the other world they were supposed to undertake any work demanded of the dead man. In *The Book of the Dead* the deceased, speaking to his *ushabti*, is thus introduced:

FIG. 63. EGYPTIAN "USHABTI" FIGURE IN FAIENCE

> O Image, if I be summoned and appointed to do any work whatsoever of the labours which are done in the underworld, and if at any time I be appointed to sow the fields, to fill the watercourses with water, to bring the sands from the East to the West, then do you say: "Here am I."

The custom of providing *ushabti* figures for the dead was so deeply rooted that even those Egyptians who embraced Christianity, instead of renouncing it, preserved it in slightly altered form. In the graves of Akhmim Panopolis, belonging to the period from the fourth to the seventh century, are to be found tin figures 4½ cm. high, representing Lazarus shrouded in bands. He serves as a funeral symbol of the Resurrection.

No other land, even distantly, can be compared with Egypt in respect to riches of this kind, but it is probable that this is due to the nature of the soil, especially adapted for the preservation of perishable objects; other ground of a less favourable condition would not protect them in the same way. The Greeks certainly knew the use of the grave image, for graves of the archaic period have yielded little figures, similar to those of the Egyptians, engaged in all kinds of useful work—stamping corn, kneading dough, and baking bread. Among them are female mourners, others with pitchers, and still others making music with flute or tympanon, and so on. Archæologists believe that these terracottas formed a substitute for the retinue which the deceased had in life, serving instead of the human sacrifice customary in the heroic period. Some classical scholars, such as Adolf Furtwängler and Robert Schmidt, treat even the Tanagra

FIG. 64. BARBER
Terra-cotta grave figure
from Tanagra

FIG. 65. HANDWORKER
Terra-cotta grave figure
from Tanagra

FIG. 66. HOUSEMAID
Grave doll from Eretria

figures, which have so rapidly and so justly become famous, as genuine grave images.

FIG. 67. WALKING GIRL
Terra-cotta from Tanagra
*Sabouroff Collection*

FIG. 68. GIRL WITH HAT
Terra-cotta from Tanagra
*Sabouroff Collection*

Greek clay sculpture flourished in Corinth, Thisbe, Megara, and Myrina; it was a considerable article of export to the Crimea, Crete, and other neighbouring localities. Since the seventies of

F

the last century Tanagra, in Bœotia, has been added to the already known centres of manufacture, and, because of the high artistic quality of its ware, it has cast all the others into the shade, since 1873–74 the necropolis on the Kokkali hill near that city having yielded many of those little figures which in refinement of form, in easy grace, and in elegance of appearance have not been surpassed even by the porcelain art of the eighteenth century. In

the first enthusiasm for this newly discovered source of antique beauty it was believed that we had here to do with products of the age of Praxiteles, but a critical examination of style and technique has served to remove the Tanagra figures from these by a century. They could hardly have existed before the first half of the third century B.C., and so belong to the period of Hellenism; although Furtwängler is perfectly right in saying that they are the finest extant specimens of Greek art after the time of Alexander the Great.

Like other Greek terra-cottas, they were shaped in moulds, with freely modelled heads and limbs joined on separately. The lines of these Tanagra figures are particularly fresh and sharp; one can see how the clothing has been worked over with the modelling stick. The cold colours are carefully and tastefully conceived. The subjects are generally beautiful girls in the bloom of youth; boys and young men appear but rarely. All move on the border-line between the ideal and reality, borrowing their motives from contemporary pictorial art. The usual subject is a young woman endued with an undeniable charm, sitting or standing, holding in her hand a distaff, a ball, a fan, a mirror, an apple, a letter-board, a bunch of grapes, a mask, a lyre, or some similar object. Within their own limits the modulation and beauty could not be surpassed. The terra-cottas from Myrina, in Asia Minor (second and third centuries B.C.), vie with those of Tanagra. Here special attention was devoted to figures in movement: figures of Eros, goddesses of victory, dancing youths of effeminate appearance, hermaphrodites, satyrs, alongside of many caricatures. Of these Greek

GIRL WITH FAN
Terra-cotta from Tanagra
*Sabouroff Collection*

terra-cottas only a small fraction have been discovered in private houses; the majority were found in graves, so that we are justified in concluding that all of them were grave images.

The Romans shared with the Greeks the custom of making offerings at the grave; among them, indeed, it is authenticated even at the beginning of the imperial period. Most of the extant Roman clay figurines too have been found in graves, some of which contained as many as thirteen pieces. They were manufactured in the mass by hand; in Pompeii shops have been unearthed in which images of this kind were exposed for sale —gods, porters, gladiators, toga-clad citizens, and so on. The custom of the homeland was, of course, carried over to the distant provinces. On the Rhine, especially in the neighbourhood of Mainz, numerous figures of Mars and Mercury, some about 6 to 13 cm. high, made of bronze and silver, and others in a cheaper quality, of white clay, have been unearthed. The workshop of Servandus, which flourished in the second half of the second century at the barley market in Cologne, produced figurines of Bacchus, Venus, Diana, and Mercury which were so popular that

FIG. 70. STATUETTE OF A CHINESE CONJURER
Earthenware. Han Dynasty

they were copied in other districts. The habit of making grave offerings endured into the early Middle Ages, being first condemned as a heathen practice in the Carolingian epoch.

In China, where the death sacrifice was widely practised, the offering of living persons was abolished, then reintroduced, and eventually disappeared completely after the time of Confucius (551–478 B.C.), its place being taken by images. It seems that even before the time when living persons were sacrificed straw or paper images were burned at the funeral and then placed in the grave—a practice that endured up to recent times. The reform instituted by Confucius consisted in the substitution for the human offering of a wooden doll with movable limbs, which was placed in the grave of the deceased. Whereas, too, in the past part of the actual possessions of the dead man was sent to the flames, now men were satisfied with representations in paper of the objects of value. Marco Polo, who visited China about 1280, records this, and speaks too of the male and female paper figures which were burned with the corpse. These once real, but now fictional, offerings spring from fear inspired by the dead man's spirit. Men were convinced that the soul looked around

FIG. 71. SPIRIT CONJURER
Earthenware. Han Dynasty

FIG. 72. A YOUNG MAN
Earthenware. Han Dynasty

for means of subsistence, and that if these were refused it proceeded forcibly to procure them by tormenting the survivors. Consequently, for the sake of their own quiet, men provided the dead man's soul with whatever it might require. On his part, the deceased received a kind of guarantee that his descendants continued to care for him and to make sacrifice to him.

Out of this conception has arisen an artistic activity of high æsthetic value. Beginning under the Han Dynasty (206 B.C. to A.D. 220), and continuing during the Tang period (A.D. 608 to 922), it was barely extinguished before the fourteenth century. These long centuries, of course, have provided a vast quantity of such images; the extant examples number thousands, and presumably only a few of the actual graves have been opened. As in all human affairs, here too vanity entered in. Owing to the custom of exhibiting the grave offerings before the funeral, rivalry among the rich and aristocratic soon made itself evident, until eventually the authorities decided that action must be taken to control these funeral luxuries. In 741 the Tang Emperor Kao Tsung issued an edict prohibiting the use of offerings made of gold, silver, copper, tin, or even wood, only clay objects being permitted. Even the number of offerings was specified: those who stood above the fourth class might be given ninety pieces, those over the sixth class sixty pieces, those over the tenth class forty pieces, while the common people were allowed only fifteen objects. These decrees had the result which comes of all unenforcable laws—they were circumvented, until an edict of 1372 allowed of only one object as a grave offering.

FIG. 73. CHINESE WOMAN IN FESTIVE CLOTHES
Probably Tang Dynasty

While grave sculpture during the period immediately following the Tang era was mostly carried out in wood the Tang figures themselves are of clay, and in the early Ming period the terra-cottas again form an exception. The better-class ware was made of a finely granulated, baked, and glazed clay, executed in various shades. The humbler ware was only roughly baked and left unglazed; this was painted when cold, and sometimes with many colours. Hollow moulds were used for the making of the figures; after the moulding the seams were covered over, but remain visible, the figures being hollow within. Owing to the great demand, there must have been a genuine mass production of these grave images, but there were among the modellers some outstanding artists who introduced an individual style into their work. The wealth of models, so far as forms represented is concerned, is extraordinarily great. All branches of Chinese

culture over a period of 1500 years appeared here in countless
variations. Among the male figures are horsemen who act as
bodyguards in front of and behind the coffin, detachments of

FIG 74. CHINESE WOMEN WITH LOTUS BLOOMS IN THEIR HANDS
Earthenware. Later than Han Dynasty

soldiers in full armour, civilians in respectful attitude, bands
of musicians, wrestlers, boxers, clowns, and actors. The forms
are naturalistically conceived, and the figures are often shown
with dramatically seized attitudes. The love—indeed, we may
say the passion—of the artists is, however, for the women, who

not only are represented much more frequently than the men (in some graves have been found hundreds of female figures), but are characterized in greater variety. Harem women, dancing girls, servants with fan or spittoon, are here in diverse forms. Often they wear highly fantastic costumes and headdresses, and they are conceived in every possible attitude; but never are they represented as naked. The artists have brilliantly delineated the peculiarly charming and rich dresses and gestures of these women. *Così fan tutte* beyond death and the grave. The gleam of the varnish preserves their coquettish laughter and the unfathomable glance of their hollow eyes—a strange escort on the way to eternity. Another class is consecrated to divinities whose duty it is to protect the grave from demons and the corpse from the defilement of evil spirits. These so-called guardian gods for the most part are fashioned in grotesque, and occasionally in bizarrely contorted, forms. In Japan too, the culture of which is closely allied to that of China, it was the custom on the death of an emperor to bury alive with him his entire retinue. Shikune, under the Emperor Suimin, is said to have been the first, in 24 B.C., to prohibit this practice, substituting for the sacrifice of living persons the offering of clay images.

So far we have been engaged in a sphere where the doll has a magical significance. The *rôle* which fell to its lot as a magical figure was no small one; but it had other important tasks to fulfil in the ordinary life of the citizens—above all in religious cult. Throughout the whole of antiquity the employment of images in divine service was common. As a supreme example of this Schlosser adduces the presentation of the body of Adonis, an originally Oriental divinity, whose worship was celebrated by Greek women in processions where figures of the lovely youth were borne around. At the Roman *lectisternium* the gods were solemnly entertained, figures with wax heads and real clothes taking the place of the divinities. Images, too, were sometimes used for the purpose of executing justice or wreaking vengeance. Thus Trebellius Pollio relates that on one occasion a figure of the usurper Celsus, whose body had been thrown to the dogs, was strung up on the gallows, as a visible symbol to all of the ignominy with which his memory should be regarded. Many centuries later Pope Pius II took a similar revenge on one of his political opponents, Sigismondo Malatesta, of Rimini; failing to capture this man, he got a speaking likeness of him burned with due solemnity in front of St Peter's, Rome.

The symbolic expression of scorn and vengeance by means of the image, when the guilty person is not at hand, has remained

alive up to the present day. Gersau was once the smallest
Swiss republic and, as a sign of its sovereignty of justice, had a
gallows in front of its gate. To annoy their neighbours the
Lucerners, on one occasion in the eighteenth century, hanged a
straw image on this gallows, but the people of Gersau got the
laugh on their side by dressing up the figure as a Lucerner in his
official costume. Not long before the outbreak of the War a
Russian monk Iliodor, a close rival of Rasputin in sanctity, got
a great image dressed in a Jewish caftan to be carried round in
processions he organized at Zarytsin. Ulrich von Wilamowitz-
Möllendorf in his reminiscences relates that when he visited
Schulpforta, about 1860, a straw figure dressed like a scare-
crow was made by the third-form boys at the conclusion of the
autumn examinations and then was carried round the building
on a pole as the 'examiner.' In January 1929 the English
League against Imperialism held a meeting in London at
which Saklatvala, the Communist member in the House of
Commons, "protested" against the "activities of British
Imperialism in Afghanistan" and against the part played there
by Colonel Lawrence under the guise of Aircraftsman Shaw.
Amid the acclamations of the audience a life-size image representing Colonel Lawrence was burned.

The trade in clay images at Rome was very large; whole
streets were occupied by their manufacturers, and there were
special markets where they were sold. Because of the great
demand they were usually made in moulds over a wood base or
left hollow; when, as was rare, they were formed by hand the
figures were made solid. During the excavations at Pompeii,
according to Kekule, it was noticed that these small clay images
were not to be found in the more opulent houses; the palaces
in the Strada di Mercurio and the Strada di Nola contained
hardly an example worth speaking of. The nearer an approach
is made to the excavations in the Strada Stabiana, which was the
centre of the industrial and commercial life of the city, the richer
become the discoveries. A mass of heterogeneous cheap ware was
unearthed in the dwellings of the slaves, many more in the bar-
racks of the gladiators and in the poorer houses. It is rather
touching to note that in the confusion of the city's ruin the people
in their flight sometimes snatched up nothing but their clay
dolls; among the bodies found in the Foro Triangolare were
unearthed clay figures which they had taken with them in
preference to all their other goods.

Aristocrats and rich people were not content with the cheap
clay figures; they got great wax images made, clad in real gar-

ments. According to the statement left by Kallixenus concerning the *pompa* of Ptolemy Philadelphus, there were in the King's pavilion groups of such figures, representing ancient actors, placed in separate niches. These images seem to have been indispensable, especially at the obsequies of distinguished people. The custom originated from the practice of exhibiting the corpse to the public gaze for some time (in Rome, for example, seven days) before the burial or cremation—a practice which, in warm climates, necessitated special precautions. Thus, just as the Egyptian mummies were furnished with portrait-masks, death-masks were put on the faces of corpses in Nineveh, Phœnicia, Carthage, Greece, and Italy. These were made of bronze, iron, or clay—in Mycenæ even of gold. In Cumæ a grave of the Diocletian period was unearthed containing two skeletons which, in place of the heads belonging to them, had wax heads fitted with glass eyes. A remarkable parallel is provided by the mummies from the New Hebrides preserved in the Berlin Völker-Museum. The bodies of bamboo, moss, and bark, painted in naturalistic colours, bear real human heads. On the island of Bali, even at the present time, it is customary to burn corpses, but as this is expensive they are often allowed to remain lying for a considerable time; in the tropic climate, however, they rapidly decompose, and a palm-leaf image is burned in their stead. This custom is in use also for those who die far from their homes. Great solemn funerals, especially of kings and princes, demanded long preparations and such a lapse of time as often led to the decomposition of the body. Wherefore from the merely masked corpse a step was taken toward the image representing the dead man and magnificently arrayed. On the great Diplyon vase found at Athens, belonging to a period between 1000 and 800 B.C., it is clear that the artist has depicted a funeral procession bearing a corpse wrapped in cloths on a hearse, while the dead man is represented once more as an image lying on his death-bed.

This custom the Romans inherited from the Greeks. At Cæsar's funeral, according to Appian, the statue of the murdered man was made of wax; it showed the twenty-three bleeding wounds inflicted by the conspirators, and was so contrived as to turn to all sides during the processional march. At the funeral rites of Germanicus the body was unobtainable, and accordingly a clothed wooden image with a wax head was substituted for it. At the entombment of Pertinax there were two images of the Emperor, representing him respectively as awake and asleep; pages warded off the flies from these just as if he had been living.

Ammianus Marcellinus, in describing the obsequies for the son of the Chionite king, Grumbates, who had fallen in the year A.D. 359 before Amida, tells how the prince lay on a high catafalque, surrounded by ten biers with figures representing his retainers.

Imperial Rome bequeathed this 'funeral sculpture,' as a prerogative of the high aristocracy, to the Middle Ages; during the feudal period it survived even the most violent political turmoils. England and France are the two countries where these peculiar funeral ceremonials, when for the corpse is substituted an image, were raised to a fine art. To these rites belong, too, those connected with the *chambre de parade*, in which the image was put on a bier, the table set, and the food served daily before the burial. Since the lord was treated as though he were still alive, every attempt was made to render the image as naturalistic and lifelike as possible. The figures were life-size, the bodies made of wickerwork, hard-boiled leather, oak, and, in order to reduce the weight, left hollow, with straw over a wooden base and the whole

FIG. 75. FUNERAL FIGURE OF KING EDWARD III OF ENGLAND (*d.* 1377)
*Westminster Abbey*

FIG. 76. FUNERAL FIGURE OF QUEEN CATHERINE DE VALOIS
*Westminster Abbey*

covered with stucco. Head and hands were of coloured wax; arms were generally movable. Hair and beard were provided, and the figures were dressed in garments from the dead man's wardrobe. There is documentary evidence for the use of these figures from the first half of the fourteenth century, but the earliest extant example is that of King Edward III of England, who died in 1377. A large collection of such figures, so far, at any rate, as England is concerned, is preserved in the Islip Chapel at Westminster Abbey, where their tattered appearance has given them the nickname of 'the ragged regiment.' Clad in their State robes, they stand in glass cases—kings and queens and other historical celebrities such as Cromwell, Pitt, and

90

Lord Nelson in the uniform he wore at Trafalgar. They would have been of great value for the history of costume had they not been restored, but when James I visited Westminster Abbey in 1606 along with his brother-in-law, King Christian of Denmark, the dean got all the existent figures newly clad, a procedure that was repeated in the eighteenth century. Queen Elizabeth, for example, whose costume must have been exceedingly interesting, was entirely redressed in 1760.

In France there is documentary evidence for the use of the funeral image from the death of King Charles VI in 1422. At the obsequies of Henry II, who died from a wound received in a tournament, the King's image, set on a throne, was carried round in a procession lasting several days. These figures came from the hands of artists: Jean Perréal made those of Louis XII and Queen Anne, François Clouet those of Francis I and Henry II. When Henry IV was murdered three sculptors immediately set to work. Malherbe saw one of the examples, and described it as similar to "the bodies made like dolls in the Palais"—that is to say, like a mannequin of the fashion shop then established in the Palais de Justice. The head and hands were of wax, realistically formed: the dress a red silk vest and a royal mantle of purple velvet embroidered with golden lilies; crown, sceptre, and *main de justice* were also provided. This image lay in state for eleven days. Twice daily meals were brought to it by officers of the Crown, these being subsequently given to the poor. Louis XIII was the last monarch to have his death solemnized with this great funeral pomp in the olden style. The custom was revived when the dissolute Marat was stabbed on July 13, 1793, by the dagger of Charlotte Corday. On that occasion there was exhibited, not the hideous corpse of the incurable leper, but an image made by the famous painter David.

The images of the English kings were preserved in Westminster Abbey; those of the French monarchs were kept in Saint-Denis. There the German travel-writer Johann Jakob Volkmann saw the whole series of funeral images from Charles VIII to Louis XIII, clad in ermine mantles, crowns on their heads and sceptres in their hands, sitting large as life, on chairs in glass cases. During the Revolution the iconoclastic rage of the mob destroyed these remarkable relics, the head of Henry IV alone surviving the ruin; this is now preserved as a bust in the Musée Condé at Chantilly. The high aristocracy and the clergy followed the example of the Court. When, for instance, the obsequies of the two Guise brothers, murdered in the Château de Blois by command of Henry III, were solemnized at Toulouse in 1588, three different images of the Duke and of the Cardinal respectively were exhibited to the public. One represented them as they were being murdered; in another they knelt in prayer; and in the third they lay on the catafalque. These images are said to have been on show at Toulouse for a long time.

Other countries too followed this custom. The doges of Venice down to the last, who died in 1797, were honoured in the same way. When the celebrated painter Elisabetta Sirani died at Bologna in 1665—of poison, as it was believed—a full figure of the artist sitting at her easel was shown at her funeral in the church of S. Domenico. Frederick William I of Prussia himself, who hated all foreign things, and in particular detested the French from the bottom of his heart, did not escape this foreign ritual. When he was buried at Potsdam in 1740, there was exhibited in the *chambre de parade* an easy chair on which was placed "the likeness in wax of the highest-souled king." The last known example seems to have been that of King Victor Emmanuel of Italy. In January 1878 a life-size wax image of the dead monarch, leaning against a wall in a room of the Quirinal, was exhibited at his funeral.

## VII

## WAXWORKS AND THE MANNEQUIN

FROM these exhibitions developed the waxworks, for it was but a step from this spectacular art of the aristocracy to the booth art at the annual fairs of the people. This descent, if so it be called, carried to extremity that desire for naturalistic representation which has been associated with the wax image from the very start. Those engaged in this work did not seek merely for a reflection of reality; their object was complete illusion. The votive figures had this quality; it was emphasized too in the funeral image; and the waxworks simply carry this almost painful tendency toward naturalism, to use Schlosser's happy phrase, "to the verge of indiscretion." The lineaments are represented in such detail (down even to the small hairs of the beard), and such a startling lifelikeness is aimed at, that there can be no possibility of any æsthetic appreciation. The oldest panopticons were the churches, with their naturalistically reproduced votive figures. The first genuine secular collection of life-size wax figures was that shown at the Doolhof in Amsterdam, apparently as early as the sixteenth century. There there were groups and single figures, among them William the Silent, Henry IV of France, Gustavus Adolphus (and, later, Queen Christina and Cromwell), who were gazed at in astonishment by travellers as great spectacles.

Works of art so well calculated to suit the popular taste appeared as profitable business propositions to the promoters themselves. Among the itinerants in Germany were many who travelled about with wax figures which they exhibited for money. In 1605 a certain Ambrosius Müller, of Erfurt, wished to show at Nürnberg the figures, "made in wax," of John Huss, Luther, and Melanchthon, but the magistrates packed him off, "since there have been idols enow here already." In the following year Christoph Gagler, of Klagenfurt, fared no better with his "idol work." At Paris in 1611 François de Bechefer got up a similar show, in which was to be seen the lately murdered King Henry IV. Here we come on that element of the horrible which seems to have formed so great an attraction of these waxworks from that time onward. This interest in the waxworks went along with a fashion in Society circles for portraiture in wax. In the seventeenth and eighteenth centuries those who could pay for it liked not only to be painted, but to be moulded in wax; the life-size figures dressed in real clothes exercised apparently an extraordinary fascination. Antoine Benoist, wax-embosser to Louis XIV, became famous for his life-size portrait in wax of Queen Anne of Austria with her Court ladies. They were represented as standing, richly clad, "for all persons of rank deemed it an honour to honour the artist with their finest clothes for this purpose." Considerable numbers of images of this kind have been preserved in various art-historical collections; thus Peter the Great is shown in the Hermitage at Leningrad, and the great Prince Elector King Frederick I in Schloss Monbijou, where, too, may be found some children's toys belonging to a Hohenzollern prince who died in infancy. From the end of the seventeenth century comes the wax figure of Luther, still to be seen, clad in the dress of a Protestant minister, in the Marienkirche at Halle. He sits before a table, his clenched hand placed on a Bible; formerly he wore a peruke, but this has now been replaced by a cap. On the death of Frederick the Great Johann Eckstein made two wax figures of that monarch, although these were no longer used for a funeral parade. One of them went to the Hohenzollern Museum; the other, clad in the uniform worn by the King in the Seven Years War, went to Brunswick.

In Paris during the second half of the seventeenth century there must have been several waxwork collections open, on payment, to the public, for the aforesaid Antoine Benoist in 1668 succeeded in securing from the king a special privilege for his waxworks, a privilege which was renewed from time to time and in 1718 continued in favour of his son for a period of twenty years. Unless there had been competition such a privilege would not have been required. A wax-sculptor of uncommon talents was Johann C. Creutz, who, since he lived in Paris, called himself Curtius. He was specially renowned for the marvellous anatomical models in wax which he executed with a master's hand. In 1783 he opened his waxworks, in which the Caverne des Grands Voleurs provided a special attraction for a novelty-seeking public. On July 12, 1789, his exhibition was stormed by the mob, and the busts of Necker and the Duc d'Orléans were carried off to be borne in triumph through Paris. The artist got his niece, Marie Grosholtz, to come to Paris, where he instructed her in his art; she modelled many heads after the life, and gave lessons to Mme Élizabeth, the sister of Louis XVI. In the year 1794 she married a certain M. Tussaud, from whom she was separated six years later. In 1802 she moved to London, taking with her the whole of her uncle's vast collection. Tussaud's waxworks, carried on by the son, grandson, and great-grandson of the foundress, has remained one of the chief spectacles in London for well over a century, the Chamber of Horrors in especial forming a centre of attraction, the interest of which is augmented with every new murder. The original collection was destroyed by a great fire in 1925. After reconstruction the exhibition was reopened in 1928.

FIG. 77. MANNEQUIN OF
. TUT-ENCH-AMUN

End of XVIIIth Dynasty (about 1350 B.C.). From *Tut-ench-Amun*, by Carter and Mace

*Photo Harry Burton*

At the same period that Curtius opened his panopticon in Paris the Hofstatuarius Müller, who was in actuality a Count Deym of Strítez, founded his show in Vienna at the Stock im Eisen. It included all the celebrities of the time—the entire royal family, the potentates of Christendom—Frederick II, Catherine of Russia, Louis XVI, Marie-Antoinette, the Dauphin, and others. It gained additional brilliance from a number of *galant* automata in such settings as the bedroom of the Graces. The artist died in 1804, but his collection survived him. The Musée Grévin, in Paris, and Castan's panopticon, in Berlin, have retained their popularity right down to the present time. Up to about 1880 wax sculpture was practised as a free art in Mexico, where *mestizos* at the annual fairs improvised wax figures. These were painted and clothed and sold at moderate prices. In 1878 A. Montanari brought a selection to the Paris exhibition, where they were much admired on account of the peculiar vigour of their style.

These wax figures always move "on the threshold of art"— one step more and we arrive at the mannequin. The invention of the dress-doll used by tailors to aid them in trying on dresses, and serving as an excellent advertisement in fashion shops because of the exact fit of the clothes, has been ascribed, but wrongly so, to Poppæa, the beloved of Nero. She was not needed

95

to invent it, for this useful article was in existence long before her time. In the grave of Tut-ench-Amun, dating from about the year 1350 B.C., there was discovered, alongside the great carved, gilded, and painted death image of the King, his dress-figure sharply cut off at the middle and above the elbows. This

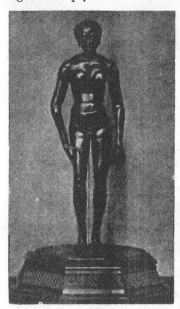

FIG. 78. LIMBED DOLL, FROM THE
BEGINNING OF THE SIXTEENTH
CENTURY
Erroneously ascribed to Dürer

is life-size and is painted white, obviously to suggest a shirt; unquestionably it was used to try on Pharaoh's garments. Near by in the grave was found the dress-chest. When the tyranny of Galeazzo Maria Sforza, Duke of Milan, became at last too terrible to be endured a conspiracy was formed among the aristocracy, as a result of which he was murdered in 1476 in the church of S. Gottardo. So as to be absolutely certain of success, these conspirators practised on the Duke's dress-figure. The popularity of these mannequins has not waned. Edmond de Goncourt knew a French duke who possessed twenty-five mannequins, on which all his wardrobe was set out so that his suits should not take on false forms or creases. The masters of the *grande couture*, whether they are settled in Paris, in London, or in Berlin, keep mannequins of their foreign customers on which they can execute their orders.

Closest akin to the mannequin is the lay figure, the aid of the prentice painter and sculptor. It is difficult to determine its age, but it is first mentioned in Filarete's work on architecture, written about 1460. In Germany it does not appear before Dürer's time. These lay figures were of various sizes. Vasari relates that Fra Bartolommeo got a life-size wooden figure made in order to study the folds of drapery; this interesting object is still preserved in the Accademia delle Belle Arti at Florence. G. B. Armenino, of Faenza, and Bernardino Campi, of Cremona, both of whom wrote in the second half of the sixteenth century, give plentiful instructions concerning the manufacture and use of these modelling figures. The smallest kinds were employed by painters engaged in sketching out compositions containing many figures, so that they might get an impression of the physical reality, carry through difficult foreshortenings in the building up of groups, and regulate the positions of single figures so as to give a clear idea of distance. Such things could not be studied so easily on the living model—at any rate when a view

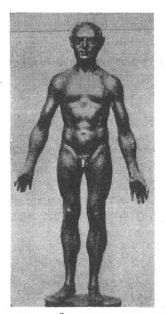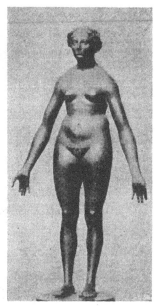

FIGS. 79, 80. GERMAN PROPORTION FIGURES CARVED FROM WOOD
Frankish work, about 1530
*Hofmuseum, Vienna*

from below was desired. Paolo Uccello, in the first half of the fifteenth century, was said to have employed little horses of this kind for his battle scenes. These figures were usually modelled. in clay and then cast in wax from a mould; by kneading and bending they could be put into any attitude desired. Drapery was represented by wet paper or pieces of cloth. Perugino was said to have ordered the figures he required from Sansovino, who also made the models for those of Andrea del Sarto. Antonio Begarelli, a celebrated clay-modeller, was credited with having made the little figures required by Correggio when he was engaged in painting the cathedral dome at Parma. Michelangelo himself, it is said, employed such figures when engaged on *The Last Judgment* in the Sistine Chapel. Tintoretto

G

97

carried out his studies in light by aid of small clay and wax figures made and dressed by himself. From him his talented pupil El Greco acquired the habit of working with figures; Pacheco recounts that he saw in the master's *atelier* in Toledo a whole cupboard of figures which had been made by the artist himself.

FIG. 81. THE PAINTER IN HIS STUDIO
Ostade
*Dresden Art Gallery*

Since these painters' lay figures were made of clay or wax they must have been immovable, but the extant modelling figures of the sixteenth century are of wood and have movable limbs. The German examples have been ascribed to Albrecht Dürer, but wrongly so. It is certainly true that Dürer, on his journey to the Netherlands in 1520, presented "a carved little child" to the Portuguese agent at Antwerp, but this was not necessarily of his own workmanship. The Nürnberg master, as several of his drawings and woodcuts prove, worked much with ball-limbed lay figures, but assuredly he did not make any of these. In the collection of Count Valencia de Don Juan is preserved a small modelling figure, very carefully fashioned of beech-wood, 23 cm. high. Neck,

98

body, arms, and legs, even fingers, toes, and jaws, are movable. An old inscription ascribes it to Dürer. The female counterpart, likewise of beech-wood and likewise movable, in 1864 belonged to Alexander Posonyi in Vienna. This came from the Nürnberg art collection of Paul Praun and was also ascribed to Dürer, but the fact that the proportions do not accord with Dürer's militates against this assumption. Emil Michel suggests Conrad Meyt as

FIG. 82. THE PAINTER WITH TWO LAY FIGURES
D. Chodowiecki
From Basedow's *Elementarbuch*

the maker of the male figure. Another female figure of this kind was preserved in the Leipzig collection of Hans Felix; it was modelled with delicacy of feeling, but its face, with its rigid features, was quite unlike Dürer's. The Kunsthistorische Hofmuseum in Vienna possesses three wooden proportion figures, representing man, woman, and child, which Schlosser conjectures must have originated in Franconia about 1530. Two wooden modelling figures, 25 cm. high, belonging to the beginning of the sixteenth century are also preserved in the Ferdinandeum at Innsbruck. The most beautiful and masterly of all extant examples are, in the opinion of E. F. Bange, the two beechwood figures in the possession of the Akademie der bildenden Künste in Berlin. These are 19 cm. high, with ball-joints which render even the fingers and toes movable. Bange suggests that the carver was one of the Regensburg-Salzburg school connected with the master J.P.—possibly even that master himself. The Kaiser-Friedrich-Museum, too, possesses a female wooden specimen of this type in addition to an anatomical male lay figure carved from wood, with movable limbs; the latter probably belongs to the second half of the sixteenth century and is derived from the anatomical figure made by Prospero Bresciano. These objects must have been very common in the Renaissance period; several examples are included in the inventory of Margaret of Austria in 1524. Since they mostly appear in pairs, is it possible that they were amorous toys?

The lay figures have not yet disappeared from the painters' and sculptors' studios. As time passed by they were gradually improved. At Paris in the eighteenth century Anciaume was especially famed for their manufacture. On April 18, 1774, the widow of the copper-plate engraver Gravelot advertised that she had for sale three English lay figures, each 2½ ft high, with copper joints and various coloured costumes.

In spite of the fact that the naturalistically treated wax figure will always remain a difficult problem for the student of æsthetics, it yet has some connexions with fine art. A group of Spanish sculptors carried this naturalism to extremes in their plastic work. Endeavouring to secure absolute truth to reality, they aimed not at any artistic impression, but solely at the illusion of immediate realism. The *imagenes de vestir* of the Spanish churches, figures set up at certain ecclesiastical festivals, have this end in view. The sculptor supplied only the head, hands, and feet; the costumes, for the most part over-rich and costly, were made of real cloth and gold embroidery. To secure the realistic impression real hair as well as glass eyes and glass tears were utilized, while the colouring went to extremes in its naturalistic representation of blood and wounds. All the large and many of the smaller Spanish churches possessed sets of such dressed-up images representing the persons connected with or suffering in the Passion; these, arranged in groups, were carried around in the processions of Easter week. They were called a *paso*. The greatest Spanish artists occupied themselves on work of this kind. The *Paso del gran poder* of Montañes and Zarcillo's *paso* in the Ermita de Jesús, Murcia, are works widely famed and reverenced, more closely associated with Spanish feeling than the white marble alone admitted by the æsthetics of the academicians. "This was the last time in Europe," says Sobotka in reference to these works, "that fine art was also a popular art." The highly renowned *Cristo de Burgos* is distinguished by naturalism of the crudest sort; in this cathedral Crucifixion the realistic representation of bleeding and festering wounds is carried to such a disgusting extreme that a legend has arisen to the effect that the figure had a human skin. It is, however, really covered with cured and painted leather—which, to be sure, is bad enough!

FIG. 83. CHRIST ON THE PALM ASS
Carved wood. Lower Bavaria
*Kaiser-Friedrich-Museum, Berlin*

The contemporary art of sculpture on this side of the Pyrenees did not go to such extremes of naturalism. The figures of the Sacro Monte of Varallo, the Crucifixion of which was executed by Guido Mazzoni under the direction of Gaudenzio Ferrari, are much more tasteful in form and colour. German sculptors too avoided these excesses of the Spaniards. The chief image in the Palm Sunday processions has always been the 'palm ass'— Christ sitting on an ass run on rollers. This group appeared at Augsburg as early as the time of St Ulrich, who died in 973, but all the extant examples in public collections belong to the fourteenth and sixteenth centuries. In some specimens (for instance, that in the Georgianum at Munich) the figure of Christ is carved naked, and is wrapped in a cloth mantle. They were so richly decorated at the festival that an Austrian proverb speaks of being "dressed up like a palm ass." At the Nonnberg in Salzburg there was an especially famous palm ass which was so decked out at the processions with rose-wreaths of coral, garnets, etc., that it was rumoured to be worth a whole kingdom. In 1782 Archbishop Count Colloredo ordered it to be broken up for firewood. In 1780 the custom of bearing round the palm ass in procession was denounced "because it offends against good taste." This anathema reached even to the palm ass of the church of St Peter in Munich. The people there clung to it with such tenacity that, in spite of all decrees, it was not abolished until a functionary of the church, on March 17, 1806, solemnly ordered it to be sawn in pieces. Small palm asses were given as toys to those children who, sitting behind and in front of the figure of Christ, took part in the procession. A palm ass was, according to Strele, still in use in his time at the convent of the Dominican nuns at Lienz; the figure of Christ there was clad in silk.

# VIII

## TOY DOLLS IN ANCIENT TIMES

IT is certain, then, that the image is of boundless antiquity, but it is doubtful whether the toy doll is as old. For there is this to be borne in mind—that no dolls have been discovered in childrens' graves of the prehistoric period. Of course, there might have been such made of perishable material; in defence of this view may be adduced the striking fact that, while no dolls have been discovered in neolithic settlements or in the Swiss lake-dwellings, there has been found a number of dolls' utensils. The arguments put forward by Walter Hough must here be taken into account. He draws attention to the fact that the oldest dolls known to us—the ancestor image and the idol—were objects having a religious and magical significance, and were handled only

FIG. 84. BYZANTINE DOLL'S TUNIC, OF COLOURED WOOL, FROM THE CEMETERY OF AKHMIM

by priests and medicine-men. Everything militates against the supposition that, at a time when men believed in the magical properties of the artificial human figure, children would have been permitted to play with objects so enwrapped in dangerous mysteries. The possibility, however, remains that the little figures, as belief faded and they lost their place in the rite, were handed over as toys to children. The play doll might easily have developed from the idol in the course of time, one and the same piece perhaps serving different purposes in ages of differing beliefs.

A progress of this kind is to be noted among the Hopi Indians, who, at the conclusion of their ceremonies, give their cult images to children to play with. Similar examples, too, have been recorded in the history of modern civilization. Roger Edgeworth, Canon of Bristol Cathedral, complained in 1544 that Catholic churches were being plundered, the figures of the

103

Madonna and of the saints being handed over as dolls to the children. In any case, the toy doll is the youngest sister of the

image. As such, however, it does not belong to the primitive possessions of human culture; it is not spread throughout the entire world, but is confined to civilized peoples. There are savage races (or were, at least) which do not possess toy dolls; Richard Schomburgk in British Guiana and Forbes in the Malay Archipelago came across tribes whose children do not know how to play. American ethnologists have demonstrated that the Indians first adopted the toy doll from emigrants in the time of Queen Elizabeth. In most of the Indian tongues there is no word for 'doll'; in others it is identical with the word 'baby.' It is evident at the first glance that the objects made for their children by some of the nature peoples of to-day betray European influences.

FIG. 85
WOODEN DOLL
OF IMPERIAL
ROME FROM THE
CEMETERY OF
AKHMIM
Height, 40 cm.

Toy dolls, then, exist only where there is civilization, but, while it is almost certain that they were not known among primitive peoples, they are to be met with fairly freely among the various civilized races of antiquity. The Vorderasiastische Museum in Berlin possesses a little alabaster doll which certainly does not belong to a religious cult; its arms are missing, but from the holes in the shoulders it is evident that these were movable. Apparently, too, it was designed to be dressed. Among the extraordinarily rich array of figures left by the ancient Egyptians there are many which were obviously used as toys. These are made of wood or linen stuffed with papyrus strips, the facial features being embroidered and the hair represented by threads. Some specimens are clad in woollen dresses or loin-cloths, and the arms and legs are often movable. Occasionally these dolls have portions added in wax; neckcloths, armlets, and rings on the feet are frequently

FIG. 86. GREEK TERRA-
COTTA LIMBED DOLL
FOUND IN THE CRIMEA

supplied. The least shapely in appearance are the drollest—
Wilkinson thinks for the purpose of catching the attention of
small children. Indeed, they are sometimes so rough that only
a child's fancy is capable of recognizing in them a human form.
There are also dolls made movable in the style of puppets,
representing women slaves at their washing or harvesting, etc.

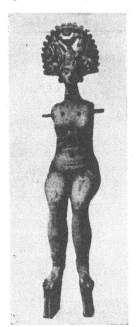

FIG. 87. APHRODITE
Terra-cotta dolls from Myrina

The Agyptische Museum in Berlin has a little limbed doll of
this kind dating from about the year 1900 B.C. In the necropolis
of Akhmim Panopolis, belonging to the sixth and seventh centuries A.D., Robert Forrer unearthed many large toy dolls made
of cloth and wood; their hair was fixed by means of asphalt,
their faces were painted, and they were clothed with woollen
costumes. There, too, were found single articles of dolls' dress
and dolls' utensils.

The oldest example of a Greek toy doll is a clay rattle box
made in female shape, but of which the head is missing. This
was found by Schliemann in one of the lower strata at Troy. In
children's graves too of the Mycenæan and of other archaic
periods are to be found small female dolls, often representing

women with children in their arms. It is to be observed that most Greek dolls represent women. The wax doll was called *dagynon* in Ionic, *dagys* in Doric; *plaggon* was the designation for

FIG. 88. EARLY GREEK PAINTED CLAY DOLL FROM A BŒOTIAN GRAVE
*Louvre, Paris*

'doll' in general. The manufacture of these objects was a widely disseminated trade; doll-makers were called *koroplastoi*. Most were made of clay, but plaster and wax were also employed, the

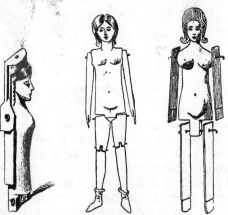

FIG. 89. GREEK LIMBED DOLLS

latter being spread on a wooden base and then worked over by hand. The arms and legs of the figures were frequently movable. Throughout classical antiquity Sardis, the capital of Lydia, was renowned for its manufacture of such toys. In Athens the

106

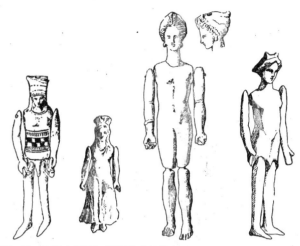

FIG. 90. EARLY GREEK LIMBED DOLLS FROM ATHENS, MYRINA, RHODES
Children's toys. Terra-cotta

merchants had their stalls in the *agora*, where they sold their articles to the children. Better-class examples were often executed with pains-taking care—these were of fine light-brown clay, only lightly baked and painted when cold. While heads and breasts were generally modelled in careful detail, the body was left rough, since it was intended to be covered with garments. Demosthenes, Lucian, Dio Chrysostom, and Suidas—all have left us some information about the Greek doll. Plutarch tells a pretty story of how his two-year-old daughter Timoxena begged her nurse to give milk to her doll as well as to herself. The little girls found pleasure in making clothes for their dolls, and the young Greek maidens, who were wont to be married at twelve or thirteen years of age, played with them up to the time of their betrothal, when they dedicated the dolls and all their wardrobe to Artemis or the nymphs. There are still extant gravestones of Greek girls who had died young on which this dedication of dolls is recorded. Sappho, according to Athenæus, dedicated her doll to Aphrodite: "O Aphrodite, despise not my doll's little purple

FIG. 91. GREEK CLAY DOLL, IN THE SHAPE OF A CHILD, FROM A GRAVE
*Biardot Collection*

107

neckerchief. I, Sappho, dedicate this precious gift to you!"
The *Anthologia Palatina* has preserved an epigram in which
Timarete consecrates her doll with its accessories to Artemis
Limnatis.

> Timarete before her marriage has offered up to Diana her
> tambourine, and her valued ball, and her cap, the defender of her

FIG. 92. GRAVESTONE OF A
GREEK GIRL
Avignon

FIG. 93. GRAVESTONE OF A
GREEK GIRL
Athens

> locks, and her dolls, O Limnatis, as is fitting for a virgin to a virgin,
> and her doll's dresses. And do thou, daughter of Latona, place thy
> hand over the girl Timarete, and preserve holily her who is holy.[1]

The Latin for the newborn child before it has been given a
name is *pupus* or *pupa*; from these words *Puppe* is derived, and
this has been adopted as a loan word in several languages to
signify the plastic representation of a little child. The Roman
toy dolls were for the most part made of clay; their manufacture
was widespread, and the products were a staple article of commerce. More carefully worked figures were made for the rich.
In the grave of a little girl in the Prati di Castello at Rome was
found a carved wooden doll, 30 cm. high, with movable limbs.
The hands were carefully executed, but the arms and legs were

---

[1] Translation from *The Greek Anthology*, by George Burges (Bohn's Classical
Library), pp. 412–413.

represented only by smooth strips of wood. In the sarcophagus of the Empress Maria, a daughter of Stilicho and wife of the Emperor Honorius (384–423), which was opened in 1594, there was discovered a beautifully ornamented little ivory doll. The Roman girls, like their Greek predecessors, were wont to dedicate their dolls to a goddess on the eve of their marriage. According to Persius they made an offering of these dolls to Venus or to the *lares*. Dolls were at that time no less dear to the hearts of Christian children than they were to the little pagans; several examples have been found in childrens' graves in the catacombs.

FIGS. 94, 95. ROMAN LIMBED DOLLS
FOUND IN ITALY
Children's toys

# IX

## EARLY TOY DOLLS IN EUROPE

THE toy doll did not disappear in the medieval child world. Although no extant examples exist from the earlier centuries, literary records testify to their importance. In the *Indiculus Superstitionum*, belonging to the eighth or ninth century, rag dolls (*simulacra de pannis*) were mentioned. The word for a doll in

FIG. 96. NÜRNBERG DOLLS OF BAKED CLAY,
FOURTEENTH TO FIFTEENTH CENTURIES
*Germanisches National-Museum, Nürnberg*

Old High German was *Tocha*, in Middle High German *Tocke*. From the fifteenth century the word *Docke* was adopted, while Geiler von Kaiserberg had already used the word *Puppe*, which rapidly won popularity. *Tocke* apparently at first meant a little block of wood, which makes us believe that the oldest German dolls were rather primitive things. In its acquired sense the word was widely used. Wilhelm von Oestreich, Oswald von Wolkenstein, and *Der jüngere Titurel* loved to compare beautiful young girls with lovely *Tocken*, naming them *Sommertocken*. Neidhardt von Reuenthal called his Vriderun a *Tocke*; Hugo von Langenstein called St Martina a heavenly *Tocke*; and when

Clara Hatzlerin wishes to give expression to her ill-humour at decked-up peasant girls she calls them village *Tocken*. Luther, in rebuking female vanity, speaks of woman as a pretty *Tocke*.

The toy doll as such is a familiar subject among writers. *Mai und Beaflor*, Hadamar von Laber, and *Virginal* refer to the children's *Tocken*. Wolfram von Eschenbach refers to them

FIG. 97. CLAY DOLLS, FOURTEENTH TO FIFTEENTH CENTURIES
*Germanisches National-Museum, Nürnberg*

oftener than other poets, since in his little daughter, with whom he loved to play, he had, of course, a real child before his eyes. In the *Titurel* he makes the young Sigune beg that her dolls be not forgotten when she is going on a journey, and in conversation with Schionatulander she asks whether she may still keep on loving her doll. In the *Willehalm* he is describing the beauty of coats of mail: "Here came the sun's gleam on many coats of mail; my daughter's *Tocke* is hardly so lovely." This shows that these dolls were dressed up as richly as possible for their little owner. Geiler von Kaiserberg, the Strasbourg preacher, alludes to this when he accuses parents of teaching their young daughters "to be proud of their dolls." A century

III

later Fischart complains that women decked themselves up as girls decked up their dolls, and Simplizissimus says of himself, "she decked me up like a French doll." Guote, the daughter of Rudolf von Habsburg, married in her teens to Wenzel von Böhmen, had nothing of greater interest to tell her husband than how she had dressed her doll.

The extant examples, however, in no wise give an impression of special magnificence. The oldest of all, belonging to the

FIG. 98. NÜRNBERG DOLL-MAKER AT HIS WORK
From the *Hortus Sanitatis*, Mainz, 1491

thirteenth century, is made on the model of the Trojan dolls, mentioned above—a rattle box of baked clay in the shape of a wreathed and smiling woman. Similar specimens originating in the thirteenth century have been discovered in the soil of old Strasbourg. In Nürnberg too some clay dolls, dating back to the fourteenth century, were brought to light in 1859 under the pavements—children in swaddling clothes, monks, little men, and lovely women dressed in the fashion of the time with large hoops. Some of them have a remarkable circular hollow on the breast about the size of a florin, apparently designed to hold a christening gift. Hefner-Alteneck found numbers of such figures in the course of excavations at the city of Tannenberg. These little clay dolls are, however, of the simplest pattern, not necessitating the use of clothes. This must have taken from the children a great part of the charm of these dolls when regarded as toys. Such dolls found in the cities were apparently not single articles, but seem to have been shop stock—a fact proving that the manufacture of dolls must, even at that time, have been a rising industry. In 1413 at Nürnberg, which has remained a principal centre of this industry up to the present day, a doll-maker of the name of Ott is recorded, and another, named H. Mess, is mentioned in the year 1465. Amusing and instructive are the illustrations in the various editions of the *Hortus Sanitatis,* a favourite fifteenth-century work dealing popularly with medical subjects. These show the doll-maker at his trade and,

XLVII.
Ein Handtwerck̄sfraw in der Schlesien.
Jn was klaibung vnd gebaht.    Die Handtwerck̄sfrawen einher gehn.

FIG. 99. WOODCUT BY JOST AMMAN, 1577

although they have no pretensions to photographic exactitude, indicate that dolls with movable arms are intended.

In the sixteenth century the iconographic records increase. Jost Amman, Tobias Stimmer, the artist using the monogram J.R., and other illustrators of civic life have immortalized in many of their sketches little girls playing with their dolls. The doll must then have been a popular article, for Fischart ironically ejaculates: "What marvel is it that wives manage to get round their husbands so easily? From their childhood they are used to play with dolls; they merely continue their game with their husbands after marriage!" These pictures reveal the fact that all the little girls played with dolls which impersonated women, invariably dressed in the contemporary fashion; dolls representing children had not yet made their appearance.

In 1584 Margarethe Schleicher, a little girl of Nürnberg

received a present of a doll dressed like a real Nürnberg bride, with her large peculiar head-gear. At Christmas 1619 Frau

FIG. 100. PRINCESS MARIE OF SAXONY
Painting by L. Cranach. About 1540

Löffenholtz presented her seven-year-old daughter Barbara with a large doll and a *hennsla buben* (a male doll, the word *hennsla*

114

being connected with *Hänschen*); her five-year-old and three-year-old children also received dolls.

The wax doll appeared in Germany during the seventeenth

FIG. 101. CHILD WITH DOLL
Historical Exhibition of Ancient Art, Paris, 1879
*Albert Goupil Collection*

century. Joachim von Sandrart praised the products of Daniel Neuberger in Augsburg: as hard as stone were these, and so marvellously coloured that they seemed to be alive. In 1632 the town of Augsburg presented King Gustavus Adolphus with a sumptuous art cabinet costing 6500 reichsthalers. The designer,

115

the well-known Philipp Hainhofer, inserted in it a pair of dolls which to-day are to be found preserved in Upsala—a cavalier and his lady, 9½ and 11½ cm. high, holding each

FIG. 102. DOLL AS A COSTUME MODEL
Height, 75 cm. Beginning of the seventeenth century. French
*Figdor Collection, Vienna*

other's hands in readiness to dance by means of a mechanism no longer operative. The gentleman has movable head and arms; he wears a tunic and silken breeches trimmed with silver braid, a pointed lace collar, a grey broad-brimmed hat, high boots of brown leather, and a sword. Around his waist he has a yellow silk sash with silver fringe; over his right shoulder a blue cloak with silver lapels. The lady's head unfortunately is missing, but her dress, consisting of a yellow silk damask costume ornamented with silver braid and a sash of rose-coloured silk with silver fringes encircling the waist, has been carefully preserved. Since this was a gift to a king it certainly represents the

FIG. 103. AUGSBURG DOLLS
From the art cabinet of Gustavus Adolphus in Upsala. About 1630

best in the doll line which could then be obtained in Germany. Hainhofer, who was active as a connoisseur, an art-collector, and an art-dealer, supplied also a large set of toy dolls with another of his art cabinets which he sold to Duke Philip II of Pomerania in August 1617, and which is now to be found in the Schlossmuseum at Berlin. This represented a farmyard full of dolls, including soldiers, girls, farm servants, carriers, cavaliers, and peasants of both sexes. One woman was seated milking a cow, and even a "closet," "in which a girl is sitting doing the needful," was included. There were many animals, and the various kinds of poultry were even covered with real birds' feathers. The model, 210 cm. long, 165 cm. wide, and 120 cm. high, was made by Mathias Kager, the animals modelled by Johann Schwegler. Among ladies of quality these farmyards

117

were popular toys—and also expensive, for they cost from 500 to 800 gulden. Duke William of Bavaria gave several of them as

FIG. 104. BEDROOM IN A DOLL'S HOUSE
Seventeenth century
*Bayerische Landesgewerbe-Anstalt, Nürnberg*

FIG. 105. KITCHEN IN A DOLL'S HOUSE
Seventeenth century
*Bayerische Landesgewerbe-Anstalt, Nürnberg*

presents; he sent various specimens to the Queens of France and Spain, some archduchesses, and other princesses, but these have all now disappeared. Only a few scattered examples of seventeenth-century dolls' houses have been preserved, all certainly the property of adults, for their well-preserved condition

FIG. 106. LARGE NÜRNBERG DOLL'S HOUSE (EXTERIOR)
Eighteenth century
*Germanisches National-Museum, Nürnberg*

testifies to the fact that they have never fallen into children's destructive hands. Duke Albert V of Bavaria got a sumptuous doll's house made for him; this was placed in the art gallery of

119

the Residenz in Munich, but unhappily is not now extant. In 1631 at Nürnberg Anna Käferlin set up a complete doll's house,

FIG. 107. LARGE NÜRNBERG DOLL'S HOUSE (INTERIOR)
Eighteenth century
*Germanisches National-Museum, Nürnberg*

including even a library, an armoury, and a music room, which she exhibited on payment. Paul von Stetten records in 1765

From the "Gallerie des Modes," 1780

that at Augsburg there were dolls' houses which had cost 1000 gulden and more. Doll-making remained a free, unincorporated trade, in which all kinds of hand-workers participated. In

Dockenmacher von Pappen Zeuch.
Reichthum, Schönheit, Stärck, istnur Pappen Werck.

Ihr Kinder inder Eitelkeit,
wann wollt ihr euch der Docken schämen?
Sieht nicht, was endlich Tod und Zeit,
leicht wieder wissen weg zu nehmen,
wann euch des Sterbens dunckle Nacht,
das Grab zum Gitter-Bette macht.

FIG. 108. FROM WEIGEL'S "HAUPTSTÄNDE," 1698

Nürnberg alone there were seventeen workshops devoted to the manufacture of dolls. The council of that city on November 17, 1600, gave permission to Barbara Beuchin, daughter of Georg Breitner, of Bamberg, to display for sale the dolls of her own making in the market-place near the Schönen Brunnen. In the year 1700 there were six master doll-makers in Nürnberg.

The toy doll in France, one need hardly remark, was an

*Dockenmacher von Trachant.*
*Liebt und begehrt, was ewig währt.*

*Mein Schatz, und meiner Freude Ziel*
*ist Gott, soll meine Seele sprechen.*
*Des Reichtums buntes Docken-Spiel*
*kan leicht ein Unglücks Stoß, zerbrechen,*
*Vergnügung fehlt ihm die es weiß,*
*wie dem Trachant-Bild Menschen Geist.*

FIG. 109. FROM WEIGEL'S "HAUPTSTÄNDE," 1698

esteemed object. A traveller who visited Paris in the middle of the fifteenth century saw some exhibited for sale:

> Non desunt puppæ gratissima dona tenellis
> Virginibus miro culta formaque decora.

Antoine Astérau, who wrote a description of Paris in the same century, saw on the stalls of the Palais de Justice, where various articles of luxury were regularly set out for sale, "charming and attractively dressed dolls." In the year 1455 Raoulin de la Rue supplied Princess Madeleine, daughter of King Charles VII,

FIG. 110. DWARF WITH
PERUKE
Eighteenth century
*Bayerisches National-Museum,
Munich*

FIG. 111. GENTLEMAN
WITH SWORD
Wooden doll. Seventeenth century
*Bayerisches National-Museum,
Munich*

with a doll representing a woman on horseback attended by her foot servants. In the sixteenth century Paris played an important part in the doll trade. Emperor Charles V, in spite of his hatred of France, ordered dolls to be sent from Paris for his little daughter. In 1530 he paid Jean Beauvalet, chaplain of St Gudule's in Brussels, ten francs—then a large sum—for this purpose. King Henry II got six dolls sent from Paris to his daughters; these cost him nine francs. In 1571 Duchess Claudia of Lorraine instructed P. Holman to get for her in Paris four to six of the most beautifully dressed dolls he could find. They had not to be too large, however, since they were destined for her newly born granddaughter, the Duchess of Bavaria.

FIG. 112. DOLL IN WALKING DRESS
First half of the eighteenth century
*Germanisches National-Museum, Nürnberg*

No definitely authentic example of French workmanship of this period has been preserved. That particular doll which has become well known through its appearance at various exhibitions and in prints, and which was shown first in the Albert Goupil Collection at the world exhibition of 1878, is not an original, but is an ingenious patchwork made up of various old parts. The dress is a sixteenth-century child's dress of silk (originally white) with embroidered underclothing, which had belonged to the wardrobe of a statue of the Madonna in a Venetian convent. There Bardini, the dealer in antiques, procured it. In the Vanutelli Collection in Florence he found the

FIG. 113. DOLL'S SUNSHADE OF RED SILK
Eighteenth century
*Germanisches National-Museum, Nürnberg*

marble head of a child doll which had been made in the fifteenth century, perhaps in Donatello's studio itself, or, at any rate, somewhere near. This he bought and provided a fine head for the costume by making a smaller painted replica of the marble. The body, arms, and legs of the figure were made of new material, the collar and cap to fit it being supplied out of the lining of the dress. The small doll is thus a Neapolitan crib-figure of the eighteenth century for which a dress in the style of the sixteenth century has been made out of old cloth. In this way, out of antique material which came from Venice, Florence, and Naples—all, without exception, of Italian origin—was created a 'French' doll. A pretty game, which, however, didn't succeed in deluding the experts.

In 1604 Sully sent the young Dauphin, later Louis XIII, a state coach filled with dolls. In 1605 the Prince received a male doll, and in 1606 a very beautifully dressed little noble;

in 1608 he was presented with a Capuchin monk of earthenware. In certain rhymes put into the mouth of the clown Gros-Guillaume in 1619 reference is made to a plaster doll which he promises to Dame Perrine. Dolls of this material must have been the finest quality; the better class went in for luxuries in dolls as in other things. Richelieu gave the Duchesse

FIG. 114. AUGSBURG WOMAN:
WOODEN DOLL OF THE
EIGHTEENTH CENTURY
*Bayerisches National-Museum, Munich*

FIG. 115. LADY OF THE
EIGHTEENTH CENTURY
*Bayerisches National-Museum,
Munich*

d'Enghien a doll's room with six dolls, all of which could be dressed and undressed—grandmother, mother, child, midwife, nurse, and lady's maid. Cardinal la Valette d'Épernon presented Mlle de Bourbon, later Duchesse de Longueville, with a magnificent doll together with a rich wardrobe. It cost him 2000 thalers, a sum which in the first half of the seventeenth century represented a small fortune. When a little Spanish Infanta came to France in 1722, to be brought up with the young

Louis XV and later to be married to him, the Duchesse d'Orléans presented her with a doll which had many changes of clothes; this cost her 22,000 francs. In 1779 Mme de Montholon paid twenty-five louis d'or for a doll. Esther Singleton believes that

FIG. 116. THE CHILDREN OF THE DUC D'ORLÉANS
Engraving by Joullain after the painting by Coypel. About 1760

we must conclude from the evidence of the fairy-tales of the Baronne d'Aulnoy that the French dolls of this time had movable heads and even movable eyes. This development, however, was not reached till a century later; in the year 1700 it can have existed only in the imagination of the authoress.

We must picture for ourselves the dolls of past centuries—whether they be German or French or English—as simple and fairly primitive objects. The body often consisted of a bundle of rags, to which arms and feet were attached by tape; sometimes it consisted of a leather bag filled with bran or sawdust. A step forward was marked when the arms and legs were jointed, and so made movable. Occasionally, however, the legs were left out altogether, the whole doll resting on a hoop petticoat.

FIG. 117. CHILD WITH DOLL REPRESENTING A MONK
Engraving by Ingouf after the painting by Greuze. About 1760

The old Nürnberg toy dolls were made entirely of wood covered with cloth, the heads being always carved and painted. The English dolls were characterized by disproportionately large heads.

Alongside of these dolls designed for the children of the higher class there were others of a wholly inartistic sort which came from the hands of the folk. These contented themselves with a simple reproduction of bodily and facial forms, providing for the childish imagination merely the barest indication of the

128

FIG. 120. WOODEN LIMBED DOLL
FROM THE GRÖDNER TAL
*Spielzeug-Museum, Sonneberg*

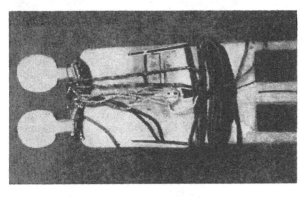

FIG. 119. TWIN DOLLS OF THE
HAUSSA NEGROES
*Spielzeug-Museum, Sonneberg*

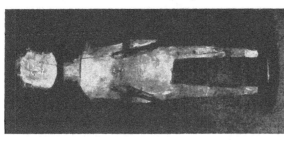

FIG. 118. PRIMITIVE
WOODEN DOLL FROM
TRANSYLVANIA
*Spielzeug-Museum, Sonneberg*

human image. This is thoroughly characteristic of pastoral art, which for the most part makes use of wood as a medium of expression, no matter whether its home is in the Alps, Thuringia, the Erzgebirge, or the Carpathians. Even the actual specimens

FIG. 121. OLDEST SONNEBERG WOODEN TOYS

produced in different districts resemble each other in an extraordinary manner. Bohemian wood-carved or turned dolls are so similar to those from the Grödner Tal that the one could be taken for the other, and the Christmas angels from the Saxon

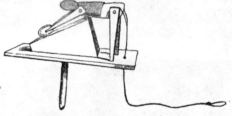

FIG. 122. EGYPTIAN CHILD'S TOY
*Leiden Museum*

Erzgebirge might be their sisters. Typical of all of these is the cone shape, and the same taste, with its passion· for bold colours, is to be traced in the painting of the figures. The famous toy industry of Sonneberg, the beginnings of which are to be found in the fourteenth century, originates from the work of the hunters, charcoal-burners, and woodmen of the district.

About the middle of the eighteenth century arose in Paris the vogue of that type of doll named, after the place of its origin,

DOLLS OF THE PERIOD OF THE FRENCH REVOLUTION
From a catalogue of toys. Reproduced in Henri René d'Allemagne's
*History of Toys*

*pantin.* The diarist Barbier mentions that these were first seen in children's hands in 1746, but that it was not long before adults took delight in the toy. In 1747 they were to be found in all the best houses. D'Alembert writes concerning them:

> Posterity will find difficulty in believing that there were in France people of mature judgment capable of spending time, in a fit of

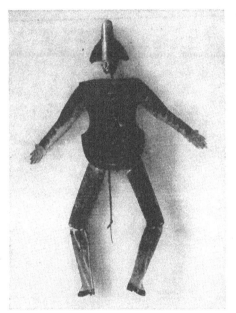

FIG. 123. WOODEN "HAMPELMANN," PAINTED IN
VARIOUS COLOURS
Eighteenth century. Height, 89 cm.
*Germanisches National-Museum, Nürnberg*

weakmindedness, with this ridiculous toy, and that with an ardour which in other countries would hardly be pardoned in tenderest youth.

Artists devoted themselves to it; the famous Boucher made a painting of a *pantin* for the Duchesse de Chartres, for which he was paid 1500 francs. The popularity of the toy endured until 1756. At last the police interfered and prohibited it, ostensibly "because the women, under the lively influence of this continual jumping, were in danger of bringing children into the world with twisted limbs like the *pantins*."

It is not surprising that French authors have assumed that the

131

*pantin* was an invention of Paris, "the city of light," and there is really no need to deny it to them; but the French were not required to invent this puppet. It was known in classical antiquity; the principle of moving a figure by means of a thread attached to the loose limbs was practised by the Egyptians for their toy dolls. Plato, Herodotus, Horace, and Apuleius—all

FIG. 124. CRIES OF BERLIN
Etching by Rosenberg. About 1786

refer to them, and literary records testify to their early existence in Germany. In the sixteenth and seventeenth centuries they were called *Hampelmann*, and in Thuringia also *Zappelmann*. In an account drawn up for the Saxon Court at Torgau in 1572 these puppets are mentioned—"stuffed dolls which are pulled with strings." Schwieger says in the *Geharnischte Venus*: "common *Hempelmänner*, these little toy dolls are often more sought after than things brought from both the Indies." In 1710 Amaranthes writes of "how one can decoy good money out of people's pockets just as one can decoy children with the *Hampelmann*." The word *Hampelmann* was often applied to simpletons, while "giggling like a *Hampelmann*" was said of silly laughter. This toy was a favourite object of comparison in a derogatory sense. Thus Heinrich Heine speaks of Wellington as a *Hampelmann* whose strings were pulled by the aristocracy. In 1848 was published at Frankfort a very witty satire on parliamentary rhetoricians:

132

# EARLY TOY DOLLS IN EUROPE

*Michel's March Acquisitions, Toys of Right and Left for Old and Young. Published by Eduard Gustav May.* In this the orators of that gathering which had been greeted with such extravagant hopes, and which had ended so dismally, were represented as puppets—Beckerath as a bag of money, Mittermaier in Court dress, Heckscher as a lackey, Dahlmann as a toad, Robert Mohl in a dressing-gown, M. Mohl as a groom, Radowitz as a monk, Jahn with a very long beard, Rösler as a canary, and so on.

FIG. 125. " ZAPPELMANN " : CONDUCTOR
Richard Gräff
*Werkstätte für den Hausrat, Theophil Müller, Dresden*

133

# X

## THE FASHION DOLL

MORE skilfully than any other nation the French utilized dolls as a profitable means of propaganda, employing them freely in the service of their trade in ladies' fashions. French fashions,

FIG. 126. "HAMPELMANN": PEASANT
GIRL IN PARTS
French engraving. About 1750

FIG. 127. "HAMPELMANN": BALLERINA
IN PARTS
French engraving. About 1750

and not by chance, are highly favoured by women of all the five continents. Yet only rarely are these fashions real inventions of Paris; usually they come from other sources; but there they are executed with so much taste, and the French women know how to wear their clothes with such a peculiar charm, that Paris fashions capture all eyes and are eagerly imitated. The French never spare themselves self-praise, and just as some-

134

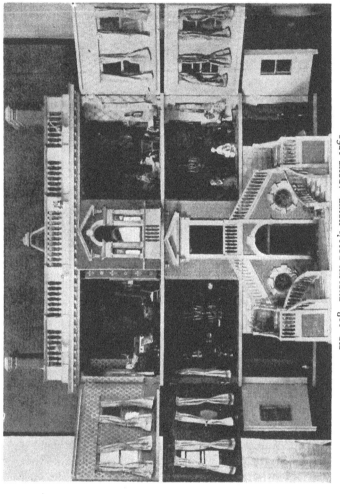

FIG. 128. ENGLISH DOLL'S HOUSE, ABOUT 1760
Lent to the Bethnal Green Museum, London, by Mrs Walter Tate
*By permission of the Victoria and Albert Museum*

thing always remains in the mind when we hear slander of others, so this general and constantly repeated self-praise never misses its mark, the hearer always having it impressed on his memory. At a time when as yet the press was non-existent, long before the invention of such mechanical means of reproduction as the woodcut and the copperplate, to the doll was given the

FIG. 129. THE BREAKFAST (DETAIL)
Engraving by Lépicié after the painting by Boucher. About 1740

task of popularizing French fashions abroad. The fashion doll first makes its appearance in the account books of the French Court. Queen Isabeau of Bavaria got dolls sent to the Queen of England to give that youthful monarch an idea of the fashions of the French Court. In 1396 Robert de Varennes, the Court tailor of Charles VI, received 459 francs for a doll's wardrobe executed by him. As this was a considerable sum, it is to be concluded that the dolls were life-size, made to the measure of the English Queen. The next record dates from a century later. In 1496 Anne of Brittany, the then reigning queen, ordered a great doll to be made and dressed for the Spanish Queen,

136

DOLLS OF THE PERIOD OF THE FRENCH EMPIRE

About 1800-10

Isabella the Catholic. Isabella was then forty-three years old, an age which in a period when girls were wont to marry at fourteen years seemed to be on the threshold of senility, but was very smart and particular about her dress, never giving audience to foreign ambassadors twice in the same costume. This fact

FIG. 130. CHILD WITH DOLL (NUN)
J. B. S. Chardin

must have been well enough known in the French Court; the actual dress put on this doll was deemed to be wanting in perfection, and it was decided to re-equip it with a much costlier *ensemble*.

Marie de' Medici, when Henry IV, no longer in his first youth, took her as his second wife, was full of eagerness to learn all about the prevailing French fashions. "Frontenac tells me," writes the King to her, "that you wish to have samples of our fashions: I am therefore sending you several model dolls." In the seventeenth century this export of dolls, hitherto left to chance, was systematized and organized. Furetière in his *Roman Bourgeois* informs us that in the *salon* of Mlle de Scudéry, the well-known novelist, there used to stand two dressed dolls—the one a large *pandora* in full costume, the other a small *pandora* in *négligé*. Fashion dolls of this kind were first sent to England and then to other countries. As early as 1642 the Strasbourg

FIG. 131. GERMAN DOLL
Stuffed body with a china head (1850–60), dress, and *coiffure* (1878).
Height, 68 cm.
*Germanisches National-Museum, Nürnberg*

satirist Moscherosch ridiculed the German women of his time for getting dolls sent to them from Paris in order that they might copy costume and *coiffure*. Still more sharp expressions appeared in the anonymous lampoon of 1689 called *Der deutsch-französische Modegeist* (*The Spirit of Franco-German Fashion*). "And the worst of it is," we read there, "that not only do our women-folk themselves travel to France, but they pay as many thalers for their models, these dressed-up dolls, to be sent to them, as would serve them to emulate the very frippery of the devil." Such satire, however, did not trouble the German ladies. A certain A. Leo, who from 1671 to 1673 accompanied a Herr von Lüttichau on the Grand Tour, in

1673 sent from Paris to his pupil's aunt, Frau von Schleinitz, a doll "which he had got made in the latest fashion, especially in so far as the head and hair were concerned."

FIG. 132. WAX DOLL: TOWN LADY, MUNICH, 1877
*Spielzeug-Museum, Sonneberg*

The fashion doll penetrated as far as Venice. At the Sensa, the fourteen-day fair in the Piazza S. Marco, was annually exhibited a doll clad in the latest Parisian fashion, and for a whole twelve months this remained the dressmakers' model.

139

The chief destination for these exported fashion dolls was England, and even war could not hinder their passage. Writing in 1704, the Abbé Prévost observes:

> By an act of gallantry which is worthy of being noted in the chronicles of history for the benefit of the ladies the ministers of both Courts granted a special pass to the mannequin; that pass was

FIG. 133. THE CHEVALIER DE PANGE
Painting by Drouais. About 1760

> always respected, and during the times of greatest enmity experienced on both sides the mannequin was the one object which remained unmolested.

Such announcements appeared in the English papers as "Last Saturday the French doll for the year 1712 arrived at my house in King Street, Covent Garden." During the Regency the French Ambassador in London was Dubois, who later became Cardinal, and, in order to win favour with the English ladies, he wrote to the dressmaker Mlle Fillon in Paris, ordering her to send a large mannequin designed to show how the French women were dressed and coiffeured and how they wore their underclothing. His nephew, however, in reply to his order stated that this was not such a simple matter, that it would cost at least 300 francs, and that neither Mme Law nor Mlle Fillon

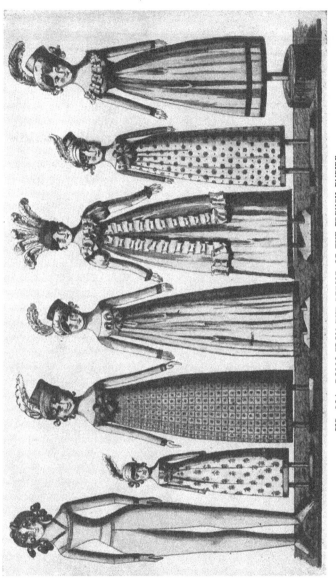

FIG. 134. DOLLS FROM THE PERIOD OF THE FRENCH EMPIRE
About 1800–10
From *Histoire des Jouets*, by Henri d'Allemagne

would risk the expense unless they were sure of being reimbursed. In 1727 Lady Lansdowne sent to Queen Caroline's ladies-in-waiting a mannequin in Court dress with the request that, after

FIG. 135. BRIDE (NÜRNBERG), MIDDLE OF THE NINETEENTH CENTURY
*Bayerisches National-Museum, Munich. Photo Kester and Co.*

it had circulated among them, they should dispatch it to Mrs Tempest the dressmaker.

In his trade lexicon of 1723 Savary mentions the beautiful dolls, elaborately coiffeured and richly dressed, which were sent to foreign Courts. No longer were they called, as formerly,

142

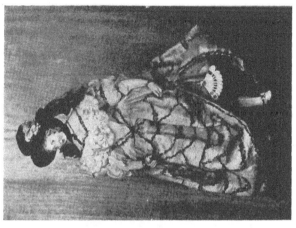

FIG. 136. DOLLS IN ROCOCO DRESS
*Bayerische Landesgewerbe-Anstalt, Nürnberg*

by the name of *pandoras*, being styled now 'dolls of the Rue Saint-Honoré,' a street which in the eighteenth century was the centre of the Parisian tailors, just as the Rue de la Paix is to-day. They were also called the *grands courriers de la mode*, under which title they were invoiced as having arrived at Dover in 1764. These fashion dolls were made life-size in order that the clothes with

FIG. 137. ENGLISH DOLL OF THE REIGN OF QUEEN ANNE
*Victoria and Albert Museum*

which they were dressed might be immediately worn. "The *chic* imparted to fashion by French hands," writes Mercier in his *Tableau de Paris*, "is imitated by all nations, who obediently submit to the taste of the Rue Saint-Honoré." Mercier, a good journalist, once took a stranger who doubted the existence of the fashion doll to Rose Bertin in order to convince him that it was a reality. Rose Bertin was the dressmaker of the elegant world; she worked for the Queen, and neither she nor the other Court dressmaker, Mme Éloffe, neglected the dressed-up mannequins. In 1777 Bertin clothed for Prince Rohan-Guéménée a large, beautifully coiffeured doll in a ball dress of white-and-rose silk

144

over the hoop petticoat. It was to have cost 300 francs, but that sum was never received by the dressmaker, for the Rohan family went bankrupt in millions. Mme Éloffe supplied the Comtesse Bombelles on August 18, 1788, with a life-size mannequin in Court dress for 409 francs, 12 centimes. Marie-Antoinette took pleasure, through the good offices of the furniture-designer

FIG. 138. ENGLISH DOLL'S SHOP, ABOUT 1850
Presented to the Bethnal Green Museum, London, by Miss Lester Garland
*By permission of the Victoria and Albert Museum*

David Röntgen, of Neuwied, in sending to her mother and sisters dolls dressed in the latest Parisian styles. Risbeck too, who visited Vienna in the last decade of the century, mentions them: "French fashion rules here despotically. Periodically mannequins are sent here [Vienna] from Paris and serve the ladies as models for their dresses and head-gear."

Not only dressmakers, but hairdressers made use of dolls. Thus on one occasion Mme de Sévigné promised her daughter a doll coiffeured according to the latest mode, while Melchior Grimm described in his well-known correspondence how the hairdresser Legros, who was the most popular Parisian 'hair-artist' in the time of the Pompadour, had many enemies, and how these had

K

145

been silenced by the exhibition of thirty coiffeured dolls at the annual fair of Saint-Ovide in 1763. These beautiful dolls, to which was entrusted so important a cultural mission in the spreading of French fashion, have even found poets to sing their praises. Algarotti, in his Italian epistle to Phyllis, celebrated in song the

FIG. 139. ENGLISH WAX DOLL,
ABOUT 1780
Presented to the Victoria and Albert
Museum by Miss Ethel Diton

FIG. 140. ENGLISH DOLL WITH WAX
HEAD, ABOUT 1800
Presented to the Bethnal Green Museum, London,
by Mrs Greg

*By permission of the Victoria and Albert Museum*

charm of the French mannequin, and Delille, a fashionable French poet of the day, in 1786 praised Rose Bertin's dolls:

Et jusqu'au fond du Nord portant nos goûts divers,
Le mannequin despote asservit l'univers.

The French example did not remain unimitated. *The Gentleman's Magazine* contained a note in 1751 to the effect that several mannequins with different styles of dress had been made in St James's Street in order to give the Tsarina (Elizabeth) an idea of the manner of dressing which at the moment was in fashion among the English ladies. Catharine II designed articles of an absolutely unique cut for the young grand dukes, and in order to show King Gustavus III of Sweden how she clothed her grandchildren she got dolls made and dressed according to her directions. In the end the Parisian fashion mannequins succeeded in reaching North America. In *The New England*

FIG. 141. GIRL WITH DOLL
Sir Joshua Reynolds. About 1785

*Weekly Journal* of July 2, 1733, appeared the following advertisement:

At Mrs Hannah Teatt's, dressmaker at the top of Summer Street, Boston, is to be seen a mannequin, in the latest fashion, with articles of dress, night dresses, and everything appertaining to women's attire. It has been brought from London by Captain White. Ladies who choose to see it may come or send for it. It is always ready to serve you. If you come, it will cost you two shillings, but if you send for it, seven shillings.

147

In similar manner, only in a less flowery style, two dressmakers of Irish nationality in New York advertised in 1757 to the effect that the latest mannequins had arrived from London. In 1796 a certain Sally MacKean wrote to her friend Dolly Madison, "Yesterday I went to see a mannequin which has just come from England to give us an idea of the latest fashions."

FIG. 142. ENGLISH DOLL, ABOUT 1860
Presented to the Bethnal Green Museum, London, by Mrs Greg
*By permission of the Victoria and Albert Museum*

It need not, however, be concealed that very soon the suspicion developed abroad that the Parisian tailors and dressmakers were making use of these mannequins merely for the purpose of getting rid of their old stock. Horace Walpole wrote from Paris on September 22, 1765, to George Montague: "The French have become very plain in their dress. We English still pray to their old idols." Even Prince Henry of Prussia, who in 1769 asked Darget to get him some cloth from Paris, thought it necessary to add a warning that he did not wish for such as had been made for German princes and barons, but the sort which the Prince

148

FIG. 143. MALE AND FEMALE PEDLARS (PORTSMOUTH), ABOUT 1810
Presented to the Bethnal Green Museum, London, by Mrs Greg
*By permission of the Victoria and Albert Museum*

FIG. 144. FLAT PAINTED FIGURES
Lady with fan, man smoking, man with a muff. Eighteenth century
*Bayerisches National-Museum, Munich*

de Conti and the Marshals Contades and d'Estrées were then wearing. The wars of the French Republic and of Napoleon I put an end to the free passage of the mannequins, nor were these so necessary now that the fashion journals provided a complete substitute. Their use, however, has not wholly ceased. French fashion mannequins cost eighty francs before the War, and many

FIG. 145. ENGLISH MOVABLE FASHION DOLLS, ABOUT 1830

such figures, about a metre high, along with complete *trousseaux*, were supplied for the harems of some Oriental grandees.

England was responsible for the invention of one particular kind of figure used for the purpose of displaying new fashions in dress. Up to comparatively recent times the English tradition in regard to the toy doll is remarkably meagre; indeed, it seems that originally English dolls had no special name allotted to them. They were simply called 'little ladies' or 'babies,' and it is only in the eighteenth century that the expression 'doll' begins to be used. The English themselves are in doubt con-

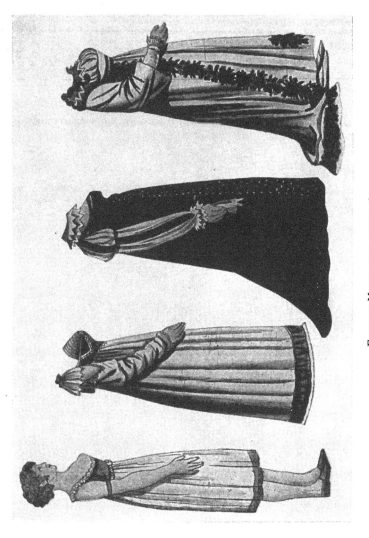

ENGLISH MANNEQUIN, ABOUT 1800

cerning the etymology of this word. Some consider that the term 'doll' is connected with the diminutive of endearment

FIG. 146. ENGLISH WAX DOLL, MIDDLE OF THE NINETEENTH CENTURY
Presented to the Victoria and Albert Museum by Frank Green

'Dolly' (for Dorothy); others think it is a derivative from 'idol'; still others turn to the Norse *daul*, which signifies a female domestic servant. Even though we know almost nothing about the older periods, it must be presumed that the little English girls

151

had their dolls. The portrait painted about the year 1600 of
Lady Arabella Stuart as a child shows her with her doll dressed
exactly like a grown-up woman, just as were the German and

FIG. 147. TRICK DOLLS OF PRESSED AND CUT-OUT CARDBOARD
(METAMORPHOSES)
*Germanisches National-Museum, Nürnberg*

French toy dolls of that time. Only toward the end of the
eighteenth century did England enrich the doll world with new
inventions. Silhouettes cut out of paper had been known for a
long time in Germany; in the Germanische National-Museum,
in Nürnberg, is a picture-sheet of the seventeenth century with

152

fashion-plates intended to be cut out; but the English made out of this something entirely new. They invented the one-sided figures to be cut out of paper, for which many different garments were provided, the costumes thus being rendered changeable. These paper figures, 8 in. high and supplied with six sets of clothes, were put on the market in 1790 by English firms. In the *Journal des Luxus und der Moden* of 1791 they are called attention to, and Bertuch, who was always on the look-out for novelties, at once proceeded to imitate them. Such a figure, with its wardrobe of six changes, cost then three shillings. The French adopted this invention as a means of cheap advertisement for their fashions; Gavarni, for example, lithographed a whole series of such fashion-plates intended to be cut out.

FIG. 148. MANNEQUIN

# XI

# THE TOY DOLL IN THE NINETEENTH CENTURY

ONLY in the nineteenth century does a real improvement in technique become apparent. Greater demands from the public led to greater efforts on the part of the producers; pleasing devices came to improve the doll, and eventually factory pro-

FIG. 149. ELISA, PRINCESS RADZIWILL
Etching by Haller. About 1810

duction, because of a careful specialization of labour, reached an accurate elaboration of even the tiniest details, and evolved something of perfection in its own kind. The leather bags were better stuffed, being now filled, not with bran, liable to pour out when the least injury was done to the cover, but with animal hair or seaweed and finally with fine wood shavings. The coarse leather used in past times was replaced by thin sheepskin to which were affixed arms and feet of porcelain. *Papier mâché*, the invention of which is by some ascribed to Italy and by others to France, was used in Sonneberg in 1810, and by its means, with the use of casts from sulphur moulds, dolls were made, although it is true that these were still somewhat clumsy in shape. In

# THE TOY DOLL IN THE LAST CENTURY

1850 gutta-percha took the place of the leather bag. The flexibility of the limbs, which until then was somewhat fettered, was improved by the introduction of ball-joints; Jumeau and Son in Paris invented the movable neck, and after that innovation greatest attention was paid to the head. The wooden head with hair indicated only by paint was replaced by the China head, and the hair marked only by modelling was replaced by as

FIG. 150. SUSANNE VON BOEHN
Sketch by Ulrich von Sulpius. 1858

realistic substitutes as were possible—flax, untwisted silk, and mohair of the Angora goat, sometimes even real human hair. An unmistakable revolution ensued from the introduction of the wax head with glass or enamelled eyes. By 1826 eyes that could close had been invented. For long England enjoyed the fame of producing the best and prettiest wax dolls. At the Parisian world exhibition of 1855 the English dolls modelled by Napoleon Montanari aroused great enthusiasm. To-day we have our dolls' heads with real hair, eyelashes, and eyebrows, fitted with teeth and movable eyes. To the inventor of the metronome, Mälzel, we owe the first speaking doll. In 1827 he took out a patent in Paris for a doll which could say " Papa " and " Mamma " when it was squeezed. The first doll which could walk by itself appeared in 1826. These early experiments, of course,

155

have long been superseded, for now we have dolls which can speak, sing, and cry at will.

Up to the nineteenth century all dolls were made to represent grown women. About 1850 the limbed baby doll, or *Gelenktäufling*, was introduced from England into Germany. This term signifies

FIG. 151. PORTRAIT OF THE DAUGHTER OF HERR ARTUS
Painting by Chaplin. 1878

a baby doll of flesh-coloured *papier mâché* dipped in a wax solution to give an impression of the human skin. The limbs are movable, and the dress is only a little chemise. In 1855 at the Parisian world exhibition these baby dolls were for the first time introduced to a large public. Since then they have won great popularity, and have almost entirely ousted the dolls representing women.

The specialization of work has greatly facilitated and improved the manufacture of dolls. In the Parisian workshops of the forties of the last century a doll was reckoned to consist of ten

FIG. 152. SONNEBERG LEATHER DOLL, 1820

separate pieces, but to-day we have gone far beyond that. In the doll industry there are indeed more separate branches than

· FIG. 153. "PETITE DRÔLESSE! VOUS ME FEREZ MOURIR DIX ANS AVANT MON TERME"
Lithograph by Randon. 1860

157

in any other trade. There are eye-cutters, eye-setters, arm- and leg-moulders; such advertisements as "A moulder of small hands wanted" serve to indicate the wide scope of this specialization of labour. Much toil and care is demanded for the assembling of the parts, for the painting, where various problems involved by the conjunction of different kinds of materials have

FIG. 154. SPEAKING LIMBED DOLL, NINETEENTH CENTURY
*Bayerisches National-Museum, Munich*

to be surmounted, and finally for the costuming. Formerly the purchaser of the doll's body had to attend to the clothing herself, or the little girl to whom it came as a present had to take that business into her own hands.

A good example of this is provided by Queen Victoria; until she was fourteen years old she used to play with her dolls, and found amusement in associating herself in the dressing of the otherwise very simple figures. Of the one hundred and thirty-two specimens she possessed she clothed thirty-two herself. Only

ENGLISH DOLL, ABOUT 1830
Presented by Miss M. A. Rooth to the Victoria and Albert
Museum, London

FIG. 156. "MA SŒUR, REGARDE DONC MA JOLIE POUPÉE"
Engraving by Noël, 1806

FIG. 155. MA POUPÉE
Engraving by Noël. Paris, 1806

about seven or eight were dressed as men; for the rest the young owner found her models in her ladies-in-waiting and in the famous singers, dancers, and actresses of the time, these including such persons as Marie Taglioni, the Duchess of Clarendon, and

FIG 157. SONNEBERG LEATHER DOLLS WITH CHINA HEADS, 1840
*Spielzeug-Museum, Sonneberg*

Lady Bedford. The late Queen was truly a little pedant, for when she was a child she kept a catalogue of her dolls, with careful enumeration of their names and dresses.

Apparently at that time only the French dolls were put on the market all ready dressed; about 1850 there were in Paris several workshops engaged solely in supplying articles for the doll's wardrobe. Natalis Rondot, who prepared a report on the

160

# THE TOY DOLL IN THE LAST CENTURY

French exhibition of 1849, speaks in laudatory terms of the work of the French artists engaged in this branch of the doll industry. He writes:

> So far as dolls' costumes are concerned, the Parisian dressmakers have no equal. With great dispatch and wonderful skill they are able to make use of the smallest pieces of cloth, producing from these elegant attires. The doll's cloak and dress are correct

FIG. 158. ROCOCO DOLL
About 1750. Height, 50 cm.
*Germanisches National-Museum, Nürnberg*

replicas of the latest fashions; the doll dressmakers are not only skilled in the cut, the preparation of underclothing, and general outfit; they show taste in the selection of materials and colours. Thus these dolls are not only dispatched into the provinces and abroad as samples of fashion; they have become indispensable for the general export of fashionable novelties, for it has been realized that without the aid of the doll the tradespeople do not know how to sell their goods. The first little cloaks sold in India, for example, were there worn on the head until the fashion doll arrived at Calcutta to show the ladies their mistake.

Paris here indulged in great luxuries. At the world exhibition of 1867 dolls were exhibited with real cashmere shawls costing over six hundred francs. The dolls which thirty years later were presented in Paris to the daughters of the Tsar cost several thousand francs.

FIG. 159. GENTLEMAN WITH STICK. PEASANT WOMAN WITH ROSARY
Wooden dolls. Eighteenth century
*Germanisches National-Museum, Nürnberg*

In 1870 Germany introduced the wholesale factory method in the production of dressed dolls, and through this innovation the German firms took a leading position in the doll market. Even in the Middle Ages there had been a considerable exportation of dolls from Germany: "Toys from Nürnberg hand go to

162

FIG. 160. OLD MUNICH DOLL

*Bayerisches National-Museum, Munich. Photo Kester and Co.*

every land " was a proverb of the time. The Sonneberg industry, which had already shown good promise in the fifteenth century, reached fruition in the sixteenth century, but was for a long time disorganized because of the Thirty Years War. Augsburg and Nürnberg, however, recovered quickly, and by the eighteenth century these towns were producing toys wholesale. In the nineteenth century this dominating position of Germany was

FIG. 161. DOLL'S HEAD OF PAPIER
MÂCHÉ
*Bayerische Landesgewerbe-Anstalt, Nürnberg*

FIG. 162. THURINGIAN
EMPIRE DOLL
About 1810. Height, 56 cm.
*Germanisches National-Museum,
Nürnberg*

strengthened, so that, according to the impartial view of Jeanne Doin, "before the War the German doll reigned everywhere." This was a result which Germany, again according to the testimony of this French lady, "owed to a methodical and patiently conducted effort." "The irresistible activity of inventive Germany," she continues, "was equal to the requirements of the moment." She goes on to say that:

All countries drew thence their supply of china heads, for Saxony supplied these post paid at ten centimes a piece, while in France they cost forty centimes on the spot. The material was

DOLL, ABOUT 1865
Sketch by Walter Trier

perfect, the work careful, the dispatch prompt and regular. This competition, added to facilitation in the payment of accounts, was irresistible, and ruined the French doll industry.

The French industry otherwise had been very active since 1862. The total value of the toys produced in Germany was

FIG. 163. ALTENBURG AND WENDISH DOLLS

raised from thirty-six million marks in 1894 to one hundred and forty million in 1913. A third of these amounts came from the

FIG. 164. NÜRNBERG-FÜRTH TRAIN WITH DOLLS IN COSTUME
*Spielzeug-Museum, Sonneberg*

sale of dolls alone. In present-day Germany the most important centres of the doll industry are Sonneberg, Nürnberg-Fürth, Ruhla, Waltershausen, Ohrdruf, Giengen, on the Brenz, and the Saxon Erzgebirge—the headquarters being in Bavaria, Thuringia, and Saxony. Some of these factories have been in

165

existence since about 1880. It will be understood that the making of dolls at home by hand labour, with only very little mechanical assistance, has almost completely disappeared. In the year 1910 in the Meininger Oberland alone twenty-five thousand persons were engaged in the manufacturing of dolls. At that period Germany's dolls dominated the world market; of the total

FIG. 165. CRIES OF BERLIN
Etching by Rosenberg. About 1786

European products more than two-thirds were supplied by Germany, and even of all the dolls annually made throughout the entire world Germany contributed more than half. As Privy Councillor Crämer has pointed out, this industry was the more important for Germany in that its profits for the major part were represented in wages, which was of deeper significance for the national economy than if the manufactured articles had been themselves of greater intrinsic value. The actual amount of wages may be estimated at from 70 per cent. to 75 per cent. of the total value of the goods.

The War temporarily interrupted this development, and led to the manufacture of these goods in other countries; non-German firms then flourished, since the strongest competitor had been put out of action. The Japanese factories in Kioto and Osaka stepped forward, and in August 1914 France had begun to

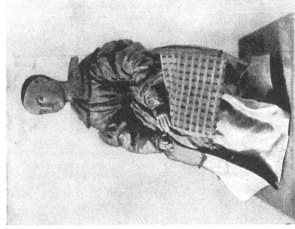

FIG. 166. DOLL OF THE BIEDERMEIER PERIOD
About 1840. Height, 76 cm.
*Germanisches National-Museum, Nürnberg*

FIG. 167. DOLL OF THE BIEDERMEIER PERIOD
About 1835. Height, 60 cm. The wig is missing.
*Germanisches National-Museum, Nürnberg*

FIG. 168. FRENCH DOLL REPRESENTING A CHILD
About 1760

FIG. 169. "PUTZENBERCHT"
Etching by Göz, 1784

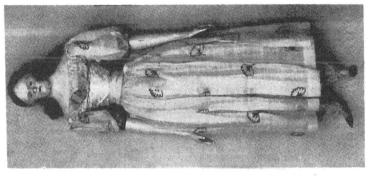

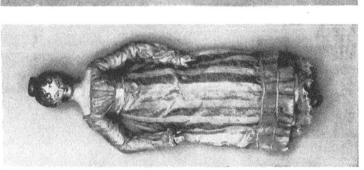

FIGS. 171, 172. DOLLS, ABOUT 1830
*Metropolitan Museum, New York*

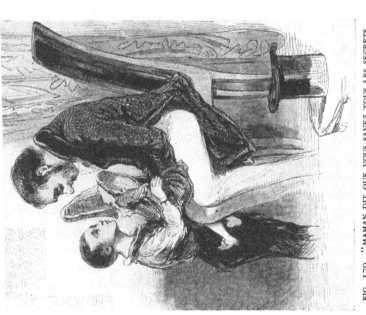

FIG. 170. "MAMAN DIT QUE VOUS SAVEZ TOUS LES SECRETS
DE POLICHINELLE, MOSIEU D'ALBY: QU'EST-CE QUI PEUT
DONC LUI AVOIR ABÎMÉ LE NEZ COMME ÇA . . . DITES?"

Sketch by Gavarni

think of the "Renaissance of the French Doll." The manufacturers began by imitating the cloth dolls of Margarethe Steiff,
of Giengen, which resulted in the abandoning of paths hitherto
trodden in France and in transference of attention from the
elegant fashionable lady to the simple child. Whether these
efforts will have a success remains to be seen.

FIG. 173. DOLL, ABOUT 1830
*Bayerisches National-Museum, Munich*

# XII

## THE TOY DOLL IN THE MODERN PERIOD

ALTHOUGH the toy doll has been in existence for several centuries, it was discovered by science and art only about the year 1900. It was at that time that the educationists began to get interested in it, and hand in hand with them came the artists,

FIG. 174. PLAYING WITH DOLLS
After the sketch by Chodowiecki. From Basedow's *Elementarwerk*

who believed that it was their duty to reform the doll. This was the period when, with a great flow of rich rhetoric, attempts were made to raise domestic furniture to artistic levels, when fashions themselves had to submit to reformation on the part of architects and painters; and clearly the doll had no claim to special indulgence. For the high educational significance with which it is invested the doll has to thank the fact that it is a representation of the human form. Because of this it satisfies the awakening instincts of the child, and develops these into lasting

171

emotions. Touching and seeing, the growing soul comes to an understanding with the world around it, and then with that which exercises the greatest influence upon it—with man. For this reason the doll takes the highest place in the imaginative play world of the child. The child who does not possess a doll

FIG. 175. THE YOUNG PHILOSOPHER (DETAIL)
After the painting of L. Boilly. 1790

will very soon make a substitute out of rags, a broom, sticks, bottles, pillows, which the realizing power of its imagination will endow with life. The moment of illusion, the autosuggestion, the self-deception—whatever it may be called—is so powerful that the child looks upon the doll of its choice as a living part of itself, and takes it to its heart with a passion which is but the greater the uglier the actual object is in reality. When she was a child Carmen Sylva played with her mother's footstool as if it had been a doll, and when Queen Elizabeth of Prussia, on a visit to the palace, made use of this footstool, the little Princess pushed her away, tore the stool from under her feet, and cried in an outburst of rage, "You mustn't put your feet on my child." The child's imagination does not need a naturalistic

FIG. 176. GIRL WITH DOLL
Macout, Paris. About 1800

representation of reality; an indication of the most superficial kind is for it quite sufficient.

The more highly, then, did the professional pedagogues estimate the educational value of the toy doll, which not only provides a welcome soil for the thriving and blossoming of the childish imagination, but is also regarded as a concentration of all the functions making for serious thought and act. "Where all the thought and feeling of the child are directed toward the doll as an object of love," says Paul Hildebrandt, "the educationist has an easy job, for there is to be discovered already existent in embryo deep feeling, true inner culture, and sensibility for art." Unquestionably the development of the maternal

173

instinct in the little girl is deeply influenced by the interest she takes in her doll. George Sand and Victor Hugo provide us with examples—indeed, Konrad Lange goes so far as to assert

FIG. 177. NEW YEAR'S PRESENTS AT PARIS
Anonymous engraving. About 1800

that "Women who have not played much with dolls in their childhood are distinguished in their maturity by low taste in matters of art and especially by lack of feeling." It seems, however, that that is going too far. One must here keep

ENGLISH DOLL, ABOUT 1875
Presented by Mrs Galloway to the Victoria and Albert
Museum, London

well in view the precise nature of the doll. A doll representing a woman, dressed up like an adult, such as formerly were by far in the majority, cannot awaken maternal feelings in the little girl, for she cannot easily descry her child in the shape of a lady of fashion. The importance even of the dolls representing children is minimized by some writers; thus James Sully, G. Stanley Hall,

FIG. 178. COPTIC WOODEN DOLL
About 600 B.C.

and others are of the opinion that the "maternal feeling" aroused by playing with dolls may be grossly overestimated. The sheer joy taken in clothing dolls and in attending to them, which includes dressing and undressing, has at least a good deal to do with the child's love of the doll, and besides this there is the pleasure taken in imitating grown-ups and in exercising authority on one's own. For the development of the child's psychology the actual make-up of the doll is unimportant; the amount of life attributed to it by the child, as Robert Breuer rightly remarks, decreases in proportion to the elaboration of its form; the meanest shape and the simplest outlines release the

175

noblest ideas and energies. In view of this the Russian congress
which was held concurrently with the exhibition of dolls at St

FIG. 179. ABYSSINIAN CHILDREN'S DOLLS
*Ethnographisches Rijksmuseum, Leiden*

FIG. 180. SILESIAN BAST DOLLS
*Spielzeug-Museum, Sonneberg*

Petersburg condemned the large French dolls, and protested
against their power of walking, speaking, and singing. These do
not leave the smallest scope for the play of the child's imagination,

and demonstrate that the simpler object succeeds in its aims far better than the complex.

It was here that the reformers stepped in. The naturalistic doll was recognized as the phenomenon of our satiated, artistically unproductive, wholly unimaginative civilization, and it was felt that a remedy must be found. Not in vain do we live,

FIG. 181. MODERN SWEDISH DOLL MADE
ENTIRELY OF WOOD
*Photo Kester and Co.*

according to the unfortunate catchword of the charming Swedish woman in the *Century of the Child*; we make much of the life of the child; we take pains to educate it as little as possible, to make it prematurely vain and conceited, to awaken in it not the slightest feeling for duty; and consequently we are inevitably forced to bother our heads with its toys. The idea of reforming the doll arose from the desire of opposing mass production and of creating a characteristic, if possible individually conceived, toy doll. In the elegant fashion doll the children no longer were to get an unnatural object into their hands; the superabundance of the all too concrete details was to be opposed. The child itself was asked what it wanted, and then, when it was seen that it made no special demands, and when the insignificance of the

M

stimulus which it needed to arouse its imagination was realized, adults began to imitate children. Not only was simplicity aimed at, but even technical imperfection itself was pleaded for; it looked almost as if nothing could be too simple for the child.

The reforming movement in the doll trade originated in the artistic circles of Munich, and later was followed up by Berlin,

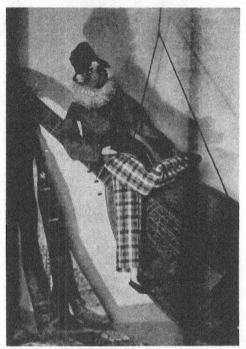

FIG. 182. ART DOLL
Else Kollmar-Hecht

Dresden, and Karlsruhe; it proceeded in the usual way to offer prizes and to arrange competitions and exhibitions. The astonishing discovery was then made that the pieces which gained the first prize were not favoured by the children. They were, indeed, made too childishly to be able to attract them—"super-toys," as Paul Hildebrandt calls them. They were freely stylized, always beautifully primitive and geometrical, and were considered to be as naïve as the child itself, because the child is in the habit of finding simple substitutes for dolls. But to become consciously naïve is to become affected; the purely literary idea of reform has turned out to be fruitless. Something notable has

178

FIG. 183. HUGO AND ADOLAR
Designed and executed by the sculptor Buchholz, Züllichau
*Kunstgewerbehaus H. Schwerdtfeger, Berlin. Photo Delia*

FIG. 184. PEASANT AND PEASANT WOMAN
*Bonbonnière* in *papier mâché.* Designs by Fritz Kleinhempel
*Deutsche Werkstätten, Dresden,* 1911

certainly been created in the doll line by these reformers, but
such dolls make a greater appeal to the grown-ups than to
children. Thus wooden dolls have been produced in Munich
with the idea of endeavouring to secure the simplest possible
forms; these fit like boxes into one another, one nest of boxes
representing the royal family, another, the same shape only
differently painted, showing little Snow-white and the Seven

FIG. 185. MR BANKER
*Bonbonnière* in *papier mâché*. Fritz
Kleinhempel
*Werkstätte für den Hausrat, Theophil Müller,*
*Dresden*

FIG. 186. ROCOCO LADY
*Bonbonnière* in *papier mâché*. Fritz
Kleinhempel
*Werkstätte für den Hausrat, Theophil Müller*
*Dresden*

Dwarfs or the peasant women of Dachau. It is the Dresdeners and
the Viennese, however, who have gone to the greatest lengths
in stylization. The character dolls of Fritz and Erich Kleinhempel in Dresden and the creations of the Viennese workshops are
equally far removed from the actual world of the child. After
sketches of Kolo Moser, Fanny Zakucka, Minka Podhabka, etc.,
wooden dolls have been turned and painted in which the principle of 'style at any price' seems driven to extremes. Even
their cloth dolls were strictly geometricized. They may have
introduced fresh *nuances* of feeling, may even have attained those
"highest reaches of cultured taste" and that select composition
of form which Adolf Braig asserts for them (no one will dis-
pute that), but when this critic is able to find praise for "a
180

FIG. 187. ART DOLLS
C. Heinrich, Nürnberg

FIG. 188. CAR MASCOTS
Josephine Baker. Designed and executed by Brunhilde Einenkel
*Kunstgewerbehaus-Schwerdtfeger, Berlin*

decidedly languid beauty" it becomes clear at once that these creations are certainly in their wrong place when considered as dolls. In the year 1903 the Bayerische Gerwerbemuseum, in Nürnberg, offered a prize for sketches of characteristic wooden toys designed to arouse and stimulate the taste and

FIG. 189. SPANISH COUPLE
Anna Bauknecht

the imagination of children. Among the works sent in those of August Geigenberger and Bernhard Halbreiter, of Wasserburg, were particularly felicitous, as were those of Marie von Uchatius, of Vienna. In the following year the Dresden handicraft workshops made an appeal for designs to express old familiar children's toys in new forms, and were answered by artists such as Riemerschmidt, Urban, Kirchner, Wenig, Eichrodt, who sent in sketches,

the marked stylization of which the critics of the time praised
or condemned according to their individual points of view. For
a time the groping and the searching proceeded. The first real
success was achieved by Munich artists, who in 1909 instituted
an exhibition of toy dolls in the warehouse of Hermann Tietz;

FIG. 190. PEASANT WOMAN WITH BASKET OF EGGS
Anna Bauknecht

here they aimed at and reached simplicity, naturalness, and
genuine childishness. The dolls exhibited were equally far
removed from triviality and from coarseness; the golden mean
between the rude naturalistic style and the sweetly unreal style
in the formation of dolls was gained at last. Here for the first
time was heard the name of Marion Kaulitz as a doll artist. Her
dolls are full of individuality and character and yet always
remain children, so true-hearted and bright, so charmingly pert
and rakish. The heads, of *papier mâché*, were modelled by Paul
Vogelsanger and painted by the artist, who also made the dresses.

183

# DOLLS AND PUPPETS

The same heads, when given different wigs and dresses, provided a series of entirely different impressions. With her Lilian Frobenius, Alice Hegemann, and Marie Maré-Schur, won distinction with their dolls, made lovingly and with insight. While it could be believed, when looking at Kaulitz's dolls, that one was gazing at real boys and girls, the dolls of Josef Wackerle move in a clever, piquant realm which, it is true, gives them charm for grown-ups, but debars them from the sphere of toys.

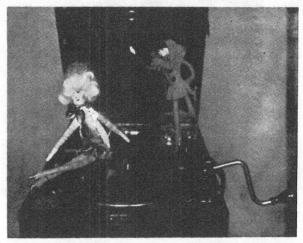

FIG. 191. AMUSING CLOTH DOLLS FOR THE GRAMOPHONE
*Photo Delia*

The example of Munich gave the Berliners no rest; they also had to have their exhibitions of dolls, with that flaring advertisement and that lack of taste which is so typical of all the Berlin institutions of that period. Because of that the whole thing fell flat, as such things always will in these circumstances. And yet it was in Berlin that at an exhibition of home-made toys held in 1912 was discovered an artist whose name, both in Germany and outside, is immediately called to mind whenever German dolls are spoken of—Käthe Kruse. Her maternal instinct has led her to the invention of new types of dolls. At first she made dolls only for her own children, making use then of raw potatoes as material for the heads. All her dolls arise from tender and intimate understanding of the child's mind—hence the great immediate and universal success which she yet enjoys. She has naturally replaced the potatoes with a more durable material, and now makes indestructible dolls. It is possible that the

184

clever creations of other women artists arrest greater admiration in this sphere, but the dolls of Käthe Kruse compel love, and that is greater than admiration. The lively interest taken in her work has given the artist occasion for expressing her own views. Writing in 1923, she says:

> My dolls, particularly the little baby ones, arose from the desire to awaken a feeling that one was holding a real little baby in one's

FIG. 192. MUNICH ART DOLL
Designed and executed by Marion Kaulitz, Munich

arms. I must say, however, that this idea did not originate in my brain, but sprang from that of my sculptor father, who all his life long was concerned with the problem involved in the effect created by plastic form. Strange to say, the consideration of the emotional effect to be aroused and the recognition of the necessity of working on one's emotions is virgin soil for the doll. But it is always so; wherever there is creativeness a start must be made at the beginning in so far as there is a desire to solve the problem. And the problem of the doll, tantamount to education in maternal feeling, education in womanly act and in womanly bliss, perhaps even in a better understanding between mother and child, between mother and mother—this whole problem of the doll has certainly sufficient interest in itself.

185

# DOLLS AND PUPPETS

At all exhibitions held since her discovery the dolls made by
Käthe Kruse have been universal favourites, unrivalled by any
competitor.

FIG. 193. DOLLS
Käthe Kruse

FIG. 194. MUNICH ART DOLLS
Designed and executed by Marion Kaulitz, Munich

As the German manufacturers were actuated by educational
motives, French firms in 1902 offered a prize, principally with
the object of finding ways and means of meeting the over-
whelming German rivalry. Artists of renown, such as the
sculptor Frémiet and the painters Détaille and Gérome, sent in

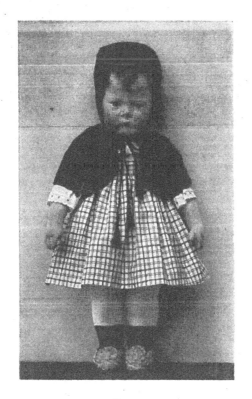

DOLL
Käthe Kruse

sketches, but this attempt resulted in nothing, for commercial circumstances do not allow themselves to be led by purely æsthetic considerations.

The attempts at reform have imparted new and powerful impulses to the interest taken in the toy doll; at a certain period

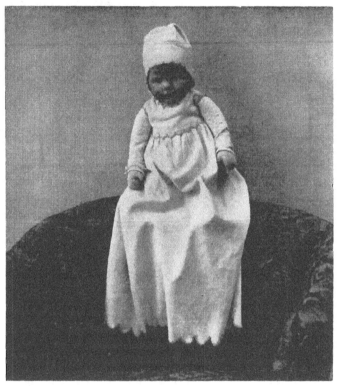

FIG. 195. DOLL: "DU MEIN SCHUFTERLE"
Käthe Kruse

the exhibitions came literally in crowds. At Brussels in 1892 the celebrated impresario Schürmann organized an exhibition of dolls which he believed required a charitable object as its excuse, but the doll-shows held in St Petersburg and in Vienna could renounce that pretext and were organized for their own sake. In 1905 at Leipzig six hundred dolls were collected together. Rich in types was the 'international' doll exhibition organized in October and November 1911 at Frankfort by the Frankfort Women's Club. Outside of Germany the Amis des Arts got up in 1926 at the once more alienated Strasbourg an

187

Exposition de Jouets Anciens, which showed much that was lovely, mainly from the collection of Robert Forrer. In the winter of 1927–28 the Märkische Museum in Berlin presented a cleverly and beautifully arranged exhibition of old dolls, mostly originating from the environs of the capital.

Formerly only the ethnographical museums had indulged in the collection of dolls, and these, as was natural, concentrated

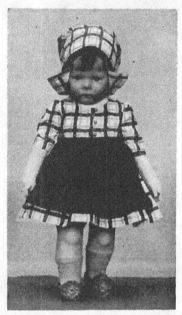

FIG. 196. DOLL: "MARINA"
Käthe Kruse

more on the exotic types, but now the other public collections freely indulge in the displaying of these objects. The Industrie-museum in Sonneberg, which must be given first place in this regard, possesses an important collection of toy dolls, including examples both of dolls and of dolls' heads dating from the year 1735. The museums of Berlin, Frankfort, Nürnberg, Prague, and Stuttgart have all directed their attention to this interesting object, and it seems to have a special fascination for the museums in the United States. The Metropolitan Museum in New York, the Children's Museum in Detroit, the Heye Foundation in New York, the Essex Institute in Salem, Massachusetts, the Fairchild Collection in Madison, Wisconsin, have permanent sections showing dolls arranged in complete series, following thus

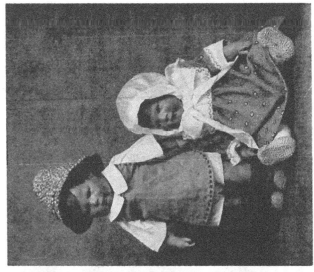

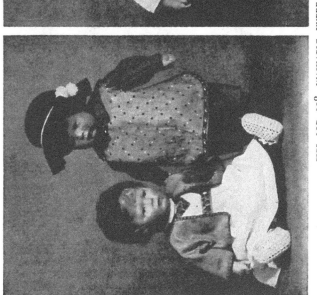

FIGS. 197, 198. WASHABLE, UNBREAKABLE CLOTH DOLLS
Käthe Kruse

the example of the private collectors. Carmen Sylva possessed a splendid collection of dolls; that of Elisabeth Lemke passed into the hands of the Volkskunde Museum in Berlin; Rodman Wanamaker founded that of the Musée Carnavalet in Paris; while others, such as George Savile Seligmann in Paris and

FIG. 199. DOLLS
Dora Petzold
*Photo Kester and Co.*

Frau Wenz in Munich, carry on their collecting activities with love and ardour.

This ardour seems sometimes to overshoot the mark; the serial arrangement of dolls, such as was for a long time popular, has only a narrowly specialized value. The collection of dolls designed to provide a survey of local costumes arranged in 1893 by Dutch women in the Dutch East Indies as a present for the young Queen Wilhelmina was truly an undertaking of unquestionable value for the study of the customs of the Dutch colonies, of double value indeed, because the natives themselves joyously participated in it. The Sultan of Sambas commissioned one of

190

FIG. 200. DOLL: "THE GERMAN CHILD"
Käthe Kruse. After Julius Hübner's *Portrait of a Girl*

his relations, Pangeran Amar di Radja, to supervise the making of various figures painted by F. J. Duchâteau. These, in the opinion of experts, were excellently made, and the dolls are to be regarded as genuine miniature replicas of Malays and Dayaks.

FIG. 201. ITALIAN DOLLS (LENZI DOLLS) MADE OF FELT
*Photo Kester and Co.*

It is quite a different matter, however, when an historical object is on view. Thus in 1892 Mme Piogey at Paris exhibited sixteen dolls which were supposed to represent French feminine fashions from the year 1000 to the year 1890. At the world exhibition in Chicago in 1893 a similar collection of twenty-five dolls was on view, also designed to show the history of feminine dress in France. These attracted much attention then, but on looking at

FIG. 202. MALAYAN DOLLS

Left to right: Malay chief; Malay chieftainess; Malay in festive clothes; Malay woman ir festive clothes
From the Padang Highlands of Sumatra

illustrations of the various figures now, we are compelled to describe them as merely toys, of absolutely no value from an historical point of view. Not only do the childish faces of the dolls fail to fit the *rôles* apportioned to them, a criticism which can generally be levelled at all the dolls supposed to represent women of older periods, but even the costumes themselves are

FIG. 203. BRIDEGROOM AND BRIDE FROM JAVA

only approximately correct, as is demonstrated by their measurements and by the lack of real old material. Fancy dress dolls they are, nothing more.

French women, however, have found great amusement in this game. Mme Charles Cosson in 1893 exhibited at Paris sixteen similar costume dolls, embarrassing the unfortunate Musée des Arts Décoratifs by presenting them to it. Mme Martet reproduced the figures of Balzac's *Comédie Humaine* in dolls; Mme Pulliche made six Venetian women of the eighteenth century

DUTCHMAN

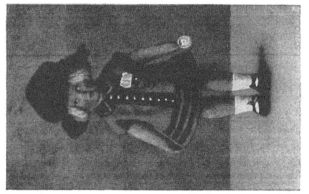

GISELA

Made in the factory of Heinrich Zwanzger, Nürnberg

after the sketches of Georges Barbier, these later going to the Metropolitan Museum in New York. This institute possesses also a doll review showing seven centuries of fashion, which Miss

FIG. 204. COSTUME DOLL: WOMAN PILGRIM (JAVA)

FIG. 205. COSTUME DOLL: HADJI (JAVA)

Frances Morris executed from the paintings of old masters. The Unions des Arts in Paris has established a collection of dolls which represents the most celebrated actresses on the Parisian stage—Sarah Bernhardt, Mme Réjane, Segond-Weber, Bartel,

Sorel, Granier, etc.—in their characteristic *rôles* and costumes.
The wax heads were modelled by Mlle Lifraud and were painted

FIG. 206. PARISIAN COSTUME
DOLL: MARQUISE DE POMPADOUR

FIG. 207. PARISIAN COSTUME
DOLL: MERVEILLEUSE
(DIRECTORY)

FIG. 208. DOLLS IN PARISIAN POPULAR COSTUMES
Martin Guelliot
From the exhibition "L'Art pour l'Enfance" in the Musée Galliera

by Mme Claude Marlef. Mmes Lafitte and Désirat presented to
the Musée National de la Guerre, in Vincennes, dolls designed to
show women's fashions from 1914 to 1918; Mme Myrthas Dory

FIG. 209. FRENCH COSTUME DOLLS AT THE WORLD EXHIBITION AT
CHICAGO, 1893

in a similar set has traced the costumes of women war workers during the War years. "These will preserve for the future a memory of one of the most critical periods in French history,"

FIG. 210.  DUTCH DOLLS FROM SEELAND
Nineteenth century.  Presented to the Victoria and Albert Museum by
Miss Elize Frere

writes Mme Calmettes. During the War Mmes Paderewski, Lazarski, and Fiszerowni carried on propaganda by means of Polish dolls which they sent to Paris. American museums by means of dolls have exhibited all kinds of European local costumes and those of all the native Indian tribes. M. and Mme Martin Guelliot in Paris are said to possess more than six

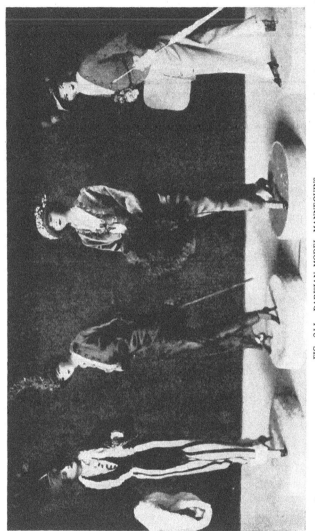

FIG. 211. PARISIAN MODEL MANNEQUINS
Anne Lafitte Désirat
From the exhibition "L'Art pour l'Enfance" in the Musée Galliera

FIG. 213. SCHWABING PEASANT WOMAN

*Bayerische Landesgewerbe-Anstalt, Nürnberg*

FIG. 212. "DER ALTE FRITZ"

*Spielzeug-Museum, Sonneberg*

hundred dolls, between 30 and 50 cm. high, representing all races of the world. Marie Koenig has been able to collect several hundred dolls from all countries for the ethnographical section of the Trocadéro. Such costume dolls have no more significance for scientific study of the folk or for the history of culture than a modern historical novel has for the study of history—that is to say, none at all. They remain embellished toys possessing value only in so far as they amuse the persons who make them and those who see them.

FIG. 214. DOLLS IN NATIONAL DRESS
Left to right: date, 1840; date, 1810; middle of the eighteenth century; beginning of the nineteenth century

# XIII

## DOLLS OF EXOTIC PEOPLES

It is quite another matter with toy dolls of exotic peoples and of those classes among European nations which have not been influenced by town culture, and hence are inspired by their own imaginations. These possess a certain definite psychological interest.

In them are reflected the talents and disposition of the various peoples. From these productions landscape and climate can be guessed at; from the manner of composition can be gauged the handicraft and the power of technical invention; from the forms the power of imagination and the artistic ability.

The elementary, or, as it may be called, the basic, doll consists of a stick, with a thickening at the end as a head; it has preserved the essentials of the human shape—the upright form. When another stick is introduced, placed cross-wise on the first, the line of the shoulders is indicated, and at once a great anatomical advance is attained. A second generation of dolls is represented in the soft bag, in which head and limbs are produced by tying up parts with string. Elisabeth Lemke found these rag dolls or 'patchwork dolls' (*Fleckerldocke*) from Sicily to Transylvania and beyond to the Ober Pfalz. In this style and manner the Hungarian children make their dolls; for the nose they use a grain of corn, with oats or pepper seeds for the eyes. At Plattensee the children pull down the petals of red poppies, wind round a blade of grass, and thus make the body and dress of a doll; the seeds form the head. The main principle remains always the vertical line, a principle which has influenced modern creative artists as well, so much so indeed that their dolls look more like wooden sticks than human figures. This primitive shape too appears in the oldest wooden dolls of Sonneberg, which reflect the human figure only in coarse outlines.

In all the five continents a survey of the toy doll will always lead us back to the three essential basic forms, and will always reveal anew the fact that toy dolls as well as magical dolls are prevailingly of the female sex. In Sanskrit the words for a doll all signify 'little daughter'; from these the words *putteli* and *puttalika* (Richard Pischel is quoted here) have survived in folk speech. The ancient Indian dolls consisted of wool, wood, buffalo-horn, or ivory, and seem to have attracted much attention among the young girls, for in the *Mahabharata* two of these ask some warriors to bring back pretty clothes for their

FIG. 215. INDIAN DOLLS
*Spielzeug-Museum, Sonneberg*

dolls as booty from the field of battle. The girls must have been devoted to this amusement up to the time they were marriageable, as Vatsyayana counsels boys and youths, when they desire to win the maidens' fancies, to join them in their playing with dolls. This lively interest in doll play has survived to our own times; in 1873 a doll's marriage was publicly celebrated with great festivities at Dacca, in Bengal.

Toy dolls in Siam are remarkable because they are exceptionally delicate, and the children there must either be improbably gentle or else these refined images are not intended to be played with at all. They are made of baked clay, the dresses being either represented by painting or made of real cloth; ear-rings and jewellery are rendered in silver wire. Their bearing follows the smooth elegance of the adults, although among them there are to be found some dolls representing children with the hair done up in tufts in the way characteristic of the young. The Siamese have also dolls of wood and paper.

In the Chinese and Korean languages the word 'doll' comes

FIG. 216. CLAY DOLLS FROM TIENTSIN, CHINA
*Staatliches Museum für Völkerkunde, Munich*

from the same root as the words for idol or fetish. This seems to confirm what Gustav Schlegel has observed; he says that little girls in China never play with dolls, these having always been regarded as endowed with magical power. Only in the last decades have come toy dolls, of puffed-out silk with heads of oiled paper and hands and feet of sepia (cuttle-fish); there are also others made of clay and *papier mâché* in the European style, but possibly these are intended only for export. In China the tumbling doll is a very popular toy; this is called in Chinese "Stand up, little priest."

According to Schlegel toy dolls were first introduced to Japan by the Dutch, nor do the great annual doll festivals of girls and boys disprove this statement, since the dolls used there could never be regarded as toys in the ordinary sense of the word.

FIG. 217. CLAY DOLLS FROM TIENTSIN, CHINA
Long Life, Wealth, and Good Fortune in Children
*Staatliches Museum für Völkerkunde, Munich*

The girls' doll festival takes place on the third day of the third month and lasts three days. Every better-class family in Japan possesses a series of dolls for this festival, these being handed down from generation to generation as treasured heirlooms. They are set on the steps of a platform, the highest always

FIG. 218. JAPANESE DOLL (TOKYO), NINETEENTH CENTURY
*Victoria and Albert Museum*

reserved for the Emperor and Empress. The whole is proceeded with according to certain ceremonial rites, and when the festival is over, the entire set is once more carefully packed away. The boys' doll festival takes place on May 5. The chief doll here is the Empress Jingo, a heroine of the olden days; indeed, all the dolls used in this festival are of an historical character. Japanese artists such as Hokusai delighted in depicting these festivals, which seem to have descended from an old Shinto purification feast originally held on March 3. On these occasions the whole family went to the river, and each member rubbed his body with

FIG. 219. CLAY DOLLS FROM TIENTSIN, CHINA

*Staatliches Museum für Völkerkunde, Munich*

a piece of paper cut by the priests in the semblance of human form, in the belief that his sins would thus be transferred to the dolls, which the boys then threw into the water. The girls' dolls

FIG. 220. ESKIMO DOLLS
*Spielzeug-Museum, Sonneberg*

belonged to a plastic tradition; they were the so-called 'sons of heaven'—that is to say, magical dolls which, according to popular belief, took voluntarily on themselves all possible misfortune a woman might encounter in her life. Originally the pair of dolls set highest on the platform was only a married couple, supposed to give the little girl some conception of marriage, but later the

FIG. 221. THE DOLL FESTIVAL IN JAPAN

After Siebold's *Nippon*, 1840

O

royal couple was placed there. These Japanese dolls are diverse in kind; some, such as the *Ilinasama* figures from the Ryukyu Islands, are very roughly made of folded paper; others have heads of bamboo fibre. The ancient type consisted of a roll of paper with long threads instead of a head, but this material must originally have come from the province of Satsuma. To recog-

FIG. 222. MODERN RUSSIAN DOLL
*Spielzeug Museum, Sonneberg*

nize a doll in this shape one had to be told what it was. The Japanese doll festivals created a great sensation in the United States in 1927 when the Committee of World Friendship among Children, a branch of the Federal Council of the Churches of Christ in America, sent 11,000 representative dolls to the girls' festival on March 3. Thousands of these were previously exhibited at the Plaza Hotel in New York, and the finest were awarded prizes. In Tokyo the doll ship was ceremoniously received and befilmed, and there followed the usual exchange of cablegrams containing the most charming assurances of friendship. But will this "great social and educational mission" break down the difference between the United States and Japan in California and the Pacific?

In the Malay Archipelago toy dolls are made of lontava-leaves, of strips of palm-leaf plaited diagonally, or of a very roughly carved yellowish wood; they are also sewn together from cotton and palm-leaves and ornamented with glass beads. Rag dolls too, made out of a patterned cotton sacking, are to be found there. In spite of the prohibition of the Koran, the

FIG. 223. DOLL OF THE APACHE INDIANS
*From the collection of A. L. Dickermann*

Mohammedan children do not allow themselves to be deprived of their dolls. Mohammed himself was forced to recognize this, for his wife, Ayesha, at the time of her marriage only nine years old, brought her dolls with her to her husband's harem, and the prophet permitted her to play with them to her heart's content. The Turkish races inhabiting Russia give their children dolls made of bark, straw, and rags.

The Samoyedes make their toy dolls out of ducks' beaks, leather, or wood, and dress them in cloth; in spite of their primitive appearance they bear such resemblance to the civilized doll that we must regard the latter as their model. The Liberian dolls look like small furry creatures, somewhat similar to the Eskimo dolls, which also have connexions with the European dolls. In the Northern regions the fur doll predominates, for its dress, like that of the European dolls representing ladies, is based on the dress of the adults. Nordenskiöld met with many examples of these among the Tschuktchi, in Alaska, in East Greenland, and among the tribes of North-western America; similar toy dolls have been found in graves belonging to races long extinct.

The Indian tribes of the United States possess a great wealth of diverse kinds of toy dolls. Several scholars, such as C.

FIG. 224. DOLLS OF THE ZUÑI
Man and woman
*From the collection of A. L. Dickermann*

Steffens, support the view that the original discoverers of America must have found dolls already existent among these tribes, and that the Indians consequently had no need to learn from the settlers how to manufacture them. This theory, however, seems to be invalidated by the fact that the extant dolls are clearly copies of European models, using native technique and material certainly, but borrowing their shapes from abroad. Even now not all the tribes have toy dolls, and it is to be suspected that others make their dolls not so much for their own children as for foreign collectors. The Cheyennes, Iroquois, Sioux, and Apaches are said to be ignorant of the toy doll, but not so the Prairie Indians and those of the Dakota and Blackfoot tribes. These make their dolls of leather and embroider them with glass beads; the faces are grotesque, and the very carefully executed dresses seem based on models from the Old World. The Zuñi use a clay figure as a basis. The Katschina dolls of the Hopi Indians have already been referred to in another connexion; these are half cult dolls and half toy dolls, and remind us too of European types. The Pima, a Nearctic race in the south-west of the United States, have clay dolls which they paint

FIG. 225. TOY DOLL OF THE PIMA (SOUTH-WEST OF THE UNITED STATES)

and ornament with beads, with a bast apron and a girdle of wool.

In Mexico there have been discovered clay dolls, marked with the insignia of the sun, appertaining to the cults of the ancient Aztecs, supposed to belong to about the year 1000 B.C. The Indians of present-day Mexico in their exceedingly skilful way model little dolls of wax or put them together of rags and decorate them with flaxen ornaments. They also cut out of paper dolls which are very close to the prehistoric 'board idols.' The modern dolls of the natives in Guatemala, Bolivia, and Chile, which they are accustomed to crochet or knit from coloured wool over a wire frame and embellish with hair and glass beads, clearly betray Spanish influence. In Bolivia there are also primitive specimens in wax dressed in cloth or made of resin with a paper costume, and Columbia has its clay rattle dolls representing both men and women. Bone dolls with eyes of mother-of-pearl are to be found in the Rio Negro district, alongside others of plaited bark, painted and decorated with feathers in the likenesses of the local masked dancers. The Kadiueo, South American Indians, carve remarkably lifelike dolls out of wood;

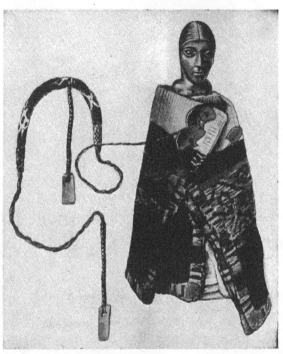

FIG. 226. ANCIENT PERUVIAN DOLL, MADE OF GOLD-LEAF AND · DRESSED IN CLOTH, FOUND NEAR LIMA

the Borero have male dolls made of narrow, rectangular strips of palm-leaf laid together and female dolls made of broader strips, neither the face nor the arms and legs being indicated. The dolls of the Karaya likewise dispense with head, arms, and legs; an indentation, however, marks the mouth, and the shape of the breasts is indicated in black wax. The most completely developed dolls of South America are those of Guatemala; these are small, but are most carefully dressed. The roughly carved wooden dolls of the Chaco Indians, in Paraguay, obviously derive from the sacred images which were introduced by the Jesuits, who were in power there in the eighteenth century.

214

FIG. 227. ANCIENT PERUVIAN CLAY DOLLS

Children's toys from the cemetery of Ancon

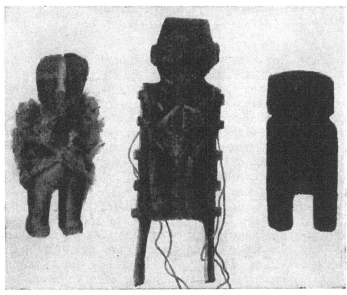

FIG. 228. ANCIENT PERUVIAN WOODEN DOLLS

Children's toys from the cemetery of Ancon

In ancient Peru, with the richly developed civilization it enjoyed before the entry of the Spaniards, there existed a doll-making art of a very high standard. Massive gold female dolls have been found there, dressed in cloth, as well as silver male dolls with three skirts and three wallets made of real cloth. When the Peruvian children died their toys were put in their graves, and the dry earth, for the most part permeated with saltpetre, has preserved them marvellously. These toy dolls were made of all conceivable materials; some, manufactured of clay pressed in moulds, had exceptionally large heads and stiffly extended

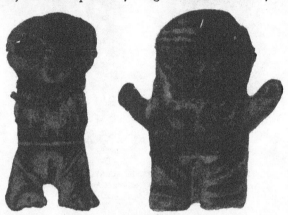

FIGS. 229, 230. ANCIENT PERUVIAN CLAY DOLLS
Children's toys from the cemetery of Ancon

limbs. They were intended to be dressed in cloth, while openings in the upper part of the head served for the securing of feathers, shells, or other ornaments. The ancient Peruvians seem to have set great store by durability. Some of the dolls which have been found there are so naïvely executed that they must have been made by the children themselves. Sometimes the faces were painted. Besides the clay dolls there were also toy dolls of carved wood, of wool, of Cabuya fibre, or of straw plaited into fairly rough shapes, in which eyes, mouth, and teeth were only indicated by indentations.

The modern toy dolls in the United States need hardly be differentiated from the European, but there are to be found among them some characteristic types. Leo Claretie bought in Kansas City a doll made out of iron wire and gutta-percha in the shape of a skeleton. This is typical, for we learn from Caswell Ellis, for example, that American children delight in playing at illness, death, and burial when they amuse themselves with their dolls. During the Revolution French children, too, played with a dolls' guillotine, and even to-day Parisian shops offer for sale *chemin de fer à catastrophes* with plentiful dead and injured.

The toy dolls of African negro tribes, like those of the American Indian races, are undeniably influenced by the European. This is proved particularly by the examples originating in the Sudan, where the body is made of wood, the head and limbs of clay, and the hair of wool. The dress is of cloth, and ornaments of coins and glass beads are added. So far as the African doll has preserved its independence, generally it presents human forms only in rudest outlines. Thus the wooden dolls of the Ashanti, with bead hair, look more like shapeless chess-men than human beings; those of the Yoruba resemble blocks of wood even when they have heads attached. The dolls of the Basuto consist of bandages wound round a wooden base and provided with threads and strings of beads. These are cone-shaped, without any distinguishable head. The dolls of the Haussa are of wax, but, in spite of the nose ornaments of glass beads, they show little likeness to human form. The bone doll of the Somali has a cloth head, the hair is of wool, and the facial features are indicated by sewn-on glass beads. In Togo there are glass-eyed clay dolls which show clearly the male and female organs.

FIG. 231. ANCIENT PERUVIAN
CLAY DOLL

## XIV

## DOLLS USED FOR DECORATIVE PURPOSES

THE reform in the toy doll has created a strong reaction even among adults. It is not merely that the doll became a collector's object, making an appeal, after all, only to a small circle; it became fashionable, and that is a thing which always attracts the crowd. In America for a time grown-up women themselves took out dolls, and, when President Roosevelt was popular, teddy bears as well, for their daily walks. Among the follies emanating from Hollywood is the wearing of a doll as a pendant. This is attached to a silk cord and hung round the neck, a fashion truly so absurd that it deserves to be copied by female highbrows in other countries. German women are, however, content to play with their dolls indoors, taking rubber dolls with them to their baths. The tea-cosy dolls in particular, the fashion for which raged for several years, gave the greatest scope in this direction. These are common enough in the shape of a bulky balloon dress with a tiny porcelain upper part for the body, the one out of all proportion to the other. Their rapid popularity was due to the fact that they displayed fine workmanship; not being designed simply as toys, but serving a strictly practical purpose, they really depended entirely on the skill shown in making them. Apart from that they had the advantage of rapidly gathering dust and of so becoming unattractive, thus providing a welcome excuse for the preparation of a new *toilette*. While German women were still content with their tea-cosy dolls the Americans went much further, for they used the doll as a decoration for their rooms. Since a doll, from its resemblance to the human form, always retains something of a living being, when used as a piece of decoration it imparts to a room a kind of spiritual animation which no other small object of art can in any way equal. In the United States favour is given to burlesque puppets for adding an individual note to the drawing-room. These grotesque dolls are made out-of-joint; the limbs are too long, the faces repelling, the eyes squinting. In Germany Staudinger has made such dolls for the delectation of grown-ups. Emma von Sichart, of Munich, using porcelain heads of Nymphenburg manufacture, has dressed very charmingly and tastefully clad figures in the tea-cosy style; Betty Krieger, of Frankfort, made series of costume dolls, in replicas of Bavarian, Hessian, and other peasant dresses, with love and accuracy; Hella Bibrawicz and Clarisse Spiegel at Nürnberg in 1921 held an exhibition of attractively attired drawing-room dolls. Clever fingers have composed all kinds of pretty things, but this type of doll first became art under the hands of Lotte Pritzel.

When this artist first introduced her work she came as a revelation; it was as if the curtain, hitherto concealing a completely unknown sphere of art, had been suddenly drawn. One hardly dares to use the term 'doll' for these creations, since this word so easily leads one astray. These figures possess a psychological strength, in marked contrast to their delicate butterfly-like forms. "They came to life," as H. Rupé says very beautifully, "like improvisations of the subconscious. Lotte Pritzel must herself feel surprised at her own fancies." Her methods are extraordinarily simple: a wire frame, a little slip of silk or *chiffon*, some glass beads or spangles, and at the top a wax head. And with these she creates works of art which, once seen, can never be forgotten. They recall Aubrey Beardsley and the canvases of Greco, yet they are inspired by a wholly individual note, a tremblingly

FIG. 232. THE SWORD-DANCER
Lotte Pritzel
*Photo Delia*

fervent rhythm. The artist has baptized her fantasies with the names of Simonetta, Ganymed, Bajadere, Chichette, the Unveiled, Hamlet, Adoration, and so on; these names originate from the difficulty of finding an expression for complexes of sentiment which are experienced, but cannot be defined. They are there so soon as the figure is seen; they have no binding motive, for Lotte Pritzel works freely, without any backward glance at artistic conventions. If one seeks the counterpart of these enigmatical figures in the world of the known, one might perhaps find it most fittingly in music. They shape themselves as harmonious tones, fleeting memories, half-forgotten dreams, ever threatening to vanish into the nothingness of which they were born. The faces are visionary, morbid; the figures are exaggeratedly slim; the attitudes are strained.

FIG. 233. DOLLS
Relly Mailander

Fascinating, bewildering, tormenting, if you like, is the sexlessness of these dolls; in their expression and in their indeterminate dress they possess something excitingly ambiguous. The secret they hold can never be reached. All the perversions of a soulless, hopeless species drowning in sensuousness are here carried to extremes, a ghostly existence in the world of reality. Lotte Pritzel's dolls have more of the essence of our age than a whole glass palace full of modern pictures. That word, then, so much misused is here in its proper place; every doll made by this artist is an experience for the person who looks at it, and an experience need not necessarily be merely one of pleasure; it can also sometimes arouse reflections. Before she discovered her own style Lotte Pritzel experimented in making

FIG. 234. ORPHEUS
Lotte Pritzel
*Photo Delia*

the heads of her dolls out of chestnuts; then she turned to toy
dolls with movable limbs, and, after developing her talents,

FIG. 235. DOLL
Relly Mailander

came at last to the wire skeleton, which granted her a flexibility
that does not belong to this world. The wax heads she models
and paints herself. She has found success from her very first

222

appearance (at Munich (?) in 1909 (?)); she has held exhibitions and received general recognition. The cultural section of the Universum-Film dedicated a whole film to her dolls. The sensitive, subtle art of Lotte Pritzel is, like everything genuinely

FIG. 236. DOLLS OF WOOL
*Spielzeug-Museum, Sonneberg*

original, incapable of imitation; maybe because of that so many have tried to imitate it.

The dolls made by Erna Pinner, to which she gives such titles as the Superior, the Elegant, the Distinguished, the Resolute, Woman of To-day, are made of cloth and have movable limbs; the head too is of cloth and painted. They are not fragile works of art like the dolls of Lotte Pritzel; on the contrary, they gain by being taken in the hand, although they remain creations of the drawing-room, far removed from the nursery. The

223

Pritzel dolls are unrivalled in their own sphere, just as the Käthe Kruse dolls in theirs; perhaps only the paper dolls of Erna Muth, of Dresden, can be considered artistic creations worthy of being compared with them. Erna Muth first exhibited her works in 1919, at a time when there was the greatest lack of

FIG. 237. PAPER DOLL
Erna Muth, Dresden
*Photo Kester and Co.*

materials, limiting herself to the cheapest substances, wire and silk paper. She succeeded both in surmounting the external difficulties inherent in the process of fashioning the materials at her command and in getting over the poverty of the stuff with which she worked, wresting effects from it which possibly costlier and more supple material would not have offered her. The flexible wire allowed the artist to give her dolls an attitude full of the suggestion of powerful movement; indeed, the further she went in that direction, the greater was the success of her figures.

# DOLLS FOR DECORATIVE PURPOSES

Surprisingly simple in technique yet rich in appearance and worked out with sovereign skill, the dolls of Erna Muth make us regret nothing save their perishability.

The drawing-room doll of grown-ups is a fashion like all other fashions; it will vanish again from the vitrines as once it entered them. And that will not be the first occurrence of this phenomenon. It is to be remembered that eighteenth-century society likewise played with dolls, in point of fact even with the same sort of dolls, for the porcelain figures then in fashion could just as little be placed in the hands of children as could the dolls made by Pritzel and Erna Muth.

FIG. 238. GROTESQUE CLOTH DOLL REPRESENTING MEPHISTO
*Photo Kester and Co.*

## XV

## PORCELAIN FIGURES

THE art of porcelain had been introduced to Europe only a few years when modellers set to work on plastic objects as well as on crockery, and, indeed, reached immediately to a perfection

FIG. 239. CHINESE PRIEST
F. A. Bustelli
*Staatliche Porzellan-Manufaktur,*
*Nymphenburg*

in form through which the artists expressed by the means of porcelain the finest ideas of their period. Winckelmann, it is true, wrote disrespectfully at the time, declaring that "Porcelain is mostly used for making ridiculous dolls," but to-day we pass a different judgment. Indeed, this porcelain now appears to us, in the words of Max Sauerlandt, to be "the most perfect material for the self-portraiture of the eighteenth century." It became the real factor which, by settling style and giving direction, influenced rococo art; to-day it would be difficult to form

226

a mental picture of that epoch without the help of its china, just as it would be difficult to picture the *Biedermeier* age without its lithography or the Second Empire without its photography. From the very beginning porcelain, on account of its delicacy, was fit for the use of a pampered society, and this delicacy has been assumed by the shapes into which it was formed, being,

FIG. 240. DOLL WITH PASSAU CHINA HEAD
Emma von Sichart

indeed, imposed upon them by the fragility of the material. The shaping of the models was by no means a simple affair; even the smallest figure had often to be divided into numerous little pieces, later set together. The seams were then plastered; little details were touched up by hand; the whole was worked over with the modelling stick; and even then the firing could bring completely unexpected surprises, for the figures shrank by a third in the oven. This circumstance influenced the attitudes taken by the figures, and compelled little arms and legs to assume twists not always intended, but certainly through these means was produced a contour, the arbitrary nature of which

227

attained to what the rococo art desired and strove after. The gleaming lights which play so constantly over the reflecting glazed surface, and often change the emphasis so marvellously, produce that capricious modulation of expression, that constantly shimmering ebb and flow of light, that precious coquetry, which was so peculiar to the whole society of the time—a society whose elders rouged and whose young powdered themselves white.

FIG. 241. CAVALIER AT A PEDESTAL
F. A. Bustelli
*Staatliche Porzellan-Manufaktur,*
*Nymphenburg*

FIG. 242. LEDA
F. A. Bustelli
*Staatliche Porzellan-Manufaktur,*
*Nymphenburg*

The material itself, thus newly bestowed on European art, possessed great advantages—the pure white of its substance, the animating shimmer of its glaze, and the permanence of its colours. Happy chance, too, brought it immediately into the right hands. The first modeller of Meissen ware, Johann Joachim Kändler, was a commanding artistic personality, to whom it was granted to conjure up elegance and grace, the ideals of the life of his time, into porcelain plastic form. He found worthy followers in the rival factories which sprang up so rapidly during the period. Dominik Auliczek and Franz Anton Bustelli in Nymphenburg, Johann Peter Melchior in Höchst, Karl Gottlieb Lück in Frankenthal, Wilhelm Beyer in

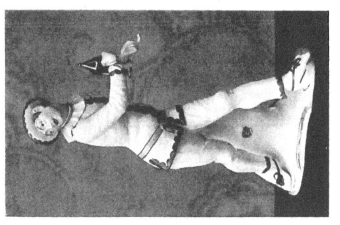

PIERROT WITH LANTERN

ISABELLA

Franz Anton Bustelli

*Municipal Porcelain Factory, Nymphenburg*

Ludwigsburg, Simon Feilner in Fürstenberg, besides many others who might be named, brought a great deal of talent to their work. To them all belongs a surprising power in invention and in the shaping of forms and a truly inexhaustible imagination. The models of china dolls emanating from German factories may be counted in their thousands, and perhaps as many more have

FIG. 243. SCARAMOUCHE, FROM THE ITALIAN COMEDY
F. A. Bustelli
*Staatliche Porzellan-Manufaktur, Nymphenburg*

perished. In their multiplicity these plastic motives comprehend the whole world of rococo life—cavaliers and their ladies, gods and goddesses, figures of the Italian comedy, dancers, singers, soldiers, Turks, and Chinese. Whatever names they were given, whether they were taken from real life or had only a mythological significance, whether they took their conception from the higher spheres or descended to the lower orders of hand-workers, peasants, fishermen, huntsmen, shepherds, gardeners, is of no import; they all belong to the Court circles, an exclusively aristocratic style being reflected in their deportment and dress.

229

Spirit, taste, temperament, *joie de vivre*, and amiability seem to have united to produce in these china dolls a smiling reflection of eighteenth-century society. The interest in the rococo period, still so vital in our own time and still exercising such a powerful charm on cultured people, is mainly inspired by this porcelain plastic art which gives to the epoch such a high importance. No other period and no artists so gifted as these had such

FIG. 244. LADY IN A HOOPED DRESS
F. A. Bustelli
*Staatliche Porzellan-Manufaktur, Nymphenburg*

material at their disposal. We grant to the ladies and gentlemen of that long-vanished age a pre-eminent charm; we like to dream of their superior grace and their playful mastery of all that concerns social intercourse. But who knows whether these beloved dolls do not deceive us and lead us astray? Do we not attribute to their models merits which perhaps spring only from the artists' imaginations? Were the Upper Bavarians whom Auliczek and Bustelli saw before them about the middle of the eighteenth century really so utterly different a type of people from what their descendants are to-day? Were they indeed so slim and agile, so bewitching in every movement, so expressive in every gesture? Was it not really but the spirit of the creative

230

artist which incidentally granted to these dolls that charm through which they yet exercise their fascination? Have they not perhaps borrowed charms which assuredly could not have been justified by sober reality? Kändler, Melchior, Bustelli, and others are those from whom rococo art borrows the transfiguring glitter which shines around it; from them the little gentlemen take their bold gallantry, the little ladies their

FIG. 245. CHINAMAN WITH A LUTE
F. A. Bustelli

coquettish reticence; from them come the artlessness of the little affectations of the figures and the grace of their artificiality.

The modellers, too, were those who found in these porcelain dolls an expression for the entire temper and culture of the period, who, with their modelling sticks in their hands, traced all *nuances* of feeling, and accompanied their contemporaries from the wantonness of courtly gallantry to the bliss of sentimental *bourgeois* tears, starting with polite inuendoes and finishing with little funereal monuments. But seldom has such a sovereign skill been applied to objects of so narrow a range and of so playful a tendency, and Georg Hirth is unquestionably right when, in his enthusiastic praise of this German art, he wishes to compare it with the Tanagra figures of classical Greece alone. In

231

their bold conception they resemble these ; in the care with which they are executed they surpass the classical dolls. This truly is

FIG. 246. WOMAN FROM TEGERNSEE
J. Wackerle
*Staatliche Porzellan-Manufaktur, Nymphenburg*

a precious province of rococo art through which Germany has enriched the whole art of the eighteenth century.

When rococo art had died away in a riot of colour and movement, and the antique style gained predominance, this porcelain

FIGURE OF A HORSEMAN, AFTER LEONHARDI
Theodor Kerner
*Staatliche Porzellan-Manufaktur, Nymphenburg*

plastic art lost its charm. The white, unglazed, and unpainted biscuit china was given preference by those who raved about the

FIG. 247. LADY WITH A MUFF
J. Wackerle
*Staatliche Porzellan-Manufaktur, Nymphenburg*

marble whiteness of Greek sculpture. The precious rococo plastic was accused of tastelessness, and, as of old the images of gods, the ancestor images, and the idols had ended as toy dolls, about the beginning of the nineteenth century these irreplaceable

233

porcelain figures were put into the hands of ignorant youth and destroyed. Marie von Ebner-Eschenbach relates that in her father's palace the old Meissen crockery was handed over to the domestics; the family ate only from pressed English earthenware, this being considered more modern and elegant. In the *Biedermeier* period the Viennese manufacturers produced a new sort of very charming china doll, but the dolls of Thüringer ware brought the porcelain of the time into disrepute. Very beautiful costume figures, the subjects of which came mostly from the old town of Ulm, were made by the potter and embosser J. J. Rommel and his sons Septimus and Nonus in Ulm during the first half of the nineteenth century. These were made of clay, baked and painted.

# XVI

## UTENSILS IN DOLL FORM

THE china plastic ware of the eighteenth century, in addition
to its uncommon richness in ornamental figures, took up another
style which had been popular from ancient times as an element

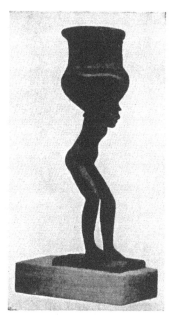

FIG. 248. EGYPTIAN
IVORY PAINT-BOX IN
HUMAN SHAPE

FIG. 249. EGYPTIAN WOODEN
PAINT-BOX IN HUMAN
SHAPE

in decoration; this was the making of various utensils in doll form.
It is generally assumed that the old Egyptian 'stick figures'
show the first beginnings of the introduction of the human shape
into various utensils. However that may be, it is certainly met
with at an early date in all parts of the world and at all stages of
culture. For the classical period there is sufficient evidence to
show that dolls were used in diverse ways as supports and

handles for vessels and lamps. Large Greek vases are extant which are decorated with small clay dolls.

How closely the ideas harmonize is shown by a comparative glance at remnants of ancient art in this kind. The Romans, for example, loved to make their bronze weights in the form of little figures, a custom which is also to be found among the Ashanti negroes in Africa. For the weighing of gold-dust the

FIG. 250. KOKA-EATER—CLAY VESSEL
Chan Chan Chimu civilization, Peru

latter make brass weights in the shape of little men and women, between 3 and 5 cm. high. The natives of New Guinea give human form to the hooks they make for hanging up their food in order to protect it from being devoured by wild beasts; and in the shape of vessels the human form is to be discovered in all latitudes. The Bakuba, in the Belgian Congo, carve wooden goblets in the form of dolls, but the most extraordinary testimony of this style, carried out absolutely systematically, is provided by the New World. The Chimu civilization of ancient Peru had hardly any vessels except those made in human shape; they even introduced cripples and blind men in this way. Similar pots and other utensils were made by the Tzapoteks in prehistoric Mexico.

The Middle Ages inherited this taste from the ancients. While the art of sculpture on this side of the Alps was making its earliest,

FIG. 251. CLAY VESSELS IN HUMAN SHAPE FOUND IN COLUMBIA

tentative experiments the Germani were already engaged in making their utensils in plastic rounded human forms. They thus loved to give human appearance to cast vessels, reliquaries, candlesticks, and other similar objects of daily utility. The Renaissance, baroque, and rococo periods adopted and transformed this

FIG. 252. CANDLESTICK, ABOUT 1400
*Louvre, Paris*

*motif* in their art work. During the sixteenth century the virgin goblet provided a popular pastime. This represents in precious metal a full-length figure of a woman dressed in the fashion characteristic of the time, with large hoop dress. With both its hands this figure holds aloft a little cup, which is on a swivel. When the goblet was in use the large vessel was first filled and then the smaller. The gallant endeavoured to empty the large one to the dregs, and if he succeeded the lady drained the smaller. In a drink-loving age such pastimes formed a pleasant spice for the stupid carousals to which it did homage. In the Castle of

238

Rosenborg is preserved a silver goblet representing King Christian IV racing on horseback. The horse's head forms the cover, the forelegs the handle, and the body the goblet. The whole thing was made at Brunswick in 1596. Similar drinking toys (Diana on a stag, for example), sometimes fitted with clockwork, are to be found to-day in almost all collections concerned with the history of culture.

FIGS. 253, 254. SKETCHES FOR GOBLETS
Water-colours by Jakob Mores, of Hamburg. About 1570

The cheapest earthenware proceeded on the same path. In this ware were produced tankards fitted with lids, intended to be emptied before being set down. Karl Simm refers to a goblet made in this shape by a Cologne tile-baker of 1550, as well as to others representing monks, nuns, and other figures of the time transformed into drinking vessels. The Tirol clay-modeller Christoph Gandtner, of Innsbruck, who worked about 1585, was particularly skilful in inventing such things. He has foot-soldiers, girls, Franciscan monks, women innkeepers, and so on, all glazed in variegated colours and all made to be used as tankards. In the seventeenth century the glass-works too made goblets in human form out of bottle glass; in this blown-glass style monks formed a favourite subject. There are also lady

239

tankards intended to be emptied without being set down; sometimes their dresses were decorated with glass threads. During the seventeenth and eighteenth centuries the pockets of elegant ladies and gentlemen were filled with all kinds of little useless trinkets which commonly assumed human form. There were,

FIG. 255. LARGE VIRGIN GOBLET OF
FRIEDRICH HILLEBRAND
Nürnberg. 1580

for instance, tobacco-grinders, by means of which one could grind one's own snuff. These were made of ivory, box-wood, or bronze, and represented shepherds, shepherdesses, drinkers, Italian comedians, and so on. The smoking tobacco too required its little trinkets: pipe-cleaners of silver in the shape of chimney sweeps or harlequins, pipe-fillers of amber in the shape of beautiful girls or crouching little men. As was natural, the greater proportion of these pretty treasures was intended for the ladies. The chief place was taken by the perfume bottle, which it was difficult to do without at a time when no one bathed and no one washed save in exceptional cases. There are peculiar and pretty examples of these in plenty: King David in amber, young girls in ivory, squatting men, often in not very decent postures, in box-wood, but the greater proportion are in porcelain. The manufacturers in Meissen, Höchst, Veilsdorf,

FIG. 256. AQUAMANILE, AFTER 1300
*National Museum, Copenhagen*

and Vienna produced in every conceivable shape little dolls designed to be used as flagons—babies in swaddling clothes, gentlemen, ladies, Moors, Savoyards, pierrots—painted in various colours and mounted in gold and silver. Even Shakespeare was made use of as a flask in Chelsea ware.

Another object utilized by women was the needle-box, which in the hands of the peasants, during all periodical changes in style, preserved its original shape of a child in swaddling clothes. This object is closely connected with the nutcracker and the smoking mannequin, which too have been preserved in the houses of the peasantry. The latter is made to resemble a

*Rübezahl* (a fabulous mountain spirit). In its empty stomach is placed a fumigating pastille, the vapour of which comes through the open mouth, giving the illusion that the little man is smoking.

FIG. 257. AQUAMANILE, FOURTEENTH CENTURY
*Bargello, Florence*

The nineteenth century discovered the daily use of water and soap and thus made the perfume bottle superfluous, but in its place it provided good society (before the invention of the electric bell) with the table-bell. The Musée Rétrospectif of

242

NUTCRACKERS, EIGHTEENTH CENTURY
*Bayerisches National-Museum, Munich*

the Paris exhibition in 1900 succeeded in bringing together a multitudinous array of these handbells, the most popular shapes among which were those of ladies in hooped dresses of all styles, from the sixteenth century down to the period of Louis-Philippe of France, although there were also dozens of figures representing, in the greatest possible variety, characters as different as charwomen, Jeanne d'Arc, and Napoleon I in his cloak. To a certain extent this exhibition drew attention to their value as collectors' objects. Candle-extinguishers well deserved to be placed alongside of these. Such extinguishers, indispensable at a time when one dared not blow out a tallow candle for fear of the unpleasant smell it caused, represented monks, nuns, hermits, *curés*, and ladies, making us admire the inventive spirit which had been expended so fruitfully on this trivial object. We ought, however, to consider ourselves lucky that we can now collect without having to make use of them.

FIG. 258
NUTCRACKER
Erzgebirge

The doll gave its form to some objects; it gave its name to others. In heraldry the common representation of a human body with mutilated arms is called a *Docke*, and in several parts of Germany, in Thuringia and Saxony for example, a bundle of yarn, since it looks like a doll, is called a *Döckchen* of yarn, in spite of the fact that that word otherwise has long disappeared from both colloquial and written language. The proverbial expression in Berlin for something far distant is 'as far off as the dolls.' This is explained by the fact that in the eighteenth century the Grosser Stern in the Tiergarten was embellished with statues, and when the citizens wanted to take a long Sunday walk they went 'as far as the dolls.'

The peasant, of course, knows the doll as well as the townsman. In Silesia, Bohemia, and Slovakia the beehives are often made to assume human shape by the use of branches of poplar- or lime-trees, and scarecrows are obviously made to resemble human beings. In Bavaria the latter are called *Tadema*, which, according to Schmeller, derives from *tattern*, which is synonymous with *zittern* ('to tremble'). Grimm, however, thinks that a derivation from *Tatar* (wild, dissolute fellows) is more probable. These

**243**

figures always retain the original shape of the doll—the stick with a cross-piece attached, completely covered with clothes. At harvest time too one speaks of 'dolls,' although in this connexion the word is used only by students concerned with matters appertaining to folk-life, and not by the peasants themselves.

FIG. 259. BEEHIVE FROM HÖFEL

In some districts, as, for instance, Lippe, both for the sake of drying the corn and for its easy handling, the sheaves are bound into a bundle by the reaper, such a bundle being referred to as a 'doll' because of its doll-like appearance. One of these sheaves is then set up perpendicularly with its stump on the ground; usually eight other sheaves are arranged round about it in a circle, and the whole is covered with a large sheaf, the ears of corn hanging down like thatch over the others. In the shadow these 'dolls' of corn ripen, and the grain is protected from heavy rains.

# XVII

## THE DOLL AND THE STAGE

THE theatre has not been able to do without the doll. The medieval stage made use of the doll in its production of mystery plays; at that period the representation of martyrdoms and other horrors was popular, and, as such scenes could not well be interpreted by living actors, for these particular episodes the actors were replaced by dolls, described in French texts as *feinctes*. The stage directions for the *Mystère des Trois Doms*, which was produced at Romans in 1509, devoted special attention to the costume of the dolls utilized for this purpose. The materials for the dresses on that occasion cost thirty-seven florins, a sum equivalent to about forty pounds pre-War.

Dolls were essential, too, for the rich entries and pageants of that time. When, for example, Duke Borso of Milan entered Reggio in 1453, a pretty little girl, dressed as Fides, greeted him and allegorically destroyed Heathen Idolatry, which was represented by a doll on a pedestal.

Even to-day the stage cannot get on without dolls; many dumb parts fall to these, in particular those of very little children. Up to the closing years of last century the *rôles* of little children at the Hoftheater in Weimar were taken by the great toy doll Frieda, which belonged to a family which lived at Frauenplan. One of Frieda's loveliest memories was of the time when Privy Councillor Goethe once found her in the park and sent her back to those who had lost her.

The doll is indispensable at many folk pastimes and festivals, such as have survived up to at least a short time ago. To the Christmas ceremonies in Mexico was attached the *pinata*, a clay-headed doll which blindfolded children sought to seize and break. At the New Year there was a certain sport practised in the factories of Basle, when a doll, the 'Silvester bag,' was given to the workwoman who was the last to arrive. On Twelfth Night in the Sarntal of Switzerland *Glöckelsinger* ('bell-singers') used to go in procession through the village carrying with them a female straw doll and asking for gratuities. At the conclusion the figure was beaten into shreds. Most common were the

245

so-called *Winteraustragen* at the close of the carnival. This particular custom has survived longest in Italy, Spain, and Portugal. There the doll in the shape of an old woman used to be carried over the boundaries and then burned or thrown into the water. In Oporto a straw doll in female dress used to be carried through the streets to the door of the oldest woman inhabitant and then burned in the market square.

On this side of the Alps too there were to be found, not so very long ago, traces of this ancient custom. In Baden Sauerland and in Lower Austria a hideous straw doll was carried out of the village and buried in snow or dung. In the region of Glogau, in Silesia, on Mid-Lent Sunday a doll made of straw or wood was borne in procession and then was beaten, burned, or thrown into the water. The *Sechseläuten* ('Six Strokes of the Bell') in Zürich was, or is, a very similar custom. On one of the last Mondays in April there used to be a great procession of the guilds there with carts and horses. At the conclusion the *Bögg* was burned at the lake on a pile of wood, this *Bögg* being a grotesque doll, representing winter. The festival was called *Sechseläuten* because of the big bell rung then and not again until September. Among the Saxons in Transylvania the girls dress up a pretty doll in festival clothes and carry it through the village to a girl who represents life. To her they present the dress and throw the doll itself into a brook. In Mexico during Passion Week life-size dolls, often beautifully dressed and sometimes representing negroes, were until recently burned publicly under the name of Judas. This custom is to be found also in some Catholic districts of Germany. On Whit Sunday the peasants in Prignitz used to organize a dolls' riding match; in the Altmark the doll used to be placed on a cow. On Whit Sunday in Steiermark a life-size doll clad in rags, the so-called *Pfingslötter*, is placed before the window of any girl who sleeps in past sunrise.

About 1850 Harry Phelps, an eleven-year-old lad in Stratford, Ontario, Canada, amused himself by making dolls stuffed with old clothes so that they resembled human beings and might be transformed into 'spirits.' The thing created such a sensation that Andrew Jackson Davis was dispatched to investigate the matter. In such harmless way was born the American spiritualism of to-day. In 1873 a 'spirit photographer,' famous in his own time, Buguet by name, made use of dolls, enveloped in sheets, for his pictures. He was certainly condemned for his rude fraud, but that did not make much impression on those who believed in him.

# XVIII
## EDIBLE DOLLS

THAT dolls—that is to say, objects resembling human form—can be made of all possible materials was shown at the exhibition at Frankfort in 1911. Here there were not only imitation bottles and work-bags made in doll shape, not to speak of the inevitable tea-cosy, but also little cork dolls which had originated from a competition organized by the wine stores of Matheus Müller in Eltville. This exhibition showed many similarly clever toys, such as dolls made of balls of cotton, short sticks, fish bladders, and fir-cones. Whether they had edible dolls there we do not know, although these might well have had a place, for they are at least as old as the toy doll. Technically this kind of bakery is called 'picture bread.' The articles baked generally represented domestic animals and were used as substitutes for these when sacrifices were to be made. Human figures of this kind were, of course, by no means rare, these being mainly connected with annual and family festivals. Herodotus heard of them in Egypt, and they were popular too in Greece. When Christianity succeeded in quelling idolatry the idol figures continued to be copied in bakery at least. This superstitious custom, connected with the New Year, was reproved by St Eligius (588–659), while the Synod of Liptinæ, in 743, prohibited the making of idols of sanctified flour.

The *Indiculus Superstitionum*, of the eighth or ninth century, speaks of "simulacra de consparsa farina," which perhaps refers to gingerbread. *Frithjof's Saga* tells how the heathens baked idols at the *dîsa blôt* and smeared them with oil; through Frithjof's error or misfortune a baked *baldur* dropped into the fire, the flames fell on the fat, and the house was burned down.

Perhaps it was on this account that Norwegian laws of the thirteenth century prohibited the ceremonial baking of bread in human shape. The severest punishments were meted out to those in whose houses dough offerings in the shape of the human form were found concealed. Such an one was declared an outlaw and was exiled after being deprived of his possessions.

In ancient Mexico the edible doll was utilized at certain high feasts in connexion with divine service. For the main feast of Huitzilopochtli, in the fifteenth month of the year, a large image of that god was made by the temple virgins out of seeds and the blood of children, and on touching it men were supposed to receive absolution from their sins. After the offering of human sacrifice a priest in the dress of the war-god shot an arrow at this image and divided the separate pieces among the people, the king receiving the heart. He who ate of it pledged himself to Huitzilopochtli in regard to certain services, sacrificial presents, and acts of penitence.

FIGS. 260, 261. GINGERBREAD FIGURES
Dresden. About 1810

The gingerbread doll had a tenacious life, perhaps because it appealed to the stomach and not to the spirit. The shapes which it assumed remained the same for centuries. Thus, the three holy virgins St Einbede, St Warbede, and St Willebede have long survived the worship once devoted to them; generations ago that became merely mythical, but in the shape of cakes, which are still to be found to-day, they continue to give delight both to children and to grown-ups. On his eleventh birthday Schreiber received a gingerbread man which was as large as himself. In the Middle Ages sweets in the form of small figures used to be offered for sale in the streets of Paris. Vasari records that Jacopo Sansovino made sugar figures for artists' feasts, and legend declares that the genius of Thorwaldsen was discovered by this means when he modelled a dough-cake figure for a dinner. At the great feasts of the courts little figures made of sugar or marzipan continued popular for long; porcelain took the place of these substances for the first time in the eighteenth century. In his description of the "spectacular dishes" which were provided at Munich in November 1613 for the nuptials of the Duchess Magdalene and the Count Palatine Wolfgang, Philipp Hainhofer ·tells us that several of the figures were made to move, in spite of the fact that they were eatable. The devil, always thought of as connected with St Nicholas, is still made, under the name of *Kletzenmännlein*, *Krampus*, or *Klaubauf*, out of chocolate, gingerbread, baked fruit, or raisins. These once used to be sold at the Fair of St Nicholas in Vienna, held on December 6, some of them being even life-size. The *Zwetschgen*, or *Kletzenkrampus*, consists only of two sticks put together in the shape of a cross and ornamented with dried plums, dates, figs, etc. August Geigenberger, of Munich, used to make these up very cleverly, dressing them in costumes of tissue paper.

At Warmbrunn, in the Riesengebirge, there is a *Tallsacken* fair held on Palm Sunday. The *Tallsack* is a human-shaped figure made of dough with eyes of currants, holding an egg at the breast. Both sexes are represented in this type of baking, the male sex being distinguished by a little beard of thread.

## XIX

## THE DOLL IN LITERATURE

It is, indeed, only natural that play and play dolls—two such important elements in the life of the child—could not remain without an echo in fine literature. One need but refer to Andersen's charming fairy-tales to see how great a part is taken there by little dolls representing girls and by tin soldiers. The much more powerful poetic genius of Clemens Brentano, in whose *Gockel, Hinkel, und Gackeleia*, too, "a beautiful figure of art" is the chief centre of interest, has been completely eclipsed by the great success of the Danish writer.

In his tales Hoffmann often makes dolls and nutcrackers the main characters of his stories, and by their means the whole romantic spirit of his riotous imagination is thrown into relief. These, however, were not written for children. For the latter Cosmar's *Puppe Wunderhold*, written in the *Biedermeier* period, with illustrations by Luise Thalheim, was much more suitable. This is a German forerunner of Lewis Carroll's *Alice's Adventures in Wonderland*, and was not less dear to little German girls than Alice was to English childhood.

Dickens's humorous and warm-hearted genius delighted in dolls and in their makers, but the *Fitzebutze* of Richard Dehmel, who regards "the childish toy in the higher, philosophical perspective of eternity," made only a slight appeal to children.

Playing with the doll, which, although it is a lifeless being, may yet exercise so strongly suggestive a power, has led to playing the doll. In the ancient Indian *Kamasutra* a game is referred to which is named there the "imitation of the doll," and this indeed consists of naught else than the imitation on the part of the players of doll-like actions and movements. In the eighties E. Rathgeber wrote a ballet, *Spielwarenzauber* (*The Magic of Toys*), the subject of which was based on a fairy-tale from *Fantaska*, where the dolls in a shop come to life and discuss the purchasers each of them would desire.

The greatest and most lasting success, however, was gained by the ballet of Josef Bayer, *Puppenfee* (*The Doll Fairy*), which

# THE DOLL IN LITERATURE

appeared on the stage about 1890 and is still being played after the passing of so many years. At New York in 1914 Anna Pavlova danced as a doll, dressed in a costume which Albert Rutherston had designed for her.

FIG. 262. FIRST LESSONS IN RIDING
After the lithograph by Francis, 1832

# PART II: PUPPETS

## I

## AUTOMATA AND MOVABLE IMAGES

By careful moulding in wax and by clothing it in real cloth the doll could be made to assume an almost perfect resemblance to a human being, but before there could be any question of absolute illusion two difficulties had to be surmounted—movement and speech had to be artificially introduced. For centuries men struggled with this problem, which, however, has only comparatively recently found a solution. Now we have our automatic figures which can walk, move, and speak—indeed, when necessary, deliver lengthy orations.

The road which had to be traversed before this goal was reached, starting as it did in dimmest antiquity, was a long and weary one. Two methods there were of providing this creature of art with what might be called free will—one by using human force and the other by using mechanical force, it being necessary, of course, for both to work in concealment. The releasing of the impulse through the human hand, being the simplest, must have been the oldest method. Herodotus records that at the festival of Osiris Egyptian women were in the habit of carrying around images of the god, each of which had an exceptionally large phallus which could be moved up and down by means of a string, while at the processions of Jupiter Ammon twenty-four priests brought in a statue of that deity which, by a movement of its head, indicated the direction in which it desired to be borne, and similar phenomena were recorded from the temple of Heliopolis. Indeed, the priests of every religion have known the value of movable images for influencing the imagination of the credulous. At Roman processions there was carried about a figure named Manducus, which, like our nutcrackers, could open and shut its gigantic under-jaw. The Norse sagas also mention animated divine images, presumably with men placed behind them. Tricks of a similar kind were by no means unknown in the medieval Christian Church. Many were the crucifixes which moved their heads and showed blood oozing from the wounds in their sides, as well as Madonnas which shed tears. These hand-controlled images, which at big feasts played a part in the service, first disappeared from the English churches at the Reformation; in Catholic France they maintained their position in the church up to the seventeenth century. The *mitouries* celebrated at the Assumption of the Virgin, in August, at the church of St Jacques in Dieppe were widely renowned. On such occasions living persons and images performed together, and the angels which flew about flapping their wings and blowing their trumpets aroused great enthusiasm. These spectacles were finally suppressed in the year 1647.

Of such displays the only relics are the gigantic figures used in some processions particularly associated with those territories in Western and Southern Europe down to the Alps which were originally inhabited by the Celts. Cæsar and Posidonius relate that among the Celts sacrifices were made every five years by the Druids, that on these occasions giant images of wickerwork, wood, and straw were set up, filled with men and sacrificial animals, and then burned. At a much later period in the Ile de France similar giant images, dressed as soldiers, were burned after being carried round at religious processions. In Hainaut between 1456 and 1460 giant figures took part in processions organized during plague years; these made their appearance also at Amiens, Metz, Nevers, Orleans, Poitiers, Laon, and Langres. There they were styled *papoires*, and often were accompanied by dragons, likewise set in motion by concealed men. The majority of the towns in Flanders and Brabant possessed such giants, which the people used to dress up as Goliath or Christophorus. At Douai there was the giant Gayant with his wife and children—figures made of wickerwork, with brightly painted wooden heads, the father 21 feet high, the mother 18 to 20, and the children 12 to 15. Ten or twelve persons were required to move the largest. When Matthieu de Montreuil went with Cardinal Mazarin in 1660 to the royal wedding on an island at the mouth of the Bidassoa he saw at San Sebastian, in Spain, seven gigantic figures carried round during the Corpus Christi procession; these were made of wickerwork and painted canvas, and were intended to represent the Moorish kings and their wives. They were so tall that they reached the roofs of the houses, and each was carried by two or three men concealed inside it. Quite recently processions of this kind were held at Pamplona, when gigantic figures, representing Moors or Normans, visited the town hall in festive procession, bowed before the image of the Blessed Virgin, and danced in front of the cathedral. Similar shows are to be found in Sicily, while at Salzburg the giant Samson was still accompanying processions in the second half of last century.

Primitive races have remarkably similar customs. For their masked dances, apparently designed in honour of the dead, the Baining of New Britain, Oceania, prepare gigantic figures on a

FIG. 263. THE DANCE OF GIANTS
Masquerade of Emperor Maximilian I. From the *Freydal*

light cane framework, covered with oxhide and provided with painted faces. These figures may be as much as 45 m. high, and are carried on bamboo poles. Dancers, panting and stamping their feet, support the figure on their dance spears, and when the leader of the throng sinks down after a few steps under the weight of the forepart of the image, which rests on his head, they let it fall to the ground. The onlookers tear it into fragments, taking the pieces home with them as amulets possessed of magical properties.

The delight taken in the giant-show must have been universal. The romantically minded "last of the knights," Emperor Maximilian I, a somewhat pleasure-seeking and frivolous monarch, who took great pains in the planning of his masquerades, once disguised himself and his fellow-dancers as giants, in comparison with whom their partners cut a pretty comic figure, since they looked just like children. Even as late as the last Tsar's coronation, in May 1896, a procession of gigantic images of this kind was organized in the Khodinskoie Plain —a procession which gained a tragic fame because of the terrible catastrophe which occurred on that occasion.

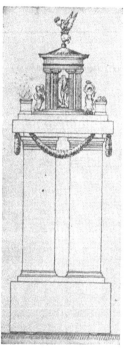

After human power as a controlling force comes the use of material substances. These, such as sand, water, and quicksilver, can alter an object's centre of gravity and bring it back once more to its original position. We know that the Chinese and the Greeks were acquainted with this property of quicksilver and utilized it. It is said that by means of quicksilver Dædalus made a wooden image of Venus move. Among the ancients, however, there is no doubt that water played the chief *rôle* as a controlling force; here water-pressure, warmed air, and steam have all to be taken into consideration. The Egyptians in especial were renowned for the construction of automata. At a festival of Bacchus which was held under Ptolemy Philadelphus (285–247 B.C.) there was carried in a figure of the god which dispensed wine from a golden goblet. At that period in the town of Nysa there was an allegorical statue which rose

FIG. 264. HERO'S AUTO-MATON

automatically, poured milk from a gold shell, and sat down again. Hero of Alexandria, the most famous mechanician among the ancients, who lived presumably in the second century B.C., has left a treatise concerning automatic theatres in which he describes his own inventions. Wilhelm Schmidt, basing his account on Hero's works, thus describes the movements of a group of his automatic figures. A platform, fitted with three wheels, bearing the apotheosis of Bacchus moved by itself upon a firm, horizontal, and smooth surface up to a certain point and then stopped, at which moment the sacrificial flame burst forth from the altar in front of which Bacchus stood. Milk flowed from his *thyrsus*, and from the goblet

255

he held streamed wine which sprinkled a panther crouched at his feet. Suddenly festoons appeared all round the base of the platform, and figures representing the Bacchantes, to the beating of drums and the clanging of cymbals, danced round the temple within which Bacchus was placed. Then the god turned round to another altar, while a figure of Nike, set on the top of the

FIG. 265. HERO'S AUTOMATON
After the sketch by Wilhelm Schmidt
*Neue Jahrbücher für das klassische Altertum*, II, 1899

temple, turned in the same direction. The second altar flamed forth, the *thyrsus* and the goblet flowed again, and the Bacchantes danced. After all these movements had been carried out automatically the platform returned of its own accord to its starting-point.

These automatic shows were carried still further. At the end of the second century B.C. a five-act play, *The Tale of Nauplius*, was produced by Philo of Byzantium in a regular automatic theatre, which had a vertical partition dividing it into machine-room and stage. In the first scene were shown twelve Greeks standing in three rows, as if they were engaged in repairing ships—sawing, cutting timber, boring holes, and hammering. In the second scene appeared the launching of the ships. The third scene displayed a moving landscape. The fleet passed by, with dolphins diving up and down. A storm came on. In the fourth scene Athena made her appearance to Nauplius, who held a torch aloft. The fifth scene introduced the shipwreck; Ajax tried to save himself by swimming, but Athena cast a thunderbolt at him, and he vanished in the waves.

These automata, driven by water-power, were still being made use of during the seventeenth century in the laying-out of gardens. A good example is that of Salomon de Caus in the Schloss park, at Heidelberg, especially famous before the outbreak of the Thirty Years War. Archbishop Markus Sittichus, Count Hohenhembs, got similar automatic playthings introduced into the Hellbrunn park, near Salzburg. These are still to be seen, and continue to give delight to naïve souls. The description which Prince Max of Hohenlohe has given of them is so beautifully expressed that it may be quoted here:

Some centuries ago the princely magician Markus Sittichus laid out a rare and marvellous garden near Salzburg. In this luxuriant place, shaded by magnificent trees, subterranean streams murmur soft melodies between long alleys and spacious flower-beds and make strange play in magic grottoes. As we step into these moist, dark caverns, all at once a loud warbling of birds, like the song of a thousand nightingales, breaks upon our ears; in the depths small, strange figures begin to move over concealed wells—figures of men and animals, of airy spirits and deities, of clumsy goblins and teasing water-sprites. Water drips from the stone stems of creeping stalactites, and the gleam of all the precious jewels in Aladdin's garden sparkles in the light of the magic lamp from *The Arabian Nights*. And above, over the gurgling grottoes and the singing springs, Markus Sittichus, among other things, built a magnificent pavilion, almost enclosed by an iron curtain.

With what excitement did we children wait for the moving of that curtain in anticipation of the wonders it concealed from us! At last the magic veil was lifted; the curtain rose, and before our enchanted eyes stood, in a small compass, a completely strange world, a theatre of life.

There stood palaces and houses, strange buildings with high, glistening domes and Eastern cupolas, narrow streets, and wide boulevards, all of them filled with little men and women, motionless certainly yet deceitfully lifelike, in their strange, old, multi-coloured dresses, and near them horses, cats, and dogs. Before the town hall stood soldiers all ready to march, commanding officers, citizens thronging in rich, heavy garments; in the market-place

R

257

merchants were chaffering and drivers speeding. The most extra-ordinary thing, however, was that we could see, too, through the walls of the houses into the interiors and watch what was going on within—how the bakers baked, how the washer-women washed, how the millers prepared their bright, golden-yellow flour and the cooks got ready their tasty dishes. One could see here the maids sweeping the floors, here a husband and wife fighting with one another in their room, here the children playing, here the teacher giving his lessons from open books, and many things besides.

Suddenly, at a magic knock, a strain of subterranean, mysterious music vibrated from the depths, and at that moment the whole town began to take life, all the figures commenced to move. The officers gave their orders, the soldiers marched off, the citizens really began to crowd along and the merchants to carry on their business. Men ran and speeded by; in the house the bakers started baking, the washer-women washed, and the maids did their ironing. The married couple fought in earnest, the children romped, and the teachers gave their lessons. Everybody, every single one, started moving, really and truly, and lived, and was marvellously real, and the dream was no longer a dream, but genuine pulsating life. The mill creaked and the hens cackled; the girls moved in circles; entertainers and jugglers led fettered bears into the square and made them dance.

Then we children noted with fear that suddenly the clock on the town hall forgot to strike, and all the chimes died away, and one figure after another became automatically slower in movement until it gradually grew rigid. Then all at once everything stood still, and the wonderful music ceased to play. Before we were aware of it the iron curtain sank before our gaze, and with the vanishing of the last houses in the town the strange dream vanished, and all that was true, all that we had believed in, passed again into the realm of the fairy-tale.

The art of making automata was in existence as early as the third century B.C.; small automata must have been known even in Aristotle's time, as his *Physics* proves. Of such objects there is no lack of record. Homer speaks of Vulcan's twenty tripods which automatically entered the banquetting hall of the gods and rolled out again. Archytas of Tarentum, who lived about 390 B.C., is said to have invented a mechanical flying pigeon, but this, of course, is very doubtful. In the great Indian fairy-tale collection of the *Somadeva*, which belongs to the eleventh century, but includes matter of a much earlier date, mention is made of puppets moved by mechanism; one fetched a wreath, another water, a third danced, and a fourth is even said to have spoken. Petronius refers to a silver doll which could move like a living being. Oriental and Byzantine sources are especially rich in their records of such automata. Several caliphs are said to have been in possession of trees on the branches of which mechanical birds sat singing and flapping their wings. The Emperor of the East, Constantine VII Porphyrogenitus, owned not only such a tree, but also a huge, mechanical, roaring lion. Descriptions of these wonders aroused the imaginations of Western poets. Thus the Tristan saga has its automaton, a

FIG. 266. AUTOMATIC TOY OF THE EIGHTEENTH CENTURY
*Collection of Henri d'Allemagne, Paris*

temple with the figure of Isolde, on whose sceptre sits a bird flapping its wings and at whose feet lies a dog shaking its head. In the Middle Ages these things were very popular. The sketch book of Willars de Honecourt, which belongs to about the year 1245, contains a drawing of an eagle which could move its head when the deacon read the epistle in the church. Albertus Magnus, who died in 1280, is said to have made an automaton— a lovely woman who could speak—which the zealous Thomas Aquinas destroyed, declaring that it was the work of an evil spirit.

Clocks with automatic figures appeared at quite an early date, and these too the poets (for example, in *Der jüngere Titurel*) loved to describe. The huge clock in Strasbourg Cathedral in 1352 showed the three kings bowing and a crowing cock. The so-called *Männleinlaufen* on the clock of the Marienkapelle in Nürnberg, which was constructed between 1356 and 1361, was famous. There the Emperor Charles IV was shown sitting on

259

his throne, and when the clock struck twelve the seven prince electors passed before him and bowed. The man who struck the hours with a hammer on a bell was well known by about 1380, and the clocks at Lubeck, Danzig, Heilbronn, Bern, Ulm, and elsewhere displayed a variety of other mechanical movements—crowing cocks, bears that shook their heads, a king who turned a sand-glass, and the twelve apostles moving in a circle. That these playthings have lost none of their attraction can be denied by no one who at 11 A.M. has watched the mechanism of the great clock which the merchant Karl Rosipal erected on the tower of the new town hall in the Marienplatz at Munich.

Regiomontanus in the fifteenth century is said to have made a fly which fluttered round the room, and similar wonderful inventions are recorded in Spain. Don Enrique de Villena, a reputed magician, made a head which could speak. In the cathedral of Toledo Don Alvaro de Luna, who ended his days on the scaffold in 1453, was reputed to have got tombstones made for himself and his wife which were so artfully contrived that, when Mass was said, the recumbent figures raised themselves and knelt. Isabella the Catholic is supposed to have ordered the destruction of these remarkable mechanisms on the ground that they were unsuitable for the dignity of the place and the solemnity of the occasion. Leonardo da Vinci, who took a keen interest in all sorts of mechanics, constructed in 1509 a lion which could walk about and which could open its breast, to reveal within the lilies of France. Emperor Charles V sought to while away time in his old age at the cloister of Yuste by playing with automata. The Milanese engineer Giovanni Torriani helped him in this; it was he who constructed an automatic wooden male figure which went daily to the archbishop's palace at Toledo and thence fetched bread.

In the wine-loving sixteenth century men liked to use automata as so-called drinking clocks, interesting examples of which are to be found in the Grünes Gewölbe, at Dresden. One of these, a mechanical toy, represents St George engaged in freeing Princess Aja of Lybia from the dragon. It is wound up and allowed to run on its wheels along the table, and it is a rule that one must empty one's glass before it comes to a stop. The other, made by a native of Nürnberg, C. Werner, is a gilded silver centaur engaged in carrying off a woman. When the clock is going the eyes of the two figures move, but if the base of the concealed mechanism is pulled twice the two foremost hounds spring up, the clock runs round in a circle on its wheels, and the

THE MECHANICAL CLOCK ON THE TOWER OF MUNICH TOWN HALL

centaur shoots at the guests arrows which are taken from his quiver and placed in the bow, and whoever is struck must give proof of his drinking capabilities.

Already in this century automatic devices were included in the equipment which wandering showmen took round to exhibit for money. In 1582 Peter Döpfer, of Schneeberg, displayed in Nürnberg a mechanical mine. In 1587 the town council of Nürnberg gave permission to Daniel Bertel, of Lubeck, "to show for three days at the price of a pfennig his mechanical pieces and toys, as first a fleet of galleys with Turks and Christians fighting on the sea, also merry Swiss and German dances and pretty acrobatics." In November 1611 "two foreign wax-modellers, who have brought here some figures which move by themselves," were allowed to exhibit their wonders for three days in Nürnberg.

Gottfried Hautsch, who died in 1703, was already well known as a maker of tin soldiers when he constructed in Nürnberg a mechanical automaton with many figures, which was nicknamed his "little world." This is a kind of automaton which, to distinguish it from others, is technically indicated by the term *theatrum mundi*. The *theatrum mundi* for centuries provided the traditional afterpiece of the wandering marionette theatres; by means of small movable figures running on rails it showed a diversity of scenes, such as the creation of the world and Noah and the Flood. Flockton's show, which was exhibited in England at the end of the eighteenth century, utilized five hundred figures, all employed in different ways and manners. Here there were movable figures of a peculiarly ingenious kind: swans, for example, which dipped their heads in the water, spread their wings, and craned their long necks to clean their feathers. Even in 1803 Reichardt was expressing admiration in Paris at the mechanical theatre of Pierre, who previously had been settled in Vienna. It was only with the success of the film that these mechanical shows declined, but not so long ago one could still see, as a lively and boisterous afterpiece to a popular puppet-show, the battle of Sedan, the siege of the Taku forts, sledging, storms at sea, etc. In the seventeenth century there was another motion-mechanism likewise connected with the toy doll: this was of the type of the automatic figures in Hainhofer's art cabinet already referred to. In the first years of the eighteenth century Abraham a Sancta Clara, the well-known Viennese preacher, speaks of "dolls so ingeniously contrived that on being pulled, pressed, or wound up they become animated and move by themselves as desired." Corvinus, who wrote under the name of Amaranthes, could describe in 1716 the "costly and ingenious dolls which display *actiones* by means of concealed clockwork"; these were then a speciality of Augsburg and Nürnberg, "which are rapidly filling the entire world with them." Such moving dolls, *la jolie catin*, were shown in France on the streets by itinerant girls.

The eighteenth century, when automata seem to have been

FIG. 267. LA CHARMANTE CATIN
Etching by Bouchardon. From the *Cris de Paris*. About 1750

particularly popular, produced masters of this kind of art. The first was Jacques de Vaucanson, who constructed his automata, which rapidly became world-famous, between 1738 and 1741. One was a flute-player who had a repertoire of twelve selections; still more admired was a life-size duck which waddled and quacked, moved its wings and neck, ate corn, and drank water, then, having digested its food, dropped a mass looking like excrement. It was remarkable, too, for the skilfulness with which its plain copper plumage was put together so as to resemble the lovely shimmering shades of a real duck. These automata were exhibited all over Europe and eventually came into the possession of the well-known aulic councillor Beireis, of Helmstedt, in whose rather disorderly collection Goethe saw them in 1805 in a somewhat dilapidated condition. Feldhaus knew of a similar automaton—a peacock constructed fifty years before by a French general, which could also walk, eat, and digest with palpable success.

The position occupied by Vaucanson was later taken by the two Droz, Pierre Jaquet Droz, the father, and Henri Louis Jaquet Droz, the son, of La Chaux de Fonds. The former in 1760 made a child doll capable of writing, and the latter in 1773 constructed two figures, one of which could draw and the other play the piano. All three are still preserved in the museum at Neuchatel. The third of these skilled inventors is Wolfgang von Kempelen, who in 1769 made a chess-player, which he exhibited with the greatest success; no one then could discover the secret of its mechanism. In 1809 Napoleon played a game of chess with it and lost. Here, however, we are not dealing with a pure automaton, for in the box on which the figure was mounted was concealed a man who, by a system of mirrors, could see the chess-board and the movements made by his opponent. Another speaking figure, this time a real automaton, was made in 1778 by Kempelen. It is curious to observe that Tippoo Sahib, Sultan of Mysore, who had every reason to hate the English, got an automatic group constructed for his pleasure; this included a life-size tiger which rushed roaring ,to devour an Englishman in uniform. After the death of the Sultan, in 1799, this proof of his sentiments was found among the treasures at Seringapatam.

That to-day we have performing dolls which can not only move, but speak and sing (by means of an inserted gramophone) has already been mentioned in the section dealing with the development of the toy doll. It is not very long ago that a record performance by one of these automata was vouchsafed us. In September 1928 an exhibition of model engines was to have been opened in London by a prominent man. At the last moment he had to decline. A mechanical man, clad like a robber knight, in full armour, took the chair on the platform in his stead. Calmly he waited till the audience assembled; then he rose, took a few steps backward to the speaker's desk, and began to address them. He spoke clearly and precisely, in a tone which carried farther than any human voice could have done. He referred to the wonders of the exhibition and to the future of engineering, putting himself forward as a fitting example of this science. His eyes sparkled, his lips moved a little to reveal sharp teeth, resembling those of a beast of prey. It is reported that a partner is being made for him, a mechanical figure of a woman. The impertinent fancies of *Simplizissimus* concerning mechanical tsars are thus far outdistanced by the reality.

# II

## THE ORIGIN OF THE PUPPET-SHOW

THE child that occupies itself with its doll is playing, without knowing or desiring it, at a theatre, and thereby is poetically and dramatically active. It puts itself in the place of the doll; it is artist and public in one person; it creates the object of art and appreciates it at one and the same time. Herein lies the basis of the puppet theatre, for the first child which played with its doll as if it were a living being may be regarded as the originator of the marionette stage. When and where this happened we naturally do not know, even as little as we know where and at what period adults first perceived this tendency of the child's mind and created an art form out of its naïve play.

Some scholars, the chief representative of whom is Richard Pischel, seek the home of the puppet-show in India. From there it is said to have gone to Persia, and to have reached Europe through the medium of the Arabs. Against this theory it may be justly argued that proofs of the existence of the puppet-show in ancient Greece carry us back to very much earlier times, and that consequently India cannot possibly assume the credit of its invention. When we note the existence of the puppet-show during early centuries spread over all civilized lands, and when we reflect that in truth no great intelligence was required for its invention—indeed, all men had to do was open their eyes and observe their own children—we may think of autochthonic development, and assume that the puppets must all have resulted in general and independently from the preliminary condition— the child's play—which was everywhere existent. Philipp Leibrecht, however, rejects this highly illuminating conception, since he observes that not only the similarity of the persons represented, but also the likeness in the matter pertaining to the shows, testifies undoubtedly to an international connexion. This connexion must be granted, even if we are uncertain as to what way the transition from people to people came about.

It is possible, at least not impossible, that in the puppet-show we have before us the most ancient form of dramatic representation. Certain it is that this puppet-show best harmonized with·

the intelligence of the people at large, for it came to meet the popular conceptions and appealed to their instincts. On that account the puppet-show is "often a much clearer mirror of the thought and feeling of the people than poetry, and not infrequently is the bearer of ancient traditions." When we try to follow the history of the puppet-show, however, there arises one great difficulty—namely, the lack of precision in the documentary evidence relating to its technique. To-day, following the example of Dr Alfred Lehmann, we classify the puppet-play according to the following plan:

(1) puppet-shows with flat figures: (a) the shadow theatre, (b) the *theatrum mundi*, (c) the theatre of figures.

(2) puppet-shows with rounded figures: (a) the hand-puppet theatre, (b) the marionette theatre: one worked from below and the other from above.

The records preserved in old texts only rarely provide justification for this division, for the simple reason that the individual author had in his mind only one or the other type of puppet, and for the time being that signified for him *the* puppet-show in general. To this system of classification may be added still another species. Lehmann's grouping takes into consideration only the movable puppets, but we might include also those that are immovable—the kind of show which, when it is represented by human beings, is called *tableaux vivants*. With inanimate figures, this special type may be defined as the mass arrangement of dolls, to which naturally the word *vivants* cannot be applied. The group includes table decorations, Christmas cribs, and tin soldiers, all utilizing a large number of figures.

# III

## TABLE DECORATIONS AND THE CHRISTMAS CRIB

EVEN in the fifteenth century, in order to add to the pleasures of the table, decoratively constructed dishes of food used to be served up; these, intended for the eye alone, were designed to satisfy the æsthetic and literary pretensions of a society proud of its learning. For making the figures themselves *Tragant*, a composition of flour, water, and paste, was regularly used, the whole group being under the supervision of a skilled *chef* trained in the moulding of forms.

Allegories and symbolic shapes in table decorations made special appeal to the taste of the age. Porcelain was utilized for this purpose in the eighteenth century, and then may be said to have been the first true flourishing time of this type of art. During this period it was a common practice to have the little figures modelled in sets, these sets being intended for arrangement on the table. One of Kändler's masterpieces was just such a table set, called the *Temple of Honour*, which consisted of 123 separate pieces and, when put together, occupied a space 1·16 m. high, 86 cm. wide, and 60 cm. deep. Yet, large as it was, it served merely as the centre piece of a still larger decorative set, in which appeared seventy-four other white figures.

All the porcelain-manufacturers competed in providing magnificent examples of this kind. In 1767 the convention of the Zwettl monastery presented Abbot Reine Kollmann with a set of Vienna ware, 4 m. long and 50 cm. deep, representing the arts, virtues, and crafts. Charles Eugene, Duke of Württemberg, ordered in Ludwigsburg a gigantic table set which showed Neptune with a great retinue of Tritons, naiads, dolphins, fish, etc., the whole built up in a basin of water to be placed in the centre of the table. A table set was part of the service which in 1772 Frederick the Great presented to Catherine II; this displayed the Queen sitting on a canopied throne, completely surrounded by representatives of all the Russian races under her dominion. In 1785 the Prince Palatine, Charles Theodore, presented Cardinal Antonelli with a service of Frankenthal

267

porcelain, which included as table decorations thirteen groups, sixty single figures, forty animals, and thirty-six vases on pedestals. In 1791 a table set of Berlin ware was produced which symbolized nature with all its powers and mysteries in figures of divinities, temples, altars, and obelisks. The confectionary of Count Brühl, the superintendent of which had control of the table decorations, contained not only dozens of figures, but also a number of accessories, such as four churches, two temples, fifty-one town houses, thirteen peasant houses, sheds, stables, niches, gondolas, goats, pyramids, grottoes, reservoirs, cornices, vases, altars, pillars, pedestals, flower-jugs—all designed for use in the building up of table decorations. Even in 1808 Napoleon I, when his friendship with Alexander I was at its closest, ordered for that monarch a Sèvres service in Egyptian style, consisting of temples, obelisks, sphinxes, etc. This set had an advantage over those which had hitherto been usual in that it was capable of being varied, and could be set up, as fancy dictated, now in one way, now in another. The famous table sets of Johann Melchior Dinglinger, in spite of their richness in figures, had not been adaptable in this manner. His most renowned work, representing the Court of the Great Mogul in Delhi and made as a table set for Augustus the Strong, has been called a doll's house, so crowded is it with little gilded and enamelled figures. On this the master himself, together with his family and fourteen apprentices, is said to have worked from 1701 to 1708, and for it he is said to have received 58,485 thalers.

Important in a much deeper sense is the Christmas crib, commonly made up by the utilization of a number of small figures. The crib itself testifies to a genuine, strong religious sentiment, powerful enough to arrest our attention now by its form of expression, while the extant examples of ancient manufacture form valuable and interesting documents for a study of social life in past times. The artists who made these crib-figures took pains to render them as realistic as possible; they accentuated expression, bearing, and gesture so acutely that often they approached caricature. These cribs provide a very effective, even though silent, theatre, so that Rudolf Berliner has every justification for placing the crib-figure alongside the marionette.

The custom of exhibiting a crib at Christmas is a very old one, and those who attribute its invention to St Francis of Assisi are certainly mistaken. That saint, having ever striven to bring closer to the hearts of his contemporaries the human element in the Christian faith, arranged Christmas festivals which approached as nearly as possible to the events in Bethlehem, with a real

268

child, a real manger, and real animals, but the puppet-crib existed long before his time. It is, indeed, as old as the Christmas festival itself, which was first established by Pope Liberius in the year 354. There are extant sermons delivered about the year 400 by St John Chrysostom and St Gregory Thaumaturgus in which references are made to the existence at that period of a crib with figures of the Holy Family, even with figures of an ox and an ass.

FIG. 268. ITALIAN CRIB-FIGURE OF THE EIGHTEENTH CENTURY

From *Denkmäler der Krippenkunst*, by R. Berliner (B. Filser, Augsburg)

*Bayerisches National-Museum, Munich*

The ancient Church loved such shows, and these produced a much more powerful effect on uneducated folk (probably also on educated people as well) than the Mass and the sermon. The procession with the palm ass has been mentioned elsewhere in another connexion; similar ceremonies were carried out on Good Friday, at Easter and Whitsuntide. The Christmas crib, half a toy and half an object of devotion, just as it is to-day, seems to have its home in Italy and in particular in Naples, where it was to be found in its richest and most artistic forms. The oldest specific record of the crib which Georg Hager can adduce comes from Naples, where in the year 1478 a certain Jaconello Pepe gave a commission to two sculptors, Pietro and Giovanni Alamanno, to make a crib for his family chapel in S. Giovanni a Carbonara. The individual pieces are fully detailed: the Blessed Virgin with a crown, St Joseph, the *Bambino*, eleven angels, two prophets, two sibyls, three shepherds, twelve sheep, two dogs, four trees, an ox, and an ass. In 1507 a crib of twenty-eight figures was ordered from

Pietro Belverte, of Bergamo, for the church of S. Domenico Maggiore in Naples, while in 1558 the nuns of Sapienza commissioned Annibale Caccarello to make a crib of fourteen figures, for which they paid 140 ducats.

By the sixteenth century the crib is to be found on this side of the Alps; an inventory of 1537 relating to the Carmelite monastery in Bruges mentions two cribs, while by the seventeenth century the Jesuits had introduced them to Munich; in 1607 for the first time the fathers installed such a crib in the Michaelshofkirche, and provided for it incidental music. In old Bavaria the crib was very greatly beloved and became extremely popular. The Benedictine nuns at Frauenchiemsee in 1627 obtained their first crib, which was built up as a 'mountain,' so as to provide the greatest possible space for figures, animals, and so on. The crib, like porcelain ware, flourished most in the eighteenth century, receiving special attention in Naples and in Sicily, where a playful temperament, artistic talents, bigotry, and an inexhaustible imagination combined to create the most extraordinary and the most charming specimens of the type. The figures were made by distinguished sculptors, such as Giuseppe Sammartino, who had won such fame through his *Christus* in the chapel of the Princess Sangro, Domenico Antonio Vaccaro, Matteo Bottiglieri, F. Celebrano, Niccolo Somma, Lorenzo Mosca, all of whom were at the same time the modellers of the Capodimonte porcelain ware. The heads were made of terra-cotta, with glass eyes, the hands and feet of wood set on wire limbs, which permitted them to be placed in any desired position. The painting of the skin was carried out on a chalk ground, with an under wash in tempera, and finished off with oil-colour varnish—a technique which not only gave opportunity for a rich variety of flesh colours, but also produced a fine varnished surface. They were constructed according to the rules of perspective, the larger figures of the foreground not exceeding 37 to 40 cm. in height. The bodies of the animals were made of terra-cotta, the legs of lead, the ears of tin, while the buildings for the most part were constructed of wood or cork.

For the dresses of their crib-figures the Neapolitans used real cloth, the seams of which were edged with wire thread so as to secure a more plastic effect; the gold and silver ornaments too were often real. The Sicilian figures were carved from limewood; the dresses were of linen saturated with glue and paste. The material was starched after modelling and then realistically painted. The artists were given the greater scope for their efforts in that a very extensive series of subsidiary themes was

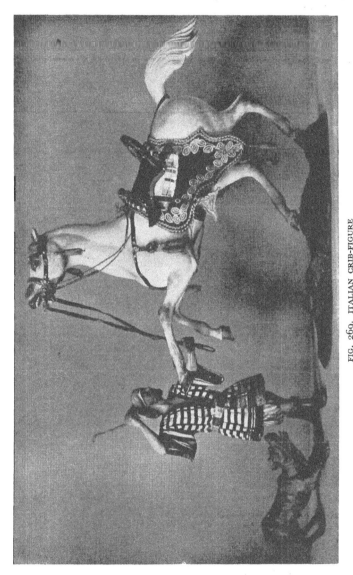

FIG. 269. ITALIAN CRIB-FIGURE

From *Denkmäler der Krippenkunst*, by R. Berliner (B. Filser, Augsburg)

*Bayerisches National-Museum, Munich*

there to stimulate their imagination. Legend declared that at the time of Christ's birth an annual fair was being held at Bethlehem; there was not a being between heaven and earth who was not present at it. There were peasants, shopkeepers,

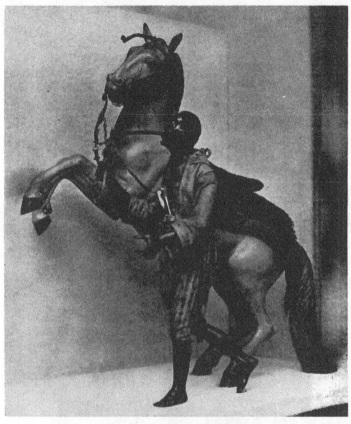

FIG. 270. ITALIAN CRIB-FIGURE
Naples
*Bayerisches National-Museum, Munich*

workmen, landowners, merchants, beggars, cutpurses, **fighting**, dancing, playing, music-making children, domestic and **exotic** animals, accompanied by an improbable wealth of *finimenti*. Here, too, were all sorts of food—vegetables, fish, bread, fruit, cheese, sausages, eggs, oysters, lobsters, macaroni, etc.—besides musical instruments, gold and silver plate, and so on. Still further opportunities were offered by the arrival of the three

272

kings and their magnificent retinue. All these figures were transplanted to the eighteenth century and to the Gulf of Naples, so that these cribs can be regarded as mirrors of the contemporary life of the people. The illusion of time and place was the greater because the artists liked to make use of local scenery and to present, with all the illusion of perspective,

FIGS. 271, 272. ITALIAN CRIB-FIGURES, EIGHTEENTH CENTURY
The procession of the three kings. In the original the two sections here shown are continuous.
*Bayerisches National-Museum, Munich*

its ruins, peasant houses, inns, brooks, waterfalls, and bridges. Automata were also sometimes employed, and travellers who saw the Christmas cribs in Calabria refer to them as theatres of moving puppets.

The Christmas crib was a sport in Naples to which all, high and low, from royalty down, paid homage. Charles III liked to make his cribs with his own hands, and his queen, a Saxon princess by birth, made the dresses for her husband's dolls. Families were in the habit of visiting each other's cribs, some of which, it is said, cost as much as 30,000 ducats. All those who visited Naples at this period—Goethe, the Abbé de Saint-Non, Gorani, Friederike Brun, etc.—are full of praise for them. "The

s                                                                   273

artistry displayed completely defies description and passes the
bounds of imagination."

Whereas the Neapolitan cribs were concerned in particular
with the exceedingly vivid folk scenes, the multitude of figures
completely distracting attention from the main incident—the
birth of Christ—the Sicilian cribs preferred the gruesome. On

FIG. 273. ITALIAN CRIB-FIGURES, EIGHTEENTH CENTURY
From *Denkmäler der Krippenkunst*, by R. Berliner (B. Filser, Augsburg)
*Bayerisches National-Museum, Munich*

that account they liked to bring within the scope of their
subject-matter the massacre of the innocents as well as the
Nativity. In wealth of captivating detail and art of arrangement the Southern Italian cribs of the eighteenth century are
unsurpassed, but the art was not neglected in the rest of Italy,
being especially encouraged in different centres by the Franciscans and the Capuchins. In 1709 a rich prelate in Rome
had a whole houseful of crib-figures, the entire collection being
valued at about 8000–9000 thalers. Among the cribs in Roman
churches those of S. Francesco a Ripa and S. Maria Ara
Cœli were deemed to be the most lovely. The latter was built
round the famous *Bambino* and, influenced by local tradition,
included the Emperor Augustus and the sibyls among its figures.

FIG. 274. ITALIAN CRIB-FIGURES, EIGHTEENTH CENTURY
Group of shoemakers. From *Denkmäler der Krippenkunst*, by R. Berliner (B. Filser, Augsburg)
*Bayerisches National-Museum Munich*

In æsthetic beauty and in richness the German cribs cannot be compared with the Italian; but maybe the German examples have one advantage, in that they were dear to the heart of the people. The dramatic instinct of simple folk as expressed in the cribs succeeded in creating a wholly unliterary but, in the best sense of the word, popular art. It sprang from the hands of the folk themselves, and hence was able, without the necessity of any explanation or interpretation, to count on the full understanding of the crowd. In order to display the wealth of figures on a wider scale subsidiary events were appropriated from Biblical history, the crib being so divided into five groups: the Nativity, the shepherds' offering, the visit of the three kings, the flight into Egypt, and the Holy Family in Nazareth. Such scenes as the massacre of the innocents and the marriage at Cana could be added *ad libitum*. Legends too could be introduced there to the heart's content, and since the cribs were usually on display from Christmas to Candlemas the ambition of the artists was fully satisfied, and to those artists belonged every man who could use a wood-carving tool and every woman who could sew and embroider.

In old Bavaria, the Tirol, Upper Austria, and Styria peasants and hunters moulded and carved during the long winter evenings, year in and year out, for a genuine crib was never really finished—it could always be made still more beautiful and brought nearer to perfection. There are, indeed, cribs which took a hundred years and more to complete. In the Tirol not only did every church possess its crib, but in many villages every house had its own example. In the towns too the cribs had their amateurs who, if they could not carve themselves, would buy the figures from others. In Augsburg crib-figures were already articles of commerce in the eighteenth century, while in Munich there was even a regular crib market. A priest at Volkmannsdorf, near Moosburg, in 1678 ordered from an itinerant wood-carver a crib that took two years to finish. The figures, 30–35 cm. high, were wooden dolls with detachable limbs, movable heads, glass eyes, and wigs. In Munich the cribs of the Michaelshofkirche, with their figures 1 m. high, enjoyed great fame, and similar renown attached to those of St Peter's church and the church of the Franciscans.

In the convents these cribs were a welcome diversion, giving the nuns employment the whole year round. One of the most valuable belonged to the Ursuline convent at Innsbruck. Its oldest figures dated from the beginning of the eighteenth century; these were 20 cm. high and made of wood, with legs and arms

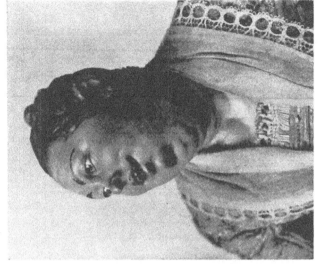

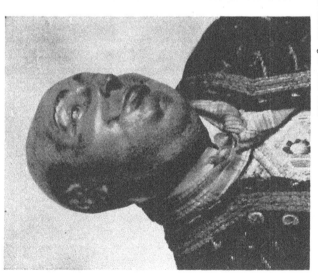

FIGS. 275, 276. HEADS OF ITALIAN CRIB-FIGURES

Host and hostess  From *Denkmäler der Krippenkunst*, by R. Berliner (B. Filser, Augsburg)

*Bayerisches National-Museum, Munich*

of the same material rendered movable, and thus adjustable to any position, by means of wire joints. The heads were moulded

FIG. 277. ALPINE WOODEN DOLL
Eighteenth century. German crib-figure
*Bayerisches National-Museum, Munich*

in wax, with hair of flax or wool; the bodies were wrapped round tightly with thick linen, and then dressed in real cloth garments of an exceedingly rich sort in the rococo theatrical style. The angels thus appeared with short hooped dresses and

278

laced sleeves, like the *ballerinas* of the time; they wore velvet
and silk trimmed with ermine, embroidered with gold and silver,

FIG. 278. WOODEN DOLL: PEASANT BOY
Eighteenth century. German crib-figure
*Bayerisches National-Museum, Munich*

ornamented with beads and stones, some with crowns containing
real jewels. The retinue of the three kings boasted the uniforms
of the queen's guards. Armour, weapons, and accoutrements were
of metal—some even of precious metal. A private individual,

279

even at that time, could not easily rival such a display, but the wood-carvers had the power at least of providing infinite variety in their figures. There were the three kings, with their retinue of servants, horses, camels, and elephants, besides shepherds, hunters, wagon-drivers, butchers, woodmen, hermits, beggars, men and women of the peasantry, cows, sheep, chamois, hares, etc.—all carved with care and either painted or dressed. In

FIG. 279. CRIB-FIGURES OF LIME-WOOD DRESSED IN CLOTH
Tirol. Eighteenth century

one of the most famous cribs—that at the church of Birgitz—the figures were so expensively clothed that a mantle of one of the kings cost thirty-six florins.

The accumulation of architectural detail is as characteristic of the Tirol cribs as the superabundance of figures. The crib belonging to the Jaufental family, of Wilten, which has been placed in the Österreichische Museum für Volkskunde, in Vienna, mingled dwellings of the Tirol Alps with architecture of the Renaissance, temples, and a hill castle. For the six scenes it represented it utilized twenty-four buildings, 256 human and 154 animal figures. Its origin is to be traced to the year 1700. As automata were by that time widely known, these were eagerly seized upon for the purpose of animating the figures. Paul von Stetten saw such automatic cribs at Augsburg in 1779. When

FIG. 280. CRIB OF THE STIFTSKIRCHE IN ADMONT
J. Thaddäus Stammel. Painted by Pötschnick, 1755

thus equipped they might cost anything up to several thousand guilders. Canon W. Pailler in the reminiscences of his youth describes a large mechanical crib which he saw in Upper Austria; all trades were represented there—smiths, cabinet-makers, tanners, millers, threshers, turners, shoe-makers, tailors, carpenters, etc., engaged in their respective activities.

The pleasure taken in the representation of popular life wholly surpassed that taken in the sacred episodes. There is a saying in Upper Bavaria, describing a general hotchpotch, which runs: "There's as much hash here as in a crib." For this reason an episcopal ordinance at Regensburg in 1789 prohibited the display of popular accessories in the cribs, and others banned them completely. Thus, Count Thürheim in 1803 forbade the exhibition of the crib in Bamberg, on the ground that the inhabitants of the Frankish provinces were too enlightened for such frivolities. When the reaction set in against the preceding rationalism there was a brief renaissance of the crib in the nineteenth century, but this was only a waning gleam, a last flicker before coarse-grained materialism overwhelmed or destroyed all the natural springs of folk life.

Yet still were there artists at work whose charming creations were able to hold the public interest in the crib and to provide it with ever new life. Roman Anton Boos, a distinguished sculptor, was a maker of crib-figures, and above all there was that Ludwig who died in 1830 and who, in Hager's judgment, produced the best figures ever made by Munich crib-makers. His figures, 26 cm. high, with movable heads and jointed limbs, were delicately and carefully carved to show muscles, veins, and wrinkles, like the late Gothic wood statues. Even then large sums were given for them by amateurs. The Court musician Zink in 1838 paid forty-one florins for three shepherd figures, and the crib belonging to Heindl, director of the mint, was valued in the sixties of the century at 1500 florins. About this time, however, interest in the crib began seriously to diminish. With Andreas Barsam, who died in 1869, disappeared the last artistic carver of crib-figures at Munich, and Sebastian Habenschaden, who died in 1868, was their last skilful painter.

The crib maintained itself longest, as an object of real popular affection, in the Alpine Tirol and in the Salzkammergut, where wood-carving as a home occupation is pursued from sheer love of the thing itself. So long as the carvers took the baroque statuary as their model their figures retained the lifelike movements and the rich clothing of that style; the first indication of a decline is marked about the year 1800 in the work of Johann

# THE CHRISTMAS CRIB

Mühlmann, who looked for his model to contemporary religious painting, with its anæmic and academic rigidity. The *naïveté* of the conception declines, for, although the display of figures is certainly not less rich, these are no longer so free from restraint as formerly, their deportment being now clearly determined by the episode at the manger. In place of individualized figures appear types of a wholly general sort; the fantastic baroque

FIG. 281. CRIB-FIGURES OF LIME-WOOD DRESSED IN CLOTH BY
JOHANN KIENINGER IN HALLSTATT
Nineteenth century

landscape which predominated in the eighteenth century takes on a simpler form, which is nearer akin to reality, and often preference is given to a background of one simple tone. As the foreground of the general panorama was rendered plastically and the background merely painted, great care was taken to secure an illusive transition from one to the other.

The Tirol, with its wood-carved and painted figures, remains the true home of the crib, and has produced in many homely workers artists in their own kind. Such an one was discovered at Hallstatt in the person of Johann Kieninger, who died in 1899, at the age of seventy. The Österreichische Museum für Volkskunde, in Vienna, possesses a mountain crib made by him, which, in Haberlandt's words, is

a wholly charming work, in which the mixture of popular tradition and individual inventive spirit is worthy of special note. Unsur-

283

passable and inimitable is the admixture of traditional and personal conception in this work, which impresses the observer with a sense of childish innocence and of native homeliness.

An artist of similar powers was Josef Partsch, in Engelberg, who died in 1886, at the age of seventy-five. His speciality was the Christmas crib with multitudes of participant figures. Praise has been given to his work for its touching simplicity in spite of its religious profundity and its great technical skill. Partsch tinted his figures in water-colour; the smaller ones were cast in plaster from stone moulds.

In the Salzburg district dressed figures were preferred, for they were, according to Mühlmann, far more national. The heads were hand-moulded of flesh-coloured wax, with eyes of glass, the bodies themselves being concealed under the stiffly extended folds of cloth. These clothes, with their trimmings of gold spangles, beads, and precious stones, made a rich show. Composition in groups, a popular method in the eighteenth century, was here more rarely employed, each figure standing by itself, without any direct relation to its neighbour. The most magnificent crib in the Tirol style is that splendid one of the master tanner Moser in Bozen, which is now in the possession of the Bayerische National-Museum; this was made in the forties by its former owner and by Johann Pendel in Meran. Here a richly fantastic architectural setting is equipped with all kinds of mechanical devices, such as clocks and water-falls, while the staffage includes several hundred little figures varied in size from 2 to 10 cm. in accordance with the rules of perspective. This work of art cost its owner 10,000 florins. In the Tirol the wood-carvers had been in the habit of wandering about at Christmas with their works—Annunciation cribs, the three kings, and Easter plays—exhibiting them for a trifle, but about the year 1900 this custom came to an end, and the crib sank into being a museum piece.

The Riedinger Collection, in Augsburg, containing many hundred figures, was deservedly famous. Larger and more varied was the collection of Max Schmederer, particularly rich in Southern Italian cribs. These were offered by the owner to the Bayerische National-Museum, in Munich, but the then director of the museum rejected this valuable gift, and only a Press campaign, inaugurated by the Munich *Neueste Nachrichten*, succeeded in getting this collection, which is unique in its own way, accepted and put on exhibition. Since that time it has formed one of the most noteworthy sections of the museum.

Art and science first paid attention to the crib when it had already ceased to play a part in the life of the people; since then the cribs have been collected by museums and regarded as valuable documents for a knowledge of the folk. Friends of the crib in all quarters have banded together, and out of their confederation a working society has been formed. In Munich the architect de Crignis conducts a crib school every winter, and P. Simon Reiter, of the Order of St Francis, has written a practical textbook on the subject. The Salzburg Crib Society (*Krippenverein*) in 1919 organized a large exhibition of ancient cribs in St Peter's Monastery, while in the winter of 1928 an exhibition of cribs, arranged by the German Catholic Women's League, was held at Berlin, a place which we usually associate with crude materialism. Alongside Oberammergau cribs from the carving workshops of the well-known portrayer of Christ, Anton Lang, were to be seen works of the progenitor of the German crib art, Sebastian Osterrieder, of Munich. The Innsbruck sculptor Kuen showed a wood-carved crib panorama; Knapstein, of Cologne, a Rhine citizen crib; the wood-carving school of Warmbrunn a crib by Professor Del Antonio; and the art school of Münster several works by the director of their sculpture class, Professor Guntermann, in which the group of Mary and the child captured attention by its divine beauty. The wood-carved crib-figures of Melchior Grosseck in Silesian popular dress made a lively and naïve impression; deeply rooted in Westphalian sentiment were the homely lines of Mormann's figures. A large Christmas group with artistically carved jointed figures by Lamers-Vordermayer was on loan from a private collection, as were also a Westphalian crib from a convent of Poor Clares and a beautifully cut wood crib frieze. Works of Tirolese, Ukrainians, and Berliners stood here side by side. Majolica cribs and wooden cribs made by machinery (among them one made after Dürer) were to be seen here beside reliefs and religious scenes executed in needlework. These had as great an interest for their reflection of folk customs as for that of folk dress, which no organization in the world can now revive.

The crib with automatic figures approaches close to the puppet theatres. Such cribs with moving figures were once so common in Aachen that the expression *Krepche* ('crib') simply signified a puppet-show. In Poland too boys used to tramp round with the *Schopa*, a box with a crib, in front of which danced various kinds of dolls. In the second half of the eighteenth century the puppet-crib-plays were a favourite amusement for high and low in Vienna, Schönholz styling them the "most beloved miniature theatre with thumbnail actors, all movable." Maria Theresa patronized Frau Godl, whose real name was Barbara Müller, and who had set up her stage in Lerchenfeld. Her principal scenes were those of the three kings, the flight into Egypt, the massacre of the innocents, Holofernes' tent, and Saul's palace, while the puppet theatre At the Metal Tower (Beim Blechernen Turm) in Wieden presented with special care Joseph's flight into Egypt, Daniel in the lions' den, and David and Goliath. In Vienna only scenes from the Old Testament were allowed; when the painter Sacchetti, in 1806, desired to present Christ's Passion by means of wax puppets permission was denied him.

It seems that in France preference was always given to cribs with automatic figures. The Theatines in Paris even in the seventeenth century were accustomed to set up a Christmas crib with movable wax figures at the door of their cloister, and as late as the eighteenth century the crib scene and the Passion were represented and played with similar puppets on the Petit Pont de l'Hôtel Dieu. This kind of crib-puppet-show was disseminated throughout the whole of France, gaining special popularity in the south at Marseilles. The cribs in Lyons too must have been more like marionette theatres than the motionless groups such as appeared in Italy and Germany. It is assumed that they were a relic of the old mystery-plays, with which indeed they share one peculiarity—the introduction into their text and personnel of comic elements expressed in lower-class dialect. In Lyons these were represented by Father and Mother Coquard, who mingled with the shepherds at the crib and spoke in the Lyonese *patois*. They sang a duet in which the mists of their native place were referred to, and which ended with an exhortation to the youthful spectators to behave themselves well. Thus in France, as in Germany, the crib, by quick transition, turned into the puppet-show.

## IV

## THE TIN SOLDIER

So far as we have referred hitherto to the toy doll we have been concerned (whether directly expressed or not) with the toys of the little girl. About 90 per cent. of toy dolls are of the female sex, and they are treated as playthings almost exclusively by girls. James Sully has asserted that boys are not generally inclined to play with dolls, and, if they do turn to dolls, they

FIG. 282. LITTLE HORSEMAN
Terra-cotta. Cyprus

FIG. 283. LITTLE HORSEMAN
Terra-cotta. Tanagra

(so far, at least, as the boyhood of the United States is concerned) like only such as are out of the ordinary—clowns, for instance, negroes, and Eskimos—and prefer even animal toys to these. Evidence of this can be found even in the distant past. It is recorded from early medieval Iceland that the six-year-old Arngrim Thorgrimsson presented his little brass horse to his four-year-old uncle Steinolf Arnorsson since he himself was then too old to be still playing with it.

The boyish toys of past centuries were mostly dolls representing warriors and horsemen, large numbers of which, made of wood, clay, and metal, have been preserved from various epochs of civilization. Even in late classical days little Trojan horses with warriors on them, whether as toys or mementoes of a journey, were sold on the site of ancient Ilium. Innumerable are the extant figures of little knights made of baked clay or

287

glazed stoneware, the playthings of German boys of the fifteenth and sixteenth centuries. The earliest pictorial record we possess of the existence of such German toy dolls is a miniature from the well-known Codex of the Herrad von Landsperg, which in 1870 was destroyed by fire in the Strasbourg Library. In this late twelfth-century manuscript a couple of boys were shown making two knights, held on horizontal strings, fight with one another. This "knightly toy," which made tenderest childhood

FIG. 284. LUDUS MONSTRORUM
About 1160. A children's toy or a puppet-play?
Painting from the Codex of the Herrad von Landsperg

acquainted with its future duties, lost, in the course of centuries, nothing of its popularity. Emperor Maximilian, the "last of the knights," who had his life written and illustrated in the *Weiss-kunig*, commissioned Burgkmair in 1516 to execute a picture which shows how as a boy he used to play with a friend at tilting. They are seen pushing two mounted knights in armour set on wheeled frames one against the other, each endeavouring to unhorse the other with his lance. The Emperor took delight in this toy even in his old age, for he ordered from the armourer Koloman, helmet-maker in Augsburg, two such knights in so-called tilt harness set on wooden horses. They were intended for the young King Ludwig II of Hungary. Several similar toys have been preserved—for example, in the Museum Ferdinandeum at Innsbruck, at Burg Kreuzenstein, and elsewhere. In the Vienna Kunsthistorische Hofmuseum there is a toy of this kind certainly earlier than the sixteenth century, representing chargers and knights of cast brass ready for the tourney. These can be

288

drawn toward each other with strings so that their tilting lances meet. The finest example, however, is to be found in the Bayerische National-Museum, in Munich. This must belong to about the year 1556 and bears the arms of the Nürnberg family Holzschuher. The horse's neck and feet are movable; the knight

FIG. 285. EMPEROR MAXIMILIAN, WHEN A BOY, AT PLAY
Woodcut by Hans Burgkmair. From the *Weisskunig*

is made of wood and is fully accoutred. Armour and weapons are technically correct down to the minutest detail, so that the doll may be regarded as a model of contemporary harness for man and charger. Less expensive must have been the "little wooden man which when pulled can fight" with which about this time the six-year-old Felix Platter was presented as a *Dockenhansl* ('gift'). Even as late as 1600 the old Duke William of Bavaria was accustomed to give princely persons "little tilting horsemen which were moved by clockwork."

The warrior doll has, it is true, remained a toy beloved of boys, but it has been considerably simplified in recent times. The more or less complicated mechanism of the plastic figure has given place to the flat figure, represented in the tin soldier. Originally the flat figure was made of lead, but as that substance

FIG. 286. MAN ON HORSEBACK WITH THE HOLZSCHUHER CREST
About 1556
*Bayerisches National-Museum, Munich*

was too soft and had too little power of resistance it was replaced first by tin and then by an alloy of tin and antimony. Robert Forrer and Theodor Hampe have traced back through centuries the genealogical tree of this little flat figure, and have rummaged out for it a very respectable ancestry—in which they count not only the so-called *schardana* figures of the close of the third century B.C., but the primitive metal warrior dolls found in Etruria, Greece, and Istria. In the Hallstatt period, about the year 1000 B.C., the records increase. At Karnten, near Rossegg, a primitive little horseman was discovered in a grave-mound; even thus early it was made of a mixture of lead and tin. In some graves near Frögg eighteen similar horsemen were found. The famous bronze chariot of Strettwag, in Steiermark, which belongs to the later Hallstatt period and the significance of which even now has not been quite explained, seems to be full of such dolls. The horsemen, measured with their shields, are 13 cm. high, the foot-soldiers 10½ cm. Very similar figures were known in the Chibcha civilization. From the lake of Siecha, Cundinamarca, Columbia, was fished up a golden group representing a raft with a high priest and his retinue of ten persons. The little figures, conventionally flat, like tin soldiers, measure 3 to 7 cm. in height.

FIG. 287. ROMAN TIN FIGURE
FOUND ON THE RHINE
Legionary of the Imperial period
*British Museum*

The Romans were also acquainted with flat soldiers made of tin and lead. In a grave at Pesaro was discovered a figure of Cæsar on horseback, and at Mainz was found a one-sided cast

FIG. 288. LEAD SOLDIERS
Fourteenth century

tin figure of a Roman legionary of the Imperial epoch, with short sword, large shield, greaves, and helmet. This art was not lost in the Middle Ages, but it is not at all clear whether the little figures which have come down to us from that time were devotional objects, the so-called 'pilgrims' badges,' or toys. Perhaps they may have been both. Little cast figures of lead and tin belonging to the thirteenth and fourteenth centuries have been found in the Seine; these, about 6 cm. high, represent horsemen such as St George and St Martin, and are finished only on one side.

Theodor Hampe mentions a Schlüsselfeld table decoration of 1503, a famous goldsmith's work of Nürnberg provenance, which represents a ship made animate by the presence of many little figures. These were made of precious metal and enamelled; they show, at any rate, that men knew at that time how to make toy figures of the tiniest form. Whether they were made then in cheaper material to serve as toys is not known. It is said that Louis XIII in 1610 played with lead soldiers which were 7 cm. high. These lacked foot-plates and must consequently have been stuck on to the table. In 1650 an army of soldiers was made of silver for the twelve-year-old Louis XIV, Georges Chassel, of Nancy, sketching the designs, which were carried out by the goldsmith Merlin. The cost of this royal toy came to 50,000 thalers. When the King and Colbert a few years later wanted a number of toy soldiers for the Dauphin they sent to Nürnberg, as the most famous manufacturing centre of toys of all kinds and of inventions connected therewith. At the King's order the goldsmith Johann Jakob Wolrab made several hundred silver cavalry soldiers and infantry. It is believed that the famous Vauban was sent to Nürnberg expressly for the purpose of supervising the work. The 3½-inch figures were equipped by the compass-maker Hans Hautsch and his son Gottfried with an automatic device which aroused great admiration. In 1698, about twenty-five years after it was completed, Weigel writes of it from memory:

> ·They went through the usual war manœuvres very ably; they marched to left and to right, doubled their ranks, lowered their weapons, struck fire, shot off, and retreated. Then the lance-men tried to knock the cavalrymen out of their saddles, but these were quite prepared to defend themselves by firing their pistols.·

Another army, of cardboard figures, consisting of twenty squadrons of cavalry and ten battalions of infantry, was made by Pierre Couturier, called Montargis, between 1670 and 1671 and by Henri Gessay between 1669 and 1670. It cost 28,963 francs, and is still to be seen in the public collections in Paris.

The tin soldier was not a common thing in the seventeenth century. When in 1670–75 the Prince Elector of Bavaria desired

# THE TIN SOLDIER

a military toy for his son, who later won fame in war as Maximilian Emmanuel, he ordered the carver Matthias Schütz to make him some wooden infantry and cavalry. *Papier mâché* must also have been in use for this purpose, for the father of the well-known painter of hunting pictures Johann Elias Ridinger made some soldier dolls at Ulm of that material. The tin soldier is a creation of the eighteenth century, and owes its being, like the contemporary porcelain plastic, to Germany. All authors are in

FIG. 289. OFFICER AND TROOPERS OF THE LÜTZOW CORPS
Painted tin figures of the eighteenth century
*Germanisches National-Museum, Nürnberg*

agreement that it arose as an "echo of the victories of Frederick the Great." At any rate the mass production of these figures begins with the Seven Years War. From these cultural efforts the Fatherland gained at least one benefit in that the lead-soldier industry throughout the nineteenth century remained specifically German. By the year 1900 there were about twenty German tin-soldier factories with an annual output of a million marks. "Germany," remarks the well-known French social historian Henri d'Allemagne, "in particular has improved this toy. Skilfully she has taken advantage of its influence on the upbringing of the child—to set alight and to nourish the flame of patriotism and to keep alive the traditions of honour and bravery."

With the toy soldier too Nürnberg asserted its old pre-eminence as the centre of the toy industry. Andreas Hilpert, of Coburg, in 1760 settled in Nürnberg, and was able to make this toy popular by means of his technical and artistic ability. He invented the small flat figures with a standing plate such as

293

we have to-day, and created in the diverse types a genuine art form—"these most artistic tiny rococo figures," as Hampe calls them. About forty different kinds of Prussian, French, Russian, and Turkish soldiers came from his skilled hands; his activities, however, were not confined entirely to military figures, but included also representatives of civil life. After the artist's

FIG. 290. WOOD-CARVED FIGURES OF SOLDIERS
Eighteenth to nineteenth centuries
*Germanisches National-Museum, Nürnberg*

death the firm was carried on successfully by his family. In the illustrated catalogues of the great toy-shops of that time, that of P. F. Catel at Berlin in 1790, and that of Georg H. Bestelmeier at Nürnberg, issued between 1798 and 1807, the tin soldiers are fully represented. At the same time the picture sheets intended to be cut out became popular. About the year 1810 a baker named Boersch at Strasbourg cut out of paper all the regiments of Napoleon's Great Army, painting them carefully and correctly. He was said to have compiled in this way about five thousand figures. These sheets were once very common and were often designed by well-known artists. War-painters, like Adam, were, of course, in special demand for this kind of work, but the picture sheets of Pettenkofen, Schindler, Kriehuber, Zampis, and others are also noteworthy for their boldness of treatment.

294

# THE TIN SOLDIER

In the first half of the nineteenth century the Nürnberg industry found open competitors in Northern Germany. The firm of G. Söhlke was founded at Berlin in 1819, and this name for long generations remained dear to the children of that city.

FIG. 291. TIN SOLDIERS
About 1820

This firm produced, in addition to soldiers, figures for fairy-tales, for *Gulliver's Travels*, and for *Robinson Crusoe*; keeping fully abreast of the time, it manufactured toy trains when as yet the railway had hardly gained its footing, and accommodated itself, too, to the success in fiction of *Uncle Tom's Cabin*. In 1830 J. E. Dubois founded his business at Hanover, producing figures of the Hanoverian legion, the Napoleonic guards, etc., magnificently executed in design, modelling, and painting. In spite of all this, æsthetic and commercial precedence remained with Nürnberg, for Ernst Heinrichsen, who set up business in 1839, outstripped all competitors. He it was who introduced figures of standard sizes, fixing these at 3 cm. for infantry and 4 cm. for cavalry; formerly the figures with muskets had been 11 cm. high and the Prussian guards 8 to 9 cm. He himself was a very skilful designer and engraver, and he was able to attract famous artists to work for him; he got Camphausen, for example, to sketch for him Gustavus Adolphus's Swedish troops. In addition to this, he followed the tendencies and interests of his time with a keen eye to commercial opportunities. He prepared tin figures for Cooper's Indian tales, for polar expeditions, and for African explorations besides others for the Trojan War, the Crusades, and bull-fights; the militia of 1848, the Crimean War, the Boer War, the Great War, and, lastly, the Reichswehr have all been represented accurately by this old-established firm, for it is still in existence. In addition to Heinrichsen must be mentioned Johann C. Allgeyer, of Fürth, whose firm has been carried on by his son and grandson, and J. C. Haselbach, of Berlin, who made over 5000 different moulds for figures representing soldiers in the English wars in India, the French wars in Mexico, and the war of 1870–71.

Playing with soldiers is by no means confined to boys; it has been popular also with those monarchs who wished to advance militarism among their subjects. Certainly we may not count among these Tsar Peter III, the first of the Holstein family to sit on the Russian throne, for, although this half-witted prince liked to play with toys, he did it in a wholly childish way; once, indeed, he ordered a rat which had eaten two of his soldiers of *Tragant* to be tried and sentenced to death according to martial law. The tin soldiers which he played with are still preserved in one of the small palaces of Oranienbaum. In the style of the tin soldiers was the war game invented by the Polish general Mieroslawski and practised seriously both at headquarters and among the rank and file, although it was not played with figures, but with little stones. Tsar Nicholas I was said to have excelled in this game and to have beaten even his brother-in-law, who later became Emperor William I, at the "battle near Bautzen." Hampe declares that for this Tsar Heinrichsen made tin soldiers representing the mounted regiments of the Russian guard.

The Prussian monarchs, on whom the spirit of militarism was so deeply impressed, have left in their model dolls valuable evidence relating to the old Prussian army. Of these the arsenal and the Hohenzollern Museum in Schloss Monbijou possess extensive collections, and to them Adolf Menzel has devoted a careful examination. The oldest piece is a great red-and-black-striped wooden doll belonging to the first years of the reign of Frederick William I. It represents a grenadier of the red life-guards about to throw a grenade. Then come models in very much smaller style, for the most part representing officers and men of the Prussian army in the second half of the eighteenth century, very delicately and accurately formed, with wax heads and cloth hats, bearing real plumes. Frederick William III possessed dolls of this kind 20 cm. high, moulded in lead, and then painted in perfect likeness of the uniforms and accoutrements worn in all the regiments of his army. Emperor William I too had a doll army, each a careful model of a soldier from one of his regiments. The Armee Museum in Munich has a similar collection of little toy soldiers representing the former Bavarian army.

What originally was only a plaything for half-grown boys—no less a person than Goethe refers to it in his *Dichtung und Wahrheit*—has gradually become, thanks to careful modelling and equipment, an aid to students of military history and a valuable museum piece. The Germanische National-Museum, in Nürnberg, made a start in the collection of these objects, and its example has been followed by various other local museums. In the Landes-museum at Dresden whole battlefields are reproduced by means of tin soldiers. The Great War much stimulated interest in this representation of reality. A Berlin factory in 1915 had window displays in which the most famous historical battles, beginning with those of the Egyptians and concluding with the battle of the Masurian Lakes, were reproduced by the employ-ment of 35,000 tin soldiers. In the same year an exhibition of 50,000 tin soldiers was held in Vienna at the KK. Österreichische-Museum, in the Stubenring; art students from Professor Breitner's school undertook the preparation of the various landscapes necessary. The battles of Custozza, Sedan, and Mars-la-Tour were shown by the utilization of some 8000 figures.

To-day the tin soldier has almost wholly lost its position as a toy; it is now preserved by the collector in the vitrines. These collectors are so numerous and so zealous in their activities that they have formed societies, and have established special periodi-cals devoted to their sport. The tin-soldier museum of the aulic councillor Anton Klamrot in Leipzig is justly famed: "German antiquarians and students of folk life truly owe much to him because of his energetic activities in the collection of these objects; in this he has shown real historic sense."

# V

## THE PUPPET-SHOW IN ANTIQUITY

WHEN we turn to the history of the marionette theatre we are often, as noted already, in doubt whether we are dealing with the hand puppets or with the marionettes on strings. Inferences, however, may be drawn when the references to the marionettes occur in metaphors where they are introduced as objects of comparison. When Aristotle writes that those who direct the

FIG. 292. ACTOR (MESSENGER) AND COMIC ACTOR (DANCER)
Terra-cotta. From Myrina

marionettes need only pull their strings in order to set in motion first the head and hands of the little being, then its eyes, shoulders, and limbs, all so delightfully obedient, it is quite clear what sort of puppets he alludes to. Apuleius describes the strings in the same way. Galen likens them to men's muscles, and Plato relates them to our passions, which pull us this way and that. Horace compares in his satires (*Duceris ut nervis alienis mobile lignum*) the human lack of free will with the stringed marionette.

Puppets with movable limbs have been preserved from ancient times in considerable numbers, but genuine marionettes controlled by strings are certainly not among them—not to mention puppets with movable eyes. Perchance they have all perished, for the material of which they were made—wood—is especially liable to decay; this is particularly unfortunate, for we know that the puppet theatres were very popular in Greece. Xenophon, in describing a visit he paid in 422 B.C. to the house of Kallias in Athens, refers to a Syracusian who came with his puppet theatre to entertain the guests, but who could not capture Socrates' attention. In the time of Sophocles the marionette theatres must have appeared frequently in Athens. In his

FIG 293. WINGED DOLLS
Terra-cotta. From Megaris and Tanagra

*Deipnosophists* Athenæos reproached the inhabitants of that city because they had handed over the theatre of Dionysos to the marionettes of the *neuropastes* ('string-puller') Potheimos, and because they took more delight in these than in Euripides' plays. The Emperor Marcus Aurelius likewise interested himself in these puppets; he, like Horace, makes comparison between their strings and man's free will. This comparison, however, is so obvious that no special ingenuity is demanded for its invention. The Indian *Mahabharata* also mentions the string-controlled marionettes, and compares their servile condition with human beings. Rajah Sekhara, writing at the beginning of the tenth century A.D., makes two movable puppets take part in one of his dramas. The name given to the puppet-showman was *sutradhara*, which means literally 'string-puller,' and this name eventually

299

passed over to be applied in general to the theatrical producer —a proof that puppet-plays, which even to-day still form the only dramatic entertainment of Indian rural communities, must be more ancient than the theatre of human actors.

The Fathers of the Church did not fail to connect their cheap moral reflections on mankind with the mechanism of a well-made puppet. Considering, indeed, the great antipathy they displayed toward all manifestations of heathen culture, including the theatre, it is astonishing how tolerantly they dealt with the marionette. Clement of Alexandria, Tertullian, Synesius, all of whom condemned the theatre, said nothing against the puppets, which, we must assume, could not have been so obscene as, for example, the mime.

FIG. 294. WINGED
EROS
Clay doll from Myrina

How and when the puppet-play came to Germany we do not know; perhaps we may agree with Philipp Leibrecht in assuming that the introduction of this art was due to the jugglers who followed the Roman legions over the Alps. Evidence in favour of this theory is provided by the fact that an Old High German gloss identifies *Tocha* (the modern *Docke*, or doll) with *mima*. Its existence, however, cannot be definitely proved before the twelfth century, and even then proof is forthcoming only if we take the picture in the Codex of the Herrad von Landsperg, which belongs to about the year 1170, not as a children's toy, as it seems to be, but as a puppet theatre. Immediately after this date, on the other hand, records begin to multiply, demonstrating clearly that this thing must by then have become universally popular. In 1253 the minnesinger Meister Sigeher compared the way in which Pope Innocent IV behaved toward the German princes with a puppet-play—a comparison which unfortunately was only too fully justified. Ulrich von dem Türlin, Willehalm von Oranse, Thomasin von Zirclaria, writing in the thirteenth century, agree in styling "mundane joys a mere puppet-play." Hugo von Trinberg, who finished his great didactic poem *Der Renner* in the year 1300, relates that the jugglers used to bring small puppets from under their cloaks, making the spectators laugh with their antics. They were called by various names—*Kobold*, *Wichtel*, and *Tatermann*. The laughter occasioned by their jests gave rise to a proverb—'laughing like a *Kobold*.' Apparently

300

these puppets—and here one must think rather of hand puppets than of stringed marionettes—contributed much to strengthening the popular belief in pigmies and little imps. In the Redentin Easter play which a Cistercian, Peter Calf, composed in 1464 at the village of Redentin, near Wismar, Luzifer speaks of those "who play with puppets and cheat fools of their money." In the German translation of the French heroic poem *Melagys*, which belongs to the fifteenth century, a scene lacking in the original is inserted wherein the Fée Oriande performs a play with two puppets—in all probability hand puppets.

FIG. 295. GREEK CLAY DOLL FROM A GRAVE
Marionette?
*Biardot Collection*

The oldest picture, moreover, which we possess of the puppet theatre on this side of the Alps shows figures of this kind worked by hand. These are, as might be supposed, figures in the head of which the performer places his forefinger, while he moves the arms with his thumb and middle finger. Only three-quarters of the puppet accordingly is seen, and, since usually but one performer with two hands at his disposal operates them, only two puppets appear at one time. In the manuscript of a French heroic poem, *Li Romans du Bon Roi Alixandre*, written in 1338 and illustrated with miniatures in 1344 by the painter Jehan de Grise (a native of Flanders?), are to be found two pictures of a puppet-show. In one of the little pictures three maidens watch a performance which some scholars have attempted to connect with Punch and Judy; in the other four little male spectators watch a scene of slashing and stabbing. In these oldest illustrations is to be observed an element which has remained a property of the hand-puppet stage up to the present day, preserving its force of attraction from of old—the motive of quarrelling and conflict and cudgelling. This codex is in the Bodleian Library, Oxford.

The general popularity of the puppett heatre is proved too by the attitude of popular writers. Luther, for example, once called the papacy "a public puppet-show," and speaks elsewhere of the "holy puppets." Direct references, however, in illustrative form and text are in reality extremely few, but for this there is a double reason. The itinerant jugglers with their puppet-shows did not belong to any "respectable trade," and therefore scholars, in whose hands rested the literature of the day, were ashamed to confess that they had found any pleasure in the activities of a vagabond class of society. They held it beneath their dignity to take notice of jugglers and puppet-showmen, and if on occasion a comparison involving these did slip from their pens, as in Luther's case, it was only incidental.

FIG. 296. GREEK CLAY FIGURE FROM A
GRAVE
Marionette?
*Biardot Collection*

We know that puppet theatres certainly existed before the sixteenth century, but it is impossible to tell how they were constituted or of what sort were their puppets and repertoire. All documentary evidence, unfortunately, is silent on these points. We learn that Count Jan von Blois in 1363 ordered a puppet-show to be given in Dordrecht, that in 1395 a man was paid for such shows, that he had presented a puppet-play before the Count of Holland, that in 1451 a ban was laid on puppet-shows during Easter, but beyond that the records do not go. What plays were given then and what sort of puppets were employed we cannot tell. No doubt Rabe is right in assuming that they were hand puppets exhibited in a kind of Punch-and-Judy show.

Considering the miserable conditions of the wandering entertainers whose bread and butter depended on these shows, we may well assume that all the stage arrangements were as primitive as could be. As regards the nature of the repertoire, however, only conjectures of a wholly general sort are possible.

302

All those authors who have occupied themselves with this question assume with Gustav Freytag that fighting and buffeting must have come first in the programme. This is the more

FIG. 297. NIKE IN TERRA-COTTA
Marionette? From Myrina

probable in that performances of the kind still hold their charm for the common people. The buffoon was certainly there; he could not be banished even from the serious mysteries.

These comic characters are similar to one another in all countries. The Indian Vidusaka, the Greek *mimos*, the Javanese Semar, the Turkish Karagöz, the German serving-lad Rubin,

303

from whom Hanswurst and later Kasperle derived, all belong to one family. One and all they are ugly, dirty, vain, impertinent, greedy, cowardly, and coarse; their chief activity lies in giving sound cudgellings, in return for which they receive, if possible, sounder beatings. About the end of the fifteenth century and the beginning of the sixteenth the expression *Himmelreich* ('kingdom of heaven') was introduced into Germany for the puppet-show (or perhaps only for the box of the puppet-showman). It is to be found, for example, in Thomas Murner's

FIG. 298. MEDIEVAL PUPPET THEATRE
Miniature by Jehan de Grise, from a manuscript, apparently Flemish, *Li Romans du Bon Roi Alixandre*. Painted between 1338 and 1344
*Bodleian Library*

*Die Narrenbeschwörung* and in various Nürnberg civic degrees of the fifteenth and sixteenth centuries, and is transferred even to the players in the form of *Himmelreicher*. No plausible explanation of this word has so far been offered. T. Hampe believes that it is not impossible that the title was conferred on them because of their repertoire, which commonly derived its material from Biblical sources, known by the showmen to be popular among their audiences. Thus, a certain Heinrich von Burgund in 1510 wished to produce in Nürnberg his puppet-show of Christ's Passion, but the town council refused to give their permission. Leibrecht, working on old German civic decrees of the second half of the sixteenth century, has published a whole series of records relating to performances of religious puppet-plays in Nürnberg, Lüneberg, Nordlingen, Augsburg, Danzig, and Berlin; these amply demonstrate the great popularity of this kind of show. Not one of the texts is now known; no doubt they were handed down by oral tradition. There was only one sixteenth-century German author who wrote for the puppet stage, and that was Hans Sachs. The artistic level of the pieces of the Nürnberg shoemaker lies fairly low, and we must assume that the performances of the puppet-showmen of that time raised still slighter claims to literary worth, the less indeed in that a good many of them must have been improvised. In point of fact there is no real evidence that these puppets were introduced with dialogue at all; some historians, such as Magnin and Maindron, are of the opinion that the puppets appeared only in pantomime, and that a man in front of the stage related the course of action.

# VI

## MARIONETTES IN THE SIXTEENTH TO THE
## EIGHTEENTH CENTURY

In the sixteenth century there developed out of the puppet type the special form of the marionette. Our knowledge of its existence at this period comes from a man who was then widely famous as a scientist—Hieronymus Cardanus, an Italian, whose book *De Varietate Rerum* appeared in 1557 at Nürnberg. He writes there:

> I have seen two Sicilians who did real wonders with two wooden figures which they made to move. A single string was carried through both. It was attached on one side to a fixed post and on the other to the leg which the showman moved. The string was stretched at both sides. There is no kind of dance which these figures could not execute. They made the most astonishing movements with their feet, legs, arms, and head—all with such varied gestures that I am unable, I confess, to render an account of such an ingenious mechanism, for there were not several strings, some tight, some loose; only one went through the figures, and that was always tight. I have seen a good many other wooden figures which were set in movement by several strings sometimes tight and sometimes loosened; that is no marvel. I must add, too, that it was a really pleasant thing to see how the gestures and steps of these puppets synchronized with the music.

In *De Subtilitate Rerum* the author returns to this subject, remarking:

> If I were to relate all the wonders which are carried out by those stringed puppets popularly called *magatelli* a whole day could not suffice for me, for they play, fight, hunt, dance, blow trumpets, and attend artfully to preparing their meals.

The puppets which the scholar describes with such ardour belong to the kind which the French call *marionettes à la planchette*. In Italian they were called also *fantoccini*, whence comes the French *fantoches*. They were known everywhere, especially in Italy, where they seem to have been invented and whence wandering entertainers took them beyond the Alps to display their activities at annual fairs. The showman, who made the puppets dance by moving his limb, accompanied their steps on some kind of instrument—flute, tambourine, or bag-pipes. They were even taken across the Channel to England, Hogarth

FIG. 299. ITALIAN MARIONETTES "À LA PLANCHETTE"
Etching by J. Dumont. 1739

introducing them in the print which represents the annual fair at Southwark in 1733. The German traveller Adam Olearius, who in 1633 made a long journey by Russia to Persia, met them too in the farthest eastern parts of Europe.

In the sixteenth century the puppets supported on and moved by strings or wires received the since commonly accepted name of ' marionette.' In Italy, where they originated, they were given various names—*fantoccini, burattini, pupazzi, bambocchie*—but it is impossible to determine what distinctions these titles indicated.

Seemingly the puppet-showmen came from Italy to France with the actors of the *commedia dell'arte*. For many years Catharine de' Medici, herself a Florentine princess, played, as the Queen Mother, the chief *rôle* at the French Court and patronized

FIG. 300. MARIONETTES "À LA PLANCHETTE"
Anonymous French engraving. About 1800

Italian fashions and entertainments. The name 'marionette' is to be discovered first in a work of Guillaume Bouchet, *Les Serées*, about the year 1600. Its etymology is uncertain. Magnin is inclined to regard 'marionette' as a diminutive of ' Maria,' since small statues of the Virgin have sometimes been so called, but how the movable and, for the most part, comic puppets could have received their name from a motionless object of devotion he does not explain. In the second edition of his excellent book the same scholar conjectures that it may be derived from ' Marion,' the pet-name of the heroine in one of the Robin and Marion pastorals. These dance songs of the twelfth century, however, must have long been forgotten by the sixteenth century, and could hardly have afforded the occasion for the invention of a character name. Magnin also notes the similarity

308

"LES PETITES MARIONETTES"
From *Goût du Jour*, Paris, about 1810

of the word to *marotte*, the fool's sceptre or baton, while Frisch in his *Lexicon* of 1741 refers to the connexion of the word with the medieval fool names *morio, morione*. The etymology, as has been stated, is still not absolutely settled; all we can say is that about the end of the sixteenth century and the beginning of the

FIG. 301. MARIONETTES "À LA PLANCHETTE"
Lithograph after a sketch by Carle Vernet. About 1820

seventeenth the name is in regular use and accepted everywhere. In Germany the movable puppet was called *Dattermann* or, as Konrad von Haslau gives it, *Tatermann*, a title which has now sunk into entire oblivion.

In Italy during the sixteenth century attempts were made to perfect the marionettes. Federigo Commandini, of Urbino, who died in 1575, and Giovanni Torriani, of Cremona, who accompanied Emperor Charles V into a monastery, are mentioned as improvers of the mechanism, but it seems that their efforts were directed principally toward the perfection of automata. Their creations, however, were so startling that Torriani was immediately suspected in Spain of being a magician, while in France public accusations were made against certain wizards who possessed little devils, called marionettes, to which they offered sacrifice and from which they sought counsel. This testifies, at any rate, to the excellent quality of the puppets, which, we must suppose, appeared extraordinarily lifelike.

FIG. 302. MARIONETTE THEATRE
Engraving of the eighteenth century
*Germanisches National-Museum, Nürnberg*

In 1573 the first permanent theatre of Italian marionettes was established in London; this made an impression on Shakespeare, for he mentions these puppets repeatedly, and on one occasion makes Hamlet wish to be the speaker for a marionette stage. Many, indeed, were the supporters of the puppets. Ben Jonson in his *Cynthia's Revels* makes a woman say: "As a country-gentlewoman, [I should] keep a good house and come up in term to see motions." In 1609 a new puppet theatre, in which French marionettes were shown, was opened in London. They must have been of great perfection, for Ben Jonson has occasion to refer to their movable eyes. The first English puppet-showman known by name is Captain Pod in 1599. In England these marionette theatres seem to have aimed directly at strong stage effects; at least in the second half of the sixteenth century the

310

accusation is made that they aimed too much at deluding the eyes of the spectators. They introduced plays dealing with such subjects as the fall of Sodom and Gomorrah, the destruction of Jerusalem, and the burning of Nineveh, in addition to much later subjects, bringing thus on their boards the murdering of the Guise brothers, the Gunpowder Plot, etc. During the performances a showman spoke in front of the curtain, explaining the actions on the stage—a method which is the same as that employed in the Spanish marionette theatres. Thus, in the second part of *Don Quixote* Cervantes describes a marionette performance where the *titero*, being behind the scenes, moves the strings unseen by the audience, while a boy in front relates the events. The puppets, he adds, were so charming that the pitiable knight was deceived and came to aid the unfortunate princess against the insolent Moors.

FIG. 303. WITCH
Movable. Of lime-wood dressed in cloth. Eighteenth century
*From a peasant theatre in Steiermark*

In the permanent puppet theatres of the larger Spanish towns, in order to create a greater illusion by keeping the showmen out of sight, the custom began of providing the puppets with a dialogue of their own—a development which makes its appearance also in England. To alter the tones of his voice, and so differentiate the various characters, this showman made use of a small instrument which he put in his mouth when interpreting certain parts. It was made like a *cri-cri*, of two pieces of metal, tortoise-shell, or ivory tied together with strips of cloth. In speaking it was held between the tongue and the roof of the mouth, and the showmen were always in danger of swallowing it. In Spain it was called *pito*, in France *sifflet-pratique* or simply *pratique*, and in Italy *fischio* or *pivetta*. The Italians must have used it for various parts; in Germany, however, according to Rabe, it was reserved for devils alone.

Although there is no doubt that in the second half of the sixteenth century puppet theatres were established in France, the first reliable records concerning showmen known to be actively engaged at certain places and at definite times come from the second half of the seventeenth century; these records relate to a family named Brioché (Jean, Charles, and François), who were apparently Italians by birth and whose original patronymic was Briocci. They gave their shows on the Pont Neuf, in Paris, and had the honour in 1669 to be summoned to Saint-Germain for the purpose of entertaining the Dauphin.

FIG. 304. OLD WOMAN
Marionette. Modern

The Briochés have always been referred to by French authors as marionette-players, but it seems, however, that they worked with hand puppets, an opinion which Rabe shares. The fact that a masked ape, Fagotin, took part in their shows indicates the latter, for such a performer would only have caused confusion among string puppets. This famous beast was stabbed to death by Cyrano de Bergerac, but it had many successors; all French puppet-show-men of that time got monkeys to aid in their performances, and they were all named Fagotin. Later on a cat was introduced into the French Guignol in the same way as the Hamburg Kasperle theatre introduced a dove, the English Punch a dog, and the Viennese Wurstl a rabbit. One of the Brioché family was so skilled in his art that during a tour in Switzerland he was suspected at Solothurn of being a wizard, and was able to escape with his life only by an immediate flight. Indubitable string marionettes were those with which the director La Grille produced his operas from 1676 in the Marais district. In the year following his house was named the Théâtre des Bamboches, and attracted spectators because of its richness in costume and stage setting. Its machinery permitted him to give even fairy operas with ballets and scenic changes. The marionettes in Paris had many adversaries, among whom were to be counted not only the clergy, including the famous Bishop Bossuet, but actors of the regular stage as well. At one time the little puppets are putting the latter to ridicule, pitilessly making them a laughing-stock, the marionettes always having the laughter on their side; and then, during the last years of the seventeenth century, the actors, thinking that their takings were being reduced by the competition of the puppet theatre, proceed to drive back the puppet stages to the markets in the Parisian suburbs.

At that time Germany was in a very turbulent state, and it need hardly be said that the wandering puppet-showmen, under the weight of circumstances, must have suffered greatly. They had also to face competition, on the one hand from the touring actors, who, as, for instance, the well-known director Weltheim,

FIG. 305. DON QUIXOTE DESTROYS THE MARIONETTE THEATRE
Engraving in a French edition of *Don Quixote*. Eighteenth century

played alternately with living persons and puppets, and on the other from the itinerant charlatans and quack doctors who sought to attract the public by all means in their power, making use even of the puppet stage. Between 1625 and 1659 the orphan asylum at Hamburg received a taxed contribution from the 'comedian-doctor' in the hop market. A comedy of the creation of the world was shown with puppets in 1644 at the Saxon Electoral Court in Dresden and in 1646 at the same Court in Moritzburg. In 1656 an entertainer gave performances in the market-place at Hamburg, showing how the King of Sweden was shot by the Poles and was carried off to hell. The puppet theatre of Michael Daniel Treu seems to have been exceptionally fine. When he visited Lüneburg in 1666 his repertoire consisted of twenty-five pieces, including *King Lear, Titus Andronicus,* and *Doctor Faust* as well as historical pieces such as *General Wahlstein,* and *Cromwell's Ghost.* From 1681 to 1685 he gave performances at Munich. At this time Leibrecht says that the town of Basle was the centre of marionette-showmen from all the chief countries of Europe, their appearance there giving a decidedly international atmosphere to the town. About the end of the seventeenth century a certain Johann Hilverding stood out predominant above the mass of puppet-showmen; from the year 1685 he worked in Vienna, made considerable tours, got as far as Stockholm, and then, once more returned to Vienna, associated himself with F. A. Stranitzky, a low-class comedian then held in great esteem. He gloried in showing over fifty comedies and operas with his figures one and a half ells high—"the figures execute all *actiones* like living persons with fitting movements."

The string puppets predominated in the sixteenth century; in the seventeenth century the hand puppets, along with their typical figures Polichinelle and Punch, took precedence. Magnin assumes that Polichinelle, in spite of his close kinship with the Italian Pulcinella, was a French creation; he may be right, for this figure, in its arrogance, its impudence, and its boastfulness, provides a brilliant synthesis of the French character. His partner was Dame Gigogne, a comic figure indigenous to the folk stage, who represented the small tradespeople. About 1650 the pair had already a permanent theatre at the Porte de Nesle, in Paris.

The first reliable German records relating to this character date from the second half of the century, and once more it was foreigners who were concerned with the entertainments. In 1649 a hydrologist, Manfredi, made his appearance in Nürnberg; apparently he was "the first to exhibit Polizinell with small puppets." In 1657 Petro Gimonde, an Italian puppet-showman, introduced the type at Frankfort. The wood-carver Matthias Schütz, besides the various toys which he made between 1670 and 1675 for the Bavarian princes, "carved also various wonderful heads for a *Meister Hämmerlein* show, and also two hands therefor which were hollow within so that one might control them by this means with the fingers of each hand." This is the earliest detailed record we possess relative to the German hand

FIG. 306. FRENCH MARIONETTE THEATRE
End of the eighteenth century. Contemporary engraving

puppets of this period, and for the first time, too, this record gives them a special name. In 1744 a lengthier definition is provided by Frisch—"*Meister Hämmerlein*: the kind of puppet-show

FIG. 307. FRENCH KASPERLE THEATRE
From an engraving. About 1820

where the hand is put inside the puppet, thereby moving the body, head, and arms; it is the *Pickelhäring* ['pickle herring']." This puppet seems generally "to have had an ugly masked face."

FIG. 308. KASPERLE THEATRE IN PARIS
About 1825

Pickelhäring is a comic figure, also called Hanswurst and, in the next century, Kasperle; the last-mentioned provided the whole show with the name by which it is still known.

The most famous member of this family is the youngest of the line, the English Punch. His name is simply Pulcinella or

316

PUNCH-AND-JUDY SHOW IN FLORENCE
Lasinio. About 1780

Punchinello adapted to the English tongue, though he seems to have taken a roundabout journey to England instead of coming straight from Italy. Whether the Stuarts brought him back with them from France at the Restoration or William of Orange introduced him from Holland is not certain; at any rate, he first appeared after the Revolution of 1688, to become, with his

FIG. 309. PORTABLE MARIONETTE THEATRE
French lithograph. About 1830

dog Toby, a favourite of the English people. In the course of years his character must have changed, for in 1697 Addison could still describe him as a jolly, somewhat blustering petticoat-hunter in French style.

In the eighteenth century the puppet theatre played a considerable *rôle* in the public life of all civilized countries—a fact amply proved by the severe attacks it met with from those who belonged to the regular stage. If they could damage it and restrain its annoying competition they did so; and if they could not succeed in that they at least slandered it and sought to discredit it in contemporary opinion. How the Parisian regular stage gave performances alongside the puppet theatres has already been seen, and the same was true of England. There the incessant attacks of the Puritans at last succeeded in getting the theatres closed, but the marionettes were overlooked or considered harmless, and so were allowed to continue their performances—whence great indignation. About the year 1577 Geoffrey Fenton had written a book to demonstrate that the puppet-showmen were as unworthy creatures as the regular actors. The actors, for their part, complained loudly because the marionettes were specially favoured. In 1642 the company of Drury Lane complained of the special privilege shown toward the puppet stage and demanded that it should be closed. In eighteenth-century France too the actors did all they could to render the showmen's life difficult. These were not permitted, for example, to produce their puppets with dialogue—only monologues were allowed, and even then not spoken in a natural voice, but distorted by means of the *sifflet-pratique*.

Their affairs in Germany were no better. To the ranks of their enemies naturally belonged all those concerned with the opera and the regular theatres, such as the Hamburg barrister Barthold Feind, to whom the opera of his native town is so deeply indebted, Count Seeau, the director of the Court theatre at Munich, who refused to permit the puppet theatre to play at the annual fairs, and, toward the end of the century, the historian of the Hamburg theatre, Schütz, who calls them "miseries," dangerous and demoralizing. "The pitiful trick puppets worked by vagabonds with thumb and forefinger"—that is to say, the Kasperle theatre—is attacked by him with special hatred. The vulgarity and obscenity in which the showmen indulged alarmed the clergy. When Sebastian di Scio played *Faust* at Berlin in the first years of the century his success was so great that Philipp Jakob Spener asked for an order of prohibition from the authorities, on the ground that he considered it dangerous for the devil to be conjured up in this piece and made to appear on the stage. The many enemies of the marionette stage had a temporary success, at any rate in Prussia. On June 3, 1794, the provincial authorities were instructed to drive off all unlicensed marionette-showmen, for "these unworthy vagabonds were seeking to win applause by indecent innuendoes."

Nevertheless the puppet stage proved itself competent to deal with all attacks made on it. It remained popular, since, in Germany, as in England and France, everything the regular theatre excluded or, at least, tried to exclude—as, for example, the German Hanswurst—took refuge on this convenient stage.

# MARIONETTES

The puppet-showmen as a class became so numerous that in the eighteenth century they were formed into a kind of guild with their own special regulations and customs; one peculiar rule was that none of the play texts was to be written out, all, including the prompter's stage directions, having to be learned by heart. As a theatrical director wore a red vest to distinguish him from the rest of the troupe, so the puppet-showmen adopted a characteristic attire, consisting of a large black cloak and a broad-brimmed hat. Many of the principal showmen gave performances alternately with human actors and with puppets, which seemingly were fairly large (Matthison notes that the marionettes at Strasbourg were half life-size); automata too were introduced, and surprise turns were given special attention. On one puppet stage the chief attraction was a soldier with a pipe in his mouth who puffed out the smoke. Reibehand, who gave performances in Hamburg from 1728 to 1752, introduced in *The Prodigal Son* a hanged man who fell in pieces from the gallows, put himself together again, and then pursued the hero. It was he who got up the *Öffentliche Enthauptung des Fräulein Dorothea* (*The Public Beheading of Miss Dorothea*); after the execution applause broke out, so the head was put back on the puppet, and it was decapitated once more. In the rich commercial towns, such as Frankfort, the puppet theatres were brilliantly fitted up and equipped with all sorts of technical devices, the finest of these being that of Robertus Schaffer at the Liebfrauenberg, which was patronized even by high society. The Margrave of Baden-Durlach had Court players in his service for his marionettes; in 1731 at Berlin their director, Titus Maas, gave a performance of *The History of Prince Menschikoff*, a highly realistic theme. In his Hungarian castle at Eisenstadt Prince Nicholas Esterhazy established a puppet stage the richness of which was in keeping with its owner's wealth. For this Pietro Travaglia made the artistically formed figures, and between 1773 and 1780 Joseph Haydn wrote for them five operettas: *Philemon and Baucis, Genoveva, Dido, La Vengeance accomplie*, and *La Maison brulée*. These were presented in pantomime on the stage, with the singers behind the scenes. Esterhazy's puppet theatre won such fame that Maria Theresa requested a special performance to be given by it at Schönbrunn.

Haydn himself had a small marionette theatre and also wrote the operetta of *Le Diable boiteux* for Bernardone's puppet stage at the Kärntner Tor, in Vienna. At Mannheim in 1767 the officers of the Palatine regiments established a marionette theatre, the dolls for which were made by the Court sculptor

Egel. It was opened with Molière's *Don Juan*; as in all the Court theatres of that time entry was gratuitous. In Vienna and Hamburg the puppet stages seem to have been more beloved than anywhere else, but even in Augsburg, which he visited in 1781, Friedrich Nicolai found at a marionette performance "much better society than he had expected."

We must not forget what a great influence the marionettes have had upon the poets. In the Christmas of 1753 Goethe

FIG. 310. GOETHE'S PUPPET THEATRE
*Goethe Museum, Frankfort*

and his sister received from their grandmother a puppet theatre which he enthusiastically recalls in *William Meisters Wanderjahre* and in *Dichtung und Wahrheit*. He himself wrote for the puppets *Das Jahrmarktfest zu Plundersweilen*, and in his first years at Weimar he was still working for them. Above all, however, "the honour is unquestionably due to the wooden theatre of the Frankfort marionettes for having sowed in the soul of the young artist the seeds which later flourished into the most important poem in German." Assuredly Leibrecht is in the right when he says that this does not cast honour on the contemporary puppet-show, for Goethe's *Faust* stands above the puppet-comedies just as the moon stands above the pond in which its light is reflected. Yet *Faust* was and has remained for the following century the piece by which the puppet-showmen have gathered their largest audiences. In Vienna it was presented, with inserted *arias* and ballets, oftener than *Don Juan*, which was *Faust's* only rival. Every puppet-showman had his own *Faust* which he

320

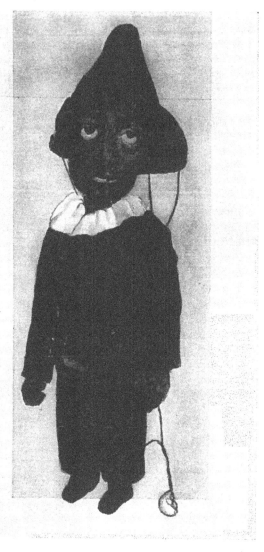

FIGURE OF KASPERLE, EIGHTEENTH CENTURY
From Karl Gröber's *Kinderspielzeug* (Deutscher Kunstverlag,
Berlin)
*Landesmuseum, Linz*

himself had adapted to meet his own requirements. Scheible in the fifth volume of his *Kloster* has published five different texts which had been written for Ulm, Augsburg, Strasbourg, and Cologne. For the success of these pieces we know the reason, which was that the chief *rôle* was taken by Hanswurst. Hanswurst, who became Kasperle at Vienna in the beginning of the eighteenth century, was always the best figure among the

FIG. 311. FAUST AND KASPERLE
Puppet-figures by Guido Bonneschky. About 1840

marionettes. He moved his head, arms, feet, and hands; he rolled his eyes; he could open his mouth and stick out his tongue. He improvised as much as he wanted, and offered the public what they delighted in most—cudgelling, vulgarity, and still again vulgarity—as much as their hearts could desire.

Magnin regards the first quarter of the eighteenth century as the most brilliant period for the marionettes in France. Men of spirit and wit, such as Lesage and Piron, wrote jolly pieces for the puppet theatres in which they indulged in mischievous sallies at the regular stage. The actor and poet Favart, who later became famous for his vaudevilles, first made his appearance in 1732 with marionettes which had the right of entry to Court, since the Duchesse du Maine, a daughter of Louis XIV, had introduced them in the entertainments she arranged at the Château de Sceaux. In one piece she had ridicule cast on the Académie; this presented Polichinelle pleading his right to be elected one of the forty immortals. The Duchesse du Maine and the Duchesse de Berry also produced farces at Versailles in which the victories of Marshal Villars were rendered ridiculous, a peculiar expression of admiration for a successful commander-in-chief. The marionettes conquered the *salons* of high society when the cardboard figures, the *pantins* mentioned already, came into fashion, and puppet-plays were improvised everywhere. The marionettes even intruded into Cirey, otherwise consecrated to purely philosophical speculations, and led Voltaire himself, as Mme de Graffigny writes in 1738, to associate himself with them and write verses for them.

From the fifties of the century public interest in the marionettes declined. Whether the players failed in fitting wit and humour, or whether preference was given to the surprising effects of mechanical devices, at any rate a change was sought for. About 1740–50 the puppet stage was imitating the much-admired scenic work of the painter engaged at the Paris Opéra, Servandoni, but the shadow theatre, newly introduced through the rococo passion for everything Chinese, supplanted for a time the simpler charm of the familiar marionettes. In the second half of the eighteenth century the Parisian puppet theatres moved over from the suburbs and from the markets to the boulevards so as to be nearer the public threatening to abandon them, and thus able to remind it of their presence. The terrible years of the Revolution did not spare them, harmless though they were. Camille Desmoulins relates that scenes were presented on the puppet stage in which Polichinelle ended his life under the guillotine; the revolutionaries, however, went even further, for in 1794 a married couple were beheaded only because their Polichinelle was considered too aristocratic and had ridiculed *Père Duchesne*—the *Rote Fahne* of the period.

In this epoch the hand-puppet theatre developed in France a distinct characteristic type of its own—Guignol—although that originated not in Paris, but in Lyons. Its inventor was Laurent Mourguet, who gave it its name, the etymology of which is uncertain. Mourguet provided Guignol with the costume of a silk-worker, and made him speak in the dialect of the common people. His hero is ignorant, but acute of ear; unscrupulous, but ready to assist; good-hearted, always in good humour, sceptical to the last degree, but when he is flattered easily led by the nose. His partner was at first Polichinelle until Mourguet invented the *rôle* of Gnafron, a character rich in not very refined jests. With the aid of a friend to whom he gave the *scenarios* Mourguet, who died in Vienna in 1844 at the age of ninety-nine, himself wrote all the pieces he played. They were considered

witty, and possessed to a high degree the flavour of Lyonese
life—a fact which guaranteed their continuous success.

In England the marionettes gained the right of entry to Court
under Charles II. From Pepys' diary we learn that on October
8, 1662, they performed at Whitehall. On August 30, 1667,

FIG. 312. ENGLISH PUPPET THEATRE
Designed by B. Pollock, with a scene, *The Silver Palace*. About 1860
Presented to the Victoria and Albert Museum by
Mrs Gabrielle Enthoven

Pepys visited a fair and to his astonishment met Lady Castle-
maine, the King's mistress, in a puppet theatre where the play
of *Patient Grizell* was being given. Themes from legend and the
Bible remained popular in England throughout the whole of
the next century, but the puppets also gave dances of jigs,
sarabands, and quadrilles. One of the most eminent puppet-
showmen in England was that Powell whom Addison and Steele
popularized in their weekly papers. He appeared alternately

in London and in Bath during the season. His strength lay in burlesque of the Italian opera, a dramatic form undoubtedly challenging satire. The dramas of Shakespeare too were adopted by the puppet stage. Samuel Johnson, whose judgment was so deeply esteemed by contemporaries, found that the marionettes played much better than living actors, giving it as his opinion that *Macbeth* was much more impressive in the puppet theatre than on the regular stage.

The eighteenth century was the period when Punch flourished in England; at this time he was the representative of English folk humour with all its degeneracy and peculiar qualities. Punch must very soon—certainly by 1731, when he is described just as he is to-day—have assumed the appearance by which he is recognized now—the bird-like features, with the huge nose, the hunches in front and at the back (for physical deformities always amuse the mob, who find afflictions of this kind ridiculous), and lastly his peaked cap and the ruff round his neck. By 1713 he had already a permanent theatre in Covent Garden—a proof of his popularity. Swift with good reason attributes this popularity to the effrontery and shamelessness of his *rôle*, but a type which receives as well as gives so many cudgellings is sure of applause. Just as no German play, however serious its theme might be, could be counted complete without its Hanswurst, so in England Punch had to appear even in Biblical dramas if these were to prove popular. Thus, in 1703 he played a part in a puppet-play *The Creation of the World* and in 1709 in a comedy *The Flood*. Yet there was a difference between the two characters. Hanswurst is a dull wag who thinks he is witty when he wallows in the mud of vulgarities and double meanings, while Punch out-devils the devil. To-day when Punch is named we think of the famous journal which bears his name, but we must not associate its polite tone with the old hand puppet. The latter's speech and action were of an unparalleled brutality; Magnin draws a comparison between the Punch of that time and Henry VIII. Punch openly speaks of atrocities, and revels in things repulsive and disgusting. He delights in paradoxes, and expresses his opinion without respect to propriety and good manners; the word 'shame' does not enter into his vocabulary. At the end of the century the puppet company was enriched by the appearance of Judy, Punch's wife, who from that time on remained a permanent member of the English troupe of hand puppets.

If civilized nations regarded the puppet stage only as a secondary kind of entertainment, the marionette theatre formed for a long time the only dramatic art among nations without their own culture, as, for example, the Czechs. In the eighteenth century Josef Winizky and Matthias Kopeckj were famous puppet-showmen among them. They were forced to write their plays themselves, owing to the fact that none except the uneducated populace understood the Bohemian tongue.

# VII

## MARIONETTES IN THE NINETEENTH CENTURY

THE early years of the nineteenth century saw German literature in the grip of a romantic sentiment which brought to the puppet theatre a still greater interest, if that were possible, than Goethe had with his attachment to classic standards. The spokesmen of the new movement, who were also responsible for the new science of Germanistics, regarded everything from a genuinely national point of view. Arnim and Brentano collected the folk-songs which still lived among the peasantry, and hoped to be able to draw materials from the puppet repertoires suitable for their purposes. They believed that the puppet theatres had a connexion with the old mysteries, and thought of the treasures which might be discovered there. These, however, did not materialize, and those things which the young poets themselves composed for the marionettes did not get very far. Like the puppet-shows given in the houses of Brentano, Achim von Arnim, etc., these were unknown outside the narrow circle of those who participated in the performances. The greatest talent for this *genre* was possessed perhaps by E. T. A. Hoffmann, whose simple humour was peculiarly adapted for the marionette style, which always hovers on the border-lines of humanity. Yet, although he occupied himself much with them in his house, he has left nothing of this kind behind him. He possessed, as Ölenschläger records, a cupboard full of marionettes which he loved to manipulate, and derived great amusement from startling his guests with them.

In various *feuilletons* there has been mentioned the "brilliant study" which Heinrich von Kleist dedicated to the marionette theatre. This reference, however, shows only that the writers had heard but half the story, and that they could not have read the article in question. This appeared under the title *Concerning the Marionette Theatre* on December 12–15, 1810, in a Berlin evening paper, but on account of the severe theatre censorship it was written purposely in a very obscure and cautious style, and has really nothing to do with the puppet theatre. The poet starts with the thesis that man, who

FIG. 313. KASPERLE THEATRE
Nineteenth century

had eaten from the tree of knowledge and had thereby lost his instinctive natural life, must return through ever broader,

FIG. 314. FAIR BOOTH, WITH NÜRNBERG PUPPETS AND KASPERLE
Woodcut by A. L. Richter. About 1850

higher, divinely striving knowledge and self-resignation to his lost innocence, regaining paradise after his wandering through the world. At all intermediate positions in this development

328

# MARIONETTES

man remains imperfect; therefore in the theatre as well only the marionette or the god is perfect. From the standpoint gained by these philosophic-æsthetic inquiries Kleist criticizes the Berlin actors and dancers. Had this article not borne so famous a name it would long ago have disappeared from the marionette literature.

The interest of the professional authors of that time is shown by the facts, for example, that August Mahlmann in 1806 published a volume of small satirical dramas for the marionettes and that the Berlin author Julius von Voss also wrote for them. Up to that time the items in the repertoire had been handed down only by oral tradition, and even then they adhered closely to certain themes, the religious pieces such as *Adam and Eve*, *David and Goliath*, *The Prodigal Son*, and *Herod* remaining in vogue up to 1840. Schütz and Dreher, whose stage was set up in Berlin and Potsdam, gave performances, in the old style, of *Faust*, *Don Juan*, ancient legends like *Genoveva*, and biblical stories like *Esther and Haman*, *Judith and Holofernes*, and *The Prodigal Son*. In the first quarter of the century the puppet theatre of Geisselbrecht was regarded as the finest in Germany. This man, a mechanic by trade, had come from Vienna and performed all over Germany. It was he who served as model for the puppet-showman in Theodor

FIG. 315. ANCIENT FIGURE OF A DEVIL FROM WINTER'S COLOGNE PUPPET THEATRE
From *Das Rheinische Puppenspiel*, by Carl Niessen

Storm's novel *Päle Poppenspäler*. Countess Line Egloffstein wrote on December 14, 1809, from Weimar to her sister Julie about his entertainments.

> Yesterday at last we saw our charming marionettes, and were so bewitched that we got quite foolish about them. Scenic changes and decorations were worthy of the greatest admiration, and the little Arlequin was so lovable he deserved to be kissed. He eats and drinks like a man, smokes his pipe, loves his Colombine, and charms every one who comes his way.

The writer of this letter betrays in her description what the public enjoyed—the lifelike appearance of the puppets. Geissel-

329

brecht's marionettes could even move their eyes, cough, and spit! These ingeniously constructed figures were augmented by trick puppets, or metamorphoses, invented by Franz Genesius,

FIG. 316. HÄNNESCHEN STAGE OF THE OLDEST STYLE
From *Das Rheinische Puppenspiel*, by Carl Niessen

FIG. 317. PEASANTS OF THE OLD COLOGNE HÄNNESCHEN THEATRE

which, by means of a certain mechanism, could be made to change their appearance; a girl dancer was thus turned into a balloon, a pumpkin into a man dancer, and a mushroom into a dwarf. Geisselbrecht's figures, too, could discharge flint-lock guns, draw their swords, pour out wine, etc.

# MARIONETTES

The marionettes provided each audience with what it desired. At Berlin in 1851 104 consecutive performances were given of a silly farce by Silvius Landsberger, *Don Carlos, the Infanta of*

FIG. 318. NOTABLES OF THE OLD COLOGNE HÄNNESCHEN THEATRE
From *Das Rheinische Puppenspiel*, by Carl Niessen

FIG. 319. THE PEASANTS OF THE COLOGNE PUPPET-PLAY
Figures from the theatre of H. Königsfeld, junior. After old models
From *Das Rheinische Puppenspiel*, by Carl Niessen

*Spain*, while the marionette stage of Weyermann at Ulm was on such a high level that the famous historian of that city, Professor Hassler, called it the "National Theatre of Ulm." The director realized where success was to be gained; he attired his puppets in

331

Ulm dress and made them speak in the Ulm dialect—types of
such a kind as were calculated to move, delight, and inspire his
audiences. Cologne owes its most original creation to the director Christoph Winter, who founded the Hänneschen Theatre in
1802, the continuous success of which is directly traceable to its
strongly marked local characteristics. The inventor of the type,

FIG. 320. HÄNNESCHEN IN THE WEHRGASSE
Painting by Passavanti
From *Das Rheinische Puppenspiel*, by Carl Niessen

who died in 1872, at ninety-six years of age, possessed a peculiar
talent for making situations and persons ridiculous without
giving offence, and for creating a comic scene without having
recourse to vulgarity. His types included Hänneschen, Marieze-
bill, Neighbour Tunnes, introducing in a jovial but harmless
manner institutions of the town of Cologne and casting a satirical
light thereon. He graduated his expressions according to the
audience he had before him, dividing these into three classes—
children, adults, and Sunday visitors. To the last-mentioned
he spoke in the roughest terms. All his plays had to end happily

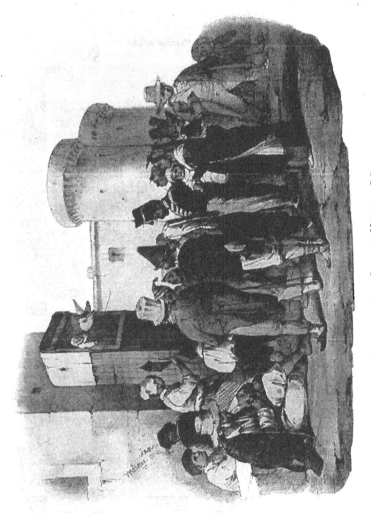

PUNCH-AND-JUDY SHOW IN NAPLES, 1828
Mörner

—even the most tragic of dramas, such as *Romeo and Juliet*, which closed with the marriage of the lovers. An attempt made by Millowitsch to transfer the Hänneschen Theatre to the regular stage met with disaster.

FIG. 321. POLITICAL CARICATURE
Cologne Hänneschen Theatre. May 1848. Sketch by Kleinenbroich

In Hamburg the hand-puppet theatre flourished in the middle of the nineteenth century, when Johann E. Rabe was yet a boy. It owed much to the actor Küper, who was specially skilful in giving his puppets characteristic local touches. He abandoned the hunchback and the large nose which the Hamburg Kasperle had inherited from Punch, and gave him instead of those the face of a Hamburg workman with a corresponding dress—a red

333

jerkin trimmed with yellow, blue trousers with yellow stripes, a white collar, and a blue peaked cap. Küper made his puppets, to which belonged Kasperle's partner, Snobelbeck, speak in the Hamburg dialect; indeed, he even set out to present all the five

FIG. 322. POLITICAL CARICATURE
Cologne Hänneschen Theatre. May 1848. Sketch by Kleinenbroich
The man with the broken sceptre and the bottle of liquor is supposed to be
Frederick William IV.

different forms of speech in the town which corresponded to the various parishes. This attention paid to the Low German speech was of considerable service to Rabe. Küper died in 1893, and when on his death-bed he ordered his puppets to be burned.

Where the showmen lacked ability to give their shows the support of local characteristics their performances were confined to a repertoire which had to count on the lowest instincts to

334

ensure a certain receipt. There was always Faust's descent into hell, together with many dramas based on pieces played on the regular stage—*Das Kätchen von Heilbronn (Kitty of Heilbronn)*, *Der Freischütz*, *Alpenkönig und Menschenfeind (The King of the Alps and the Enemy of Man)*, *Die Reise um die Erde in 80 Tagen (The Journey round the World in Eighty Days)*, *Der Müller und sein Kind (The*

FIG. 323. DOCTOR FAUST AS A VILLAGE BARBER AND MEPHISTO
AS A CHIMNEY-SWEEP
Schmid's Marionette Theatre, Munich

*Miller and his Child)*, *Der Fall Clemençeau (The Clemençeau Case)*, and so on. Next came the blood-and-thunder element—*Die Totenglocke um Mitternacht (The Death Bell at Midnight)*, *Die Leichenräuber von London (The London Body-snatchers)*, *Der Mord im Weinkeller (The Murder in the Wine-cellar)*, *Die Räuberschenke im Wiener Wald (The Robbers' Tavern in the Viennese Forest)*, *Die Teufelsmühle am Wiener Berg (The Devils' Mill on the Viennese Hills)*, etc. The announcement of scenic transformations proved always a special attraction. In 1899 a bill announced *Das Jochkreuz oder der Protzenbauer von Zehnerhof (The Cross on the Mountain Ridge, or the Insolent Peasant of Zehnerhof)*, a rural folk

335

piece, with the promise of "real water and rain," and in the same year *Der Lumpenball oder der verhängnisvolle Affe* (*The Beggars' Ball, or the Unhappy Monkey*) was advertised "with fireworks."

FIG. 324. SPANISH DANCERS
Schmid's Marionette Theatre, Munich

FIG. 325. KASPERLE AND HIS WIFE
Schmid's Marionette Theatre, Munich

Many of the old puppet-plays have been collected by Karl Engel, Kralik, and Winter. From these it is evident that the showmen, for example those of Lower Austria, while keeping to the old texts, fundamentally modernized them, bringing them

336

FIG. 326. VENETIAN MARIONETTE THEATRE, FIRST HALF OF THE EIGHTEENTH CENTURY

*Victoria and Albert Museum*

Y

into line with the popular Viennese folk songs; they thus loved the songs of Girardi. The puppet theatre in the nineteenth century found only one genuine poetic writer—namely, Count Pocci, whose activities were determined by the fortunes of the Munich marionette theatre. In 1858 the Bavarian general Karl Wilhelm von Heydeck handed over a small marionette stage to Josef Schmid. The latter opened his theatre at the Maffeianger, and

FIG. 327. VENETIAN MARIONETTE THEATRE, FIRST HALF OF
THE EIGHTEENTH CENTURY
*Victoria and Albert Museum*

in 1900 moved to a house which the city of Munich built for him in the Blumenstrasse. Schmid died in 1912, at the age of ninety-one. It is curious to notice that the manipulation of puppets seems to guarantee long life! This puppet stage owed a great deal of its success to the lovely compositions of Count Franz Pocci, who wrote for it in all forty-one pieces, which he collected in the six volumes of his amusing *Komödienbüchlein*. Pocci possessed an unconquerable humour which, although it is satirical, comes always from the heart, and not from the head. One cannot be annoyed with him, for the sarcasm which he loves to bestow on the official and scholarly world only tickles—

ITALIAN MARIONETTES
From Schmid's Marionette Theatre
*Bayerisches National-Museum, Munich*

it does not wound. His Kasperl Larifari is a jester who draws his comic spirit essentially from the contrast afforded between his fully prosaic mind, based definitely on reality, and the world of fairy-tale in which he is set by the poet. Pocci brought the puppet-play to a high level; all that old innuendo is completely banished in his pieces. His dialogue and verse are as naïve and

FIG. 328. VENETIAN MARIONETTES FROM THE MUSEO CIVICO, VENICE
Eighteenth century
*Photo C. Naya*

natural as his way of thinking; he understands the people even while he remains above them.

Josef Schmid, who through a series of decades was much honoured by young and old as "Papa Schmid," had an extra-ordinary sense for the technical as well as for the emotional side of his art. The many thousand puppets which he made were charmingly constructed and clothed with great taste. For the parts spoken behind the scenes and for the working of the puppets he had a skilled company of seven men. Among his per-formances he included operas with choruses and solos. Rapidly the marionette theatre under his direction became for Munich a genuine cultural element such as may not be underestimated.

In Italy the marionette theatre for long has maintained a position not far different from that held by the regular stage. Its success was assisted by the theatrical propensities of the people. It is not therefore mere chance that the most successful

FIG. 329. VENETIAN MARIONETTES FROM THE MUSEO CIVICO, VENICE
Eighteenth century
*Photo C. Naya*

puppet-showmen in Germany, England, and France have come of Italian stock. By the middle of the eighteenth century Abbé Dubos saw grand opera produced in Italy by means of marionettes, and the custom of presenting large shows of this kind is still maintained. The *fantoccini* of Milan used to give performances of long plays, and are said to have produced something unique in the way of ballets. The *burattini* in Rome took into their repertoire those sentimental melodramas which were in great fashion in the nineteenth century, indulging too in ballets; for the latter the puppets were compelled to wear little blue tights, similar to those which the law enjoined on the living *ballerinas*. While the regular theatres in Rome were open only during the carnival, the puppet theatres were allowed to give shows the whole year round. There they took over Rossini's operas and presented, too, a number of realistic shows. Charles Dickens saw *The Tragedy at St Helena, or the Death of Napoleon,*

FIG. 330. VENETIAN MARIONETTES FROM THE MUSEO CIVICO, VENICE
Eighteenth century
*Photo C. Naya*

played by puppets, and was highly pleased with the performance. In the drawing-room the marionettes lost all their shyness. At a private gathering at Florence Stendhal witnessed a performance of Machiavelli's comedy *Mandragola*, an unequivocal avowal of libertinism, while in Naples, under the same conditions, he saw a political satire, at that time a truly dangerous undertaking.

The Italian Kasperle theatre developed in different centres characteristic types which personified the special nature of the inhabitants. In Milan there was Girolamo, in Turin Gianduja,

341

in Rome Cassandrino, who did not hesitate to quiz heartily the almighty *monsignori* of the papal city. The Italians maintained their pre-eminence throughout the entire century; as late as 1893 the Prandi troupe won great applause in London. Of the Spanish marionettes it is recorded only that they remained true to their half-romantic, half-religious repertoire of olden times.

FIG. 331. VENETIAN MARIONETTES FROM THE MUSEO CIVICO, VENICE
Eighteenth century
*Photo C. Naya*

When, for example, *The Death of Seneca* was represented at Valencia in 1808 the blood flowed in streams (by means of red ribbons), while at the close the heathen philosopher went heavenward and made a Christian profession of faith.

The French puppet theatre could boast of pre-eminence over that of any other European country; eminent writers and artists espoused its cause or availed themselves of the opportunity afforded by it for realizing their ideals. The wandering marionettes played *Paul et Virginie* and *Atala* so long as the authors of these pieces were in fashion; then they turned to real events, such as *The Capture of the Malakoff in the Crimean War*. Apparently they did not rise above the level of the usual audience at the fairs. As in Germany and Italy the hand-puppet theatre created in diverse towns its characteristic types—types for which the *gamins*, with their colloquial tone, were taken as models. Thus,

FIG. 332. KASPERLE THEATRE IN ITALY
Engraving of the eighteenth century

Lafleur arose in Amiens—a figure said to have been invented by the workman Louis Bellette, who made him speak in the dialect of Picardy; from Lille came Jacques, and others sprang up in different centres. The famous Guignol at Lyons was carried on after the death of its founder by Louis Josserand and his family, but the most renowned French 'master' of the puppet-show in the nineteenth century was Anatole Cressigny in Paris. He was an artist in the full sense of the word. He himself wrote the *scenario* of his pieces, improvising the actual words during the

343

performance; he carved the puppets' heads with his own hands; and he is said to have been such a brilliant player that he could speak dialogue in twenty different tones. He died in 1893. In France the puppet-show was a popular amusement. At

FIG. 333. KASPERLE THEATRE IN VENICE
Etching by Zompini. 1785

Paris in 1874 there were ten booths, or 'castellets,' measuring about 2 m. square, each equipped with twelve to fourteen puppets. These were stationed in the Champs-Élysées, the Luxembourg gardens, and the Buttes Chaumont, and entertained their public with cudgellings, generally meted out to all representatives of civic authority. Rabe states that a puppet-show in the gardens of the Tuileries before 1870 could count on Sunday takings of 400 francs; Anatole made as much as 100 francs daily.

A great, indeed a passionate, lover of the hand puppets was George Sand, who in one of her novels, *L'Homme de Neige,* gives the preference to them when compared with the stringed marionettes on the ground that the latter produce a less satis-

FIG. 334. KASPERLE THEATRE IN THE RECEPTION ROOM OF THE
CONVENT (DETAIL)
J. Guardi
*Museo Correr, Venice*

factory impression in that they have a resemblance to human beings. The poetess established a complete puppet theatre in her *château* at Nohant in 1847: its history she has related in her *Dernières Pages.* Her son Maurice carved the heads, carefully but crudely, with close observation of everything that came within his experience. They were painted in oils without varnish and provided with real hair and beards; their eyes were of glass or merely indicated by black varnish, with a nail as the pupil—the latter is said to have been the more effective. By 1872 there had been presented at this theatre 120 plays, involving the use of 125 puppets, all clothed by George Sand. Generally only a *scenario* was prepared, the dialogue being improvised. The various items in the repertoire were published in 1890 by Maurice Sand; these included many parodies and skits on popular authors of the period. Another private puppet theatre like that at Nohant was established by the famous singer Duprez in 1864 at his estate in Valmondois. He made his puppets perform operatic travesties, and was given permission to produce them before the royal couple in the Tuileries. In 1861 Duranty opened in the gardens of the Tuileries a puppet theatre for which the sculptor Leboeuf made the figures. He wrote his own plays, which he published in a collected edition in 1880. They were, however, much too highbrow to be appreciated by the crowd. They had no success, and the little booth disappeared. Strange to relate, the Théâtre Érotique de la Rue de la Santé, established in 1862, fared no better, in spite of the fact that it was indecent enough to suit Parisian taste. Tissérand wrote the cynical plays presented there, and Lemercier de Neuville made the puppets. Although Henri Monnier, Théodore de Banville, Champfleury, Paul Féval, and Bizet supported this little theatre, it lasted for only one year. By 1863 it also had vanished. The publisher Poulet-Malassis wrote its history, for which F. Rops, whose talent well suited his subject, provided the illustrations. In the year that the Théâtre Érotique closed its hardly opened doors Lemercier de Neuville started a puppet theatre of his own—the Pupazzi. At the start his figures were merely flat, sharply silhouetted puppets, but afterward, with Gustave Doré's assistance, he replaced these by rounded and clothed hand puppets. Lemercier manipulated them—played, spoke, and sang, besides himself writing the plays. These were exceedingly witty comedies, characterized by a satirical tone, in which appeared various popular public characters of his day, such as Thiers, Jules Favre, Victor Hugo, Dumas Fils, Émile de Girardin. In all he composed 120 plays of this kind.

An entirely different type of theatre was projected by Henri Signoret. He made puppets worked by strings from below. The figures ran on deeply grooved rails, the heads, arms, and legs being set in motion by strings passed through the body of the puppets. Each figure had to be controlled by a mechanic, with another person singing or speaking. The scenery was painted by Rochegrosse. The inventor of this show had his first great success in June 1888 at the Petit Théâtre with *The Birds* of Aristophanes. His aims then flew high; he desired to perform more of the world's classics, making his puppets give performances of Cervantes, Molière, Shakespeare, and even Roswitha, but the public did not show much appreciation of his efforts. When the charm of novelty vanished Signoret was forced to close his theatre, in 1892. Two artists who called themselves Dickson

MARIONETTES
Walter Trier

and John Hewelt, but who in reality were two brothers of French extraction named Alfred and Charles de Saint-Genois, also invented special puppets for their productions. Alfred created a figure which was attached to his body, so that he could use both hands for manipulating it, and Charles made marionettes the strings of which were moved both from above and from below. The puppets danced like the Sisters Barrison or the

FIG. 335. THE MARIONETTES OF HENRI SIGNORET
Behind the stage. Paris. 1892

Otéros and spoke like Yvette Guilbert, and Maindron could find only one thing wrong with them, that they were too exact and left no opportunity for the unexpected. Both brothers had been stimulated by the English illusionist Thomas Holden, whose puppets were a combination of marionettes and automata. They behaved with such vitality as to create complete illusion, but in Lemercier's judgment their technical perfection was a fault, for they appealed to the eye and not to the soul, and thus possessed no individuality.

The Walloons are great friends of the marionettes. About 1900 there were fifteen puppet theatres in Brussels alone, some with comparatively large stages and often with hundreds of puppets. They presented countless sets; the costumes were

347

rich, single puppets costing between thirty and forty francs. They played still the old legends, such as *The Four Sons of Aymon*, alongside plays by Maeterlinck. The puppet-figure here corresponding to Hanswurst is Woltje, a contraction meaning 'little Walloon,' who is introduced into all the plays, be they comic or tragic.

# VIII

## THE SHADOW THEATRE IN THE ORIENT

HITHERTO we have been tracing the development of the puppet stage in its various aspects up to the threshold of the modern period. Before going further and attempting to give an account of its present position we must cast a glance at the non-European puppet theatres, which unquestionably have had a real influence on the marionette art of the Old World.

First of all comes the shadow theatre, which originated in the Far East, and entered Europe during the rococo period, at the time when China was the latest fashion. The shadow stage does not deal, like the marionette theatre, with rounded figures, but only with their shadows. Its technique is closer to the film than to the puppet theatre, since the art of the film also works, not with three-dimensional objects, but only with their two-dimensional representations. As a form of artistic expression it stands very high. "It is the art form," says Georg Jacob very prettily, "which approaches nearest the poet's dream, the creative power which reaches consummation in a waking dream; it can therefore reflect the poetic conception in all its freshness and original form, vainly striven after otherwise." Its origin is to be sought in China, where, during the Han period, in the reign of Emperor Wu (140–86 B.C.), it arose out of magical celebrations. Its scope embraces all possible incidents of the natural and supernatural worlds, intermingled with much grotesque humour and riotous fantasy. The figures are typical of the subject-matter. The good characters have human faces, the evil characters have devils' masks. These were not treated as pure silhouettes; the faces only were outlined in black. The ancient figures were made of bone or horn, transparent and painted; the modern, according to the description of Carl Hagemann, are made of stiff, oiled paper of a golden yellow colour; the bodies are cleverly built up out of a number of small planes, painted in transparent colours and superimposed on one another. Their colour effect, according to the same authority, has a subtle delicacy; for they are said to glow like stained-glass windows. These puppets are about 30 cm. high; the arms are movable at the shoulders,

349

elbows, and wrists, the legs at the thighs and knees, supported and operated by means of bamboos strengthened by wire. The representation of scenery is not without charm: hills, rocks, trees, houses, and pagodas—all are introduced. The ancient

FIG. 336. TRANSPARENT COLOURED CHINESE SHADOW-FIGURE: WA-HI, THE PRIEST OF THE TEMPLE ON THE GOLDEN MOUNTAIN
*Collection of Carl Niessen, Cologne*

texts, of which Berthold Laufer, Wilhelm Grube, and Krebs have published sixty-eight different versions, are of importance for the study of the Chinese language and people and for the history of their culture and literature. Laufer is of the opinion that the shadow-play represents the highest artistic level which dramatic representation ever reached in China, in reference, of course, to a period in the distant past. According to Carl Hagemann, it was once the refined toy of the cultured, an art for the learned, whereas to-day it is merely a hollow relic. People do not now know what to do with the figures; they cannot work them; they are stiff and inflexible or else aimlessly flop about with all their limbs; when several characters have to be introduced the player is helpless. The Chinese shadow theatre no

FIG. 337. LEATHER FIGURE OF A SIAMESE SHADOW-PLAY
*Staatliches Museum für Völkerkunde, Munich*

longer has its own repertoire; it simply takes over that of the regular stage. It has no public, and the educated classes pay no attention to it now. The Völkermuseum in Berlin possesses a complete series of artistically made ancient Chinese shadow-figures which includes fifty-one heads which could be interchanged as desired.

Japan, which is so nearly related to China, also has a shadow theatre. The figures employed there are of a simpler opaque kind, but are, like the others, grotesquely conventionalized.

In Siam the shadow-play is of quite a different sort. There only scenes from the *Ramayana* are shown, but not by means of single figures. On the contrary, the whole scene is drawn on a skin and the contours perforated. Eight to ten, even twenty or more, persons move the skin to and fro in front of a fire, so that its shadow is thrown on a white sheet hung at an angle. Two speakers explain the scene which is being shown, and the whole is accompanied by instrumental music. Although these performances are given only at high festivals, especially at the funerals of notables, a jester is not absent. The Siamese shadow-plays have been influenced by the Javanese, but their figures possess individuality.

The true home of the shadow-play is Java—at least, there it has attained its highest and finest level. Originally it must

FIG. 338. JAPANESE SHADOW-PLAY FIGURE: A BRAMARBAS
*Collection of Carl Niessen, Cologne*

have been a part of the ancient Malayo-Polynesian cult of the Javanese. The representation of the shadows of the old revered heroes and ancestors shows a clear religious colouring; only in later periods has this disappeared and the shadow-play developed into a mere amusement. As all the *termini technici* of the *Wajang* are originally Javanese it is evident that it must have been an art which arose in Java, taking over from the Chinese shadow-play perhaps only a certain amount of stimulus. The *Wajang* is classified according to seven diverse kinds, but of these only two, the *Wajang Beber* and the *Wajang Purwa* in both of its forms —the older *Purwa* and the later *Kerutjil*—fall within the category of the shadow-play. The *Wajang Beber* is a kind of primitive

JAVANESE WAJANG FIGURES

film, consisting of large sheets, 2 m. long and 50 cm. wide, on which the scenes have been painted, rolled on a wooden bar. Seven such rolls of pictures are used in one performance, which usually lasts about one and a half hours without an interval. The theme is generally a *pandji* tale, the story of a prince who experiences mythical adventures. An invisible speaker recites

FIG. 339. WAJANG FIGURE (JAVA)

the story in a monotonous voice, without the accompaniment of music. At one time the *Wajang Beber* was a festival of high importance; later it was played in fulfilment of a vow, generally relating to the illness of a member of the family; and finally it sank into being simply a children's entertainment. When in 1904 Hazeu attended a performance at Jogjakarta he noted that there was hardly any connexion between the picture and the story, the reciter having forgotten the text because he so seldom was called upon for this task.

The *Wajang Purwa*, the native shadow theatre, has been known in Java since the first half of the eleventh century. It takes its themes from the *parwas* of the *Mahabharata, Ramayana*, and the Javanese cosmogony *Manik Maja*. The nature of the pieces is always romantic, generally with a religious flavour. In

z

such cases they are supposed to serve the purpose of driving away or appeasing evil spirits, being then connected with magical and animistic rites. They introduce gods and goddesses, chieftains, princes and princesses, together with the jester Semar and his consort. Abductions are shown and battles with wild beasts, giants, wizards, and demons. The audience can never become satiated with these shows; a performance may last a whole night

FIG. 340. WAJANG FIGURES (JAVA)
(1) Semar. (2) Petruk

through, yet they do not weary. Sometimes, however, the show will continue for a whole week—pleasure and edification going hand in hand. The shadows fall on a flat white umbrella, and are cast by figures which have no equal in originality. As the Javanese people belong to the Mohammedan faith they are prohibited from making puppets in human form, and are thus limited to creatures of the fancy. The *Wajang Purwa* figures, therefore, resemble bizarre and fantastic ornaments in which a ghostly spirit is unintentionally introduced. They find an artistic parallel in certain reliefs from the *Ramayana* in the temple of Panataran in the Blitar district. The human body is in both transformed into an ornament; in the contours straight lines and edges are avoided; all is lost in curves. The figures are represented in sharp profile, with large noses and hair conventionalized in tail-like or spiral forms. Female hips are shown in front view, so that the costume can be thrust far out and the waist-line indicated as very thin. The hands and feet are shown in profile. The puppets possess hardly any likeness to humanity, but their expressions are always varied.

A centuries-old tradition has established certain definite types. Thus, a thin nose, flat brow, narrow, slanting eyes, and compressed lips indicate wisdom and high rank, while a short

FIG. 341. WAJANG FIGURES (JAVA)
(1) Japeng Reges. (2) Prince

thick nose, a rounded brow, round eyes, and broad mouth characterize the hero of powerful strength. The arms can be moved at the shoulders and elbows, and each puppet is provided with an ornamental horn support which the manipulator can control with both hands. There are also figures with movable stomachs—there are even some with exaggerated movable genitals, the phallus often consisting of nine or ten parts, with the glans shaped like a bull's head. Although the style of the figures has been established by tradition, the variety within the narrowly marked boundaries appears unexpectedly great; some *Wajang* shows, indeed, include about two hundred puppets. Originally the plays were designed for men alone; only later were women permitted to witness them, and then only when they sat at the

355

side of the showman, separated from the men. Thus, each of the two sexes sees the puppet from a different side, and this has led to the fact that the figures, originally intended only for the throwing of shadows, are painted and gilded on the side occupied

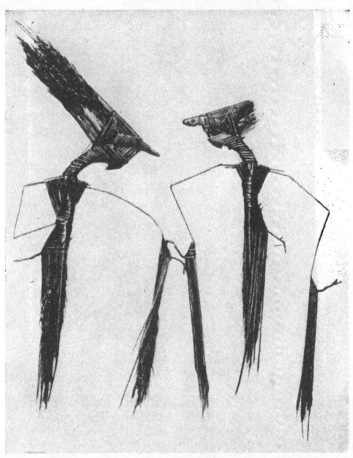

FIG. 342. WAJANG FIGURES MADE OF REEDS (JAVA)

by the showman. The upper part of the body, which is naked, as well as the arms and legs, is gilded; the hair and beard are painted black; the filigree work is coloured red, white, and dark blue. These *Wajang* figures are made of dried and smoothed buffalo hide, an art in which great skill is demanded. The tools consist of a small hammer of tamarind wood and about twenty-five to thirty different little chisels; the time taken over the work

FIG. 343. WAJANG FIGURES (JAVA)

FIG. 344. WAJANG FIGURES (JAVA)

is unlimited, several days being spent in preparing a single puppet. They are consequently very expensive; according to Gronemann, in 1913 one figure, as yet unmounted on supports and neither painted nor gilded, cost sixty Dutch guilders. This

FIGS. 345. JAVANESE WAJANG FIGURES
See opposite
*Collection of Carl Niessen, Cologne*

is explained by the fact that they are chiselled with such inconceivable minuteness, often with an almost web-like effect, so that not only the form and facial expression, but even the ornaments on the head, neck, arms, and feet as well as the finger rings and the details of the dress are clearly defined. The showman, called the *dalang*, works them with oil-lamps over his head. He is player, speaker, and singer at the same time; he is the soul of the whole performance and must know everything. He has to learn by heart the endlessly long legends and be able to improvise

358

WAJANG FIGURE (JAVA)

when required; he has, too, to execute the traditionally conventional movements of the puppets. A bell orchestra, consisting of twenty to twenty-five men, accompanies the performance. The jester has his part to make the people laugh.

FIG. 346. JAVANESE WAJANG FIGURES
The shadows of the puppets in Fig. 345
*Collection of Carl Niessen, Cologne*

Carl Hagemann gives the Javanese shadow-play a high place in the realm of applied art. He writes:

The inconceivable refinement in the outlining and distribution of planes produces a great æsthetic pleasure when we witness these plays. The arrangement of light surfaces within the shadows reveals a delicate certainty in picturesque projection, and the moving lines of the arms create such a striking impression that one may remain in no doubt concerning the artistic worth of the *Wajang*. The most cultured Europeans themselves do not grow

359

weary of watching the whole night long with amazed wonder this dramatic black and white art distinguished by its originality and æsthetic power.

The Javanese *Wajang* spread not only to Siam, but also to Bali, Lombok, and throughout the Malay States to Sumatra and the mainland.

Among the Arabs the shadow-play was known from the

FIG. 347. WAJANG-WONG
PLAYER (JAVA)

FIG. 348. THE MAN WITH
THE PEACOCK
Islamic shadow-play figure from Egypt

eleventh century; in Persia it appeared at the beginning of the twelfth century. Omar Khayyám compares human life with a shadow-drama played in a box, the lighting of which is the sun, and in which we men come and go like puppets. In Egypt the shadow theatre flourished from the twelfth to the eighteenth century, with only one short interruption, when the orthodox Sultan Tschakmak (1438–53) ordered all the puppets belonging to this kind of play to be burned. His successors were of not so severe a disposition. Sultan Selim I, who incorporated Egypt in the Turkish realm in 1517, commanded the last Sultan of the Mamelukes to be hanged, and got this event celebrated by performances in the shadow theatres. The sole relics of dramatic poetry of medieval Arabia are three texts for shadow-plays which the Egyptian physician Ibn Danijal composed in 1267. During the Turkish domination the Arab-Egyptian shadow-play languished and was driven underground by the Turkish shadow-play, the players departing from Cairo for the smaller villages of the Nile delta. The texts, dealing with folk-lore material, were learned by heart by the players and handed down by oral tradition. In this way gradually traditionalized scenes were

FIG. 349. DAHABIYA ON THE NILE
Islamic shadow-play figure from Egypt

established with certain national types. About 1870 Hassan el Quasses founded in Cairo a new Egyptian shadow theatre for which he introduced new figures of the Syrian kind. The old figures had been made by cutting out pieces of leather, the impression being secured not only by the outlines, but also by the thin, transparent, multicoloured skin which was sewn round the bare flat figures. The making of these was a great art. Paul Kahle has unearthed a whole collection in Menzabeh, the latest specimens of which are about two hundred years old. As works of art these are to be compared with Gothic stained-glass windows, but the later ones, no longer indigenously Egyptian, show the whole figure as transparent. The figures used to-day (for the sake of economy often made only of paste-board) are ½ to 1½ m. high and have movable limbs. They are pressed, by means of a palm-leaf rod 1 m. long, against a tightly stretched white sheet attached to the side wings. The repertoire

361

consists of lengthy pieces such as the *Alam u-Ta' adir* spoken of by Kahle, which includes material sufficient to enable it to be played continuously for the twenty-eight evenings of Ramadan. The crocodile play is that most popular in the Egyptian repertoire.

One feature is common to the Oriental plays, to the medieval mysteries, and to the melodramas of the eighteenth century: the comic figure, originally introduced incidentally to provide

FIG. 350. TURKISH SHADOW-PLAY FIGURES ("KARAGÖZ")

laughter for the audience, becomes in the end the pivot of the whole piece. A very good example of this is provided by the Turkish shadow-play. In the thirteenth century a Turkish word signifying 'shadow-play' made its appearance; in the sixteenth century this form of drama was popular in Constantinople, the sultans having their own private troupes, some of them highly renowned. The *Karagöz* originated in the seventeenth century; it was referred to first by the traveller Thevenot, who journeyed in Turkey between 1652 and 1657, and even in Oriental records it is not mentioned at an earlier date. From that time on, however, the shadow-play and Karagöz have become wholly identified; the comic figure has entirely pushed aside the other subject-matter. *Karagöz* means 'black eye,' which practically signifies 'gipsy.' Tradition has it that he was invented by a dervish in Brussa for the purpose of opening the Sultan's eyes to the mismanagement of his ministers, but Luschan assumes that the figure derives from Persia. He is the comedian and bearer of the title *rôle* of the shadow-play named after him. His most striking characteristics are his priapism and a very large turban,

TURKISH SHADOW-PLAY ("KARAGÖZ")

which he loses when he gets a cudgelling. By nature he is a clown, a mixture of Hanswurst and a jester, always a match for educated folks because of his mother wit, in speech more obscene than witty. His partner is Hadschi Eiwad, who represents the cheerful spirits of the better Turks. He also is a clown of lax morals, but not so rough and low as Karagöz, affecting an educated speech, and delighting in the mingling of foreign Arabic and Persian words in his conversation.

Both these *rôles* are stock types, with which are associated a few others who evoke popular laughter—the newly rich peasant, the Jewish merchant, the hypocritical and deceptive dervish, the Frenchman who murders Turkish, the Armenian, the Albanian, etc. The more ancient figures are very carefully cut from camels' skin, and are rich in design and in the planning of their joints. The outlines are sharp; the features have individuality; the colouring is varied, but executed with taste. These are often genuine works of art, whereas the modern figures are badly designed: all proportion is neglected, the painting is flaring with aniline colours, the material used is, as already noted, often only paste-board. The Turkish shadow-figures are very flexible, some of them having their limbs movable at all the joints. They are fixed on thin wooden sticks, by which they are controlled. When the showman, the *karagödschi*, has several puppets to manipulate his job becomes very difficult, for

FIG. 351. TURKISH SHADOW-PLAY FIGURE MADE OF CAMEL SKIN
*Collection of Carl Niessen, Cologne*

he often must keep his hands free in order to mete out blows, rattle castanets, etc. The *Karagöz* was at one time the chief entertainment at Ramadan, but the authorities were averse to the play, and Luschan noted a strong decline in its popularity during the eighties of the last century. The plays themselves fully reflected the physical characteristics of Karagöz; they were generally improvised from a *scenario*, and moved from the uncouth to the vulgar. Since the showman always made use of the popular speech the Government prohibited this, in an endeavour to diminish the audience. Special applause greeted the vocal tricks of the *karagödschi* when he stuttered, nasalized his words, and imitated foreign dialects.

Luschan knew of about fifty Karagöz plays, of which thirty were printed, although the fact that they were so printed did not prevent improvisation. Caustic invective and low wit directed at events and persons of the day constantly appeared here. The *Karagöz* was so dear to the Turkish heart that eventually even

FIG. 352. SARANTIDIS, VAKALO, AND YANIDI
Greek " Karagöz " shadow-play scene
*L'École Medgyès, Paris*

plays taken from the West and translated—no matter how serious they might be—had to be mixed up with comic business before they could gain success. Under Turkish rule the *Karagöz* became popular throughout the Balkans, and passed over to Algiers and Tunis. In Algiers the French suppressed it, suspecting it to be a means for the dissemination of political propaganda. The pitch of indecency was reached in Tunis in the *Karakusch* (*The Self-satisfying Swine*), where such scenes were represented on the stage as the violation of men and women. It is hardly believable that the *Karagöz*, because of its character, did not find its way to Paris long ago; it would have been excellently suited to French taste! And if it had got there, what trouble would have been taken to get it across the Rhine! It is undoubtedly the one thing lacking in the stage life of the German capital.

# IX

## OCCIDENTAL SHADOW THEATRES

EUROPE became acquainted with the shadow-play through the medium of Italy, while the French brought it into fashion as *ombres chinoises*. Georg Jacob, however, has demonstrated that it is to be met with at a much earlier date in Germany, and England too may make claims to priority. Ben Jonson ends his *Tale of a Tub* with a puppet-play in five scenes which are presented behind a transparent curtain in the manner of a shadow-play. A speaker standing in front with a magician's wand explains the action. In the West the figures are always real pure black shadows, no use being made of the Oriental application of coloured pieces. From the middle of the seventeenth century there is frequent mention of shadow-plays on the German stage—at Danzig in 1683, at Frankfort in 1692—often along with marionettes. The theatre manager Ferdinand Beck, who appeared at Frankfort in 1731, introduced between the acts of his melodramas artis-

FIG. 353. CHINESE SHADOW-PLAY:
"LE PONT CASSÉ"
French woodcut. About 1830

tic shadow-plays. In the middle of the eighteenth century a certain Chiarini gave performances of *ombres chinoises* at Hamburg; the figures were attached to strings, at the ends of which rings were tied, the rings going on the fingers of the performer, who manipulated them as if he were playing a piano. The amateur theatres too used to present shadow-plays. In 1781 Goethe got a shadow theatre built in Tiefurt, he himself and

365

Einsiedel preparing the *libretti* for the performances. The subjects dealt with in these earlier experiments are not now known, for the shadow-play could only get a footing in Germany after it had met with approval in Paris. This type of entertainment seems to have been known in Germany at an early date, but the first record we get of it is in the correspondence of Melchior Grimm on August 15, 1770. In 1775 a certain Ambroise opened

FIG. 354. CHINESE SHADOW-PLAY: PARISIAN TYPES
Beginning of the nineteenth century

a theatre of this kind, which in 1776 gave performances in London. In it was displayed a shipwreck in the midst of thunder and lightning, together with various transformation scenes, including a bridge broken into pieces, a scene which from that time on remained popular in the shadow theatre. From 1784 Dominique Séraphin, with his *ombres chinoises perfectionnées*, was a formidable rival of Ambroise. The former's puppets indicated physical features and dress by thin light strips and were much praised. "The puppets," writes Thiéry, in his *Pariser Führer*,

> represent human deportment very naturally. They dance on a tight rope and execute character dances with the greatest precision. Beasts of all kinds make their appearance here and move in their own special ways, and neither the strings nor the wires which hold and manipulate them can be seen.

FIG. 355. PEEPSHOW AFTER AN ITALIAN ENGRAVING
Beginning of the nineteenth century

FIG. 356. LATERNA MAGICA
French engraving. About 1800

Séraphin was much run after, and bore in mind the temper of his period, for from 1789 on he presented only antimonarchical pieces. He died in 1800, but his theatre closed finally only in 1870.

The Romantics loved the shadow theatre as they did the marionettes. Christian Brentano, Achim von Arnim, Justinus Kerner, Tieck, Uhland, and Mörike worked with it, while Count Pocci wrote some pretty pieces for it and designed shadow-figures. Even such an experienced theatre man as Kotzebue

FIG. 357. HOW THE FIGURES OF THE SHADOW THEATRE
ARE MOVED BEHIND THE SCENES
French woodcut. About 1840

could not resist its charm. "His large and small shadow-plays," writes Countess Julie Egloffstein in 1817, "are unique in their kind. He has grasped everything that such things possess of the beautiful, and understands the art of producing great things with limited means." In 1827, indeed, there was a regular shadow theatre in Berlin. The great success of the shadow-play between 1760 and 1830 is closely connected with the fashion for silhouettes, which was then at its height. These were worn as pendants, hung on the walls, painted on furniture and crockery; and in the shadow-play they were welcomed in movable form, accompanied even by speech and song. When the new art of lithography pushed the silhouettes aside, and still more when the mechanically produced photograph completely banished for a time all artistic treatment of such things, the shadow theatre also disappeared. In France Eudel, father of the writer Paul

FIG. 358. THE TEA-PARTY
Movable figures from a shadow-play. About 1830
*Theater-Museum, Munich*

FIG. 359. PICK-A-BACK

FIG. 360. PUNCH WITH A MASK
Movable figure from a shadow-play
About 1830

*Theater-Museum, Munich*

Eudel, was an artist who still worked for the *ombres chinoises* in a skilful way, but he stood alone. Germany possessed highly gifted designers of silhouettes, such as Konewka, but the shadow-play was forgotten.

Its modern revival is due to French artists. In the Chat Noir, a cabaret started by Rodolphe Salis in 1881, Henri Rivière began to improvise shadow-plays in 1887. Caran d'Ache,

FIG. 361. FROM RIVIÈRE'S SHADOW-PLAY "LA MARCHE À L'ÉTOILE"

Willette, Lucien Métivet, followed him without being able to rival his efforts. Rivière's art provided a fantastic fairy-tale for the eye, deeply poetic in theme, of peculiar beauty in form, the whole a dream which vanished even as one strove to capture it. The artist made use of light and colour to steep his scenes in a mood made arresting through its strange magic. Before him there had been nothing similar to this, and since the Théâtre d'Art vanished, in 1897, nothing to equal it has put in an appearance. Here there were great successions of scenes, such as the *Sphinx*, where the conquerors of all ages passed before the Sphinx, *La Marche à l'Étoile*, where the poor and lonely, beggars, shepherds, and slaves, followed the star of Bethlehem, *Clairs de Lune, L'Enfant prodigue*, in which the art of illusion reached its highest and most perfect charm. Rivière added powerfully to the impression created by his work through the utilization of light to emphasize the separate pictures. This was cast through coloured glasses which had to be controlled by ten or twelve men. The Nile landscape floated in a bluish-green twilight, Golgotha flamed forth blood-red, the Sphinx faded into a cold, misty grey, the combination of colour-tones always striking the proper psychological note. Through skilfully handled cutting and diminution Rivière secured astonishing perspective effects by simple means. Nothing is left of all his work now, but even

FIG. 362. FROM L. TIECK'S "ROTKÄPPCHEN"
Schwabing shadow-play, with coloured transparencies by
Dora Brandenburg-Polster

the careful postcard reproductions of his scenes remain yet real things of beauty.

Henri Rivière knew how to present the natural alliance of poetry and painting, to create a fairy-tale theatre which in its possibilities left the regular stage far behind; but his followers did not possess his talents. Hans Schliessmann, who was a native of Mainz, but became an Austrian subject because of his long residence in Vienna, where he had won fame as an illustrator for the comic papers, collaborated with Caran d'Ache in producing shadow-plays at the Vienna Exhibition of Music and the Theatre in 1892, but these had no more than a temporary success. Chronologically the next were the "Elf Scharfrichter" in Munich, who in 1900 introduced shadow-plays in their clever artists' cabaret. In November 1907 Baron Alexander von Bernus sought to revive the shadow-play on a broader basis. This attempt resulted from the æsthetic endeavours of the literary

371

and artistic circle to which Schwabing contributed such a peculiar tone several years before the War. "The shadow theatre," wrote Willy Rath on that occasion, "is intended for those tired of realism; in the shadow is revealed an external simplicity, the truly perfect obstacle to realism." As Bernus himself says: "The shadow theatre reflects in its purest form the intangible world of the waking dream." The stage here was a screen of white linen, 1·15 m. by 90 cm.; the puppets were 35 cm. high,

FIG. 363. FROM L. TIECK'S "ROTKÄPPCHEN"
Schwabing shadow-play, with coloured transparencies by
Dora Brandenburg-Polster

and were brought forward, unseen by the spectators, in strips. They had movable limbs, but the manipulators used restraint in giving them gesture. For illumination the petroleum lamp was preferred to electric light, since the former made the shadow soft and full, and it was possible to graduate the power of the illuminant. The figures were designed by Rolf von Hörschelmann, Dora Polster, Greta von Hörner, Emil Preetorius, and Doris Wimmer. The performances lasted from twenty minutes to an hour and a half, several speakers being engaged in the show. Bernus himself, Karl Wolfskehl, Will Vesper, Paula Rössler, and Adelheid von Sybel wrote the plays, but performances were given also of pieces from older literature, such as Goethe's *Pater Brey*, Mörike's *Letzter König von Orplid*; Justinus Kerner, Tieck, Pocci, and Hans Sach were also represented.

FIG. 364. SCHWABING SHADOW-PLAY
Munich 1907. Prologue to the Turkish shadow-play of
Rolf von Hörschelmann

FIG. 365. FROM WOLFSKEHL'S "WOLF DIETRICH UND DIE RAUHE ELS"
Designed by Rolf von Hörschelmann

FIG. 366. SCENE FROM "DIE SCHILDBÜRGER"
Otto Link. Decoration by C. Tenner

FIG. 367. SCENE FROM "HEILIGE WEIHNACHT"
Otto Link

FIG. 368. OLD GERMANY
Lotte Reininger

FIG. 369. OLD HOLLAND
Lotte Reininger

FIG. 370. OLD FRANCE
Lotte Reininger

FIG. 371. OLD ITALY
Lotte Reininger

FIG. 372. OLD SPAIN
Lotte Reininger

FIG. 373. FROM THE SILHOUETTE FILM "PRINCE ACHMED"
Lotte Reininger

FIG. 374. FROM THE SILHOUETTE FILM "PRINCE ACHMED"
Lotte Reininger

FIG. 375. FROM THE SILHOUETTE FILM "PRINCE ACHMED"

Lotte Reiniger

FIG. 376. FROM THE SILHOUETTE FILM "PRINCE ACHMED"
Lotte Reininger

FIG. 377. FROM THE SILHOUETTE FILM "PRINCE ACHMED"
Lotte Reininger

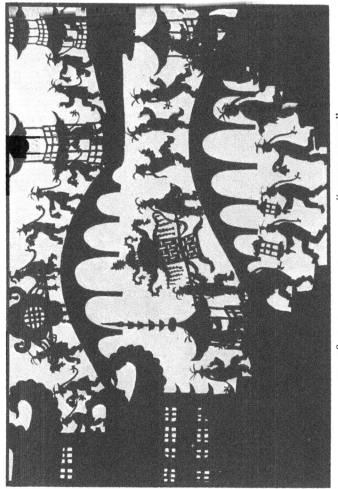

FIG. 378. FROM THE SILHOUETTE FILM "PRINCE ACHMED"

Lotte Reiniger

# DOLLS AND PUPPETS

A spinet supplied the music, and both figures and scenery were executed with great refinement; the performances were distinguished and tasteful; the imagination of the audience was aroused to a high degree; but its financial success was not such as to warrant the continuation of this theatre.

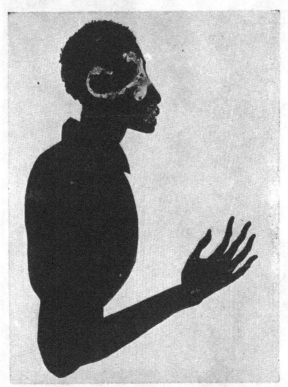

FIG. 379. SHADOW-PLAY FIGURE
Lotte Reininger

That such novelties should be copied in vulgarized forms in Berlin is comprehensible considering the ceaseless rush for sensations in that great city; such things commonly bear the mark of death on them at the very time of their birth. The Silesian shadow theatre which Friedrich Winckler-Tannenberg and Fritz Ernst opened in the Schiedmeyersaal at Breslau on November 15, 1913, looked as if it were to meet with a friendlier reception. They played *Doctor Faust*, a moral shadow-comedy in three acts adapted from the old *Faust*, Hofmannsthal's *Der Thor und der Tod*, Liliencron's *Die Musik kommt*, and other

380

FIG. 380. FAUST, SATAN, AND THE FOREST MAIDENS
From the shadow-play *Faust*. Design by Eugen Mirsky, Prague
By permission of the *Deutscher Verlag für Jugend und Folk, Vienna*

pieces, but the War brought this artistic and promising experiment to a premature end. Since then Bruno Zwiener has established a new shadow theatre in Breslau.

The peculiarly imaginative charm of the Javanese *Wajang Purwa* drew German artists too under its spell. Franz Bauer set up a shadow theatre in Bad Lausigk with figures inspired by the Javanese style; Bruno Karberg also gives performances at

FIG. 381. LOTTE REININGER AT WORK

Hamburg with puppets which are supported, like the Javanese figures, on sticks worked from below. Käthe Baer-Freyer has been influenced by Javanese art in the making of her flat wooden figures, which she paints on one side and manipulates from below. The mystical charm conjured up by the shadow-plays has ever inspired the imaginative artists to further creative activities. Thus, in 1925 Hartlaub got Flaubert's *The Temptation of St Anthony* performed at the Kunsthalle at Mannheim, with shadow-pictures made by Wilfried Otto. Kurt Scheele in Frankfort produced shadow-pictures from the fables of Hans Sachs, songs by Richard Dehmel, and folk-plays; E. H. Bethge designs and writes for the shadow theatre; Eduard Maier goes on tour from Munich with his shadow-plays; Friedrich Winckler-Tannenberg in 1920 sought by means of his *Rakete* to introduce the *Morgenstern* shadow-plays to Berlin.

# OCCIDENTAL SHADOW THEATRES

In the winter of 1925 Alfred Hahn at Munich made what seemed to be a most promising start with a shadow-play in colour dealing with the Nativity. Leo Weismantel has established an experimental shadow stage of peculiar interest in that the closely connected arts of the shadow-play and the film are here run together. In Munich Ludwig von Wiech had already put the shadow-play into a film, while Lotte Reiniger with a silhouette-film showed what could be accomplished in this style. *Aladdin's Lamp*, the fairy-tale from *The Arabian Nights*, supplied the theme for *The Story of Prince Achmed (Die Geschichte vom Prinzen Achmed)*. It was made by the Comenius-Filmgesellschaft, which between 1924 and 1926 must have taken 250,000 separate pictures, of which 100,000 were made use of. By the collaboration of the artist with Karl Koch, Walther Rüttmann, and Berthold Bartosch originated a work of art which on its production at the Volksbühne taught Berlin that this was no mere amusement for æsthetes, but represented new possibilities for the film. A short time ago the Prague silhouette artist Eugen Mirsky also tried this new path which the film has pointed out to the art of the shadow-play. In an exhibition held at Prague in June 1927 he showed silhouette figures which revealed in a peculiar mingling of the arts of the silhouette and the film a new phase, seemingly full of possibilities for the future, of the cinematographic art. His pictures are of no common sort; the step which he has taken from the merely ornamental silhouette to the naturalistic silhouette at all events may open up new prospects to the all too realistic film.

X

## MARIONETTES IN THE FAR EAST

Wᴛʜ this survey of the shadow-play we have come up to the present day, but now we must once more cast a glance at the marionettes of the Orient, if only because of their influence on the Western puppet stage. In China the theatre in which movable puppets were displayed must have been influenced by the Greek marionettes, the tradition being carried thither through Central Asia. Chinese records naturally say nothing of this. According to tradition Yen-Sze invented marionettes about the year 1000 B.C., presenting these before Emperor Mu of the Chou Dynasty. These puppets must have been very artfully contrived, for they were accused of shamelessly casting amorous glances at the ladies of the harem; for that reason the enraged monarch condemned them and their director to death. The angry potentate was with great difficulty persuaded that he had to deal here with lifeless things. Other records attribute the introduction of the puppet-play to a considerably later date, placing its invention in the year 262 B.C. At that period the city of Ping was besieged and was in danger of falling into the hands of the enemy. The prime minister then counselled Emperor Kao-tzu to get gorgeously dressed female puppet-figures led about the city walls so that by that means jealousy might be aroused in the enemy's camp, in which was the wife of the Emperor's opponent. His plan succeeded; the besieger was so much taken up with the faces of the lovely women that his wife became disturbed, and would not be appeased until her husband raised the siege of Ping and ordered his army to retreat.

There were three sorts of Chinese marionettes—those moved by strings, those manipulated by sticks from below, and the hand puppets. The first were of wood and were called *kui-lui*; the last were made of leather and named *pu-tai-hi*, which signifies 'sack-play.' These puppets played, sang, and danced love-stories, myths, legends, etc., the usual theme being that of an abducted princess rescued valiantly. The jester always took a part in these plays. There were also special pieces which were performed only before the imperial Court. The art of the

384

puppet-showman must soon have reached a high level, for Sir
Lytton Putney, the English Ambassador at Peking, was amazed

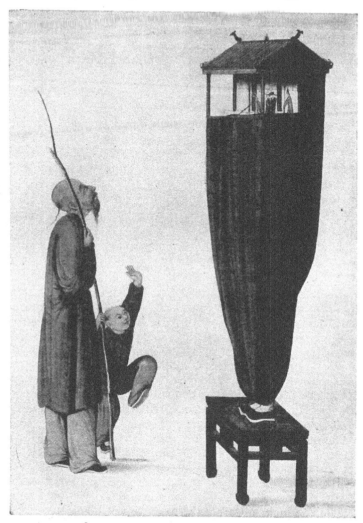

FIG. 382. CHINESE SKETCH, LATE EIGHTEENTH CENTURY
Puppet-play in the street
*Victoria and Albert Museum*

at the skill with which the showman manipulated his jointed
figures and harmonized all their movements with the dialogue.
In our own days interest in the puppets has apparently declined

seriously. Hagemann, who was unable to witness a performance —so rare have the shows become in the larger towns—attributes this to superstition. The rounded plastic puppets were no longer popular, he thinks, since they were abused for magical purposes. Sprinkled with blood, they were supposed to turn at night into malevolent demons, on which account they were feared.

The puppet theatre in Japan occupies a position entirely of its own; there is none other like it in the world. Here men and puppets share the stage together and offer a complete substitute for the living actor. Carl Hagemann holds that:

> The Japanese puppets provide the most singular, the most genuine, and the most sincere theatre operating in the present-day world. What goes on here is theatre of the last and highest grade, the finest expression of art.

And a theatre director is certainly the person best qualified to judge of such things. The same authority continues:

> The puppets play better than real actors; they make a much better theatre than men. Their performances are more powerful artistically; because of the absence of curbing humanity they are presented symbolically with the highest intensity of expression; all reality has vanished.

These Japanese puppets are not marionettes of the ordinary kind, being worked neither by the hand nor by strings, but are rather mechanical works of art manipulated by men—the female puppets by three and their male partners by four individuals. One works the head, another the arms, and a third the rods. The puppets are dressed lavishly yet with refinement, the magnificent costumes being designed by such artists as Bunsaburo. In comparison with those who control them, dressed as these are in black or dark blue costumes and with their faces muffled up, the puppets, gay in colour and light-toned in features, create a powerful impression. They are about two-thirds or three-quarters life-size, those which take an important part in the play being larger than the others. Technically the male figures take precedence over the female, for they are given greater power of expression. The men can move their eyebrows, eyes, and upper lips while the women can only roll their eyes. The colour of the women's faces is snow-white, while that of the men's is flesh-tone; their features are sharply delineated and appear to Europeans close to the grotesque. Some of the heads are said to be very old, and cannot be reproduced nowadays since the secret of the lacquering process has been lost. Hagemann describes these heads as marvels steeped in inconceivable vitality.

MINISTER FOR FOREIGN AFFAIRS    MINISTER FOR HOME AFFAIRS

Burmese Marionette Theatre

*Staatliches Museum für Völkerkunde, Munich*

They are set on ball-joints; fingers, wrists, elbows, and shoulders can be moved so that the figures can suitably manipulate their fans. Singers and reciters present the text, each figure having its own interpreter; only those of great renown for their art of delivery are permitted to deal with the dialogue between the puppets. The acting of the puppets is "inconceivably conscious,

FIG. 383. MOUNTED PRINCE
Burmese marionette theatre
*Staatliches Museum für Völkerkunde, Munich*

purposeful, inexorable." Paul Scheffer, who saw them in 1926, writes:

The artists are so powerful in their manipulation and directing, in the profound godlike attitude they assume toward the creatures in their hands, that after a moment they succeed in making us forget their presence and are no more remembered. So at last, delicately and with a sure touch, they pour their life and whatsoever of thoughts they may have concerning life and human passions and human moods into the puppets which they hold. The black figures near them are their assistants. They all move delicately and always with dignity. Yet they do not hide, as we do, that they have to make a thousand movements; the puppets are always openly surrounded by these mechanical devices, and through this they become uncanny. Before our eyes is clearly revealed the means by which the figure nods, rises angrily, throws a sharp glance to the side, or seems to laugh sneeringly; but, since all this seems to be part of its own life, it appears inevitable and indisputable. The boundaries between mechanism and inspired existence are, as it were, obliterated.

FIG. 384. HERMIT
Burmese marionette theatre
*Staatliches Museum für Völkerkunde, Munich*

This brilliant manipulation comes from the fact that the puppet-players are engaged in this trade of theirs from earliest youth; they dedicate their whole lives to the puppets. It is asserted that the living actors themselves have taken their histrionic style from the puppet theatres, and that from it they have borrowed their most impressive plays. This kind of theatre possesses a permanent stage in Osaka, founded about two hundred and fifty years ago by Takemoto Chikuyo Gidayu. He lived from 1651 to 1714, and was the most famous reciter of his time. In the middle of the eighteenth century it is said to have reached its culmination in poetical, musical, and technical form, but degenerated when the public developed a taste for the living actors. Alongside of this Ningyo-tsukai theatre is the puppet theatre called Ito-Ayatsuri, where genuine string marionettes give performances. This sort of puppet is, however, not much cared for by the public; apparently it was not indigenous to Japan, but an importation from abroad. In addition to these there are itinerant puppet-players in the form of wandering

FIG. 385. CLOWN (LEFT). MAGICIAN (RIGHT)
Burmese marionette theatre
*Staatliches Museum für Völkerkunde, Munich*

singers who hang their boxes round their necks and make their puppets dance on the top. The influence of the puppet stage on the regular theatre and *vice versa* has been traced by Carl Hagemann in Burma also. In the marionette theatres there the puppet first appeared as a reciter of prayers—a figure who appears at all public performances. The Burmese figures are made to dance just like the girls of the Pwe shows, but more grotesquely, wildly, and irregularly; the living girls, for their part, dance as though they are being pulled by strings. The puppets, with all their limbs movable at the joints, are supported on wires and strings, so skilfully that a good player not only can produce very agreeable and brilliant as well as naturalistic and

389

grotesque movements, but can attain to great variety in the arrangement of positions. At the end of the last century Burmese marionettes gave a special performance at the Folies-Bergère, in Paris, which was received with great enthusiasm. A magnificent complete puppet theatre from Burma is in the possession of the Ethnographische-Museum in Munich. The wonderfully attired puppets hang on strings, the prince supported

FIG. 386. PRINCESS
Burmese marionette theatre
*Staatliches Museum für Völkerkunde, Munich*

by eleven of these, the princess by thirteen; the trunk of the elephant is composed of five movable pieces. The faces of the human persons are full of character; those of the evil spirits are caricatured. Realism and fantasy are thus blended in the Burmese plays. A prince and a princess are supposed to be pursued and fly into the jungle. There they are persecuted by demons, given counsel by hermits, and protected by good spirits —which bring all to a happy conclusion.

In Java, apart from the shadow-play, real marionettes are also to be found. One of the types is the *Wajang Kelitik* or *Kerutjil*, wherein appear, not the shadows of the puppets, but the puppets themselves. The plays have as their main theme the hero Damar Wulan and his deeds. Then there is the *Wajang*

THE EVIL SPIRIT NATT
Burmese Marionette Theatre
*Staatliches Museum für Völkerkunde, Munich*

FIGS. 387, 388. PRINCIPAL FIGURES OF A BURMESE MARIONETTE THEATRE

*Staatliches Museum für Völkerkunde, Munich*

*Golek*, which is played with rounded, wooden, dressed puppets, with loose and movable heads. Here for the most part are introduced heroes from the Mohammedan *Amir-Hambjah* cycle. This kind is said to have completely supplanted the others and to be much beloved by the spectators.

In India the puppet theatre as a popular amusement preserved its existence up to recent times. Now, indeed, when "Europe's whitewashed mediocrity has dominated the whole world," as Carl Hagemann says, "in a few years we shall not be able any more to find in India the genuine and the native. Like a grey rain-cloud, Europe's sobriety covers the ancient magnificence of colour. Soon all days will grow like eventide." The American film, with its dreary tastelessness, will be the death of native talent in India too. The pieces played on the Indian puppet stage were amazingly long; plays of seven to ten acts were no rarities. The stock piece, *Samavakara*, had, it is true, only three acts, but of these the first act alone lasted nine and a half hours, the second two and a half, and the third an hour and a half. As an afterpiece to this endless show a farce was presented in which the Indian Hanswurst, called Vidusaka, was given the chief *rôle*. In very early times in India—Pischel says in the eighth century—the attempt was made to banish this obscene jester from the stage, but without success.

# XI

# THE PUPPETS OF TO-DAY

WE have traced the history of the puppet theatre up to the last century, a time in which its very existence was in question. It seemed then to be confined to the fairs of remote districts, and, although still retained in the nurseries, seemed rather to be tolerated there than encouraged. And just as it appeared to have died away completely, it showed that it still had life in it and still offered possibilities for artistic activity, on account of which it was seized upon from all sides. Many things contributed toward its revival. The primal impulse came from the professional artists. It will be remembered how at that period many painters, somewhat tired of the so-called 'fine' art, turned to 'applied' art, in order to find in creative work of this kind a source of satisfaction which the constant change of tendencies and the conflict of ideas denied them in the other. They discovered, accidentally, among the furniture, implements, and toys of the period of 'honest workmanship,' with which they sought to identify themselves, the old marionette theatre. This discovery seemed to them the happier in that the puppet-play apparently possessed that charm after which they all strove so passionately—the naïveté, the true simplicity of the folk. Here they were joined by those poets who had turned their backs on the prevailing dreary realism of the time in an effort to capture the romantic point of view. These were the days when there was a distinct turning away from Zola and a movement toward Maeterlinck. The dramatists greeted the puppet stage because it excelled the regular theatre in pure simplicity. Not the living actors, they opined, only the marionettes, were capable of expressing poetry without a distracting wilfulness; the human stage prohibits this, the puppets never. The marionette is naught but the expression of the artist's idea; the actor is always a man, and only too often his personality seems to place an obstacle in the way of true· expression of a thought. Support from former times was found to strengthen this idea. Jean Paul emphatically demanded marionettes instead of actors for the performance of comedy. As early as 1839 Leman had asserted that a well-equipped

393

# DOLLS AND PUPPETS

marionette theatre would be the genuine native German folk theatre, and his contemporary Justinus Kerner had spoken out against living actors on the stage. The latter writes:

> It is peculiar, but to me at least the marionettes seem much less restrained and much more natural than human actors. The marionettes have no life apart from that of the theatre. With the marionettes and the shadow-plays the illusion is rather as if events

FIG. 389. PLUTO, PRINCE OF HELL
Last work of the puppet-showman Xavier August Schichtl,
Munich (1849–1925)
*Theater-Museum, Munich. Photo Hatzold, Magdeburg*

really taking place in one part of the world were seen mirrored here in small as in a *camera obscura*.

Not only did the writers of the older generation, such as Georg Ebers, Felix Dahn, and Adolf Wilbrandt, prove themselves enthusiastic friends of the puppet theatre, but they were joined by the younger men—Gustav Falke, Richard Dehmel, and others; such a successful dramatic poet as Ludwig Fulda could confess that "puppet theatres were once my highest ideal." Schnitzler, too, and Hugo von Hofmannsthal found the regular actors who interpreted their pieces too coarse and obstinate, and they cast longing glances at the puppet theatre. Even such a great

394

actress (and director) as Eleonora Duse wrote to Vittorio
Podrecca: "I envy you. I too should have liked to be the
director of a puppet-troupe. Your actors do not talk, but obey;
mine talk and do not obey." The most pertinent thing ever
said concerning the connexion between the marionettes and the
actors we owe to Bernard Shaw. The words which he wrote
to the Italian puppet-showman Podrecca are reproduced in the
introductory note at the beginning of this book.

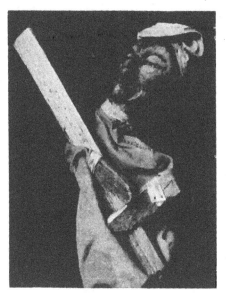

FIG. 390. KASPERLE
Hand puppet. Carlo Böcklin

To the artists and the poets came the æsthetes, with their
"homesickness for childhood," as Carl Niessen has put it so
admirably. This longing for a distant paradise led men back, as
in the eighteenth century, to the Far East, where they met with
the puppets and the shadow-plays. To those desirous of reaching
backward from the stylelessness of naturalism to style and to
powerful form the marionettes must truly have been welcome.
Instead of representing the human body and its movements
naturalistically, they deliberately diverged from the real proportions of physical nature. The true puppet is not an individual,
but a type. Its centre of gravity lies in its lead-filled feet, corresponding neither with the natural nor with the optically
apparent. This determines the nature of its movement, and it is

395

precisely the stiffness inseparable from the marionette which gives it its character. The facial expression as well as the bodily movements is typically fixed; instead of being expressive of changing moods, it provides a kind of epitome of the part. The theme and form of the marionette-play have to harmonize with these features, and from this results the last necessity of the marionette stage. The puppets are passionless; they can only

FIG. 391. THE LITTLE ROBBER
Hand puppet. Carlo Böcklin

act; such pieces alone can be performed as are developed simply, without any kind of psychological content. Psychologically the theme of the play must be limited to the representation of types, the conspicuous qualities of which must be clearly indicated. The marionettes will not and cannot give life by themselves such as it is the aim of the living actor to present, but provide an artistic reproduction of that. The special rules on which the marionette stage is based, the possibilities of expression confined within narrowly marked boundaries, demand of the audience a specific exercise of its imagination and a strong faculty of illusion not granted to every one. Even the pedagogues joined in this chorus of manifold acclamations by which the revived puppet-plays were welcomed. Writing in 1904, Paul Hildebrandt observes:

# THE PUPPETS OF TO-DAY

The puppet-play demands by its nature the greatest participation on the part of the child, and hence is one of the best and most instructive of theatrical forms, that on which adults ought to bestow the greatest attention in the interests of the artistic education of our children.

Konrad Lange too was convinced that Kasperle and marionette theatres aided the child toward an appreciation of plastic

FIG. 392. THE DEVIL
Hand puppet. Carlo Böcklin

art and of drama, providing the boy with a bridge leading to the enjoyment of other dramatic art. This philosopher complains that in so many families no attention is paid to this subject, and considers this a serious neglect in the education of children. No other occupation, in his opinion, will lead children so surely to the very core of all artistic expression as the theatre. In every family Lange would wish to see in use a small puppet theatre.

Among the patrons of the puppet-play was also numbered the Kunstwart, an organization which supported all endeavours seriously made to raise German culture. Göhler, who acted as spokesman, would recognize in the Kasperle theatre the simplest and most fitting form of art conceivable for the childish understanding, strongly shaping and limiting all the extravagant dreams of a still unyielding fantasy. If domestic episodes are

397

chosen for the subject-matter, there then arises a fine and entertaining opportunity for the appreciation of daily life and of familiar surroundings in a simplified artistic form. Then Kasperle, who truly knows the good and bad conduct of children, may with his exaggerations and his good humour transform into laughter some things which otherwise would turn to tears. Thus the Kunstwart pleads for the revival and greater cultivation of Kasperle in the nursery.

FIG. 393. OLD WOMAN
Hand puppet. Carlo Böcklin

Frankly, for this, besides goodwill and some money, talent would be required. Nothing could come of the way in which the Teachers' Union at the Leipzig Michaelmas Fair in 1912 interested themselves in the Kasperle theatre. "Kasperle as a medium of education" makes much less impression than the hero of the fairs, with all his coarseness and extravagant cudgellings; he is simply a bore. Kasperle was a grossly abandoned creature, no one can deny it—but all his pretensions against authority go back in origin to the primitive idea which brings to a good end the struggle of an intrepid man against inimical powers such as death and the devil. He conquers them since he possesses humour, in spite of it all remaining an incorrigible old sinner, for he is always craftier than his opponent. It is a

FIG. 394. FROM THE OPERETTA "DER TAPFERE KASSIAN," BY O. STRAUSS
AND A. SCHNITZLER
Figures by I. Taschner
*Marionette Theatre of Munich Artists*

FIG. 395. FROM "WASIF UND AKIF"
Executed by Leo Pasetti
*Marionette Theatre of Munich Artists*

# DOLLS AND PUPPETS

falsifying of the character of this strongly sketched personality to attempt, as the Teachers' Union does, to reduce it to a mere speaking tube which admonishes children to be good—to behave well at school, obey the teachers, study diligently, and bring home good marks. That is simply a case of getting Beelzebub to cast out the devil. The puppet-play, as the Kunstwart stated in May 1914, may become practical pedagogy, but the poetry need not thereby suffer. If the stage is turned into a *cathedra* it

FIG. 396. SCENE FROM THE THIRD ACT OF THE OLD GERMAN FAUST PLAY
BY J. BRADL AND P. NEU
*Marionette Theatre of Munich Artists*

will diminish in value; the child as such has a right to its imagination, and merely speaking about the child is not education at all. The puppet theatre should not only treat the child as a spectator, but should inspire it to participate in the play and to imitate; it should spur it on to active work of its own. If that were to succeed, then the puppet-play would be once more, as in olden days, one of the most popular forms of art—an art for which one can justly assert that it has roots in the folk, a thing which can be said of none of the fine arts at the present day.

One advantage of the puppet theatre is that it does not require the expensive and elaborate equipment which the regular stage demands, that it can produce wonderful things with the very smallest outlay. There is no lack of guidance; Leo Weismantel, Erich Scheuermann, Philipp Leibrecht, Peter Rich, Rohden, and others have given useful practical instruction concerning its use. At Easter 1925 a "Child and Theatre" exhibition, organized by the Saxon Teachers' Union in Leipzig, demonstrated all

400

FROM "Wasif und Arif oder die Frau mit den zwei Ehemännern "
BY A. T. Wegner and Lola Landau

Figures and scenery by Professor Leo Pasetti

*Marionette Theatre of Munich. Artists, Paul Brann*

the possibilities of its suitability for practical educational purposes. Stress was laid here on the hand puppets, the manipulation of which demands less time, skill, and patience than the marionettes. The puppet theatre is well advanced in the matter of practical instruction—indeed, such instruction has been actually

FIG. 397. AKIF THE ROBBER
*Marionette Theatre of Munich Artists*

established by law in Czechoslovakia. There is only one danger: that commercial interests take control of the affair and, by offering all possible 'improvements', debar children from developing and exercising their own initiative. Puppet theatres have been brought into commerce as "legally protected" novelties; the trade exhibits them equipped with cycloramas and electric lighting, and thus possessing all that a child's theatre can do without. In opposition to this the 1912 exhibition of the Munich Women Teachers' Union showed happily how children can be

FIG. 398. GALLOWS SCENE FROM "WASIF UND AKIF"

Scenery by Leo Pasetti

*Marionette Theatre of Munich Artists*

FIG. 399. FROM " DER GROSSE UND DER KLEINE KLAUS "

*Marionette Theatre of Munich Artists*

inspired to work for themselves. Professor Bradl had carved most impressive heads from celery, turnips, potatoes, and radishes, and had dressed them in multicoloured pieces of sack-cloth. These puppets gave performances against a simple blue background which could be copied by any child. Carlo Böcklin too, the son of the famous painter, possesses a peculiar talent for the puppet-show; he has made most original figures and

FIG. 400. SHEPHERD FROM THE CRIB-PLAY OF PAUL BRANN
Josef Wackerle
*Marionette Theatre of Munich Artists*

given improvised plays for his children. In his illustrated books on Kasperle he has indicated a new way in which the puppet-play can be introduced into nurseries. Beate Bonus, under Böcklin's direction, has collaborated in the writing and collecting of the texts.

The accountant Carl Iwowski, in north Berlin, owes to both the happy idea of his *Wandervogel-Arbeitsgemeinschaft*, by means of which he gives Kasperle theatre performances for poor children of this dreariest quarter of the German capital. He began by composing a Faust play and carving the figures for it himself. For this purpose he used peculiarly knotted roots which he painted, or else little blocks of wood which under his skilful

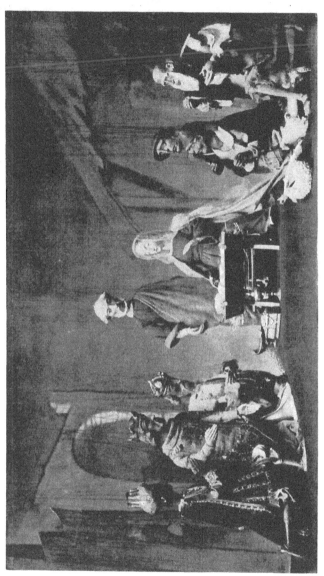

FIG. 401. THE ADORATION SCENE FROM THE CRIB-PLAY OF PAUL BRANN

Josef Wackerle

*Marionette Theatre of Munich Artists*

hands were transformed into wooden devils and other figures.
He started in 1919, and since then has developed a completely
new style in the presentation of hand puppets. He built a little
theatre of his own design, freeing his puppets from the edge of

FIG. 402. THE POLICEMAN
Jakob Bradl
*Marionette Theatre of Munich Artists*

the stage, and so giving to his figures a physical materiality
which hitherto they had been denied.

The renaissance of the marionettes is associated with two
names, Paul Brann and Ivo Puhonny. The Marionette Theatre
of Munich Artists, which has existed since long before the War,
under the direction of Paul Brann, owes its world reputation to
his puppets, the heads of which are executed by Ignatius
Taschner, Jakob Bradl, and others, and to his excellent manipulation. On his miniature stage appears a harmonious unity of all
arts, much more convincing than in the regular theatres; naïve

SCENE FROM ADAM'S COMIC OPERA "DIE NÜRNBERGER PUPPE"
Executed by Professor Jos. Wackerle
*Marionette Theatre of Munich Artists*

# THE PUPPETS OF TO-DAY

dramatic work and pleasant settings are here triumphant, precisely because lifelikeness is not demanded from his stringed marionettes. Brann wishes, to secure success, that three intellects should collaborate in his performances—those of the

FIG. 403. THE STAR SINGER
Josef Wackerle
*Marionette Theatre of Munich Artists*

manipulator, the speaker, and the puppet itself. The puppet is thus considered an intellectual force by itself, and Brann believes that much is gained by giving it free play. His own performances, at any rate, fully justify this claim and permit him a wide-ranging repertoire. This includes the puppet-play of *Doctor Faust*, the peculiar *pièce de résistance* of all puppet stages, but he presents, in addition to that, plays by Mahlmann and Pocci, Ludwig Thoma, Schnitzler, and Maeterlinck; here, too, can be seen masterly performances of little comic operas by Pergolese, Mozart, Adam, Suppé, and Offenbach. At propitious moments the illusion becomes complete; we forget that these are puppets before us.

FIG. 404. HEROD AND THE DEVILS FROM THE CRIB-PLAY OF PAUL BRANN
Josef Wackerle
*Marionette Theatre of Munich Artists*

FIG. 405. THE EXAMINATION SCENE FROM "GOETHE"
Grotesque by Egon Fridell and Alfred Polgar. Figures by Olaf Gulbransson
*Marionette Theatre of Munich Artists*

Since the deaths of Taschner and Bradl, Josef Wackerle has become the special 'house' artist of this theatre. When in 1925

FIGS. 406, 407. SINGLE FIGURES FROM "GOETHE"
Olaf Gulbransson
*Marionette Theatre of Munich Artists*

Brann wrote a crib-play after the old style, fashioning it into six impressive "blessed Christmas" scenes, Wackerle made for him a setting, so real, so homogeneous, so spiritually refined both intellectually and physically, and with such perfect harmony, as could never be attained on the regular stage. With the help of this artist, and by his own excellent artistic skill in management,

FIG. 408. THE COMPETITION DANCERS
Totalia Meschuggerowska and her partner Fred
*Ivo Puhonny's Artists' Marionette Theatre*

the director produced a powerful "unforgettable impression" which the regular stage would be incapable of. Among folk types Wackerle likes to stick fast to the people of his Werdenfels native district, and on account of that he succeeds best in those peasant types such as were so excellently delineated in the figures of the jolly play of Big and Little Klaus. Occasionally other artists too have collaborated in the work of this theatre—Olaf Gulbransson, for instance, the well-known illustrator of *Simplizissimus*, who made the figures for a travesty of *Lohengrin*.

Ivo Puhonny has placed over his puppet theatre the motto: "A good marionette is of greater value than a living mediocrity"; and he has certainly created puppets which far surpass many actors. After long preliminary studies and travels in the Orient

410

FIG. 409. PUPPETS FROM A PIECE BY WEDEKIND
*Ivo Puhonny's Artists' Marionette Theatre*
*Photo Delia*

FIG. 410. "DIE BUSSE"
Japanese farce
*Ivo Puhonny's Artists' Marionette Theatre*

he established his little theatre at Baden-Baden in 1911; he also toured with his puppets, and in 1916 gave over the directorship to Ernst Ehlert, who paid visits to every part of Germany. The unity of expression in these puppets is due to the circumstance that the artist made all the puppets and the scenery with his own hands. He has executed several hundred character puppets, and has shown himself a master of the first rank in the art of

FIG. 411. CLOWN, WITH EXPRESSIVE MOVABLE FINGERS
*Ivo Puhonny's Artists' Marionette Theatre*

puppet-carving. This is by no means an easy task, for a good marionette must not be realistic; rather must it, if it is to create the proper impression, be conventionalized without becoming too rigid. Ehlert himself observes:

> It may be said that the marionettes stray into wrong paths when an attempt is made to make them as lifelike as possible. The puppet should not imitate the human actor; it has its own laws. It need not be beautiful; it has only to be characteristic.

On this basis Puhonny makes the heads somewhat too big for the bodies and exaggerates slightly the characteristic features, thus imparting to them a certain mimic quality which proves effective in the play of his stage lighting. The singular and

412

FIG. 412. THE PIANIST
*Ivo Puhonny's Artists' Marionette Theatre*

FIG. 413. PUPPETS
*Ivo Puhonny's Artists' Marionette Theatre*

personal charm of the Puhonny marionettes, wherever they have gone in Germany, has gained them warm and sincere friends; they threw the aged Hans Thoma into ecstasy. The scope of performance of these marionettes, according to Ernst Ehlert,

FIG. 414. FROM "PRINZESSIN UND WASSERMANN"
Richard Teschner

FIG. 415. FROM "KÜNSTLERLEGENDE"
Richard Teschner

is infinite; they are capable of dealing with any scenic requirement. They venture to attempt even tragedies and works not originally intended for the puppet stage, but perhaps they produce the greatest impression when they are engaged in their own particular sphere. Puhonny and Ehlert, too, cultivate the solo-marionette successfully. They base their work on types of

414

the old itinerant marionette theatre which, thus improved, justify their right to existence as artistic creations. The Berlin Press described the "dancing Chinamen" as "the most perfect thing that has ever been shown on the puppet stage."

An artist who has long occupied himself with the problems of the marionette theatre is Richard Teschner in Vienna. Before 1909 he was settled in Prague, and there the idea of his puppet

FIG. 416. STARRY NIGHT
Richard Teschner

stage first came to him. The mysterious suggestiveness emanating from the marionette as from polychromic wax-plastic seized upon him, but the first naturalistically created puppets which he made, to serve as figures for Hofmannsthal's *Thor und Tod*, did not please him æsthetically; they were too close to nature in appearance and movement. Only after becoming acquainted with the Javanese *Wajang* did he attain, with its aid, to a style of his own. He retained its technique (the manipulation by means of thin sticks from below), but he changed the flat *Wajang* figures into rounded puppets in three dimensions, and instead of only projecting them on to a screen he put them on to an ordinary stage. Thus did he carry over the Eastern methods to the West, and he himself, besides making all the equipment, scenery, puppets, lighting, and music, wrote for his stage fairy-tales with a

415

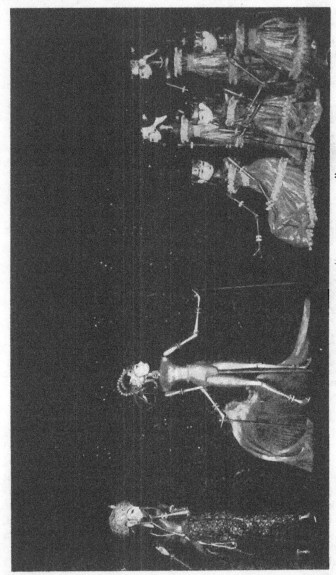

FIG. 417. STAGE OF FIGURES, FROM "NAWANG WALAN," ACT I

Richard Teschner

FIG. 418. THE SLAYER OF THE DRAGON
Richard Teschner

genuine Hoffmannesque fantasy. These puppets, which Teschner made out of polished lime-wood and then clothed, are exceedingly refined and delicate, but under his direction they give "mimic dynamic performances of such a noble simplicity and quiet power that they far surpass human actors, and it may be deemed that they will be the originators of a new style of histrionic

FIG. 419. MARIONETTE
Otto Morach. Solothurn

art." "Teschner's scene *Der Tod und das Mädchen* [*Death and the Maiden*] perhaps reveals the greatest possible refinement of the puppet-play," thinks Carl Niessen. The Viennese Kolo Moser was likewise attracted by the marionettes; in 1905 he made a puppet theatre with all the figures necessary for the performances given by Frau Lilli Wärndorfer in Vienna. At Zürich in 1918–19 a marionette theatre was established as an annex to the Kunstgewerbemuseum, in connexion with the First Swiss *Werkbund* Exhibition, and with the idea of testing on a small experimental stage the reforms for the regular stage proposed by Appia and

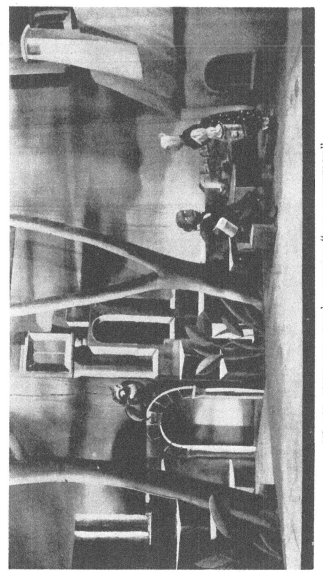

FIG. 420. SCENE FROM POCCI'S FAIRY-TALE "DAS EULENSCHLOSS"

Scenery by Max Tobler

*Marionette theatre in Zürich*

Gordon Craig. This marionette theatre works with flat and round puppets; it has found in Carl Fischer a talented carver and in Otto Morach a clever scenic designer. These artists collaborated in presenting a successful performance of *Faust*. The puppet-opera has been much encouraged in Zürich, for it was believed that by the aid of music greater possibilities of

FIG. 421. DEVIL FROM "FAUST"
Carl Fischer
*Marionette theatre in Zürich*

illusion could be attained. "The variegated rhythm of music," writes Hans Jelmoli, "corrects the primitivity of the puppet, and changes the figure into an expressive exponent of every human passion." With the aid of these "animated marionettes" performances are given of Pergolese's *Livietta e Tracollo*, Mozart's *Bastien und Bastienne*, Donizetti's operas, and an opera composed for the puppets by Manuel de Falla—*Master Peter's Puppet-show*. The Zürich enterprise has gained success, too, outside its own town and canton.

How much living power, in spite of the popular craze for the

FIG. 422. SCENE FROM A PUPPET-PLAY BY TRAUGOTT VOGEL

Scenery by Ernst Gubler

*Marionette theatre in Zürich*

cinema, is still possessed by the puppet theatre, with all the poetic possibilities it offers, is shown by the Kasperle theatre

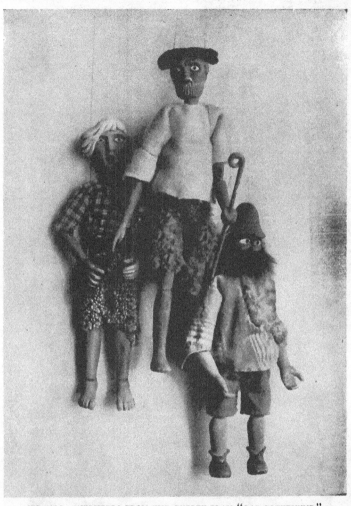

FIG. 423. SHEPHERDS FROM THE PUPPET-PLAY "DAS GOTTESKIND"
Carl Fischer
*Marionette theatre in Zürich*

founded by Dr Will Hermann at Aachen in 1919. He has created a puppet-play of a specifically Aachen character, and in Schängche (a diminutive of Jean) he has provided for it a counterpart to Hänneschen of Cologne, of such a characteristic and successful sort that this figure, animatedly reproducing the features of a canon, immediately became a freeman of his home

FIG. 424. DON QUIXOTE AND SANCHO PANZA
From *Master Peter's Puppet-show*. Otto Morach
*Marionette theatre in Zürich*

town. It is to the credit of the author that he has consciously turned aside from merely farcical elements, fully acquainted as he is, not only with the requirements of the puppet-play, but also with the life of his fellow-townsmen. But his merits were a disadvantage to him. Schängche could only express himself in the dialect of Aachen—an idiom of powerful expression within the walls of the old town, but outside of that incomprehensible. This has considerably limited his circle of admirers, and since naturally Schängche has not been without the usual lower-class competitors, counting not in vain on the baser instincts of the crowd, this enterprise, highly deserving of welcome, has not been

FIG. 425. VITTORIO PODRECCA BEHIND THE SCENES OF HIS
TEATRO DEI PICCOLI, ROME

financially remunerative, and struggles with economic difficulties which unfortunately may perhaps force it to close its doors. To-day the things that find success among the German public have to come from America. There is indeed naught else that can appeal to them.

The most brilliant marionette theatre of the present day, introducing puppets of first-rate quality, is the Teatro dei Piccoli of Vittorio Podrecca, in Rome. This is completely Italian both in manner and in style, but it has given many performances in Germany, meeting with universal applause and providing lasting stimulus to other efforts. "The Teatro dei Piccoli is welcome," writes Pietro Mascagni. "Here is an artistic show of the first rank, which deserves the applause of all who admire artistic forms which express beauty and sincerity." "Lying between dream and reality," writes the Duse with reference to this theatre, "the marionette can be perfect when

FIG. 426. MARIONETTE
*Teatro dei Piccoli of Vittorio Podrecca, Rome*

it is guided by a soul." Podrecca employs a puppet *ensemble* which has no rival in our days. His five hundred marionettes, with twenty-three people at their service, present a repertoire of operas and plays with which they have charmed the whole world. Between 1913 and 1924 Podrecca gave eight thousand performances at Rome, Milan, London, Madrid, Buenos Aires, New York, etc. He himself came to the puppet theatre from the regular grand opera stage, which had failed to satisfy him, and

FIG. 427. FIGURES FROM AN ITALIAN FAIRY-TALE
*Teatro di Ciuffettino, Florence*

it goes without saying that unity of artistic expression can be reached successfully only on the puppet stage. Podrecca's marionettes are works of art by means of which the stage fantasies of great composers and of great poets are brilliantly interpreted in a manner which could not be equalled by any singer or actor. These puppets, which are unusually large (somewhat over 1 m. high), have been modelled by artists such as Caramba, Grassi, Montedoro, Angoletta, and Pompei. The stage directing is masterly. Carl Niessen writes of it:

> The certainty with which the figures move on the stage, with which they turn, dance, romp, play at ball with one another, reach for objects, pull out handkerchiefs elegantly from their pockets and put them back again, is such that no comparison with others seems possible. Yet the performance does not aim wholly at absolute illusion. It is extremely charming when the puppet so

FIG. 428. TERESA AND HER BROTHER CATCHING BUTTERFLIES

FIG. 429. MISS BLONDINETTE WITH THE MAESTRO CAPELLACCI
*Teatro di Ciuffettino, Florence*

seriously takes the trouble to do what living people do and yet remains wholly a puppet, a great romantic toy.

Music adds to the impression made by these shows. Of old composers Pergolese, Mozart, Rossini, Donizetti, and Massenet are here represented; an attempt was made to present even Richard Wagner's *Die Feen* (*The Fairies*). The operas are all curtailed, only selections of scenes being performed, so as to

FIG. 430. "DIE ORAKELTROMMEL."
Adolph Glassgold. Head by Kathleen Cannell. 1926
*L'École Medgyès, Paris*

harmonize with the spirit and conditions of a marionette theatre. Of living composers Respighi, to take one example, has written for Podrecca's puppets his *Dornröschen*.

Alongside of the Roman Podrecca must be mentioned the Florentine puppet theatre, Ciuffettino, of Enrico Novelli, with its witty shows and clever puppets.

In the United States Tony Sarg is held to be the most talented director of puppets. The marionettes with which he has appeared in the larger cities there were made by Charles E. Searle. There they gave performances of *Rip van Winkle*, *Don Quixote*, and similar pieces.

428

FIG. 431. SCENE FROM AN OPERETTA
*Teatro di Ciuffettino, Florence*

# DOLLS AND PUPPETS

In Paris the École Medgyès devotes attention to the puppet-play. The clever marionettes here take their droll features from the skilful hands of Adolph Glassgold, P. A. Birot, Kathleen Cannell, and others.

The marionettes have created a genuine school of their own. Just as in Japan the living actors took their style from the puppets, so attempts have been made by Germany to carry over

FIG. 432. "DIE ORAKELTROMMEL"
Adolph Glassgold
*L'École Medgyès, Paris*

the technique of the puppet-play to the regular stage. In Dresden before the War, as Carl Niessen notes, the old farce of *Maître Pathelin* was produced in the marionette style. At performances of *Flohs in Panzerhause* the actors at the beginning were represented hanging on strings; in fact, in Erwin Fischer's Berlin theatre, which apes the Bolshevik style, actors and marionettes are said to have played together:

> The revolutionary Russian theatre must bring its whole being ever more and more into line with the manner of the puppet-play. The tragic clown Vladimir Sokoloff has attempted new artistic possibilities in his puppet-play—a theatre of absolutely musical dynamics.

The honourable position which the puppet theatre, thanks

430

FIG. 433. MARIONETTES
*L'École Medgyès, Paris*

FIG. 434. LE PETIT POUCET
Pierre Albert Birot
*L'École Medgyès, Paris*

to the efforts of artists and connoisseurs, has held since the opening of the century is maintained sometimes with fluctuating fortune. Marionette theatres are founded, enjoy for a short

FIG. 435. KASPERLE THEATRE FIGURES
Max Pokorny and Tilly Gaissmaier

FIG. 436. KASPERLE THEATRE FIGURES
Max Pokorny and Tilly Gaissmaier

time a certain prosperity, and then disappear, generally from lack of means. They have not wanted either partisans or assiduity and goodwill, but whether it will be possible for them, with

FIG. 437. POLITICAL PUPPET THEATRE: PODBIELSKI, BÜLOW, BEBEL, MÖLLER
From the Jubilee Number "1000" of the *Lustigen Blätter*. Berlin, 1905

FIG. 438. MARIONETTES
*Teatro Mazzini, Catania*

their refined charms designed for a wholly intimate impression
to swim against the great tide of the film, with its tempting
attractions to the public, is, alas! uncertain. A puppet theatre is

FIG. 439. MARIONETTES OF THE ARTS AND CRAFTS SCHOOL, HALLE
*Photo Hatzold, Magdeburg*

FIG. 440. R. WAGNER, A. MENZEL, BISMARCK
Kasperle theatre figures. Max Pokorny and Tilly Gaissmaier

easy to establish, but it is still easier, unhappily, to set up a
cinema, and since the film is always based on a low taste, providing the greatest attraction to dull theatre-goers and flirting
with the most evil instincts in the audiences, the mob will

434

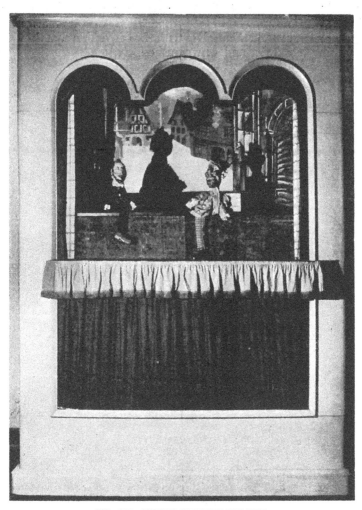

FIG. 441. MUNICH KASPERLE THEATRE
Max Pokorny and Tilly Gaissmaier

naturally give it the preference—of that there can be no doubt. Those who nowadays devote themselves to the marionette theatre must console themselves with the conviction that they are practising a refined and distinguished art, and thus serve the cause of good taste, which has always been a thing for the few alone, and in our present days is wholly an affair of the intellectuals.

Three factors which could be of high practical value have

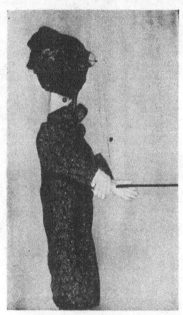

FIG. 442. FAIRY-TALE UNCLE
Puppet on sticks. Moulded in paper by Georg Zink

been recently placed in the service of the marionettes—the exhibition, the Press, and the university. At the German theatrical exhibition at Magdeburg in 1927 Dr Alfred Lehmann, of Leipzig, provided an unprecedented survey of the puppet-show in all its varieties, the greater part of the material being supplied from the well-known collection of Professor Dr Artur Kollmann in Leipzig. Since then there has not been even a small exhibition of toys which has not taken the puppet-show into consideration. Dr Alfred Lehmann also directed the *Puppentheater*, a periodical published by Joseph Bück in the interests of all puppet-showmen, which embraces within its sphere of interest both the history and the technique of the

436

PUPPET THEATRE
Walter Trier

puppets. The Union for Promoting German Theatre Culture has provided space in its official journal for a special puppet-theatre section. This paper, published by Lehmann and Schüppel in Leipzig, has been running since 1923. German high

FIG. 443. HEIDELBERG FLAT MARIONETTES
Above: Prospero and Miranda, from Shakespeare's *The Tempest*, and Austrian officer, 1750; below: fieldmouse and fox, from the fable-play by Georg Zink

'schools, which for some years past have included the 'science' of the theatre in their curriculum, are also beginning to apply themselves to the puppet-play. The Institute of Theatrical Science at the University of Cologne established a puppet-play section in 1924, and no better person could have been chosen for its director than Dr Carl Niessen. He is theoretically and practically an accomplished expert in this art, and in his hands its scientific study is well provided for.

# DOLLS AND PUPPETS

When, at the conclusion of our long wanderings through the puppet-shows of all times and of all races, we cast a glance at Germany of to-day we cannot find space to name all who deserve particular mention. A complete list it would be difficult to give, apart entirely from the fact that such a catalogue would have been in the end of very little use. An address book is not what is wanted here. Those interested in the puppets who are

FIG. 444. FIGURES MADE FROM ROOTS
Georg Zink

not referred to must not consider that the omission is due to ill-feeling or that it signifies any condemnation; they must realize that it is the result simply of lack of space.

It is but just to begin with Munich, which since the activities of the unforgettable Papa Schmid has remained the centre of serious artistic work in the sphere of the marionette theatre. The position it enjoys is due first to its artists, who have consistently devoted themselves more and more to this charming type of play, and secondly to the public, whose interest is strong enough to support several marionette theatres at one time. In Tölz the late apothecary Georg Pacher established an enchanting puppet theatre. In Graz the Kasperle theatre found many friends during the War. There Fritz Oberndorfer wrote clever texts which cast an amusing light on the commandeering of metal[1] objects, on summer-time, meatless days, etc., and satirized hoarders and War profiteers. Unfortunately this theatre has disappeared, along with the Viennese Gong. In Offenburg, Baden, the apothecary Löwenhaupt has sympathetically and lovingly devoted himself to the marionette-play. He belongs to the ranks of those who have most intimate knowledge of the puppet theatre, and he possesses a rich collection of objects relating to it.

FIG. 445. MARIONETTES
Marion Kaulitz. For Grimm's fairy-tale *De Fischer un syn Fru*

In the Heidelberg librarian Georg Zink Baden possesses another great connoisseur, collector, and promoter of the puppet-play. He works with his puppets both practically and theoretically in the interests of genuine folk education, supporting this most energetically by means of writings, exhibitions, and performances. His collections of objects relating to the history of the puppet-play and its literature, on which he has been engaged for many years, have been publicly exhibited in the theatre and music section of the town library, of which he is director. The marionette stage in Frankfort is famous for its colourful settings, for the clever manipulation of its puppets, and for its good, plain, characteristic dialogue. It indulges especially in the fairy-tale and in the solo-marionette introduced without words. In

[1] In reference to the War-time shortage of metal in Germany.

Brunswick Eduard Martens has devoted his attentions to the
puppet theatre, and has brought his *Bodenkammerspiele* ('garret-
plays') to a remarkable pitch of perfection. Many of his
puppets were carved by Hans Pfitzner. The hand puppets in
Hartenstein, in the Erzgebirge, owe their being to the merchant
Max Jacob, who wrote the plays for them himself. He is reported to have succeeded not only in fairy-tales for children, but

FIG. 446. MARIONETTE
Cläre Paech
*Theater-Museum, Munich*

also in satires of a topical sort. His puppets were made by
Theo Eggingk, a young native of the Baltic Provinces, and were
dressed by Elisabeth Grünewald. This little theatre and the
young men who assisted in its work won considerable fame by
their tours, in which they reached even to the fighting lines.
They visited German Bohemia, East Prussia, Silesia, and
Masurenland, endeavouring to bear to the Germans living there
relics of the old precious folk art. Werner Perrey directs the Low
German puppet-plays in Kiel, for which he himself writes fairy-
plays, very beautiful and very charming, but heavily burdened
with thought. As a poet Perrey demands too much—for the

FIGS. 447, 448. TRENCH PUPPETS
Made of limestone for a Kasperle theatre
*Armee-Museum, Munich*

FIG. 449. A TROUPE OF SOLO ENTERTAINERS
*Josephine and Allardyce Nicoll*

FIG. 450. SCENE FROM A MARIONETTE-PLAY: "AN INTERVIEW"
*Josephine and Allardyce Nicoll*

child's mind indeed he demands impossibilities. He makes his Kaspar speak too much and of too much. It is not possible to describe in one phrase the general tone of this theatre. In the Dessau Bauhaus experiments are being made with constructivist absolute marionettes, which consist only of abstract spatial forms created by means of wires, celluloid balls, rings, and beads. Wherever to-day creative artists are at work there the puppet theatre—be it with string puppets or only with hand puppets— finds sympathetic admirers to further its course. It is a pigmy among giants, but are not the noblest achievements in store for it?

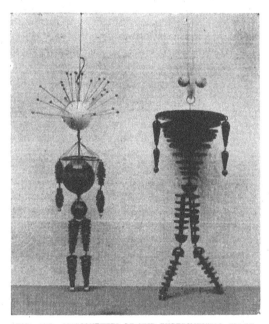

FIG. 451. MARIONETTES OF THE EXPERIMENTAL STAGE AT THE BAUHAUS, DESSAU
*Theater-Museum, Munich*

# XII

# HOW OUR MARIONETTE THEATRE STARTED

### *By* HANS STADELMANN

YES, how did it really begin? Among the bombers it was, in the lines on the Dvina, that friend Barthels, who in civil life is a Munich actor, and I, a Munich painter, got into conversation about our childhood, and neither of us could say enough about the puppet theatres which each of us had possessed. And suddenly the thought was born: What a glorious thing it would be for our dull trench life if we could introduce such a theatre there! For us the work would not be too much if only we could succeed in winning the hearts of our Bavarian militiamen, and perhaps awaken in them some enthusiasm for this genuine folk art. Yet to build a marionette theatre in the midst of a military campaign, surrounded by a thousand hindrances—that task seemed too great, and hence we decided to make the attempt only with a shadow theatre, and with that idea set at once to work. Two Kasperle comedies of Pocci's were combined, figures were carved from old military post boxes, all their limbs made movable by means of strings and wires, and in the bombers' dug-out the first performance was billed to take place; it was called *All Unnecessary Luggage must go!* And the dream of the shadow theatre was realized. After several weeks winter descended on the land; at the approach of winter the fighting round Riga was over, the advance into Livonia, patrols and outposts in the marshes, and the retreat were abandoned; again the idea of a theatre came into our minds; a few officers of the regimental staff got to know of it and were inspired by our idea, although they believed, as they later told us, that we should fail. We asked for a little support and got to work, animated only by the joy in our hearts; this time we wanted to make a real marionette theatre. "Yes, but who will carve our figures for us? We must go and see Buchner-Konrad of the 10th Company and get him to do that—he is a Munich sculptor. It's to be hoped he doesn't chuck us out when we go to ask him." So over we go to the dug-outs of the 10th Company, and carefully the whole plan is laid before Buchner. Instead of chucking us

FIG. 452. WAGNER, MEPHISTO, AND FAUST
*Eastern Front Puppet Theatre of the 2nd Bavarian Infantry Regiment*

FIG. 453. COURTIER, DUCHESS AND DUKE OF PARMA
From the old Faust play
*Eastern Front Puppet Theatre of the 2nd Bavarian Infantry Regiment*

out he flings himself into the affair with beaming joy, he rushes at once to a place in the dug-out where the clay is got for the ovens, and a couple of days later, when we again visit him, there in the corner which he has chosen as his workshop stand lifelike clay models for Mephisto and Faust. For the old puppet-play of *Doctor Faust* was that with which we desired to start. Now came active weeks. Every free minute we spent in making things—

FIG. 454. FAUST CONJURES UP THE APPARITION OF ALEXANDER THE GREAT
From the old Faust play
*Eastern Front Puppet Theatre of the 2nd Bavarian Infantry Regiment*

day and night. Buchner's hands, working with the most primitive tools, wrested one figure after another from the elder-wood; these were painted by me and in various other ways embellished. Difficult was it to obtain in the trenches the materials necessary for the costumes, miles away as we were from human habitation. And yet, with some inventiveness, we succeeded. Thus, a woollen helmet became Faust's grey mantle, a handkerchief, which was painted with flaming sulphuret of mercury, was sacrificed for Mephisto's costume. I endeavoured to glue together the whole costume for the lord Orestes from an old sand sack which was then made presentable with noble colourings. Buchner, his patience inexhaustible, made the Duke of Parma and Hanswurst too. Lovely trousers were made of the silk from the parachute of a French rocket light-ball; gilded string was used as an embellishment for the doublets, key-chains as sparkling chains of office; lead shot, matches—all came in handy.

446

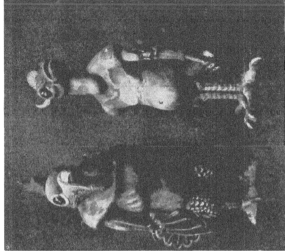

FIG. 456. TWO HELLISH SPIRITS
From the old Faust play
*Eastern Front Puppet Theatre of the 2nd Bavarian Infantry Regiment*

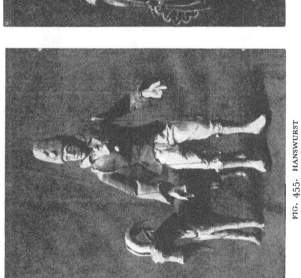

FIG. 455. HANSWURST
From the old Faust play
*Eastern Front Puppet Theatre of the 2nd Bavarian Infantry Regiment*

The buttons were indicated by glued-on peas. Unhappily, next morning we found that the rats, much to the annoyance of Buchner, had eaten them. Whereupon I gilded new pea-buttons with bronze strongly smelling of turpentine, and this took away the rats' appetite. The building of the stage itself went on at the same time. We had found a dug-out abandoned because it was in danger of collapsing, and, driven to extremities,

FIG. 457. TWO HELLISH SPIRITS
From the old Faust play
*Eastern Front Puppet Theatre of the 2nd Bavarian Infantry Regiment*

we set up our common workshop there. Between the half-rotten beams, which formed ceiling and walls, hung down great icicles. An old iron oven which smoked without giving out any warmth gave us the illusion of heat. In addition, we had a miserably functioning carbide lamp, by the irritating light of which the sculptor sat to the right busy carving, and to the left of which the painter was engaged on his backgrounds, wings, and other properties, mostly transmogrified from packing paper and pasteboard; often his colours froze on his brush.

The day of the first performance came terribly near. We had so much to do that we had no time for our meals. How much was still to be rehearsed and learned! Most important of all, the manipulation of the figures. The hours ran on mercilessly toward the first performance. All the officers, including the regimental commander, had promised to attend. The men were curious and, for the most part, as usual, indulged in abuse. "You could do something better than spend our money; your

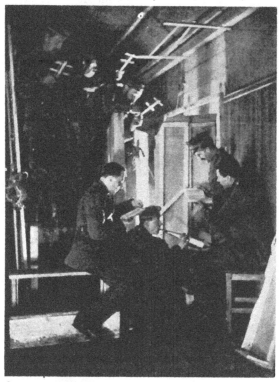

FIG. 458. BEHIND THE SCENES DURING A PERFORMANCE OF A PUPPET-PLAY
IN THE 2ND BAVARIAN INFANTRY REGIMENT ON THE EASTERN FRONT
*Eastern Front Puppet Theatre of the 2nd Bavarian Infantry Regiment*

wretched theatre has already cost six to seven thousand marks." I was speechless at such reproaches, for the whole thing had as yet not cost the regiment one penny; indeed, we ourselves had paid out of our own pockets a sum of one hundred marks for paint and material. Yet, although they indulged in abuse, they flocked in. The old shed which was transformed into an auditorium was supposed to hold one hundred, but two hundred were crammed in, and four hundred stood outside. The play began, and after the prelude we felt that we had cheered all their hearts by our work. The first scene was listened to with great attention; uninterrupted laughter filled the whole room in the scenes where Hanswurst developed his philosophy of life; and they were deeply touched at Faust's despairing end.

The regimental commander congratulated us on our success, and desired that these performances should be given daily, so that all the men of the regiment might have the opportunity of seeing them. And they came not only from our regiment, for

FIG. 459. THE DOCTOR AND THE THIEF
The former from the *Narrenschneider*, by Hans Sachs, the latter from the
*Rossdieb von Fünsing*, by Hans Sachs
*Eastern Front Puppet Theatre of the 2nd Bavarian Infantry Regiment*

they tramped as long as six hours through deep snow from the adjoining trenches; again and again new crowds filled the house down to the last seat. Hence it came to the knowledge of the divisional staff, the result of which was that one day we were ordered to give a performance with our theatre before the divisional staff and headquarters. Our play made so great an impression that several weeks later we were ordered to give a performance with our theatre at headquarters before the Commander-in-Chief, Prince Leopold of Bavaria. Then came the greatest surprise of all: an order came from headquarters that we had to make an eight weeks' tour with our theatre through the whole province of the Eighth Army in Livonia, Esthonia, and Courland, and produce our plays (we gave, besides our *Faust*, Pocci's comedies and Hans Sachs' farces) in all the towns

before the military and the civil population. The success was
so extraordinarily great in Dorpat, Pleskau, Narwa, Riga,

FIG. 460. SCENE FROM POCCI'S PUPPET-PLAY "DIE DREI WÜNSCHE"
*Eastern Front Puppet Theatre of the 2nd Bavarian Infantry Regiment*

FIG. 461. THE THREE PEASANTS
From the *Rossdieb von Fünsing*, by Hans Sachs
*Eastern Front Puppet Theatre of the 2nd Bavarian Infantry Regiment*

Mitau, and other towns that with our little stage we were able
to play to full houses every evening, the pleasant result of which
was that we were enabled to contribute quite a nice sum to our

451

regimental funds as the clear profits of our enterprise. Thus our play had a good object, and if, besides, we were successful, among the many thousands who saw our play, in calling forth, here and there, a spark which may perhaps contribute toward keeping the old marionette-play alive, we must have achieved the most ideal object of all.

FIG. 462. FIGURES FROM A
FRENCH KASPERLE THEATRE

# THE PUPPET-PLAY

OF

# DOCTOR FAUST

AN HEROI-COMIC DRAMA IN FOUR ACTS

*From the manuscript of the puppet-showman Guido Donneschky.*
*Published for the first time faithfully in its original form*
*by Wilhelm Hamm, 1850.*

## DRAMATIS PERSONÆ

FERDINAND, *Duke of Parma*
BIANCA, *his wife*
ORESTES, *his counsellor*
JOHANNES FAUST, *doctor in Wittenberg*
WAGNER, *his famulus*
KASPERLE, *a travelling genius*
MEPHISTOPHELES
AUERHAHN
MEXICO
ALEXO } *supernatural spirits*
VITZLIPUTZLI
A GOOD GENIUS
GOLIATH AND DAVID
THE CHASTE LUCRETIA
SAMSON AND DELILAH } *apparitions*
JUDITH, *with the head of Holofernes*
HELENA, *the Trojan beauty*

## ACT I

FAUST'S *study. To the left is a table on which are lying various books and astronomical instruments. In front of the table stands a magic globe.*

### SCENE I

FAUST [*sitting alone and reading*]. Varietas delecta . . . "Variety in all things shall create joy and pleasure for man." This is truly a beautiful sentence; I have read it often and often, yet it does not reach far enough for the satisfaction of my desire. One man likes this, another likes that, but we have all the impulse in our hearts to grasp at something higher than we possess. It is true that I might think myself more fortunate than many of my fellows; lacking

453

wealth, lacking support, I have attained by my own efforts to the rank of doctor, and I have carried on this profession honourably for eighteen years. But what is all this to me? Doctor I am, doctor I remain, and beyond that I cannot go in the field of theology. Ha! That is too little for my spirit, which aims at being revered by posterity. I have resolved to apply myself to necromancy, and through that to reach my heart's desire—to make my name immortal.

A VOICE TO THE RIGHT [*invisible*]. Faust! Faust! Leave off this project! Pursue the study of theology and you will be the happiest of men!

A VOICE TO THE LEFT. Faust! Leave off the study of theology! Take up the study of necromancy and you will be the happiest of men!

FAUST. Heaven! What is that? To my intense amazement I hear two invisible voices! One on the right warns me to keep to the study of theology, and says that if I do so I shall be the happiest of men; that on the left advises me to take up the study of necromancy, and says that if I do so I shall be the happiest of men. Well, then, I shall follow you, you voice to the left!

THE VOICE TO THE RIGHT. Woe, O Faust, to your miserable soul! Ha! Then you are lost!

THE VOICE TO THE LEFT [*laughs*]. Ha! ha! ha! What a jest!

FAUST. Again do I hear these two voices, one on the right bewailing and one on the left laughing at me? Yet must I not alter my purpose, since I feel that only through the study of necromancy can I bring my desires to satisfaction! Yet again, I shall follow you, you voice to the left!

## SCENE II

### FAUST *and* WAGNER.

WAGNER. I come to inform your Magnificence that two students gave me, to be handed to your Magnificence, a book which you have long wished to possess, since it deals with the study of necromancy.

FAUST. Since yesterday I have been hoping you would bring it me, and I have been eagerly awaiting it. Where is the book?

WAGNER. I have laid it in your lecture-room.

FAUST. Good! Leave me!

WAGNER. In all humility, your Magnificence, I should like respectfully to ask about something that worries me.

FAUST. Speak on, my dear Wagner! You know that I have never refused you anything that lay in my power to give.

WAGNER. Your Magnificence, I would humbly beg you to let me engage a young lad to be taken into your service, for it will be too difficult for me to manage the household and at the same time carry on my studies.

# THE PUPPET-PLAY OF DOCTOR FAUST

FAUST. Do so, my dear Wagner! It has long been my wish to see you less burdened by the management of the house so that you can apply yourself more freely to your study. You can therefore look round for a young lad, and when you have found a fit person, who can show you good testimonials, you may bring him to me, and I shall make further arrangements with him.

WAGNER. Very good, your Magnificence! I shall do all in my power to fulfil your commands.

FAUST. Then the book that the students handed over to you is in the lecture-room?

WAGNER. Yes, your Magnificence!

FAUST. Then I will go and see whether it is the same that I have vainly sought to get for so long.              [*Goes out.*

## SCENE III

WAGNER [*alone*]. What a noble-minded master is this! What would have become of me without his help? He has taken me, a lonely orphan, into his house, and has always taken such pains over my education and my progress. Can I ever repay him for all his kindness? I think not. But I will work honestly, do all I can to anticipate his wishes, and at least show him that he did not expend his kindnesses in vain, that a thankful heart beats in my bosom for him. I shall therefore go to a good friend of mine and inquire whether perhaps he knows of a suitable young man to enter his service. Accomplishment of a duty is the greatest proof for a man who wishes to show his gratefulness.              [*Goes out.*

## SCENE IV

FAUST [*who enters a little earlier with a book in his hand*]. Good man! Just remain as I have found you hitherto and I will truly strive to recompense you for your trust, and to further your fortunes so far as I can. Now, however, I desire also to carry out my resolution to devote myself solely to the study of necromancy by means of this book, and I desire immediately to test this art by a conjuration. "I charge you, you furies of hell, by hell's gates, by Styx and Acheron, to appear immediately before me! Break out, you howling storm, that Ixion's wheel may stop and Prometheus' vulture forget to torment him, and carry out my will! Despair, Fury, and Rage—hurl you at my feet!"

## SCENE V

FAUST, ALEKSO, VITZLIPUTZLI, AUERHAHN, MEXICO
[*hurled in with wild thunder and lightning*]. *Later* MEPHISTOPHELES.

FAUST. A pretty crew! Yet you are very negligent! Don't do that again to me! Tell me, you first fury of hell, what's your name?

MEXICO. Mexico.

FAUST. And how quick are you?

MEXICO. As quick as a bullet fired from a gun.

FAUST. You have a great speed, but not enough for me. Vanish!

> [MEXICO *disappears through the sky.*

FAUST. And what name have you, hellish fury, and how quick are you?

AUERHAHN. Auerhahn, and I am as quick as the wind.

FAUST. That's very quick, but not enough for me. Vanish!

> [AUERHAHN *disappears in the same way as* MEXICO *did.*

FAUST. What's your name, hellish spirit?

VITZLIPUTZLI. Vitzliputzli.

FAUST. And how quick are you?

VITZLIPUTZLI. As quick as a ship sailing on the sea.

FAUST. As a ship sailing on the sea? That is a fair speed, but with unfavourable winds it doesn't always reach its goal. Vanish!

> [VITZLIPUTZLI *goes off.*

FAUST. Say on, hellish fury—what's your name?

ALEKSO. Alekso.

FAUST. Alekso? And what's your speed?

ALEKSO. I am as quick as a snail.

FAUST. As a snail? So you are truly the slowest of all the hellish spirits? I can't make any use of you at all. Vanish!

> [ALEKSO *goes slowly off.*

FAUST. Tolerably slow!

> [MEPHISTOPHELES *comes in dressed like a hunter.*

FAUST. Ha! What do I see? A hellish fury in the likeness of a man?

MEPHISTOPHELES. You must know, Faust, that I am a prince of hell, and have the power to assume, and to appear in, whatsoever shape I please.

FAUST. You a prince of hell? What's your name?

MEPHISTOPHELES. Mephistopheles.

FAUST. Mephistopheles? That's a good-sounding name. And how quick are you?

MEPHISTOPHELES. As quick as man's thoughts.

FAUST. As man's thoughts? Ha! That is an extraordinary speed; for I can be with my thoughts one moment in Africa, another in America. Say, hellish fury, if you wish to serve me. I shall promise you to be yours, body and soul, at the end of the time I shall settle on.

MEPHISTOPHELES. Tell me the conditions, Faust, to which I must submit.

FAUST. The first condition is this, that you get me as much money as I ask from you. The second is that you make me a person of consequence among all great men and at all great courts, that you carry me wherever my desire takes me, that you warn me of all dangers. And the third condition is that you tell me before our contract comes to an end and that you obey me for four and twenty years. Are you willing?

MEPHISTOPHELES. Why four and twenty years, Faust? Half of that is enough.

FAUST. Four and twenty years—no less.

MEPHISTOPHELES. Well, I am satisfied. [*Aside*] I'll cheat him all right; he doesn't count on my skill. [*Aloud*] But, Faust, I must leave you just now to tell my prince Pluto of our agreement and ask him whether I may conclude this contract with you.

FAUST. Leave me then! But when will you return to me?

MEPHISTOPHELES. As soon as you think of me, Faust.          [*Goes off.*

FAUST [*alone*]. As soon as I think of you? I ought not certainly to enter into an agreement with a hellish spirit, but it is the only way to accomplish my desires quickly. And have I not sufficient power through my knowledge to get out of his clutches when half the time of the contract is over? Yes, so be it! Yet I feel so weary, so exhausted; this is certainly the result of the exertion of my spirit. I will go into my cabinet to rest for an hour or so, and then I shall carry on my plan with renewed energy.          [*Goes out.*

## SCENE VI

CASPER [*comes in with a bundle on his back*]. Pox on't! There's travelling for you! I have walked fourteen miles in thirteen days, and only every half-hour I've struck an inn! I've come to-day from—here. Here in my knapsack I have my whole equipage: I have the lining for a new overcoat—the cloth for it, however, is still with the shopkeeper. And here a half-dozen good stockings without heels, and a whole dozen of shirts. The only trouble is that the best of them has got no sleeve, and the eleventh is patched with the twelfth. I bought myself this fine beaver in Leipzig. It cost me twenty-one groschen, and a pair of new turned-up shoes of the latest style, the heels tipped with nails, cost me likewise seventeen groschen six pfennigs. Yes, yes, travelling costs money; I note that my purse has fallen into a galloping consumption. I've been journeying in Holland, Scotland, Brabant, England—but I've got to get there first. But in Danzig, Breslau, Vienna, Regensburg, Friessland, Nürnberg, Dresden—I've never been there at all. I was even three hundred miles behind the New World, but all at once I came on a wall and couldn't go on any farther; then I turned back, and now fortunately I find myself in Wittenberg and shall see whether I can get a situation, for I'm fed up with wandering about. When my father took leave of me said he: "Casper, try only to set your affairs a-swinging." That I've done, for my bundle is so light I could chuck it over the biggest house. But zounds! What sort of an inn is this, where neither landlord nor waiter is to be seen! Hullo, there! Wake up, household! There's a new customer here who wants to get a two-groschen bottle of wine! Mr Landlord! Waiter! What the devil's become of you! Aha! Now I hear some one coming I'll give him a good fright! *[He creeps under the table.*

SCENE VII

CASPER *and* WAGNER.

WAGNER. I'd like to know how it is that I can't find anybody who wants to go into service. The friends I was with are quite unable to recommend a suitable person to me.

*[CASPER comes out and frightens him.*

WAGNER. Oh, heavens! What is it? A strange man in my master's room?

CASPER. You're trembling like an anvil.

WAGNER. Who are you, my friend? How dare you come into this room without getting yourself announced? How did you get in?

CASPER. What a comic question! I came in on my feet, of course! But tell me—is it the habit and practice in Wittenberg for a customer to get himself announced when he wants to buy a bottle of wine?

WAGNER. My friend, you're not in an inn.

CASPER. No?

WAGNER. No, on the contrary, you are standing in the study of his Magnificence Doctor Faust.

CASPER. Well, well! What mistakes one can make! I thought, seeing so many young men go into this house here, that it must be an inn, for there also many folks are constantly going in and out.

WAGNER. That doesn't follow, as you shall hear, for all the young men you saw are students who come daily to the lectures which are delivered in this house.

CASPER. Students? And I thought they were customers! Then I made a pretty mistake! Well, I'll set myself on my feet to find an inn. *[Makes as if to go off.*

WAGNER. Wait a minute, my friend! To judge by your clothes you are a servant?

CASPER. Yes, I've got my master on my back.

WAGNER. And where have you come from now?

CASPER. From Italy.

WAGNER. Yes, my friend, but Italy is big. What I wanted to know was the precise place of your birth.

CASPER. Oh! You wanted to know the place of my birth?

WAGNER. Yes.

CASPER. I was born in Calabria.

WAGNER. What? In Calabria?

CASPER. Yes, in Calabria.

WAGNER. And what made you leave it?

CASPER. There I was engaged as companion in the house of a study-maker.

WAGNER. In the house of a student I suppose you mean?

CASPER. No, in the house of a study-maker! Surely I know best in whose house I was?

WAGNER. So you were given a situation in the house of a student?

CASPER [aside]. Oh, Jeminy! Isn't that a stupid fool! But I'll let him be. [Aloud] Yes, in the house of a student.

WAGNER. And what made you give up this situation?

CASPER. Well, do you see, that was a curious story. Every morning in Calabria I had to bring into the college for my former master his copy of Donatus, a very big book, and every day had to go over a certain plank. Now, one morning in the middle of this plank I met a pretty girl; I made her a couple of compliments, missed my footing, and let the book fall into the water. When my master heard of this he chucked me out of the job.

WAGNER. And then you started to travel?

CASPER. Yes, *per petes apostolorum*.

WAGNER. You've got some kind of a testimonial?

CASPER. Oh, yes! My master wrote a testimonial for me in black letter, chancery hand, and current script so naturally on my back with a gnarled stick that the letters will be legible till domesday.

WAGNER. Do you want to take up service again?

CASPER. Oh, yes! Do you want a servant?

WAGNER. Yes, if only you had good testimonials to show.

CASPER. Well, I've got them on my back.

WAGNER. Yes, sir, but he whose famulus I am will not be satisfied with that.

CASPER. Who are you?

WAGNER. Famulus to Doctor Faust.

CASPER. You are his famulus and want to engage me? Then I'd be a servant's servant?

WAGNER. No, you don't understand me; I will explain. My master has asked me to find a young fellow who wishes to go into service.

CASPER. Oh, that is a different story.

WAGNER. If you desire to enter his service you need only say so.

CASPER. Of course! But listen—there isn't too much work to be done here, is there? Because, do you see, I'm no great friend of work. I have so long a finger on each hand that I'm always knocking myself.

WAGNER. Oh, you'll get a very good place, with good food and wages, for my master is not married. Only one thing I must advise you about—keep secrets!

CASPER. Don't you worry about that! Just you wrap up the secrets I must keep in a piece of roast beef and a bottle of wine, for as long as my mouth has something to chew and my throat to swallow I'm as dumb as a fish.

WAGNER. Well, that will be all right. I can also tell you at once

what duties you have. In the morning you must remove the du:
from the *repositorium* and the books.

CASPER. Remove the books from the *repositorium* and the dust? Ol
that I can do; I've often done that in the house of my forme
master.

WAGNER. Then chop wood and draw water; that's all you have t(
do.

CASPER. Chop wood and draw water? Oh, the devil!

WAGNER. Don't worry about that! You'll certainly like working a!
my master's. And moreover, if only you are trustworthy and
industrious, and when we're better known to one another, then
I'll do still more for you, for I have the key of the wine-cellar in
my keeping.

CASPER. See here, Mr Famulus, how would it be if we exchanged
places? You would give me the key of the wine-cellar and you
could see to the wood-chopping and the water-drawing.

WAGNER [*laughs*]. Ha! ha! ha! That wouldn't be bad, but, as I said
just now, all that will come in time.

CASPER. Yes, yes, all that will come. But couldn't you give me something to eat and drink just now—a leg of mutton, say, or a
pheasant and a bottle of wine—for I've come from a journey and
have such a desperate hunger that my stomach is as shrunk up as
an empty tobacco-pouch?

WAGNER. Follow me! I'll fulfil your wish directly. . [*Goes.*

CASPER [*calls to him*]. Mr Famulus! Mr Famulus!

WAGNER [*comes back*]. Well, what do you want?

CASPER. Just show me a spot where I may put away my wardrobe,
so that once and for all I may take the hump out of my bundle.

WAGNER. Just come with me into another room. There you can
put away your clothes and can apply yourself to eating and
drinking. [*Goes out.*

CASPER. Rejoice, belly; now a treat's in store for you! He! he!
Mr Famulus, just take me with you! I don't know my way about
this house. [*Goes out.*

## SCENE VIII

CASPER [*runs in*]. Zounds once more! I've been in the kitchen and
have inspected what there is to eat—bacon frizzling loud and wine
from a pump! The boot-polish is good for nothing. Well, I'm
glad that I have got a new situation and that a good one. I have
taken off my knapsack and wish to look round. Zounds once
more! Where has the plum jam been put? This is a queer house,
with all the rats' tails and the piles of books, which are as big as
my grandmother's bread-board. Zounds! What is there? Is
that truly a tailor's measure? Am I then to serve a tailor? [*He
steps on to the magic circle which is traced on the ground and turns over the
pages of the books that lie on the table.*] Zounds once more! A tailor
hasn't so many books. I can read them too. What's this?

# THE PUPPET-PLAY OF DOCTOR FAUST

*Brrrr!* What's this? *Brrr!* [*Shakes his head vigorously.*] That is a
K—Katz—D, B, U, B—Pudel—Katzpudel; K–E–K——Karek
Barek, B–E–R——Berlicke! [*Three infernal spirits appear.*] Berlicke!
Berlicke! [*He looks round.*] Oh! Lord Jesus! Lord Jesus! Help!
Help! What do you black fellows want? There's no chimney to
clean here. What do you want, you charcoal-burner with the
red nose? Oh, dear god! Dear god! Zounds once more!

THE SPIRITS. Just come out of that circle, and we shall tell you. We
await your commands.

CASPER. No! no! I won't come out of this because you ask me to!
Zounds once more!

THE SPIRITS. But you must step out and give us your hand, or we do
not go away.

CASPER. Come out? Ne—give you my hand? Ne—then you'll go,
you dirty chimney-sweeps? No, I'm not coming out! I'm not
coming out! Stay as long as you will! Who asked you to come
here?

THE SPIRITS. You yourself summoned us through saying Berlicke.

CASPER. Then I'll just summon you off again. How am I to do it?
Zounds once more!

THE SPIRITS. That you must do through saying Berlocke.

CASPER. Aha! Spiritus, do you mark that? You wait, you rats'
tails! I will hunt you down now! So, now watch! Berlocke!
[*They vanish.*] Berlicke! [*They come again.*] Berlocke! Berlicke!
Berlocke! Berlicke! Berlocke! Berlicke! Berlocke! Berlicke!

[*He calls out ever quicker and quicker, the infernal spirits come
and vanish ever more swiftly, until at last they fling Casper
over the houses with woeful shrieks.*]

## ACT II

*The same room as in Act I. The chair stands on the left.*

### SCENE I

FAUST [*enters*]. Oh, heavens! What a strange dream has disturbed
me to-night and thrown my soul into torment! I thought I saw
an angel who warned me to abandon my project of entering into
an agreement with the hellish spirits, else now and hereafter I
should be utterly lost. But I cannot bring myself to change my
plan, for I feel that I am cunning enough to cheat Satan, with all
his craft and his tricks, and to cancel the bond itself whenever my
wishes are fulfilled. That vision was probably but a figment of my
troubled imagination, a phantom of the mind, designed to
frighten me as I stretched out my hand for this treasure. But the
ancients say, if one grasps it fearlessly it will vanish completely.
So I will if Mephistopheles . . .

461

# DOLLS AND PUPPETS

## SCENE II

#### MEPHISTOPHELES *enters.*

MEPHISTOPHELES. Well, Faust, have I kept my word?

FAUST. To my greatest astonishment. Have you got permissio from your Pluto to serve me?

MEPHISTOPHELES. Yes, Faust. But he requires a deed made out ii your writing, saying that you will be his property, body and soul at the expiration of the time fixed by you.

FAUST [*goes to the table*]. I will fulfil his desires immediately.

MEPHISTOPHELES. What are you going to do, Faust?

FAUST. Sign my name.

MEPHISTOPHELES. Among us of the Plutonic realm no signature with ink is valid. Among us it must be written in blood.

FAUST. But how can I get blood without cutting one of my limbs and so giving pain to myself?

MEPHISTOPHELES. Put your hand to my mouth and I will provide you with some blood painlessly.

FAUST [*gives him his hand*]. Here! [MEPHISTOPHELES *blows on it.*

FAUST. In truth, my blood flows without my feeling anything at all, and to my amazement it comes forth in two letters—an H and an F. What do these two letters mean, Mephistopheles?

MEPHISTOPHELES. What, Faust? Can't you, who are so great a scholar, interpret these letters? Well, then, these signify *Homo, fuga,* or "Man, flee."

FAUST. Ha! From whom should I fly, infernal spirit?

MEPHISTOPHELES. You must not interpret it as a bad omen—it means fly into the arms of your true servant Mephistopheles.

FAUST. If that is so I shall, without other thought, sign the document with it. [*He writes.*] "Johannes Faust"! So, now you can carry this contract to your prince Pluto.

MEPHISTOPHELES. No, Faust; henceforth I do not move a step from you. Tell me, who should carry off this document—a wolf, a bear, or a tiger?

FAUST. What should such fierce beasts be doing in my room? Let a crow take it.

MEPHISTOPHELES [*nods*]. Watch, Faust!

> [*Thunder and lightning. A crow appears, takes the bond in its mouth, and flies off.*

FAUST. But will the crow deliver the bond correctly?

MEPHISTOPHELES. You can rest assured of that. Have you now any commands for me, so that I can show you how quickly I can fulfil them?

FAUST. No. Withdraw now until I call you.

MEPHISTOPHELES. Very well, my Faust, only mention my name and in the twinkling of an eye I shall be with you. [*Goes off.*

FAUST [*alone*]. Now I should only like to know where my famulus remains so long. He could have done my bidding and been back ages ago. I hope no misfortune has befallen him; his long absence makes me very anxious. Ah! There he comes at last!

## Scene III

### WAGNER enters.

VAGNER. I inform your Magnificence that I have done everything you commanded me.

'AUST. Good, my dear Wagner. But how comes it then that you have not brought back a young lad as I gave you leave and as you yourself wished? Perhaps you have not been able to find anybody suitable?

WAGNER. Oh, yes, your Magnificence, when you bid me I'll bring him to you at once.

FAUST. Good! Bring him in! Where is he?

WAGNER. In my room. He has just come from a journey and has asked me to give him something to eat and drink. I will call him at once. [*Goes to the side.*] My friend!

CASPER [*from without*]. What is it?

WAGNER. Come here! His Magnificence wants to speak to you.

CASPER. In a minute! Let me just eat up my leg of mutton!

WAGNER. His Magnificence can't wait for you. Come at once!

CASPER. Just let me drink down this little glass of wine!

WAGNER. Don't be so rude! Come at once!

CASPER. What are you shouting about? I'm ready and waiting all the time.

## Scene IV

### CASPER enters.

CASPER. Well, what's the matter that you make such a fuss that one can't eat in quiet?

WAGNER. Here! His Magnificence wants to speak to you.

CASPER. Ah! That's quite a different matter—I'll make my compliments to him at once. Your Insolence, it gives me uncommon pleasure that you have the honour of making my acquaintance.

FAUST. Have you been in service before?

CASPER. Yes, your Insolence, in Calabria, where I was in the service of a study-maker.

FAUST. Are your parents still alive, my friend?

CASPER. I'm not quite sure. I always think that the drum-pigeons hatched me.

FAUST. You have good testimonials to show, I suppose?

CASPER. Rest assured; I have a most magnificent testimonial— [*aside*] on my back.

WAGNER. Yes, your Magnificence, he has assured me of it [*speaking confidentially to* FAUST].

CASPER [*sits on the chair*]. Ah! Here's a chair; I can make myself comfortable. [*Sits down.*] Zounds! What a charming seat This chair must be upholstered with fat steel springs! *Prr Prr!* Here one can give oneself an air of authority.

WAGNER. My friend!

CASPER. Well, what is it?

WAGNER. Get up at once!

CASPER. Why?

WAGNER. It isn't proper to sit down in the presence of his Magnificence.

CASPER. Oh, that doesn't apply to me! I've come from a journey, and he who comes from a journey is tired and desires to be comfortable.

WAGNER. But this chair is his Magnificence's own!

CASPER. Just now it is Casper's own! I don't know at all why Mr Famulus finds fault with it. Your Insolence hasn't said a single word, but every moment you, Mr Famulus, find something that doesn't seem right. I say this to you: if this goes on and once I get up my temper, then . . . [*At this moment the chair on which he sits is enveloped in flame.*] Oh! Oh! Help! Help!     [*Goes out.*

## SCENE V

### MEPHISTOPHELES, CASPER *singing.*

CASPER [*joining* MEPHISTOPHELES]. Well, who are you, *mon cher ami*? Is it good manners to come into his Insolence's room with your hat on your head?

MEPHISTOPHELES. Do you not recognize me then? I am the master's huntsman.

CASPER. The master's huntsman? And what does master want a huntsman for? He's a theologian.

MEPHISTOPHELES. But a very great lover of the hunt. I stand very high in his favour, for I catch foxes and hares with my hands.

CASPER. Zounds! Then you're a clever fellow! You know how to spare powder! What's your name?

MEPHISTOPHELES. Mephistopheles.

CASPER. What? Stoffelfuss, did you say?

MEPHISTOPHELES. Mephistopheles! Don't mutilate my name, or——

CASPER. Well, well, don't shout in that way and take on so! I didn't get it right.

MEPHISTOPHELES. Have you heard that our master is going to travel?

CASPER. Travel? Where to?

MEPHISTOPHELES. Just travel.

CASPER. Just so, travel. Where to?

MEPHISTOPHELES. To Parma.

CASPER. Oh, you can't make a fool of me! What would he want to get into a *Barme*[1] for, when he's so fat?

[1] Manger.

# THE PUPPET-PLAY OF DOCTOR FAUST

ɪEPHISTOPHELES. No! no! Parma is a principality where a great
nuptial ceremony is to take place.
ASPER. Oh! That's quite another matter. But what's a nuptial
ceremony?
ɪEPHISTOPHELES. A nuptial ceremony is a marriage.
ASPER. Do they give you much to eat and drink there?
ɪEPHISTOPHELES. Oh, yes: lots.
ɪASPER. Rejoice, my belly: there's going to be another downpour!
Is master to take me with him or not?
ɪEPHISTOPHELES. No, he has ordered that you should remain behind.
He is to journey quite alone to Parma on his robe.
ɔASPER. On his robe? That will be a pretty wear and tear.
ᴍEPHISTOPHELES. Yet I will take it on my own responsibility to take
you along with us, without his being aware of it.
ɔASPER. Oh, yes, do that, good Stoffelfuss, for I simply adore eating
and drinking!
MEPHISTOPHELES. Would you prefer to ride or go in a carriage?
CASPER. You know best. Get something sent here for me to ride.
MEPHISTOPHELES. Very well, I'll see to it at once. But I expressly
forbid you to tell anyone in Parma who our master is or what his
name is—otherwise I'll break your neck. Do you understand me?
[*Goes out.*
CASPER [*alone*]. Oh, yes, I've understood all right. One would need
cotton-wool in one's ears not to have understood. Well, I must go
and get my equipage packed up. And he will get me something
to ride on; if only he brought me here a nice little Polish or
Hungarian pony, for I like riding, and—[*A dragon enters and gives
him a knock on the shoulders; he falls down.*] What kind of behaviour
is that? [*Gets up.*] He! he! Help! help! Stoffelfuss! Stoffelfuss! Is that the horse you promised me?
MEPHISTOPHELES [*coming in*]. Just get up on it. It won't harm you.
CASPER. Oh, yes, just get up on it! That's a new-fangled horse.
I must think it over a bit. Zounds! It's got a walking-
stick behind! If the animal hits me a knock on the nose it'll
upset the applecart. It's even got wings! Won't I suffer if it
flies off? Courage! I'll get up. [*He mounts.*] That's not a bad
seat! Hi! hi! Little fox! Hi! [*The dragon gives him a knock at the
back of his head with its tail.*] Well! And who's the lout who's
given me a blow as if he wanted to knock out my four senses?
I'll put a stop to that! Well, little fox, gee up, gee up! Hi! hi!
[*The dragon gives him another blow.*] Thunder and lightning!
Some one has struck me again! [*He turns round.*] I believe it was
you with your walking-stick! Just you wait! I'll take another
seat so as to get out of the line of fire. [*He sits farther forward.*]
This beast's contrived not badly for a learner in riding, for if one
were to fall off one couldn't fall far. [*Makes movements as if he were
walking.*] But I hope there won't be bad weather to-day; I fear
this journey will cost me more in shoe leather than I get in salary.

2G 465

Now, little fox. Hi! hi! [*The dragon rises suddenly, and flies upwa*
*amid thunder and lightning. He cries out.*] He! he! Help! help
Stoffelfuss! Stoffelfuss! The animal's going up into the sky
He! he! he! [*He vanishes*

*The curtain falls*

## ACT III

### Scene I: *A garden.*

#### Duke, Bianca, Orestes.

Duke. Well, dearest spouse, how do you like my Court? Can you
find in me and my subjects sufficient recompense for the sacrifice
you have made in leaving your parents and your native country?

Bianca. Oh, my husband, how deeply you shame me in asking that
question! Have I not received proofs sufficient of your love and
of the esteem of your subjects to make me happy in the thought
of spending my life at your side?

Duke. And yet it seems to me as if a secret grief sometimes clouded
your face. Have you perhaps a secret in your breast in which you
do not feel perhaps that I am worthy to participate?

Bianca. No, I am only troubled by sorrow for my father, who was
seriously ill when I accompanied the ambassadors here to you.
Feeble and exhausted, he raised himself in his bed when I took
leave of him and said: "Be as good a wife as you have been a
daughter and my blessing will follow you always." Oh, my
husband, from that time I have been unable to repress the
anxiety which grief for my father's health occasions me. Will you
grant me a request?

Duke. Speak, dear Bianca—it shall be granted.

Bianca. Allow me to leave you now, so that I can give the ambassadors some consoling words to carry to my father, telling him of the
love and kindness which I have met with here.

Duke. With pleasure I accede to your wish. Only I beg you not to
withdraw your gracious presence overlong.

Bianca. I will hasten as quickly as I can and come to you again.
[*Goes off.*

### Scene II

#### Duke *and* Orestes.

Duke. Well, dear Orestes, what do you say to my choice of a wife?

Orestes. That you must consider yourself and the whole country
lucky to have gained so virtuous a consort and duchess, and may
Heaven grant the happiness to us all to be ruled right long by
such an excellent pair of princes!

Duke. I thank you for your wish, and hope that you will aid me
even further with your wise counsel to make my subjects happy.

ꓛRESTES. Truly, your Highness, I will try to show myself' worthy of the great favour you display towards me.

ꓱUKE. Have you prepared, as well as possible, everything that will be needed for these nuptials?

ꓱRESTES. Yes, your Highness. I have not failed to carry out your orders to the best of my ability. I have also got it announced by means of a proclamation that all artists and scholars should come here to embellish this marriage by their presence.

[CASPER *is hurled down from the sky on to the stage.*

DUKE. Good heavens! What's that?

ORESTES. Your Highness, I am amazed. This man——

DUKE. Ask him, dear Orestes, how it can possibly be that he could come down here out of the sky?

CASPER. Him! ham! hum!

ORESTES. My friend, who are you?

CASPER. Him! ham! hum!

ORESTES. How can it be that you have fallen down here out of the sky without injuring yourself?

CASPER. Him! ham! hum! Him! ham! hum!

DUKE. He seems to be dumb, if he's not dissembling. Promise him twenty ducats if he reveals this secret to us; if not, he'll get twenty good lashes.

CASPER. Him! ham! hum! Bum! bum!

ORESTES. My friend, you have heard what his Highness has promised you. If you can speak, don't delay any longer in fulfilling his Highness's desire.

CASPER. Him! ham! hum! Him! ham! hum!

DUKE. I truly believe that this man is merely laughing at us. Orestes, call the watch at once!

ORESTES. In a moment, your Highness.                    [*Prepares to go off.*

CASPER [*holds him back*]. No! no! Just wait, old sir!

DUKE. What? You can speak? You're not dumb?

CASPER. That's just the trick.

DUKE. You seem to me to be a very obstinate fellow.

CASPER. Oh, no. I'm a very good man, but I have a very bad companion, and he has forbidden me to speak.

DUKE. What's your name?

CASPER. Ah! That's what I must not tell.

DUKE. Then you must have been guilty of some terrible crime if you dare not reveal your name.

CASPER. You don't think, do you, that I've stolen anything? God forbid! Casper can go wherever you will, but no one can say that about Casper.

DUKE. So Casper's your name?

CASPER. Who told you that I was called Casper?

DUKE. You yourself.

CASPER. I? [*To himself*] Oh, you damned blubberer!

DUKE. To judge by your dress you are a servant?

CASPER. You've guessed it.

DUKE. What's your master's name?

CASPER. Ah, there's the rub! I must not reveal it, else my neck'll be broken.

DUKE. You can always tell it to me. No harm shall come to you.

CASPER. Who, then, are you?

DUKE. I am the Duke of Parma.

CASPER. What? The Duke of Parma? Pray pardon me for not having·yet made you my compliments. I am very glad that you have the honour of my acquaintance. Go on!

DUKE. Very good, my friend. Well, I should gladly know the name of your master.

CASPER. I must not tell it; but I'll show it you pantomimically.

DUKE. Well, I am content.

CASPER [raises his arm]. See here! What is that?

DUKE. That's an arm.

CASPER. Well, what is this just in front? Just in front?

DUKE. A hand, and if you close it it's a *Faust*.[1]

CASPER. Right—I serve him. But I didn't tell you.

DUKE. What? The great scholar? You're in Doctor Faust's service?

CASPER. Yes, I am. It's great to be able to speak to people and yet not give away secrets. That's the point—I am a true genius; I've always got a bunch of tricks in my head.

DUKE. Since you live with this famous man, have you not learned some of his art?

CASPER. My master learned everything from me.

DUKE. From you?

CASPER. Oh, yes! I am Faust's teacher. Haven't you heard, then, of my skill? My name has been blazoned abroad to all four corners of the earth.

DUKE. No, I haven't heard anything about it.

CASPER. Aha! Now I call to mind, we had so hard a winter then that all the sounds were frozen; but just let it thaw, and my fame will make a devil of a row.

DUKE. I should be glad to see some of your art.

CASPER. So you want to see some of my art?

DUKE. Yes!

CASPER. You shall have it directly. [*Aside*] See, Casper, if you had learned anything now, how you could have profited. [*Aloud*] Do you wish to see something big, something grand?

DUKE. Yes, something extraordinary.

CASPER. Would you like to see a great big wave come rolling in to drown all three of us?

DUKE. No, I shouldn't like to see that.

CASPER. That's a very big piece.

DUKE. I'd rather you showed me something else.

[1] Fist.

# THE PUPPET-PLAY OF DOCTOR FAUST

CASPER. Something else? Perhaps you'd like to see a great millstone crashing down from the sky to beat us down ten fathoms deep in the bosom of the earth? That's a very impressive piece.

DUKE. No, I shouldn't like to see that; my life would be endangered in this as in your first piece. Something fine, something pleasant —that's what I want.

CASPER. Oh! Something fine? Perhaps you'd like to see an Egyptian darkness wrapped up in cotton-wool? That's a very fine piece. But I need four weeks' time to pack it in its box.

DUKE. Don't go on talking such utter nonsense!

CASPER. Utter nonsense? Can you do it then?

DUKE. No—but——

CASPER. Well, you mustn't say that it is utter nonsense, for I can become offended so quickly as to make my body all run into gall when a person steps up and says it is utter nonsense, and yet can't do it himself.

DUKE. Don't be so indignant about it! Show me something else.

CASPER. Perhaps you'd like to see a devilry?

DUKE. Yes, I should like to see a *Salto mortale.*

CASPER. But what's my reward if I do show a devilry?

DUKE. I have laid aside twenty ducats for you, and these you shall get.

CASPER. I should be right glad if you gave me the money in advance.

DUKE. Why? You don't doubt my promise, do you?

CASPER. Oh! God forbid! But, do you see, when I make a devilry, usually I stay three or four months in the sky, so it would be an advantage if I had the money in advance wherewith, among other things, to pay for my lodgings.

DUKE. So soon as I am convinced of your skill you shall have the ducats—but not before.

CASPER. So I get no money in advance?

DUKE. No.

CASPER. Well, for my part, if an accident happens to me I'll have no gold with me, and you shall have it on your conscience.

DUKE. Yes! yes! Just give me a proof of your skill.

CASPER. At once! At once! Just stand a little to the side, and I will start my invocation. [*He turns always on one foot.*] *Br! br! br!*

DUKE. What does that mean?

CASPER. That's the invocation. You mustn't put me out. *Br! br! br!* Well, sirs, shut your eyes, in case things spring into your face.

DUKE. What kind of things?

CASPER. Sugar and coffee! *Br! br! br!* What do you really want to see, sirs?

DUKE. Well, a caper!

CASPER. Make it yourself! I can't do it! [*Goes off.*

DUKE. Wait, you damned rascal! Orestes, go and get the watch to arrest him and let him suffer for his villainy.

ORESTES. At once, your Highness. [*Goes off.*

# DOLLS AND PUPPETS

*Duke alone. Then* Faust. *Later little by little the apparitions.*

Duke. I will not let him be punished too severely for his audacity in having ridiculed me, for he has given me real pleasure with his droll conceits. If I'm not mistaken, a man whom I don't know is coming down the alley towards me.

Faust [*enters*]. Most serene Duke, with deepest humility I beg you to pardon me for making so free a visit. But as it has been proclaimed that all artists and scholars are invited to come to your princely marriage, I have hastened to fulfil your Highness's commands, and humbly beg that you will permit me to present here my art and my skill.

•Duke. What is your name?

Faust. Johannes Faust.

Duke. What? You are the world-famous Doctor Faust, whom all men admire, you who are able in one minute to summon summer and winter, like nature itself? You are very welcome to my Court: for long I have desired to make your personal acquaintance.

Faust. Your Highness overwhelms me with your praise, which up to now I have not done anything to deserve. Perhaps your Highness would desire to see some proofs of my art?

Duke. If it gives you no trouble, I should accept your offer with pleasure.

Faust. At all times and in every place, your Highness, I am ready to fulfil your commands.

Duke. Well, then, I should like to see here the big giant Goliath and the little David.

Faust. Your Highness shall immediately be satisfied! Mephistopheles! Do you hear? Cause the giant Goliath and the little David to appear immediately!

> [*An adagio sounds, and* Goliath *and* David *appear. The latter has his sling in his hand. After some minutes, during which the* Duke *speaks to* Faust, *the* Duke *indicates that he has seen enough.* Faust *bows and nods; the apparitions vanish; and the music ceases.*

Duke. Indeed, you have shown me these two persons beyond my expectation. I have long wondered how it was possible that this giant could be killed by a sling wielded by so small a man.

Faust. It is a proof that the strong must not always trust to their strength. What would your Highness like to see further?

Duke. The chaste Lucrece, as she stabs herself in the breast on the Capitol at Rome, since her virginity was in danger of being violated by force.

Faust. Very well, your Highness! Do you hear, Mephistopheles? Cause the chaste Lucrece to appear!

> [*He nods. Adagio.* Lucrece *appears with the dagger at her breast. Then the same dumb show as before.*

# THE PUPPET-PLAY OF DOCTOR FAUST

DUKE. Upon my honour! Most excellently do you gratify my wishes. This woman through her chastity redeemed Rome's tottering imperial throne. She will shine in history as the greatest example of womanly virtue.

FAUST. Your Highness is right! What would your Highness desire to see now?

DUKE. Samson and Delilah, as she was cutting off his hair.

FAUST. In a moment, your Highness! Mephistopheles, cause Samson and Delilah to appear!

[*He nods. Adagio. The curtain at the back opens and reveals* DELILAH *sitting in a chair with scissors in her hand; before her sits* SAMSON, *sleeping with his head laid on her bosom; she is about to cut off his hair. Then dumb show as above.*

DUKE. You are giving me more and more proof that you are one of the greatest magicians of our time. But I should like to ask for one thing more.

FAUST. Make your command, your Highness!

DUKE. I should like to see the heroic Judith with the head of Holofernes.

FAUST. Very well, your Highness! Mephistopheles! Do you hear? Cause her to appear at once—Judith with the head of Holofernes!

[*He nods:* JUDITH *appears to the music of an adagio. In her right hand is a sword, in her left the head of* HOLOFERNES. *Dumb show as above.*

DUKE. I thank you for the pleasure you have given me. You are my guest from to-day; and for as long as you stay in my Court you are my close companion. Follow me, for I wish to introduce you to my wife as the most renowned magician.

FAUST. I obey, your Highness. [*They go out.*

## SCENE IV

CASPER *and* MEPHISTOPHELES *enter.*

MEPHISTOPHELES [*dragging in Casper by the neck*]. Just you come here, you scoundrel! Why have you betrayed our master?

CASPER. Oh! oh! I haven't betrayed him. Let me alone, Stoffelfuss, golden Stoffelfuss—won't you let me go?

MEPHISTOPHELES. Why did you tell your master's name to the Duke?

CASPER. I didn't tell him a word; I just showed it to him pantomimically, and he understood at once who our master was and what was his name. But, dear Stoffelfuss, just let me go this time! Don't break my neck; I won't do it again as long as I live.

MEPHISTOPHELES. Well, it shall be allowed to pass this time. But as a punishment you will remain here in Parma alone. Master has dismissed you from his service. You'll see now how you'll perish! [*Goes out.*

CASPER [*alone*]. Stoffelfuss! He! Stoffelfuss! Golden Stoffel! Don't leave me alone! Stoffelchen! He's gone, by my soul, and left

me here! First give me at least my wages! You owe me two
months' wages. It's all in vain! The devil has taken it! Ah!
You poor Casper, how will you get on now, without a place,
without a master? And the Duke is sending round four men with
big sticks to arrest me for my magic. [*Weeps.*] Hu! hu! ha! ha!
If my grandmother knew what's happening to me I think the
good woman would weep her eyes out of her head! Hu! hu! ha!
ha!

## SCENE V

### AUERHAHN *enters.*

AUERHAHN [*descending from the sky*]. Casper!

CASPER. I thought some one called me by name?

AUERHAHN. Casper, why are you in such grief?

CASPER. And shouldn't I be grieved? My master has chucked me
out of my place. Here I am in a foreign land where I don't know
one street from another.

AUERHAHN. You are truly in a difficult position, for here there are
many bandits, who knock men dead for two halfpennies.

CASPER. Two halfpennies? And I have just threepence in my
pocket. Will they knock me dead thrice?

AUERHAHN. Yes, they will knock you dead thrice!

CASPER. Oh! oh! Poor Casper, all's over with you. Hu! hu! hu!

AUERHAHN. Listen, Casper! I really pity you!

CASPER. Well, here is one, at any rate, in the world who is affected
by my position!

AUERHAHN. Do you know? In Wittenberg the night-watchman has
died, and if you promise me your soul, guaranteeing that I can
carry it off after twelve years, I shall bring you to Wittenberg
and put you in the night-watchman's place there.

CASPER. No, nothing can come of this contract.

AUERHAHN. Why not?

CASPER. I haven't got a soul. My maker forgot to put one into me!

AUERHAHN. Don't be so silly! Don't you consider yourself a man?
Consequently you must have a soul.

CASPER. Do you really believe I have a soul?

AUERHAHN. Of course!

CASPER [*aside*]. I can cheat the silly devil in this! [*Aloud*] All right!
I remember now—I have got a soul! I don't know how I could
have forgotten. But what's your name?

AUERHAHN. Auerhahn!

CASPER. Kickelhahn? Well, my dear Kickelhahn, I promise you
my soul after twelve years—and you'll get me the night-watchman's place?

AUERHAHN. Yes, I'll get it for you.

CASPER. And bring me at once to Wittenberg?

AUERHAHN. Yes, we shall be at Wittenberg in a twinkling. Just
hold on to me.

ᴀSPER [*grips him*]. I'm holding on! [*Springs back and blows on his hands.*] Thunder and lightning! I have burned myself; my hands must be full of blisters.

ᴜERHAHN. Yes, I've got an ardent disposition!

ASPER. I've noticed that. Just cool it off a little!

ᴜERHAHN. Well, then, hold on to me once more!

ᴀSPER. Well, once more I'm holding on.

ᴜERHAHN. Say, now: Capo cnallo!

ᴀSPER. Capers and quails.

ᴜERHAHN. Capo cnallo!

ᴀSPER. Capo cnallo!                                    [*Flies off with him.*

*The curtain falls*

## ACT IV

### SCENE I

FAUST's *room as in Act I. The chair stands at the table.*

FAUST [*entering*]. Greetings, home of my earliest joy! Remove from me my depression, my ill-will! Oh, why have I renounced my hope of salvation for such an ordinary existence? Here is the wound whereby I subscribed my heart's blood to him, sure mortgage to hell. Of course, I may be of good hope, for I can laugh at Satan, since four and twenty years must pass after our contract before I become his bondslave, and now only half of that time has gone by. Yes, I shall make use of his help only for a few years more, to make myself famous, and then I shall endeavour to get out of his clutches, and seek to gain back the salvation I cast away so lightly on my abandoned path. [*He seats himself.*] But I do not know why such an overpowering desire for sleep has suddenly come on me and forces me here to take a rest. Ah! Rest—rest that since my bond has left me quite, so that up to now I have only known it as a name! [*He falls asleep.*

### SCENE II

*The* GENIUS *enters.*

GENIUS. Faust! Faust! Wake from your sinful sleep! What have you undertaken? Consider that the joys which you gain from this infernal bond are transitory, that you have destroyed thereby your hope of salvation and go to eternal damnation! Were you not born a man, and do you sacrifice yourself so wantonly to this hellish spirit? Oh, abandon the road which you have been travelling up to now! Return to virtue! You have no time to lose if you desire still to save your soul. You can break the bond, but only if you do it to-day. Oh, Faust! Follow the warning of

your guardian genius, so that I may flutter round protecting yc
as of yore!                                      [*Goes ou*

FAUST [*awaking*]. Ha! What was that? This is the second time
thought I saw my genius warning me to break my bond wit
Satan as soon as possible. Yes, yes, I will go back to the path c
virtue, and consecrate myself to it, and through it seek to mak
myself worthy of the joys of heaven. Mephistopheles!

### SCENE III

#### MEPHISTOPHELES *enters*.

MEPHISTOPHELES. What you want, Faust?

FAUST. You know that you are forced by our contract to answer all
my questions. Tell me then: what would you do if you could
obtain salvation?

MEPHISTOPHELES. I am not compelled to give you an answer to such
a question. Yet hear and despair! If I could gain eternal salvation I should climb a ladder all the way to heaven, even if every
rung were a sharp knife. And do you, a man, throw your being so
wantonly away in order to enjoy the transitory pleasures of earth?

FAUST. Ha! I am not yet in your power! Get away from me for ever!

MEPHISTOPHELES [*aside*]. Well, I will go away, and seek to bind him
to me again by some means or other.              [*Goes out.*

FAUST [*alone*]. Miserable wretch! How deep am I sunk! Yet there
is still time to repent and to regain salvation. Yes, I will follow
the words of my guardian spirit and at once relieve my heart by
an ardent prayer to God. [*Kneels down.*] All-compassionate,
look down from Your throne upon me, a sinning man. Listen to
my sighs; let my prayer ascend through the clouds; forgive me my
past sins; take me again into Your grace, and lead me . . .

### SCENE IV

#### MEPHISTOPHELES *enters with* HELEN.

MEPHISTOPHELES. Faust! Faust! Leave off praying! Here, I'm
bringing you the lovely Helen, for whom the whole of Troy was
destroyed!

FAUST. Get away, you infernal spirit! I am in your power no more!

MEPHISTOPHELES. Just look here, Faust! She shall be your own,
Faust, if only you stop praying!

FAUST [*looks round*]. Ha! What a charming shape do I see!

HELEN. Gracious sir, your huntsman told me you had some commands for me.

FAUST [*aside*]. Am I no longer myself? Ha! Are these my eyes
which are devouring her eagerly and ardently as the sunbeams do
the earth? Oh! The flame of life has blazed up in me anew; I
shall try no more to gain heaven, for the earth blooms for me in
amorous luxury.

474

EPHISTOPHELES. Look, Faust, what trouble I've taken to dissipate your ill-humour! Amuse yourself with her as you please; only banish all sad thoughts.

AUST. I thank you, Mephistopheles, for your lovely present. Now, charming Helen, are you desirous of living with me?

[ELEN. You are lord of my person, and I will not fail to carry out your commands.

'AUST. Accompany me, dear Helen; I shall show you my jewels to convince you how happy your life with me will be.

IELEN. I follow you gladly!                                   [*Goes out with* FAUST.

VIEPHISTOPHELES [*alone*]. Ha! ha! ha! He's ours now; he's got no power now to escape us! He had almost overreached me and escaped from my clutches, but a woman was the thing to put him again into our hands.

SCENE V

FAUST *runs in.*

FAUST. Oh, vanity! Ha! Damned false being! When I sought to embrace this charming form I found myself embracing a hellish fury! Oh, Faust! What have you done? Now I have provoked Heaven anew! Once more I have allowed myself to be beguiled by Satan! Ha! Cursed spirit, are you still here? Get away from my side for ever, for I shall never see you again!

MEPHISTOPHELES. Ha! ha! ha! Rage on—it hurts me not! For know that our contract is nearly at an end; without any other chance of escape you will be my property.

FAUST. The contract at an end! I your property! Yet hardly half the four and twenty years have passed since I sold my soul to you!

MEPHISTOPHELES. No, Faust, you have made a bad mistake; just count in the nights and you will see that our contract is at an end.

FAUST. Ha! Lying spirit, you have betrayed me! But rejoice not so soon! I yet feel I have the power to defy you!

MEPHISTOPHELES. I laugh at your threats; your blood is mine; the bond is ended, and soon we shall come to take you in triumph to our prince Pluto.                                        [*Goes out.*

SCENE VI

FAUST [*alone*]. Ha! Will my life's course then be ended in a few hours? [*Kneels down.*] Oh, may my prayer ascend yet once more to the all-good God! There where the rosy flames of evening soar, there is—ha! Curses! The fiery gate of hell! Listen! Never— there must I go—*Ave*—the music of the celestial choir is broken! Oh, demon, why do you twist my words so that my prayer is turned into curses? No, no, I cannot pray! The fountain of eternal mercy is sealed from me. Even if the angels were to weep tears on my account it would never be opened for me again! I can hope for mercy no more.

# DOLLS AND PUPPETS

MEPHISTOPHELES [*within*]. Fauste, prepara te!

FAUST. Ha! Now must I prepare for the last hour of my life: no must I receive punishment for my sinful life—there in the pit of hell! My heart will be fettered by Pluto's heavy chains, and th furies wait eagerly for my body in order to tear it to pieces.

[*It strikes ter*

## SCENE VII

CASPER *enters as a night-watchman with his lantern.*

CASPER [*still without*]. Grethel! Light the lantern for me. I mus start my duties as night-watchman to-day. The citizens have just given me the job, but the town council hasn't yet confirmed it; it desires first a plain proof of my worth. Well, I'll do it as well as I can. [*Enters singing.*]

> Masters all, now list to me:
> If your wives they plaguy be
> Into bed them straightway cast;
> All the quarrel will be past.
> Ten has struck.
> Dra, la, la, la, la, la!        [*Dances.*
> Ladies all, now list to me,
> You must bear much—that I see.
> Yet this is no new device—
> Sometime you've got to break the ice!
> It's been broken quite a lot.
> Dra, la, la, la, la, la!        [*Dances.*

FAUST. How dare you enter my room when I have forbidden you ever to come to my house again?

CASPER. Your Insolence, pray pardon me; I desired only to give a proof of my skill as a night-watchman.

FAUST. Very good. But stay no longer in my presence.

CASPER. And then I wish also to talk to your Insolence about the wages owing to me; for I'm pressed for money. I must buy some trade equipment in order to carry on my new duties.

FAUST. Go to my famulus and get him to pay you the money—and now begone to the street where you belong.

CASPER. Well, if you are not glad to see me, I'll go. I thought to make my affairs right if I brought my first serenade to your Insolence's house, but since it doesn't appeal to you I'll make off again immediately. [*Goes out humming.*

FAUST [*alone*]. Now at this moment I am being accused and tried by the Almighty Judge! Oh, terrible thought!

MEPHISTOPHELES [*without*]. Fauste, judicatus es!

FAUST [*springs up*]. Ha! It is done! I am judged—my sentence is passed; the Almighty has broken his staff over me! I am in Satan's power! Oh, cursed be the day when I was born!

[*Seats himself. It strikes eleven.*

476

# THE PUPPET-PLAY OF DOCTOR FAUST

FAUST, CASPER, *and later all the* FURIES.

ASPER [*within*]. Grethel, give me the lantern. It's struck again; the clock can't be quite right in its head. But pour me out first a little oil on the wick so that I can see a bit better. So! [*Enters singing.*

> All ye widowers, list to me:
> If a new wife you wish to see,
> Do not praise the first too much,
> Else you'll not get another such.
> Eleven has struck!
> Dra, la, la la, la, la!
> All ye widows, list to me:
> Truly you live in misery,
> For, alas! you have not got
> From experience you know what.
> Eleven twenty!
> Dra, la, la, la, la!

Zounds! How have I got into this room again! Pray pardon, your Insolence, that I have come into your house once more; I truly don't know how I manage to lose my path always! In a way, however, I'm glad that I have the honour of meeting your Insolence again, for I have a right big request to make to you.

FAUST. Well, what does your request concern?

CASPER. I have heard that your Insolence is to make a journey into the Plutonic realm, and I would wish to beg you to bear many compliments from me to my grandmother. She sits on the left hand as you enter hell, number one, and mends slippers.

FAUST. Get out this very minute, or I will drive your impertinence off by force!

CASPER. Well, well, don't take it so ill! I can easily go by myself.
[*Goes out hummimg.*

MEPHISTOPHELES [*within*]. Fauste, in eternum damnatus es!

FAUST [*springs up*]. Ha! Now the moment has come when I am expected in the pit of hell, where resin and brimstone burns for me, where Pluto's monsters wait for me. Soon I shall feel hell's torments in my body! The thunder rolls—the earth vomits fire! Oh, help! Oh, save me, might of Heaven! In vain! In vain is my cry for help—I must hence to a place where I have to suffer punishment for my sins. Ha! Come then, you hellish furies, rend, tear my body, and bring me to the place of my fate!
[*At the beginning of this speech thunder and lightning start. These grow fiercer. At the end the* FURIES *arrive and go off carrying* FAUST *into the sky. Slowly it grows quieter, then twelve strikes.*

# DOLLS AND PUPPETS

## Scene IX

### Casper. *Later* Auerhahn.

Casper [*without*]. Devil take it! That clock strikes as if Satan were
pulling at the rope! I must go my rounds again. Grethel, make a
couple of pans of coffee, but don't put too many grounds in it
Now give me the lantern. So! I will be back soon. See and be
quick about it! [*Enters singing.*]

> All my lads, now list to me!
> If a maiden you go to see,
> Do it nicely, do't with poise,
> See the house door makes no noise:
> Twelve has struck!
> Dra, la, la, la, la!
> All my virgins, list to me!
> Should one ask you a question free—
> "Are you, my dear, a virgin yet?"—
> Just you answer: "Yes, I regret."
> Null null has struck!
> Dra, la, la, la, la!

[*He dances and bumps with the lantern into* Auerhahn, *who has
descended from the sky.*

Casper [*shrieks*]. Kibi! Who's that?

Auerhahn. Do you not know me, Casper?

Casper. No, I don't! Who are you, *mon cher ami*?

Auerhahn. I am Auerhahn.

Casper. Oh! Let me just throw a little light on your face! [*Holds
up the lantern.*] Yes, you're right. You are Kickelhahn. What do
you want?

Auerhahn. Casper, your time is up. You must go with me to hell!

Casper. To hell? I thought the chimney was your place. I do
believe you're not right in the head! Have the twelve years
passed then?

Auerhahn. Yes.

Casper. But I made my first round as night-watchman only to-day.

Auerhahn. That's nothing. The twelve years have passed, and you
are now mine.

Casper. What do you say? As I can see, you've cheated me!

Auerhahn. Of course!

Casper. Well, you're cheated too, for I haven't got a soul! Ha! ha!
ha!

Auerhahn. And even if you haven't got a soul you must come with
me.

Casper. Listen, Kickelhahn, don't make me wild! Go your way or
my lantern will make companionship with your head!

Auerhahn. Well, you know that since you are a night-watchman
I can't get you. [*Ascends through the sky.*

478

!ASPER [*alone*]. That's charming—even the devil will have nothing
to do with night-watchmen! Well, I'll go back to my comrades,
and we'll make right merry with a can of schnaps and laugh at
the silly devils.                                          [*Goes out dancing.*

*The curtain falls*

FIG. 463. FIGURES FOR PUPPET-PLAYS

479

# BIBLIOGRAPHY

WHILE this bibliography of books and articles is not intended to be exhaustive, I have considerably expanded the list of such works given in the original German edition of this book. The present bibliography provides, I think, a fuller list of available material on the theme than is elsewhere to be found.—*Translator.*

## DOLLS

ADAMS, M.: *Toy-making at Home* (1915).

ALLEMAGNE, H. R. D': *Histoire des Jouets* (Paris, 1903).

ANDREE, R.: *Ethnographische Parallelen und Vergleiche* (Leipzig, 1889).

—— "Rachepuppen" (*Globus*, lxxvii, 1900).

—— *Votive und Weihegaben des katholischen Volkes in Süddeutschland* (Brunswick, 1904).

ANTONIELLI, U.: "Una statuetta femminile di Savignano sul Panaro e il problema delle figure dette Steatopigi" (*Bulletino di Paletnologia italiana*, 1925).

BAESSLER, ——: *Altperuanische Kunst* (Leipzig, 1902-3).

BANGE, E. T.: *Die Kleinplastik der deutschen Renaissance in Holz und Stein* (Munich, 1928).

BARTRAM, N. D.: Игрушка. Ея исторія и зналеніе (Moscow, 1912).

BASTIAN, A.: *Der Fetisch an der Westküste Guineas* (Berlin, 1884).

BAUMEISTER, A.: *Denkmäler des klassischen Altertums* (Munich, 1885).

BAUR, E. E. VOM: "Insurgents in Toyland: Frau Kruse" (*Good House-keeping*, December 1911).

BAYER, J.: "Die eiszeitlichen Venusstatuetten" (*Die Eiszeit*, I, ii, 1924).

BECQ DE FOUQUIÈRES, L.: *Les Jeux des anciens* (Paris, 1873).

BENKARD, E.: *Das ewige Antlitz* (Berlin, 1927).

BENNDORF, ——: *Antike Gesichtshelme und Sepulcralmasken* (Vienna, 1878).

BISCARI, PRINCIPE: *Sopra gli ornamenti e trastulli de' bambini* (Florence, 1781).

BLANCHET, A.: *Étude sur les figurines en terre cuite de la Gaule* (Paris, 1891).

BLÜMMER, H.: *Technologie und Terminologie der Gewerbe bei Griechen und Römern* (1897).

BOAS, K.: "Über Warenhausdiebinnen mit besonderer Berücksichtung sexueller Motive" (*Archiv für Kriminal-Anthropologie und Kriminalistik*, lxv, Leipzig, 1916).

—— "Weitere Beiträge zur forensischen Bedeutung des Puppenfetischismus" (*Archiv für Kriminal-Anthropologie und Kriminalistik*, lxviii, 1918).

BOESCH, ——: *Kinderleben in der deutschen Vergangenheit* (Leipzig, 1900).

—— "Die Puppe als Spielzeug für das Kind" (*Kind und Kunst*, i, 1904-5).

# DOLLS AND PUPPETS

BÖTTIGER, —: *Hainhofersche Kunstschrank Gustav Adolfs in Upsala* (Stockholn 1910).

BREUER, R.: "Puppen" (*Neue Revue*, Berlin, 1908).

BRONNER, I.: "Puppenmodelle in der Festtracht polnisch-jüdischer Bürgei frauen aus dem 17. bis 19. Jahrh." (*Jahrbuch für jüdische Volkskundt* 1923).

BROOK, D.: *Terra-cottas* (1921).

BRÜCKER-EMBDEN, O.: *Chinesische Frühkeramik* (Leipzig, 1922).

BRÜNING, A.: "Schauessen und Porzellanplastik" (*Kunst und Kunsthandwerk*, vii, Vienna, 1904).

BULLE, H.: "Eine altgriechische Gliederpuppe" (*Zeitschrift des Münchner Alterthums-Vereins*, N. F. x, 1899).

BUREN, E. D. VAN: *Foundation Figurines and Offerings* (Berlin, 1931).

BUSCHAN, G.: *Illustrierte Völkerkunde* (Berlin, 1924).

BUSS, G.: "Die Puppe in der Kulturgeschichte" (*Velhagen und Klasings Monatshefte*, December 1907).

CALMETTES, P.: *Les Joujoux: leur histoire, leur technique* (Paris, 1924).

CANNING-WRIGHT, H. W.: *Peeps at the World's Dolls* (New York, 1923).

CARTAULT, A.: *Terres cuites grecques* (Paris, 1890).

CLARETIE, L.: *Les Jouets: histoire-fabrication* (Paris, 1894).

CÖSTER, R.: "Lotte Pritzel" (*Deutsche Kunst und Dekoration*, xlv, 1919–20).

CRÄMER, K.: "Spielzeug und Volkswirtschaft" (*Leipziger Illustrierte Zeitung*, 1920).

CREMEANS, L. M.: "Eskimo Toys" (*Journal of Home Economics*, April 1931).

CRUICKSHANK, M.: *Dolls' Clothes and how to make them* (1923).

CULIN, S.: "The Story of the Japanese Doll" (*Asia*, October 1922).

DÉCHÉLETTE, J.: *Manuel d'Archéologie* (Paris, 1908).

DEONNA, W.: *Les Statues de terre cuite en Grèce* (Athens, 1906).

DOIN, J.: "La Renaissance de la poupée française" (*Gazette des Beaux Arts*, 1914–16).

DÖRING, W. H.: "Papierpuppen von Erna Muth-Dresden" (*Deutsche Kunst und Dekoration*, xlv, 1919–20).

EBERT, M.: "Die Anfänge des europäischen Totenkultus" (*Prähistorische Zeitschrift*, xiii, 1922).

—— *Reallexikon der Vorgeschichte* (Berlin, 1924).

EHLOTZKY, F.: *Die Herstellen von Holzspielzeug mit einfachen Mitteln* (Ravensburg, 1929).

ELDERKIN, K. M.: "Jointed Dolls in Antiquity" (*American Journal of Archeology*, October 1930).

ELLIS, A. C., and HALL, G. S.: "A Study of Dolls" (*Pedagogical Seminary*, iv, Worcester, Massachusetts, 1896–97).

ENDERLIN, M.: *Das Spielzeug in seiner Bedeutung für die Entwicklung des Kindes* (Langensalza, 1907).

ERMAN, A.: *Ägypten und ägyptisches Leben im Alterthum* (Tübingen, 1923).

FECHHEIMER, H.: *Kleinplastik des Ägypter* (Berlin, 1923).

FELDHAUS, F. M.: *Die Technik der Vorzeit* (Leipzig, 1914).

FEWKES, J. W.: "Dolls of the Tusayan Indians" (*Internat. Archiv für Ethnogr.* vii, 1894).

482

# BIBLIOGRAPHY

ewkes, J. W.: "Clay Figurines made by Navaho Children" (*American Anthropologist*, October 1923).

ishburn, T.: "Spool Dolls" (*School Arts Magazine*, November 1929).

'orrer, R.: *Reallexikon der prähist. etc. Altertümer* (Stuttgart, 1907).

'oy, W.: "Südafrikan. Zauberpuppen" (*Ethnologica*, Leipzig, 1909).

'razer, Sir James: *The Golden Bough* (third edition, 1911).

'uchs, E.: *Tang-Plastik. Chinesische Grabkeramik des 6. bis 10. Jahrh.* (Munich, 1924).

—— *Selbstzuarbeitendes Spielzeug für Knaben und Mädchen* (Leipzig, 1930).

Furtwängler, A.: *Die Sammlung Sabouroff* (Berlin, 1883–87).

Gahnay, F. von. "Rachepuppen aus Ungarn" (*Globus*, lxxx, 1901).

Goodwin, B. M.: *How to make a Doll and Other Toys in the Classroom* (1919).

Gordon-Stables, Mrs: "The Vogue of Figurines revives" (*The International Studio*, May 1923).

Gratz, P.: *Püppchens Kleidung* (Leipzig, 1930).

Grimm, J.: *Deutsche Mythologie* (fourth edition, Berlin, 1875).

Grisseman, O.: *Bastelbuch für Väter* (contains "Mädchenspielzeug," Berlin, 1929).

Gröber, J.: *Kinderspielzeug aus alter Zeit* (Berlin, 1928; translated by P. Hereford as *Children's Toys of Bygone Days*, 1928).

Gross, A.: "Ritterlich Spielzeug" (*Festschrift für Julius Schlosser*, Vienna, 1927).

Grosse, E.: *Anfänge der Kunst* (Leipzig, 1893).

Grudzinska, A.: "The Study of Dolls among Polish Children" (*The Pedagogical Seminary*, September 1907).

Grühl, M.: "Die Bedeutung der Puppen beim letzten grossen Gräberfunde von Theben" (*Cosmos, Handweiser für Naturfreunde*, xix, 1922).

Haddon, J.: *Magic and Fetishism* (1906).

Hall, A. N.: *Home-made Toys for Girls and Boys* (1915).

Hampe, T.: *Der Zinnsoldat* (Berlin, 1924).

Harris, M.: *The "Truth" History of Dolls* (1913).

Hartl-Mitius, —: "Münchener Künstlerpuppen" (*Leipziger Illustrierte Zeitung*, cxxxiii, 1909).

Havard, —: *Dictionnaire de l'Ameublement* (Paris, n.d.).

Henry, V.: *La Magie dans l'Inde antique* (Paris, 1909).

Henschel vom Hain: "Künstlerpuppen als Zimmerschmuck" (*Das Echo*, xl, No. 1971, 1921).

Hentze, K.: *Les Figurines de la céramique funéraire* (Hellerau, 1928).

Herskovits, M. J., and F. S.: "Bush Negro Art" (*Arts Monthly*, October 1930).

Hetzer, H.: *Richtiges Spielzeug für jedes Alter* (Dresden, 1931).

Hildebrand, H.: "Beiträge zur Kenntnis der Kunst der niederen Naturvölker" (in Nordenskiöld, *Studien und Forschungen*, Leipzig, 1885).

Hildebrandt, P.: *Das Spielzeug im Leben des Kindes* (Berlin, 1904).

Hillman, R.: "Kinderspielzeug in Siam" (*Globus*, lxxviii, 1900).

Höber, F.: "Alte Puppen" (*Kunst und Kunsthandwerk*, xv, 1912).

Höfler, M.: *Gebildbrote* (Leipzig, 1908–11).

HOPFGARTEN, E. VON: "Die neuesten Käthe-Kruse-Puppen" (*Das Echo*, xlii No. 2080, 1923).

HOPKINS, U. N.: "Christmas Dolls from Russia" (*The Ladies' Home Journal* December 1913).

HÖRNES, M.: *Urgeschichte der bildenden Kunst in Europa* (third edition, Vienna, 1925).

HOUGH, W.: "The Story of Dolls tells the Story of Mankind" (*The World Review*, December 1927).

HUISH, M. B.: *Greek Terra-cotta Statuettes* (1900).

JACKSON, F. N.: *Toys of Other Days* (1908).

—— "Some Old Dolls" (*The Connoisseur*, December 1927).

JENKINS, R. L.: "Industrial Art in Toyland" (*Arts Monthly*, June 1923).

JOHNSON, DOROTHY; "Theban Toys" (*The Fortnightly Review*, July 1932).

JOHNSON, G. F.: *Toys and Toy-making* (1912).

JOSTEN, H. H.: *Fulder Porzellanfiguren* (Berlin, 1929).

KARUTZ, R.: "Eine schottische Rachepuppe" (*Globus*, xlix, 1901).

KATE, H. TEN: "Eine japanische Rachepuppe" (*Globus*, xlix, 1901).

KESTER, P.: "On Dolls" (*The International Studio*, 1923).

KITTREDGE, G. L.: *Witchcraft in Old and New England* (Cambridge, U.S.A., 1929).

KRONFELD, M.: *Zauberpflanzen und Amulette* (Vienna, 1898).

KRUSE, KÄTHE: "Playing with the Christmas Doll" (*The Ladies' Home Journal*, January 1914).

—— "Meine Puppen" (*Deutsche Kunst und Dekoration*, liii, 1923–24).

—— "Aus den Kinderjahren meiner Puppenwerkstatt: eine Weihnachtsplauderei" (*Westermanns Monatshefte*, December 1924).

—— "Meine Puppen" (*Velhagen und Klasings Monatshefte*, xl, 1925).

KÜHN, H.: *Die Kunst der Primitiven* (Munich, 1923).

KUNZE, F.: "Die Puppe in der Kulturgeschichte" (*Leipziger Illustrierte Zeitung*, cxxi, 1903).

LABORDE, L. DE: *Glossaire français du moyen âge* (Paris, 1872).

LANGE, K.: *Die künstlerische Erziehung der deutschen Jugend* (Darmstadt, 1893).

LEHMANN, A.: *Aberglaube und Zauberei* (second edition, Stuttgart, 1908).

LEMKE, E.: "Spiel-, Zauber-, und andere Puppen" (*Zeitschrift des Vereins für Volkskunde*, xxv, 1915).

LEOPOLD, A.: "Alte und neue Puppen" (*Leipziger Illustrierte Zeitung*, cxxxv, 1910).

LIE, I.: "Spielzeug aus dem Erzgebirge" (*Westermanns Monatshefte*, December 1930).

LOOSCHEN, H.: "Primitive Kunst aus der Kindheit der Völker" (*Kind und Kunst*, i, 1904–5).

LOVETT, E.: *The Child's Doll: its Origin, Legend, and Folk-lore* (1915).

LOW, F. H.: *Queen Victoria's Dolls* (1894).

LOWE, M. A.: *The Use of Dolls in Child-training* (New York, 1921).

LUKIN, J.: *Toys and Toy-making* (1881).

MAKINSON, J. T.: *Toy-manufacture* (1921).

# BIBLIOGRAPHY

MARTIN, F. R.: *Sibirica. Beitrag zur Kenntnis der Vorgeschichte und Kultur sibirischer Völker* (Stockholm, 1897).

MATTHEI, A.: *Werke der Holzplastik in Schleswig-Holstein bis zum Jahre* 1530 (Leipzig, 1928).

MATZDORFF, A.: "Old Dolls of the Orient" (*The International Studio*, September 1923).

MERRIAM, E.: "Toy-making in Germany" (*Harper's Bazaar*, January 1911).

MEYER, C.: *Die Aberglaube des Mittelalters* (Munich, 1884).

MICHEL, É.: "Deux Mannequins en bois du 16e siècle" (*Gazette des Beaux Arts*, I, 1904).

MILLS, W.: "Sacred Dolls of the Italian Christmas" (*House and Garden*, December 1929).

MOLLE, S.: "Elogio della bambola" (*Nuova Antologia*, April 1929).

MONKHOUSE, W. C.: *History of Chinese Porcelain* (1901).

MOSS, A.: "A Cubist Doll-maker of Montparnasse" (*Arts and Decoration*, May 1923).

MOUNT, M. W.: "Character Dolls" (*Harper's Bazaar*, November 1911).

MÜLLER, E.: *Die Wiedergeburt des Porzellans* (Munich, 1930).

MÜLLER, M.: "Wie stehts um die bayerische Spielwarenindustrie?" (*Industrie und Gewerbeblätter*, 1927).

MÜLLER, S., and VOGELSANG, W.: *Hollandische Patrizierhäuser* (Utrecht, 1909).

MUNN, M.: "Christmas Dolls" (*The Ladies' Home Journal*, December 1929).

NASSAU, R. H.: *Fetishism in West Africa* (1904).

NOËL, A.: *Les Jeux de la poupée* (Paris, 1806).

PARSONS, E. C.: "The Toy Soldier" (*The Educational Review*, June 1915).

PARTHUM, R.: "Erzgebirg. Spielzeug aus Kinderhand" (*Die Arbeitsschule*, xliii, pp. 577–581).

PEARSON, C. S.: "Idols in Hopi Worship" (*The Mentor*, September 1928).

PERDRIZET, P.: *Les Terres cuites grecques d'Égypte de la collection Fouquet* (Nancy, 1921).

PERGER, —: "Über den Alraun" (*Mitteilungen des Wiener Altertumsvereins*, v).

PHILLIPS, A. M.: "Mme Paderewski's Dolls: designed and made by Polish Young People to help their Native Land" (*The Craftsman*, October 1915).

PICARD, M.: *Mittelalterliche Holzfiguren* (Erlenbach, Zürich, 1920).

POLKINGHORNE, R. K., and M. I. R.: *Toy-making in School and Home* (1916).

POTTIER, E.: *Les Statuettes de terre cuite dans l'antiquité* (Paris, 1890).

PUCKETT, —: *Folk Beliefs of the Southern Negro* (New York, 1926).

RATHGEBER, E.: "Die Heimat der Puppenfee" (*Signale für die musikalische Welt*, lii, 1894).

REISS, —, and STÜBEL, —: *Das Todtenfeld von Ancon in Peru* (Berlin, 1880–87).

RILKE, R. M.: *Lotte-Pritzel-Puppen* (Munich, 1921).

ROBERT, L.: *Zerlegbares Puppenhaus. Anleitung zum Bau eines modernen Puppenhauses mit Autogarage, Terasse u.a. Komfort* (Ravensburg, 1930).

ROBINSON, —: "Funeral Effigies of the Kings and Queens of England" (*Archæologia*, lx, 1907).

ROBINSON, M.: "Some Eighteenth-century Toys" (*The Connoisseur*, October 1926).

RUMPF, F.: *Spielzeug der Völker* (Berlin, 1922).

# DOLLS AND PUPPETS

RUPÉ, H.: "Neue Vitrinenpuppen von Lotte Pritzel" (*Deutsche Kunst und Dekoration*, xlviii, 1921).

SAUERLANDT, M.: *Deutsche Porzellanfiguren* (Berlin, 1923).

SCHEFOLD, M.: "Das Kind und das Spielzeug" (*Westermanns Monatshefte*, December 1927).

SCHIEBELHUTH, H.: "Puppen als Zimmerschmuck" (*Deutsche Kunst und Dekoration*, xlviii, 1921).

SCHLIEMANN, H.: *Ilios* (Leipzig, 1881).

SCHLOSSER, J. VON: "Geschichte der Porträtbildnerei in Wachs" (*Jahrbuch der Kunstsammlungen des Allerh. Kaiserhauses*, xxix, 1910–11).

—— "Aus der Bildnerwerkstatt der Renaissance" (*Jahrbuch der Kunstsammlungen des Allerh. Kaiserhauses*, xxxi, 1913–14).

SCHMITZ, G.: "Weihnachtliches Kunstgewerbe" (*Westermanns Monatshefte*, December 1925).

SCHULTZ, F. T.: "Kulturgeschichte des Spielzeugs" (*Leipziger Illustrierte Zeitung*, clv, 1920).

SCHUMACHER, F.: *Wie ich zu meiner Puppensammlung kam. Erinnerungen einer Achtzigjährigen* (Stuttgart, 1929).

SCHUR, E.: "Neue Puppen" (*Dekorative Kunst*, xvii, 1909).

SEABY, A. W.: "Toys at the Whitechapel Art Gallery" (*The International Studio*, September 1916).

SERRURIER, L.: *Kleiderdrachten in Nederlandsch. Indie vorgesteld door Poppen. Geschenk van de Dames in Nederl. Indie aan H.M. de Koningin* (The Hague, 1894).

SEYFFERT, O., and TRIER, W.: *Spielzeug* (Berlin, 1922).

SHERBON, F. B.: "The Educational Value of Doll Play" (*American Childhood*, February 1927).

SHETELIG, H.: "Statuetter fra istidens stenalder" (*Konst og Kultur*, ii, 1924).

SILBER, M.: *Die Tonfiguren vom römischen Gräberfeld am Bürglstein in Salzburg* (*Anthropologische Gesellschaft in Wien*, Mittheilungen, 1926).

SIMON, K.: *Figürliches Kunstgerät aus deutscher Vergangenheit* (Berlin, 1926).

SINGLETON, E.: *Dolls* (New York, 1927).

SMITH, C.: "Merry Figures from Vegetables" (*Better Homes and Gardens*, January 1931).

STARR, F.: "Japanese Toys and Toy-collectors" (*Transactions of the Asiatic Society of Japan*, December 1926).

STARR, L. B.: "The Educational Value of Dolls" (*The Pedagogical Seminary*, December 1909).

STEFFENS, C.: "Die Indianerpuppensammlung von Frau A. L. Dickermann" (*Globus*, lxxv, 1899).

STRELE, R.: "Der Palmesel" (*Zeitschrift des deutschen u. österreichischen Alpenvereins*, xxviii, 1897).

SULLY, J.: *Studies of Childhood* (new edition, 1903).

—— "Dollatry" (*The Contemporary Review*, lxxv, 1899).

SY, M.: *Die Thüringer Spielwarenindustrie im Kampf um ihre Existenz* (Jena, 1929).

SYDOW, E. VON: *Die Kunst der Naturvölker und der Vorzeit* ((Berlin, 1923).

—— *Ahnenkult und Ahnenbild der Naturvölker* (Berlin, 1924).

—— *Kunst und Religion der Naturvölker* (Oldenburg, 1926).

TALBOT, P.: "Some New Chelsea" (*The House Beautiful*, May 1924).

# BIBLIOGRAPHY

TALMAN, C. F.: "Little Ladies from Tanagra" (*The Mentor*, October 1923).

TAUBE, E.: *Allerlei Puppen und ihre Bekleidung* (Leipzig, 1929).

THATCHER, E.: "Doll Furniture that is a Joy to make" (*The Ladies' Home Journal*, November 1925).

TRAWNICZEK, M.: "Eingeschaffenes Spielzeug für Weihnachten" (*Die Arbeitsschule*, xliii, p. 604).

UHLE, M.: *Kultur und Industrie südamerikanischer Völker* (Berlin, 1889).

VATTER, E.: *Religiöse Plastik der Naturvölker* (Frankfort-on-the-Main, 1926).

VERSTI, V.: *Puppen und Spielzeug aus Bast und Holz* (Vienna, 1930).

VETH, —: "De Mandragora" (*Internat. Archiv für Ethnogr.*, vii, 1894).

VILLIERS, —, and PACHINGER, —: *Amulette und Talismane* (Munich, 1928).

VINCHON, —: "Le Fétichisme de la poupée et le vol aux étalages" (*Journal de Médécine de Paris*, 1914).

VOLKER, A. E.: "Puppenkunst" (*Leipziger Illustrierte Zeitung*, cxxxi, 1908).

WADE, M. H.: *Dolls of Many Lands* (New York, 1913).

WADSWORTH, B. M.: "Inspiration from German Toys" (*The School Arts Magazine*, April 1929).

WARBURG, E.: "Revolution im Kösener Puppenstaat" (*Westermanns Monatshefte*, December 1923).

—— "Kinderspielzeug in alter und neuer Zeit" (*Westermanns Monatshefte*, December 1928).

WEEKS, J.: *Among the Primitive Batongo* (1914).

WEIGLIN, P.: "Der standhafte Zinnsoldat" (*Velhagen und Klasings Monatshefte*, December 1914).

WEIXLGÄRTNER, A.: *Dürer und die Gliederpuppe*. *Beiträge zur Kunstgeschichte Franz Wickhoff gewidmet* (Vienna, 1903).

WHITE, G.: *A Picture-book of Ancient and Modern Dolls* (1928).

WILKINSON, J. G.: *Manners and Customs of the Ancient Egyptians* (1837).

WINKLER, H.: *Wertvolles Spielzeug* (Munich, 1931).

WINTER, F.: *Die Typen der figürlichen Terrakotten* (Berlin, 1903).

WITH, K.: *Chinesische Kleinbildnerei in Steatit* (Oldenburg, 1926).

WLISLOCKI, H. VON: *Volksglaube und religiöser Brauch der Zigeuner* (1891).

—— "Amulette und Zauberapparate der ungarischen Zeltzigeuner" (*Globus*, lix, 1891).

WOLDT, H.: "Kultusgegenstände der Golden und Giljaken (am Amur)" (*Internat. Archiv für Ethnogr.*, i, 1888).

WRIGHT, H. W. C.: *Peeps at the World's Dolls* (1923).

WÜNSCH, R.: "Eine antike Rachepuppe" (*Philologus*, lxi, 1902).

ZINGERLE, I. V.: *Das deutsche Kinderspiel* (second edition, Innsbruck, 1873).

## MISCELLANEOUS

"The Origin and Uses of Dolls" (*Harper's Weekly*, December 1910).

"Dolls in Old Silesian Costume" (*The International Studio*, December 1911).

"New German Dollies with Personality" (*The Craftsman*, December 1911).

"Käthe Kruse Dolls" (*The International Studio*, January 1912).

"Doll-making in Germany" (*American Homes*, July 1912).

"The Doll-head Industry" (*The Literary Digest*, January 1915).

487

# DOLLS AND PUPPETS

"Toys by a Russian Artist" (*The International Studio*, July 1915).
"The New Era in Dolls" (*The World's Work*, December 1916).
"Art in Toys" (*The International Studio*, December 1917).
"The Child and the Toy" (*The Spectator*, December 1919).
"Some French Toys of To-day" (*The International Studio*, April 1921).
"Dolls of All Nations" (*The Mentor*, December 1921).
*Das Puppenbuch* (Berlin, 1921).
"Toys of American Indians" (*Science*, January 1923).
"Indian Dolls" (*Science*, October 1923).
*Everybody's Book of the Queen's Doll's House* (1924).
*The Book of the Queen's Doll's House* (1924).
"Famous Dollies and their Home" (*Arts and Decoration*, December 1926).
"La Féerie des jouets" (*L'Illustration*, January 1927).
"Inventors turn to Toys" (*The Scientific American*, December 1928).
"Czechoslovakian Toys" (*The School Arts Magazine*, January 1930).
*Die deutsche Porzellan- und Steingut-Industrie* (Berlin, 1931).
"Toy Soldiers and Real Wars" (*The World To-morrow*, February 1931).

# PUPPETS

ABELS, H. R.: "Cinderella casts a Shadow" (*The School Arts Magazine*, February 1931).
ACHARD, M.: "Guignol" (*Annales politiques et littéraires*, April 1926).
ACKLEY, E. F.: *Marionettes, Easy to make, Fun to use* (New York, 1929).
ALBER, ——: *Les Théâtres d'ombres chinoises* (Paris, 1896).
ALBERT-BIROT, P.: *Matoum et Trévibar, ou Histoire édifiante et récréative du vrai et du faux poète* (Paris, 1919).
—— *Barbe-Bleue* (Paris, 1926).
ALFEROV, A.: Петрушка и его предки (Moscow, 1895).
ALTHERR, A.: *Marionetten* (Zürich, 1926).
AMIEUX, A.: *Cent ans après* (Lyons, 1904).
ANDERSON, M.: *The Heroes of the Puppet Stage* (1924).
B., O.: "Richard Teschner" (*Die graphischen Künste*, xli, 1918).
BAKSHY, A.: "The Lesson of the Puppet" (*The Theatre Arts Monthly*, July 1928).
BALDWIN, S.: "Dolls that come alive" (*The Woman's Home Companion*, December 1922).
BALLANTYNE, E.: "Sicilian Puppet-shows" (*The Theatre*, February 1893).
BALMER, H.: *Mein Gemüsetheater* (Bern, 1928).
BANNER, H. S.: "Java's Shadow-shows and the Kawi Epics" (*The London Mercury*, August 1927).
BARIL, G.: *Lafleur, Garçon apothicaire* (Amiens, 1901).
BARING, M.: "Punch and Judy" (*The London Mercury*, July 1922).
—— "Punch and Judy" (*The Living Age*, August 1922).
BEARD, L.: "A New Year's Punch-and-Judy Show" (*The Delineator*, January 1905).

# BIBLIOGRAPHY

AUPLAN, R. DE: "Les Poupées animées de Ladislas Starévitch" (*La Petite Illustration*, March 1930).

CKH, G. F.: *The Comedy of Marionettes, a Diary of Memories and Meditations* (n.d.).

ISSIER, F.: *Théâtre de Guignol* (Paris, n.d.).

LLOC, H.: "Marionettes" (*The Outlook*, June 1923).

RLINER, R.: *Denkmäler der Krippenkunst* (Augsburg; 1926).

ERNARD, L.: *Théâtre de Marionnettes* (texts, Paris, 1837).

ERNARDELLI, F.: "Per un teatro di marionette" (*Nuova Antologia*, April 1922).

ERTRAM, N. D.: "Das Puppentheater in der Sowjetunion" (*Das Puppentheater*, iii, pp. 161–168, 1929).

BERTRAND, V.: *Les Silhouettes animées à la main* (Paris, 1892).

BIDON, H.: "Les petits Comédiens de bois" (*Journal des Débats*, January 1930).

BIELSCHOWSKY, A.: *Das Schwiegerlingsche Puppenspiel vom Doktor Faust* (Berlin, 1882).

BIRRELL, F.: "Puppets, The Tempest, and Mr Fagan" (*The Nation*, June 1923, with reply by J. B. Fagan).

BISTANCLAQUE, —: *Guignol au Maroc* (Saint-Etienne, n.d.).

BITTNER, K.: "Beiträge zur Geschichte des Volksschauspiels vom Doctor Faust" (*Prager deutsche Studien*, No. 27, 1922).

BLACHETTA, W.: *Blachetta-Spiele und andere* (Leipzig, 1930).

BLONDEAU, H., and BUTEAUX, V.: *Guignol s'en va-t-en guerre* (Paris, 1915).

BLÜMNER, H.: "Fahrendes Volk im Altertum" (*Sitzungsberichte der k. bayerischen Akademie der Wissenschaften*, Munich; phil.-hist. Klasse, vi, 1918).

BOHATTA, H.: "Das javanische Drama" (*Miteilungen der anthropol. Gesellschaft zu Wien*, 1905).

BONAVENTURE BATANT: *Le Bottier de Saint-Georges* (Lyons, 1898).

BONNAUD, D.: *Pierrot pornographe* (Paris, 1902).

—— *Le Sacre de Clemenceau Ier* (Paris, 1907).

—— *Ulysse à Montmartre* (Paris, 1910).

—— *Venise, ou Lagune de miel* (Paris, 1913).

BOTTCHER, A.: "Vom Ausdruck des Kindes beim Handpuppenspiel" (*Blätter für Laien-und Jugendspieler*, i, 1925, 3).

BOUCHOR, M.: *Les Mystères d'Eleusis* (Paris, n.d.).

—— *Tobie* (Paris, n.d.).

—— *Noël, ou le Mystère de la Nativité* (Paris, n.d.).

—— *La Dévotion à Saint-André* (Paris, 1892).

—— *La Légende de Sainte-Cécile* (Paris, 1892).

—— *Le Songe de Khéyam* (Paris, 1892).

BOULTON, W. B.: *The Amusements of Old London* (1901).

BOWIE, A. G.: "The Story of Punch and Judy" (*The Theatre*, January 1884).

BREHM, W.: *Das Spiel mit der Handpuppe. Anleitung zur Herstellung von Handpuppen und Handpuppenbühnen und zum Spielen* (Düsseldorf, 1931).

BRESLES, J. DE: *Au Grand R. . Io . . Dé* (Dijon, 1924).

—— *Te rêves, eh Lyonnais!* (Dijon, 1925).

# DOLLS AND PUPPETS

BROOK, G. S.: "Memoirs of Marionettes" (*The Century Magazine*, Mar 1926).

BROWN, F. K.: "The Merrie Play of Punch and Judy" (*The Playgrou* July 1921).

BRUINER, J. W.: *Faust vor Goethe* (Berlin, 1894).

BRUMME, M. A.: *Das kleine Theater* (Esslingen, 1926).

BRUX, G.: "Die theatergeschichtliche Bedeutung des Marionettenspiels (*Jugendpflege*, iii, 1925, 1).

BUFANO, R.: "Puppet Anatomy" (*The Theatre Arts Monthly*, July 1928).

—— *Pinocchio for the Stage* (1929).

BUGNARD, C.: *L'École des ménagères* (Lyons, 1925).

BULLETT, G.: "Marionettes in Munich" (*The Saturday Review*, Decembe 1929).

BULLY, M.: "The Return of the Marionettes" (*Current Opinion*, liv, March 1913).

CADILHAC, P.-É.: "Guignol à Paris" (*L'Illustration*, July 1930).

CALHOUN, L.: "Another Venture in Puppets" (*Drama*, October 1920).

CALTHROP, A.: "An Evening with Marionettes" (*The Theatre*, May 1884).

CALTHROP, D. C.: *Punch and Judy* (1926).

CALVI, E.: "Marionettes of Rome" (*The Bellman*, January 1917).

CANARD, G.: *Les Classiques du Gourguillon* (texts and introduction, Lyons, n.d.).

CANARD, G., DUROQUET, A., and COQUARD, G.: *Mémoires de l'Académie de Gourguillon* (Lyons, n.d.).

CANFIELD, M. C.: "Reflections on Tony Sarg's Marionettes" (*Vanity Fair*, April 1923).

CAVAZZA, E.: "At the Opra di li Pupi" (*The Atlantic Monthly*, June 1894).

CHANAY, A.: *L'Homme qui boit* (Lyons, 1924).

CHANCEL, J.: *Le Coffre-fort de Polichinelle* (Paris, n.d.).

CHAPUIS, A., and GÉLIS, E.: *Le Monde des automates* (Paris, 1928).

CHASE, E. F.: *Ballads in Black* (Boston, 1892).

CHESSÉ, R.: "Who will come to a Marionette Congress?" (*The Theatre Arts Monthly*, April 1931).

CHESTERTON, G. K.: *Tremendous Trifles* (1909).

CHÉZEL, F.: *Pierrot-Barnum* (Paris, 1902).

CHILD, T.: "A Christmas Mystery in the Fifteenth Century" (*Harper's Magazine*, December 1888).

CLAQUERET, I.: *Chantecoine, ou la Folie de Guignol* (Lyons, 1910).

CLAUDEL, P.: *L'Ours et la lune* (Paris, 1919).

COCHRANE, M. L.: "Japan's Doll Theatre, the Bunraku-za" (*Travel*, September 1923).

COLLIER, J. P.: *Punch and Judy* (1870).

COLOMBIER, H.: *Le Bandeau d' illusion* (Brussels, 1900).

CONANT, S. S.: "The Story of Punch and Judy" (*Harper's Monthly*, May 1871).

CONY, G.: *Manuel du Marionnettiste amateur* (Nice, n.d.).

COQUARD, G.: *Deux Artistes: Laurent Josserand, Henri Delisle* (Lyons, n.d.).

CORRERA, L.: "Il presepe a Napoli" (*L'Arte*, 1899).

COURTELINE, G.: *Marionetten* (Vienna, 1902).

# BIBLIOGRAPHY

ʌIG, E. GORDON: "School: an Interlude for Marionettes" (*The English Review*, January 1918).

— "History" (*i.e.*, of the marionette stage) (*The Marionnette*, i, 1918, and ensuing numbers).

— *Puppets and Poets* (1921).

— "Marionettes and the English Press" (*The Mask*, 1929, p. 60).

ɪOZIÈRE, A.: *Le vrai Théâtre Guignol* (Paris, n.d.).

ɪDDY, M. V.: "A Third-grade Project: a Puppet-show" (*Primary Education*, October 1927).

ARTHENAY, L.: *Le Guignol des salons* (Paris, 1888).

— *Le Théâtre des petits* (Paris, 1890).

ɪAVID, É.: *El Bataille d' Querrin* (Amiens, 1891).

— *Étude picarde sur Lafleur* (Amiens, 1896).

— *Lafleur, ou le Valet picard* (Amiens, 1901).

— *Lafleur en service* (Amiens, 1901).

— *El Naissanche ed l'einfant Jésus* (Abbeville, 1905).

— *Chés Histoires d'Lafleur* (Amiens, 1906).

— *Les Théâtres populdìres à Amiens* (Amiens, 1906).

— *Vieilles réderies* (Amiens, 1920).

— *Ch'viux Lafleur* (Amiens, 1926).

DAVIS, F. C.: "Story-telling by Means of Puppets" (*The Playground*, September 1926).

DELAUNAY, E.: *Guignol du grand cercle* (Aix-les-Bains, 1912).

DELVAU, A.: *Le Théâtre érotique français sous le Bas-Empire* (Paris, 1864).

DESNOYERS, F.: *Le Théâtre de Polichinelle* (Paris, 1861).

DESVERNAY, F.: *Laurent Mourguet et Guignol* (Lyons, 1912).

DEW, L. E.: "Amusing Children" (*Harper's Bazaar*, December 1910).

DILLEY, P.: "Burattini: Marionettes that are not Mechanical" (*Drama*, October–December 1923).

DOERING, O.: "Poccis Beziehungen zum Marionettentheater" (*Magdeburgische Zeitung*, 1903).

DONNAY, M.: *Phryné* (Paris, 1891).

— *Ailleurs* (Paris, 1891).

— *Autour du Chat noir* (Paris, 1926).

DOYEN, E.: *Les Marionnettes amoureuses* (Paris, n.d.).

DRESBACH, W.: "Designing a Simple Puppet-show" (*The School Arts Magazine*, January 1927).

DUCRET, É.: *Le Théâtre de Guignol* (Lyons, 1914).

DULBERG, F.: "Bühnensilhouetten. Schwabinger Schattenspiele" (*Zeitschrift für bild. Kunst*, 1908).

DUPLATEAU, M. (AUGUSTE BLETON): *Véridique Histoire de l'Académie de Gourguillon* (Lyons, 1918).

DURANTY, D.: *Théâtre des marionnettes du Jardin des Tuileries* (Paris, 1863).

DUROCHER, L.: *La Marche au soleil* (Paris, 1899).

DUVE, H.: "Die Wiedererweckung des Kasperletheaters" (*Westermanns Monatshefte*, February 1928).

EHRHARDT, G.: *Das Puppenspiel vom Doktor Faust* (Dresden, 1905).

# DOLLS AND PUPPETS

EISLER, M.: "Richard Teschner" (*Dekorat. Kunst*, xxiv, 1921).

ENDEL, P.: *Ombres chinoises de mon père* (texts, Paris, 1885).

ENGEL, K., and TILLE, A.: *Deutsche Puppenkomödien* (Oldenburg, 1879).

F., H. K.: "Das javanische Wayang-Schattenspiel" (*Neue Mannheim Zeitung*, January 1925).

FANCIULLI, G.: *Il teatro di Takiù* (texts, Milan, n.d.).

FERNY, J.: *Le Secret du manifestant* (Paris, 1893).

FERRIGNI, P. C.: *La storia dei burattini* (Florence, 1902).

FEUILLET, O.: *The Story of Mr Punch* (1929).

FINCKH-HAELSSIG, M.: *Puppenschneiderei* (Ravensburg, 1928).

FLANAGAN, H.: "Puppets in Prague" (*The Theatre Arts Monthly*, April, May 1927).

FLÖGEL, K. F.: *Geschichte des Groteskkomischen* (ed. M. Bauer, Munich, 1914).

FOA, É.: *Mémoires d'un Polichinelle* (Brussels, 1840).

FOURNIER, É.: *Histoire des jouets et des jeux d'enfants* (Paris, 1889).

FRAGEROLLE, G.: *Le Rêve de Joël* (Paris, n.d.).

—— *Jeanne d'Arc* (Paris, n.d.).

—— *L'Aigle* (Paris, n.d.).

—— *L'Enfant prodigue* (Paris, 1894).

—— *Le Sphinx* (Paris, 1896).

—— *Clairs de lune* (Paris, 1896).

—— *Le Juif errant* (Paris, 1898).

FRANCK, P.: *Puppenspiele* (Berlin, 1931).

FROST, S. A.: *The Book of Tableaux and Shadow Pantomimes* (New York, 1869).

FULDA, FR. W.: *Schattenspiele. Erfahrungen und Anregungen* (Rudolstadt, 1923).

GABLER, E. T.: "Marionetten" (*Kunst und Künstler*, 1926).

GABRIEL, G. W.: "Opera on a Ten-foot Stage" (*Arts and Decoration*, December 1921).

GAUDEFROY, L.: *Ech Mariage d' Lafleur* (Amiens, 1907).

GENTILE, A. V.: *Teatrino per bambine e fanciuletti* (Milan, 1922).

—— *Burattini interessanti* (texts, Milan, 1925).

—— *Teatro per fanciulli e fanciulle* (Milan, 1925).

GHELDERODE, M. DE: *Le Mystère de la Passion de Notre-Seigneur Jésus-Christ* (Brussels, 1905).

GIBSON, K.: "Shadow-plays" (*The School Arts Magazine*, March 1927).

GIRADOT, MME: *Théâtre et Marionnettes pour les petits* (Paris, n.d.).

GLEASON, A. H.: "The Last Stand of the Marionette" (*Collier's National Weekly*, October 1909).

GÖBELS, H., and JÜNEMANN, J.: *Rulala, Rulala, Kasperle ist wieder da!* (Berlin, 1929).

GODART, J.: *Guignol et l'Esprit lyonnais* (Lyons, 1912).

—— *Guignol et la Guerre* (Lyons, 1919).

GÖHLER, C.: "Vom Kasperletheater" (*Kunstwart*, 1908).

GONINDARD, J.: *Guignol locataire et la Chambre syndicale des propriétaires* (Lyons, 1894).

GOUMARD, J.: *Une Partie de billard du cercle des chefs d'atelier de la Rue de Crimée, à Lyon* (Lyons, 1914).

# BIBLIOGRAPHY

RAFFIGNY, H. DE: *Le Théâtre à la maison* (Paris, n.d.).

— *Construction du Théâtre Guignol* (Paris, n.d.).

RAGGER, R.: "Deutsche Puppenspiele aus Ungarn" (*Archiv für das Studium der neueren Sprachen und Literaturen*, lxxx, 1925, 3–4).

RÄSSE, R.: "Zur Geschichte des Puppenspiels und der Automaten" (in Romberg, *Geschichte des Wissenschaften im* 19. *Jahrh.*, Leipzig, 1856).

GREGORI, F.: "Marionetten- und Schattentheater" (*Kunstwart*, xx, pp. 361–362).

GRÖBER, K.: *Children's Toys of Bygone Days* (1928).

GRONEMANN, J.: "Das Meisseln der ledernen Wajang-Puppen der Javaner in der Vorstenlanden" (*Internat. Archiv für Ethnogr.*, xxi, 1913).

GROS, DOCTEUR (JOANNY BACHUT): *Pourquoi aimons-nous Guignol?* (Lyons, 1909).

GRUBE, W.: "Chinesische Schattenspiele" (*Sitzungsberichte der k. bayerische Akademie der Wissenschaften*; phil.-hist. Klasse 28, 1915).

GRUNEBAUM, M. R. V.: "Schattentheater und Scherenschnitt" (*Jahrbuch der österr. Leo-Gesellschaft*, 1929, pp. 141–177).

GUBALKE, L.: "Marionettentheater" (*Vom Fels zum Meer*, 1905, No. 17).

GUGITZ, G.: *Der weiland Kasperl* (Vienna, 1920).

GUIGNOLET, —: *Le Théâtre des ombres chinoises* (texts, Paris, n.d.).

HAEFKER, H.: "Vom Kasperletheater. Ein Stück Kulturgeschichte" (*Der Thürmer*, viii, 1905–06).

HAGEMANN, C.: *Die Spiele der Völker* (Berlin, 1921).

HAGER, G.: *Die Weihnachtskrippe* (Munich, 1902).

HALL, M. P.: "Java's Dancing Shadows" (*Overland Monthly*, July 1928).

HAMM, W.: *Das Puppenspiel vom Doctor Faust* (Leipzig, 1850).

HAMMOND, C. A.: "The Puppet-show" (*Hygeia*, June 1931).

HAMPE, T.: *Die fahrenden Leute in der deutschen Vergangenheit* (Leipzig, 1902).

HARAUCOURT, É.: *Héro et Léandre* (Paris, 1893).

HARTLAUB, G. F.: "Siamesische Schattenspiele" (*Die Woche*, xxvii, 1925, 28).

HAYES, J. J.: (edits puppet section of *Drama*).

HAZEU, G. A. J.: "Eine Wajang-Beber-Vorstellung in Jogjokarta" (*Internat. Archiv für Ethnogr.* xvi, 1904).

HEDDERWICK, T. C.: *The Old German Puppet-play of Doctor Faust* (1887).

HEINE, C.: *Das Schauspiel der deutschen Wanderbühne vor Gottsched* (Halle, 1889).

HEMPEL, O.: *Das Dresdner Kasperle* (Leipzig, 1931).

HILL, M.: "The Theatre of Once Upon a Time" (*Kindergarten and First Grade*, November 1921).

HINOT, C.: *Le Fils à Guignol* (Paris, n.d.).

HIRN, Y.: *Les Jeux d'enfants* (translation from the Swedish by T. Hammar, Paris, 1926).

HIRSCH, G.: "Puppet Performances in Germany" (*Harper's Weekly*, April 1916).

—— "A Master of Marionettes: Ernst Ehlert" (*Harper's Weekly*, April 1916).

HIRTH, F.: "Das Schattenspiel der Chinesen" (Budapest, *Keleti Szemle*, ii, 1901).

HOLROYD, M.: "The Marionette Theatre in Italy" (*The Nation*, September 1922).

# DOLLS AND PUPPETS

HOLTHOF, L.: "Die Überreste des Goetheschen Puppentheaters und dere Geschichte" (*Freies deutsches Hochschrift*, 1882).

HORN, P.: "Das türkische Schattenspiel" (*Altgemeine Zeitung*, 112, 1900).

HOVER, O.: *Javanische Schattenspiele* (Leipzig, 1923).

HRBKOVA, S. B.: "Czechoslovak Puppet-shows" (*The Theatre Arts Monthly* January 1923).

HUNDT, P.: *Deutsche Märchenspiele* (Oldenburg, 1922).

HUSSEY, D.: "Master Peter's Puppet-show" (*The Saturday Review*, November 1924).

IRVINE, J.: "Widow Polichinelle: our First Tragedienne addresses her Audience" (*Lippincott's Magazine*, February 1913).

IRWIN, E.: "Where the Players are Marionettes: a Little Italian Theatre in Mulberry Street" (*The Craftsman*, September 1907).

JACKSON, O. L.: "A Practical Puppet Theatre" (*The School Arts Magazine*, May 1924).

JACOB, G.: *Karagöz-Komödien* (Berlin, 1899).

—— *Das Schattentheater* (Berlin, 1901).

—— "Drei arabische Schattenspiele aus dem XIII. Jahrhundert" (Buda pest, *Keleti Szemle*, ii, 1901).

—— "Die wichtigsten älteren Nachrichten über das arabische Schattenspiel" (in Littman, E., *Arabische Schattenspiele*, Berlin, 1901).

—— *Bibliographie über das Schattentheater* (Erlangen, 1902).

—— *Geschichte des Schattentheaters* (Berlin, 1907).

—— "Chinesische Schattenschnitte" (*Cicerone*, xv, 1923, 22).

—— *Schattenschnitte aus Nordchina* (Berlin, 1923).

—— "Schatten- und Puppentheater im Orient" (*Der Bühnenvolksbund*, ii, 1926, 1).

—— *Dutangade, das ist wie der Affenprinz Angada als Gesandter auszog; ein altindisches Schattenspiel* (Leipzig, 1931).

JACQUIER, L.: *La Politique de Guignol, Gnafron, et Cie* (Lyons, 1876).

JACQUIN, J.: *La Prise de Pékin* (Paris, n.d.).

JARRY, A.: *Ubu sur la butte* (Paris, 1906).

JEANNE, P.: *Œdipe-Roi* (Paris, 1919).

—— *Bibliographie des Marionnettes* (Paris, 1926).

JENKINS, R. L.: "Industrial Art in Toyland" (*Arts and Decoration*, December 1922).

JEROME, L. B.: "Marionettes of Little Sicily" (*New England Magazine*, February 1910).

JHERING, H.: "Marionettentheater" (*Schaubuhne*, vi, 5).

JOSEPH, H. H.: *A Book of Marionettes* (1922, second edition 1931).

—— "The Figure Theatre of Richard Teschner" (*The Theatre Arts Monthly*, October 1923).

—— "Puppets of Brann and Puhonny" (*The Theatre Arts Monthly*, August 1924).

—— "Römische Marionetten" (*Das Puppentheater*, i, 1924, pp. 177–181).

—— *Ali Baba and Other Plays for Young People or Puppets* (New York, 1927).

—— "Pastoral Puppets" (*The Theatre Arts Monthly*, August 1929).

# BIBLIOGRAPHY

JNGMANN, A. M.: "Marionettes Extraordinary" (*The Popular Science Monthly*, March 1918).

USSERAND, J. J.: "A Note on Pageants and Scaffolds Hye" (in *An English Miscellany presented to Dr Furnivall*, Oxford, 1901).

UYNBOLL, H. H.: "Wajang Keletik oder Kerutjl" (*Internat. Archiv für Ethnogr.* xiii, 1900).

KAHLE, P. E.: *Zur Geschichte des arabischen Schattentheaters in Ägypten* (Leipzig, 1909).

—— "Islamische Schattenspielfiguren aus Ägypten" (*Der Islam*, i, 1910, pp. 264–299, and ii, 1911, pp. 143–195).

—— "Marktszene aus einem ägyptischen Schattenspiel" (*Zeitschrift für Assyriologie*, xxvii, 1912).

—— "Das islamische Schattentheater in Ägypten" (*Orientalisches Archiv*, iii, 1913, pp. 103–108).

—— "Das Krokodilspiel, ein ägyptisches Schattenspiel" (*Nachrichten der Göttinger Gesellschaft der Wissenschaften*, phil.-hist. Klasse, 1915).

—— "Das arabische Schattentheater in Ägypten" (*Blätter für Jugendspielscharen und Puppenspieler*, i, 1924, 1).

KAHN, G. (ed.): *Polichinelle . . . précedé d'une étude* (Paris, 1906).

KALB, D. B.: "Puppets" (*The School Arts Magazine*, November 1925, June 1927).

—— "Robinson Crusoe in Shadow-land" (*The School Arts Magazine*, May 1931).

KERN, F.: "Das ägyptische Schattentheater" (in Horowitz, J., *Spuren griechischer Mimen im Orient*, Berlin, 1905).

KINCAID, Z.: *Kabuki* (1925).

—— "Puppets in Japan" (*The Theatre Arts Monthly*, March 1929).

KING, G. G.: *Comedies and Legends for Marionettes* (New York, 1904).

KLEIST, H. VON: "A Marionette Theatre" (translation by D. M. McCollester, *The Theatre Arts Monthly*, July 1928).

KOLLMANN, A.: *Deutsche Puppenspiele* (Berlin, 1891).

KRALIK, R., and WINTER, S.: *Deutsche Puppenspiele* (Vienna, 1885).

KRAUS, A. V.: *Das böhmische Puppenspiel vom Doktor Faust* (Berlin, 1891).

KREYMBORG, A.: *Puppet-plays* (1923; preface by Gordon Craig).

—— "Writing for Puppets" (*The Theatre Arts Monthly*, October 1923).

KROTSCH, F.: *Künstler-Marionetten-Theater: Bildhauer Prof. Aichers, Salzburg* (Salzburg, 1926).

KÚNOS, M.: "Über türkische Schattenspiele" (*Ungarische Revue*, vii, 1887).

—— "Türkisches Puppentheater" (*Ethnologische Mitteilungen aus Ungarn*, ii, 1889).

LAGARDE, É.: *Ombres chinoises, guignols, et marionnettes* (Paris, 1900).

LAUBE, G., and LESEMANN, G.: *Schwarzweisskunst in der Hilfsschule. Schattenspiele nach Märchen und verwandten Stoffen* (Halle, 1929).

LAWRENCE, W. J.: "The Immortal Mr Punch" (*The Living Age*, January 1921).

—— "Marionette Operas" (*The Musical Quarterly*, April 1924).

LEFEBVRE, É.: *Les Pièces de Théâtre guignol* (Lyons, 1912).

LEFFTZ, J.: "Puppenspeel im alten Strassburg" (*Elsassland*, 1929, pp. 233–237, 273–276).

495

LEGBAND, P.: "Die Renaissance der Marionette" (*Literarisches Echo*, i p. 248 *sqq.*).

LEHMANN, A: "Karagös" (*Das Puppentheater*, ii, 1925–26, pp. 46–47).

—— "Das deutsche Puppenspiel" (*Die vierte Wand*, 1927, 19).

LEHMANN, W.: "Ein türkische Schattenspiel" (*Die neue Orient*, iv, 1920, 2)

LEIBRECHT, G. P. J.: *Zeugnisse und Nachweise zur Geschichte des Puppenspiels in Deutschland* (Diss. Freiburg, 1919).

—— " Gesichtspunkte zu einer Geschichte des Puppenspiels " (*Das literarische Echo*, xxiii, 1920–21).

—— *Über Puppenspiele und ihre Pflege* (Innsbruck, 1921).

LEISEGANG, H. W.: "Marionettenspiel als künstler. Zeitausdruck" (*Das neue Reich*, xi, 1929).

LEMERCIER DE NEUVILLE: *Ombres chinoises* (texts, Paris, n.d.).

—— *Les Pupazzi au Chalet* (Vichy, 1865).

—— *I Pupazzi* (texts, Paris, 1866).

—— *Paris-Pantin* (texts, Paris, 1868).

—— *Le Théâtre des Pupazzi* (texts, Lyons, 1876).

—— *Les Pupazzi de l'enfance* (texts, Paris, 1881).

—— *Nouveau Théâtre des Pupazzi* (Paris, 1882).

—— *Histoire des Marionnettes modernes* (Paris, 1892).

—— *Les Pupazzi noirs: Ombres animées* (Paris, 1896).

—— *Les Pupazzi inédits* (Paris, 1903).

—— *Théâtre de marionnettes, à l'usage des enfants* (texts, Paris, 1904).

—— *Souvenirs d'un monteur de marionnettes* (Paris, 1911).

LEVIN, M.: "The Marionette Congress, 1930, Liége, Belgium" (*The Theatre Arts Monthly*, February 1931).

LEWIS, L. L.: "The Puppet-play as a Factor in Modern Education" (*Primary Education-Popular Educator*, June 1928).

LINK, O.: "Das Puppentheater in Rumänien" (*Das Puppentheater*, iii, 1929, pp. 173–176).

LITTMANN, E.: "Ein arabische Karagöz-Spiel" (*Zeitschrift der deutschen Morgenländischen Gesellschaft*, liv, 1900).

——*Arabische Schattenspiele* (Berlin, 1901).

—— "Das Malerspiel, ein Schattenspiel aus Aleppo, nach einer armenisch-türkischen Handschrift" (*Sitzungsberichte der Heidelberger Akademie der Wissenschaften;* phil.-hist. Klasse, viii, 1918).

LOEBER, J. A.: *Javaansche Shaduwbeelden* (Amsterdam, 1908).

LOKESCH, A. (ed.); *Alte Kasperlstücke* (texts, Berlin, 1931).

LORRAIN, J. DE: *La Barbe-Bleue* (Paris, n.d.).

LOVETT, L. S.: "Three Puppet-plays for a Rural School" (*The School Arts Magazine*, January 1931).

LOZOWICK, L.: "Exter's Marionettes" (*The Theatre Arts Monthly*, July 1928).

LUSCHAN, F. VON: "Das türkische Schattenspiel" (*Internat. Archiv für Ethnogr.* ii, 1889).

LUX, J. A.: "Geschichte und Ästhetik des Puppenspiels" (*Kind und Kunst*, 1906).

—— "Poccis Kasperlkomödien und die Marionettentheater" (*Allgemeine Zeitung*, Munich, 1909, No. 36).

# BIBLIOGRAPHY

[AcCARTHY, D.: "Marionettes and Waxwork" (*The New Statesman*, April 1923).

[ACDOWALL, H. S.: "The Faust of the Marionettes" (*The Living Age*, February 1901).

IACKAY, C. D.: "Children's Plays in Italy" (*Drama*, October 1927).

—— "Puppet Theatres in Schools" (*Primary Education-Popular Educator*, September 1928).

MAETERLINCK, M.: *Alladine et Palomides, Intérieur, et la Mort de Tintagiles, trois petits Drames pour marionnettes* (Brussels, 1894).

MAGNIN, C.: *Histoire des Marionnettes en Europe* (Paris, 1862).

MAHLMANN, S. A.: *Marionettentheater* (Leipzig, 1806).

MAINDRON, É.: *Marionnettes et Guignols* (Paris, 1900).

MAJUT, R.: *Lebensbühne und Marionette* (Berlin, 1931).

MALAMANNI, V.: "Il teatro drammatico, le marionette e i burattini a Venezia nel secolo xviii" (*Nuova Antologia*, lxvii and lxviii).

MARZIALS, A: "Puppets as Pedagogues" (*The World's Children*, 1930).

MATTHEWS, B.: "The Lamentable Tragedy of Punch and Judy" (*The Bookman*, December 1913).

—— "The Forerunner of the Movies" (*The Century Magazine*, April 1914).

—— "Puppet-shows, Old and New" (*The Bookman*, December 1914).

MAY, R.: "Aufbau eines Handpuppenspiels aus dem Stegreife" (*Volkspielkunst*, 1929).

MAYER, F. A.: "Beitrag zur Kenntnis des Puppentheaters" (*Euphorion*, vii, 1900).

MAYHEW, H.: *London Labour and the London Poor* (1861).

MAZ, G.: *Le Sarsifi Pétafiné* (Lyons, 1886).

McCABE, L. R.: "The Marionette Revival" (*The Theatre Magazine*, November 1920).

McCAIN, R.: "A Movable Playhouse" (*The Industrial Arts Magazine*, September 1919).

McCLOUD, N. C.: "Doll Play in a Doll Setting" (*The Mentor*, January 1928).

McISAAC, F. J.: "Tony Sarg" (*Drama*, December 1921).

—— "The Fun and Craft of the Puppet-show" (*The World Review*, March 1928).

McISAAC, F. J., and STODDARD, A.: *Marionettes and how to make Them* (1927).

McMILLAN, M. L.: "The Old, Old Story in Shadow-pictures" (*The Woman's Home Companion*, December 1925).

McPHARLIN, P.: *A Repertory of Marionette-plays* (New York, 1929).

—— "Anton Aicher's Marionette Theatre in Salzburg" (*Drama*, April 1929).

—— *Puppetry: A Year Book of Marionettes* (Detroit, 1930).

McQUINN, R.: "The Children's Theatre" (*The Delineator*, June 1919).

MENGHINI, M.: "Il teatro dei burattini; tradizioni cavalleresche romane" (*La cultura moderna*, 1911, pp. 39–42, 110–112).

MENTZEL, E.: *Das Puppenspiel vom Erzzauberer Doktor Johann Faust* (Frankfort-on-the-Main, 1900).

MÉTHIVET, —, and DE BUSSY, —: *Guignol musical* (Paris, n.d.).

MÉTIVET, L.: *La Belle au bois dormant* (Paris, 1902).

—— *Aladin* (Paris, 1904).

MICHEL, W.: "Marionetten" (*Dekorative Kunst*, 1919).

MICK, H. L.: "Producing the Puppet-play" (*The Theatre Arts Monthly,* April 1921).

—— "Puppets, Here, There, and Elsewhere" (*Drama*, December 1922).

—— "The Face of a Puppet" (*Drama*, January 1923).

—— "How a Puppet gets his Head" (*Drama*, February 1923).

—— "Puppets from the Neck down" (*Drama*, April 1923).

—— "Dressing and stringing a Puppet" (*Drama*, May, June 1923).

MILLS, W. H., and DUNN, L. M.: *Marionettes, Masks, and Shadows* (1927).

MODERWELL, H. K.: "The Marionettes of Tony Sarg" (*Boston Transcript*, 1918).

MOENIUS, G.: "Münchener Marionettentheater" (*Münchener Allgemeine Rundschau*, xvi, 1929, 48).

MONNIER, M.: *Théâtre de Marionnettes* (texts, Geneva, 1871).

—— *Faust* (Geneva, 1871).

MONTOYA, G.: *Les Boers* (Paris, 1902).

MOULTON, R. H.: "Teaching Dolls to Act for Moving Pictures" (*The Illustrated World*, October 1917).

—— "Toyland in the Films" (*The Scientific American*, December 1917; *The Literary Digest*, February 1918).

MÜHLMANN, J.: "Alpenländische Weihnachtskrippen" (*Kunst und Kunsthandwerk*, xxiii, 1920).

MÜLLER, F. W. K.: "Siamesische Schattenspielfiguren im Kgl. Museum für Völkerkunde zu Berlin" (*Internat. Archiv für Ethnogr.* vii, 1894).

NASCIMBENI, G.: "Le commedie d'un burattinaio celebre" (*Il Marzocco*, xv, 9).

NAUMANN, H.: "Studien über das Puppenspiel" (*Zeitschrift für deutsche Bildung*, 1929, pp. 1–14).

NELSON, N., and HAYES, J. J.: "The Dancing Skeleton of a Marionette" (*Drama*, May 1927).

—— "Trick Marionettes" (*Drama*, October–December 1927, February–April 1928).

NERAD, H.: *Kasperl ist wieder da! Ein Wort für die Wiederbelebung des Handpuppentheaters* (Prague, 1922).

—— *Eine Studie bei Kaspar Hanswurst* (Prague, 1927).

NICOLAS, R.: "Le Théâtre d'ombres au Siam" (*The Journal of the Siamese Society*, 1927, pp. 37–52).

NICOLS, F. H.: "A Marionette Theatre in New York" (*The Century Magazine*, March 1902).

NIESSEN, C.: "Teatro dei Piccoli" (*Die vierte Wand*, 1927, 18).

—— "Marionetten-Theater" (*Velhagen und Klasings Monatshefte*, xlii, 1927–28).

—— *Das rheinische Puppenspiel* (Cologne, 1928).

NODIER, C.: *Contes de veillée* (Paris, 1856).

NOETH, O.: "Die Grazer Puppenspiele" (*Das Puppentheater*, i, 1923–24, pp. 129–135).

NOGUCHI, Y.: "The Japanese Puppet Theatre" (*Arts and Decoration*, October 1920).

# BIBLIOGRAPHY

NOVELLI, E.: *Il teatro dei burattini* (Milan, 1925; published anonymously).
OHLENDORF, H.: "Schattenspiele" (*Niedersochsen*, xxxiv, 1929).
ONCKEN, H.: *Kasper för Lütt un Grot. Anleitung zum Kasperspiel, Handpuppen-spiel, Kartoffeltheater, Schattenspiel* (Oldenburg, 1931).
"ONOFRIO": *Théâtre lyonnais de Guignol* (texts and introduction, Lyons, 1865–70, latest edition 1910).
PAINTON, F. C.: "The Marionette as Correlator in the Public Schools" (*The School Arts Magazine*, December 1922).
PALTINIERI, R.: *Il teatro dei piccoli* (texts, Milan, 1925).
PARK, F.: "The Puppeteer's Library" (*The Theatre Arts Monthly*, July 1928).
PARK, J. G.: "Puppets" (*The School Arts Magazine*, May 1924).
PARKHURST, W.: "Dead Actors for Live" (*Drama*, May 1919).
PATTERSON, A.: *Shadow Entertainments and how to work Them* (1895).
—— "The Puppets are coming to Town" (*The Theatre*, September 1917).
PAUL, O.: *Neue Kasperspiele* (Leipzig, 1930).
—— (ed.): *Kasperstücke* (series of texts, Leipzig, n.d.).
PEIXOTTO, E. C.: "Marionettes and Puppet-shows Past and Present" (*Scribner's Magazine*, March 1903).
PENNINGTON, J.: "The Origin of Punch and Judy" (*The Mentor*, December 1924).
PERETZ, V.: Кукольный театръ на Руси (in Ежегодникъ Императорскихъ Театровъ, St Petersburg, 1895).
PETITE, J. H. M.: *Guignols et Marionnettes* (Paris, 1911).
PETRAI, G.: *Maschere e burattini* (Rome, 1885).
PETTY, E.: "The Trail of the Long-nosed Princess" (*Drama*, April 1928).
PHILIPPI, F.: *Schattenspiele* (Berlin, 1906).
PHILIPPON, É.: *La Bernarda Buyandiri* (Lyons, 1885).
PICCO, F.: "Lo scartafaccio di un burattinaio" (*Bolletino storico piacentino*, i, 1907).
PIERCE, L. F.: "Punch and Judy Up-to-date" (*The World To-day*, March 1911).
—— "Successful Puppet-shows" (*The Theatre*, September 1916).
PIGEON, A.: *L'Amour dans les enfers* (Paris, n.d.).
PIPER, M.: *Die Schaukunst der Japaner* (Berlin, 1927).
PISCHEL, R.: *Die Heimat des Puppenspiels* (Halle, 1900; translated by M. C. Tawney as *The Home of the Puppet-play*, 1902).
—— "Das altindische Schattenspiel" (*Sitzungsberichte der Berliner Akademie*, 1906).
PLIMPTON, E.: *Your Workshop* (New York, 1926).
POCCI, F.: *Lustiges Komödienbüchlein* (Munich, 1895).
—— *Heitere Lieder. Kasperliaden und Schattenspiele* (Munich, 1929).
POLLOCK, W. H.: "Marionettes" (*The Saturday Review*, August 1902).
POUGIN, A.: *Dictionnaire du Théâtre* (Paris, 1885).
POULSSON, A. E.: "Shadow-plays" (*St Nicholas*, July 1907).
POWELL, V. M.: "Říše Loutek, a Puppet Theatre in Prague" (*The Theatre Arts Monthly*, October 1930).
POYDENOT, A.: *Polichinelle aux enfers* (Paris, 1899).
PRAHLHAUS, J.: *Kasperle-Speil* (Königsberg, 1927).

499

# DOLLS AND PUPPETS

PROU, V.: "Les Théâtres d'automates en Grèce au Iᵉ siècle avant l'ère chrétienne d'après les Αὐτοματοποιἱκὰ d'Héron d'Alexandrie" (*Mémoires presentés . . . à l'Academie*, I, ix, 1884).

PRÜFER, C.: "Das Schifferspiel" (*Beiträge zur Kenntnis des Orients*, ii, 1906, pp. 154–169).

—— *Ein ägyptisches Schattenspiel* (Erlangen, 1906).

PUHONNY, I.: "Marionettenkunst" (*Das Echo*, xl, 1923).

—— "The Physiognomy of the Marionette" (translation by H. H. Joseph, *The Theatre Arts Monthly*, July 1928).

QUEDENFELD, A.: "Das türkische Schattenspiel im Magrib" (*Ausland*, lxiii, 1900).

QUENNELL, PETER: "The Puppet Theatre" (in *A Superficial Journey through Tokyo and Peking*, London, 1932).

RABE, J. E.: *Kaspar Putschenelle. Historisches über die Handpuppen und althamburgische Kasperszenen* (Hamburg, 1924).

RACCA, C.: *Burattini e marionette* (Turin, 1925).

RACKY, J. (ed.): *Das Puppenspiel vom Doktor Faust* (Paderborn, 1927).

RAGUSA-MOLERTI, G.: "Una sacra rappresentazione in un teatro di marionette" (*Psiche*, xiii, 3).

RANSON, P.: *L'Abbé Prout* (texts, Paris, 1902).

RAPP, E.: *Die Marionetten in der deutschen Dichtung vom Sturm und Drang bis zur Romantik* (Leipzig, 1924).

REED, W. T.: "Puppetry" (*The Playground*, June 1930).

REHM, H. S.: *Das Buch der Marionetten* (Berlin, 1905).

REICH, H.: *Der Mimus* (Berlin, 1903).

REIGHARD, C.: *Plays for People and Puppets* (New York, 1928).

RESSEL, M., and LEONHARD, P. R.: *Seid ihr alle da?* 10 lustige Stücke für das Kasperle-Theater (Muhlhausen, 1931).

RHEDEN, K. VON: "Schattenspiele" (*Velhagen und Klasings Monatshefte*, 1908).

RHEIN, J.: "Mededeeling omtrent de chineesche Poppenkast" (*Internat. Archiv für Ethnogr.*, ii, 1889).

RICCI, C.: "I burattini in Bologna" (*La lettura*, iii, 11).

RICHMOND, E. T.: *Punch and Judy* (n.d.).

RIDGE, L.: "Kreymborg's Marionettes" (*The Dial*, January 1919).

RIESS, R.: "Die Marionettenbühne" (*Gegenwart*, May 1917).

RITTER, H.: *Karagös* (Hanover, 1924).

RIVIÈRE, H.: *La Tentation de Saint-Antoine* (Paris, 1887).

—— *La Marche à l'étoile* (Paris, 1890).

ROBERTS, C.: "Pulcinella" (*The Living Age*, April 1922).

ROHDEN, P. R.: *Das Puppenspiel* (Hamburg, 1923).

ROSE, A.: *The Boy Showman* (New York, 1926).

ROUSSEAU, V.: "A Puppet-play which lasts Two Months" (*Harper's Weekly*, October 1908).

ROUSSET, P.: *Un Divorce inutile* (Lyons, n.d.).

—— *Théâtre lyonnais de Guignol* (texts, Lyons, 1895).

ROZE, A.: "A Profile Puppet-show" (*The Scientific American*, May, June 1910).

RUSSELL, E.: "The Most Popular Play in the World" (*Outing Magazine*, January 1908).

# BIBLIOGRAPHY

ℓUTHENBURG, G. D.: "The Gooseberry Mandarin" (*The Theatre Arts Monthly*, July 1928).

ŚACHOIX, L., and VERRIÈRES, J. DES: *Chante-clair Guignol* (Lyons, 1912).

—— *Cyrano-Guignol* (Lyons, n.d.).

ŚAND, A.: "Les Marionnettes de Nohant" (*Annales politiques et littéraires*, October 1923).

ŚAND, M.: *Le Théâtre des Marionnettes* (texts, Paris, 1890).

SANDFORD, A.: "Books about Marionettes" (*Library Journal*, November 1929).

SARG, T.: *The Tony Sarg Marionette Book* (New York, 1921).

—— "Domesticating an Ancient Art" (*The Delineator*, April 1922).

—— "How to make and operate a Marionette Theatre" (*The Ladies' Home Journal*, December 1927).

—— "The Puppet-play in Education" (*Kindergarten and First Grade*, December 1924).

—— "The Revival of the Puppet-play in America" (*The Theatre Arts Monthly*, July 1928).

SAUNDERS, M. J.: "A Marionette-play in Four Acts" (*The School Arts Magazine*, January 1931).

SCHELL, S.: "Czech Puppets with a History" (*Shadowland*, January 1923).

SCHERRER, H.: "Statisches zur Geschichte des St Galler Marionettentheaters" (*Das Puppentheater*, i, 1923, 4).

—— "Wege und Ziele des St Galler Marionettentheaters" (*Das Puppentheater*, i, 1923, 4).

SCHEUERMANN, E.: *Handbuch der Kasperei. Vollständ. Lehrbuch des Handpuppenspiels* (Buchenbach, 1924).

—— *Neue Kasperstücke* (series of texts, Leipzig, n.d.).

SCHINK, J. F.: *Marionettentheater* (Munich, 1778).

SCHLEGEL, G.: *Chinesische Bräuche und Spiele in Europa* (Diss. Jena, 1869).

SCHMID-NOERR, F. A.: "Maske und Marionette" (*Pastor Bonus*, April 1929).

SCHMIDT, F. H.: *Moderne Marionettenspiele* (Leipzig, 1927).

—— *Allerlei Kasparstücke. Eine Bibliographie des Handpuppentheaters* (Leipzig, 1929).

SCHMIDT, O., and HOMANN, H.: *Handpuppenspiele* (Mühlhausen, 1930).

SCHMIDT, W.: "Heron von Alexandria" (*Neue Jahrbücher für das klassische Altertum*, ii, 1899).

SCHNEIDER, N. H.: *The Model Vaudeville Theatre* (1909).

SCHOTT, G.: *Die Puppenspiele des Grafen Pocci* (Frankfort-on-the-Main, 1911).

SCHULENBURG, W. VON: "Von der nationalen Mission des Puppentheaters" (*Das literarische Echo*, xix, 1917).

SCHÜRMANN-LINDNER, H.: "Das Puppenspiel in Paris" (*Das Puppentheater*, iii, 1929, 168–172).

—— "Vom Wesen des Puppenspiels" (*Heimblätter*, vi, 1929, pp. 272–277).

SCHWARZ, A.: *Neues Kasperl-Theater* (a series of plays, Leipzig, 1928).

SCHWITTAY, P.: "Wie führe ich Schattenspiele auf?" (*Optik und Schule*, 1929, pp. 17–25).

SÉGARD, C.: *Guignol apothicaire* (Paris, n.d.).

SEIF, T.: "Drei türkische Schattenspiele" (*Le Monde oriental*, xvii, 1923).

SELDES, G.: "Grock and Guignols" (*The New Republic*, April 1926).

501

# DOLLS AND PUPPETS

(SÉRAPHIN): *Le Théâtre de Séraphin depuis son origine jusqu'à sa disparition* (Paris, 1872; published anonymously).

SERRURIER, L.: *De Wajang Poerwa, eene ethnologische Studie* (Leyden, 1896).

SEYBOLD, C. F.: "Zum arabischen Schattenspiel" (*Zeitschrift der deutschen Morgenländischen Gesellschaft*, lvi, 1902).

SHANKS, E.: "Puppetry and Life" (*The Outlook*, November 1923).

SHULTS, J. H.: "Teaching History by Puppets (*The Kindergarten Magazine*, September 1908).

SIBLEY, H.: "Marionettes, the Ever-popular Puppet-shows" (*Sunset*, November 1928).

SILVESTRE, A.: *Chemin de croix* (Paris, n.d.).

SIMOVICH, EFIMOVA: Записки Петрушечника (Moscow, 1925).

SMITH, W.: "Home Plays with Puppets" (*The Children's Royal*, December 1921).

SOMM, H.: *La Berline de l'émigré, ou jamais trop tard pour bien faire* (Paris, 1885).

SORBELLI, A.: "Angelo Cuccoli e le sue commedie" (*L'Archiginnasio*, iv).

STEMMLE, R. A. (ed.): *Das Handpuppentheater. Eine Reihe alter und neuer Komödien für die Handpuppenbühne* (a series of plays, Berlin, 1929).

STEVENSON, R. L.: *Memories and Portraits* (1887, with the famous essay "A Penny Plain and Twopence Coloured").

STODDART, A.: "The Renaissance of the Puppet-play" (*The Century Magazine*, June 1918).

STODDART, A., and SARG, T.: *A Book of Marionette-plays* (1930).

STRAUS, H.: "Puppet and Conductor" (*The Nation*, New York, February 1926).

STUDYNKA, F.: *Der rote Kasperl. Anleitung zur Kasperlstudien* (Vienna, 1929).

SURVILLE, G. DE: *Le Déménagement de Guignol* (Paris, n.d.).

SÜSSHEIM, K.: "Die moderne Gestalt des türkischen Schattenspiels (Quaragös)" (*Zeitschrift der deutschen Morgenländischen Gesellschaft*, lxiii, 1909).

SYMONS, A.: "An Apology for Puppets" (*The Saturday Review*, July 1897).

TALBOT, P. A.: "Some Magical Plays of Savages" (*The Strand Magazine*, June 1915).

TARDY, T.: *Profession libérale* (Dijon, 1926).

TAVERNIER, A., and ALEXANDRE, A.: *Le Guignol des Champs-Élysées* (preface by J. Claretie, Paris, n.d.).

TESAREK, A.: *Kasperl sucht den Weihnachtsmann* (Vienna, 1927).

THALASSO, A.: *Molière en Turquie: Étude sur le théâtre de Karagueuz* (Paris, 1888).

TICHENOR, G.: "Marionette Furioso: a Marionette-show in the House of Manteo" (*The Theatre Arts Monthly*, December 1929).

TIENNET, G.: *Le Rapide n° 6* (Lyons, n.d.).

TOLDO, P.: "Nella baracca dei burattini" (*Giornale storico della letteratura italiana*, li, 1908).

TRENARD, F.: *Quatre Pièces faciles à jouer* (Paris, n.d.).

TURNER, W. J.: "Marionette Opera" (*The New Statesman*, May 1923).

TUSSENBROEK, O. VAN: *De Toegepaste Kunsten in Nederland* (Rotterdam, 1905).

UNDERHILL, G.: "A New Field for Marionettes" (*Drama*, March 1924).

VERMOREL, J.: *Quelques petits théâtres lyonnais des XVIII$^e$ et XIX$^e$ siècles* (Lyons, 1918).

# BIBLIOGRAPHY

VISAN, T. DE: *Le Guignol lyonnais* (preface by J. Clarétie, Paris, 1912).

WALLNER, E.: *Schattentheater* (Erfurt, 1895).

WALTERS, M. O.: "Puppet-shows for Primary Grades" (*Primary Education*, September 1925).

WALZ, J. A.: "Notes on the Puppet-play of Doctor Faust" (*Philological Quarterly*, July 1928).

WARSAGE, R. DE: *Histoire du célèbre Théâtre liégeois de marionnettes* (Brussels, 1905).

WEED, I.: "Puppet-plays for Children" (*The Century Magazine*, March 1916).

WEISMANTEL, L.: *Das Merkbuch der Puppenspiele* (Frankfort-on-the-Main, 1924).

—— *Das Schattenspielbuch* (Augsburg, 1929).

—— *Das Buch der Krippen* (Augsburg, 1930).

—— *Schattenspiele des weltliches und geistliches Jahres* (Augsburg, 1931).

WELLS, C. F.: "Puppet-shows" (*The Playground*, November 1929).

—— "Marionettes, Quaint Folk" (*The World Outlook*, October 1917).

WERNTZ, C. N.: "The Marionette Theatre of Japan" (*Our World*, April 1924).

WHANSLAW, H. W.: *Everybody's Theatre* (1923).

WHEELER, E. J.: "Starling Development of the Bi-dimensional Theatre" (*Current Literature*, May 1908).

WHIPPLE, L.: "Italy sends us Marionettes" (*The Survey*, April 1927).

WHITMIRE, L. G.: "Teaching School with Puppets" (*The World Review*, March 1928).

WILKINSON, W.: *The Peep Show* (1927).

—— *Vagabonds and Puppets* (1930).

—— *Puppets in Yorkshire* (1931).

WIMSATT, G.: "The Curious Puppet-shows of China" (*Travel*, December 1925).

WITTICH, E.: "Fahrende Puppenspieler" (*Schweizer. Archiv für Volkskunde*, 1929, pp. 54–61).

WOOD, E. H.: "Marionettes at Camp" (*The Playground*, March 1930).

WOOD, R. K.: "Puppets and Puppeteering" (*The Mentor*, April 1921).

WOODENSCONCE, PAPERNOSE: *The Wonderful Drama of Punch and Judy* (1919).

YAMBO, —: *Il teatro dei burattini* (texts, Milan, 1925).

YEATS, J. B.: *Plays for the Miniature Stage* (n.d.).

YOUNG, S. G.: "Guignol" (*Lippincott's Magazine*, August 1879).

ZACCO, T.: *Cenni storici sui fantocci, sulle marionette e su altri giocucci da fanciulli degli antichi* (Este, 1853).

ZEIGLER, F. J.: "Puppets, Ancient and Modern" (*Harper's Monthly*, December 1897).

ZELLNER, H.: "Vom Puppentheater zum Heimkino" (*Westermanns Monatshefte*, December 1929).

ZIMMERMANN, O.: *So baue ich mir ein Kasperltheater* (Leipzig, n.d.).

ZWIENER, B.: *Hallo-Hallo! Hier Kartoffeltheater* (Leipzig, 1928).

—— *Das neue Schattenspiel im Freien* (Leipzig, 1928).

—— *Die neue Schattenspiele daheim* (Leipzig, 1928).

# DOLLS AND PUPPETS

### Miscellaneous

"Cassetta de' Burattini" (*The Penny Magazine*, March, April 1845).

"The History of Puppet-shows in England" (*Sharpe's London Journal*, July, December 1851).

"The Pedigree of Puppets" (*Household Words*, January 1852).

"Puppets of All Nations" (*Blackwood's Magazine*, April 1854).

"The Harlequinade" (*Chambers's Journal*, November 1856).

"Puppets, Religious and Aristocratic" (*Chambers's Journal*, December 1856).

"Popular Puppets" (*Chambers's Journal*, February 1857).

*Neues Puppen-Theaters* (Breslau, 1860).

*Punch and Judy* (1863, 1866, 1886, 1901).

*Théâtre érotique de la rue de la Santé* (texts, Brussels, 1864).

*Mr Punch* (1885).

"Puppet-shows" (*The Saturday Review*, March 1885).

*Théâtre, Saynettes et Récits, par Gnafron fils* . . . *Neveu de Guignol* (Lyons, 1886).

*Guignol à la Comédie-Française. A propos d'une visite de Coquelin au Théâtre de Pierre Rousset* (Lyons, 1887).

"A Greek Puppet-show" (*All the Year Round*, March 1894).

"A Puppet-show at the Paris Exhibition" (*The Scientific American*, November 1900).

"The Parisian Puppet Theatre" (*The Scientific American*, October 1902).

*Papyrus et Martine, Punch et Judy, célèbre drame guignolesque anglais, pour la première fois adapté en France* (Paris, 1903).

*Les Parodies de Guignol: Répertoire de Pierre Rousset, Albert Chanay, Tony Tardy, Louis Josserand, Albert Avon* (Lyons, 1911).

*La Parodie de l'étranger* (Lyons, 1913).

"The Return of the Marionets" (*Current Opinion*, March 1913).

*Le Séraphin des enfants* (texts, Epinal, 1914).

*Que de Guignon!* (Lyons, 1914).

"Punch and Judy" (*Current Opinion*, January 1914).

"The Most Immortal Character even seen on the Stage" (*Current Opinion*, January 1914).

"Puppet Warfare in France" (*The Literary Digest*, November 1915).

"Revival of the Puppets" (*Current Opinion*, July 1916).

"The Paradox of the Puppet: an Extinct Amusement born anew" (*Current Opinion*, July 1916).

*The Marionnette* (a journal edited by Gordon Craig, 1918).

"Are we forgetting Punch and Judy?" (*The Review of Reviews*, January 1918).

"How Puppets surpass our Human Actors: Tony Sarg's Marionettes" (*Current Opinion*, April 1918).

*Guignol fait la guerre* (Paris, 1919).

"Dolls knocking at the Actors' Door" (*The Literary Digest*, May 1919).

*Im Kasperltheater* (texts, Leipzig, 1919–22).

"Movies in the Time of William Shakespeare" (*Current Opinion*, May 1920).

"New Animation of the Inanimate Theatre" (*Vogue*, August 1920).

"Drama on Strings: Tony Sarg's Marionettes in Rip van Winkle" (*The Outlook*, December 1920).

# BIBLIOGRAPHY

*Das Puppenbuch* (Berlin, 1921).

"Alice in Puppet Land" (*The Independent*, February 1921).

"Play-writing for the Puppet Theatre" (*Current Opinion*, May 1921).

"Resurrecting Chinese Movies a Thousand Years Old" (*Current Opinion*, July 1921).

*La Malle* (Paris, 1922).

"How Tony Sarg performs 'Miracles' with Marionettes" (*Current Opinion*, March 1922).

"Lilian Owen's Portrait Puppets" (*Drama*, October 1922).

"Guignol" (*The Nation*, April 1923).

"Portrait Puppets" (*Current Opinion*, April 1923).

*Blätter für Jugendspielscharen und Puppenspieler* (founded 1924).

"Rubber Actors lend Realism to Movies" (*The Popular Mechanics Magazine*, May 1924).

*L'Entétation amatée* (Paris, 1925).

*Nouveau Recueil de pièces de Guignol* (Lyons, 1925).

"The Vogue for Puppet-plays" (*The Popular Educator*, January 1925).

"Behind the Scenes in a Puppet-show" (*The Popular Mechanics Magazine*, June 1925).

*Vertingo* (Paris, 1927).

*Das Puppentheater-Modellierbuch* (Berlin, 1927).

*Vom Puppen- und Laienspiel* (ed. W. Biel, Berlin, 1927).

"Our Puppet-show" (*Primary Education—Popular Educator*, January 1927).

"Les petits Comédiens de bois sur la scène du vieux Colombier" (*L'Illustration*, December 1927).

*Wir Rüpelspieler* (a series of plays, Berlin, 1927–28).

*Eduard Blochs Kasperl-Theater* (a series of plays, Berlin, 1927–30).

*Das Kaspertheater des Leipziger Dürerbundes* (a series of plays, Leipzig, 1927–30).

"Richard Teschner's Figure Theatre" (*The Theatre Arts Monthly*, July 1928).

"Telling the Story with Puppets" (*The Survey*, July 1928).

*Funsterwalder Handpuppenspiele* (a series of plays, Mühlhausen, 1928–29).

"Puppenspieler Pfingstfest in Prag" (*Das Puppentheater*, iii, 1929, pp. 129–138).

*Handpuppenspiele* (Mühlhausen, 1929).

*Höflings Kasperl-Theater* (a series of plays, Berlin, 1929–30).

*Hohnsteiner Puppenspiele* (a series of plays, edited by M. Jacob, Leipzig, 1929–30).

*Höflings Schattentheater* (a series of plays, Munich, 1929-31).

*Radirullala, Kaspar ist wieder da!* (a series of plays, Leipzig, 1929–31).

*Kasperl-Theater* (a series of plays, Berlin, 1929–31).

*Kleine Kasparspiele* (a series of plays, Leipzig, 1930).

*Ollmärksche Puppenspeele* (a series of plays, edited by O. Schulz-Heising, Leipzig, 1930).

*Der rote Kasper* (a series of plays, Leipzig, 1930–31).

"Puppets—What are They?" (*The Literary Digest*, January 1931).

*Das alte Kölner Hänneschen-Theater* (Cologne, 1931) (includes contributions by C. Niessen, O. Nettscher, R. Just, M. Hehemann, O. Klein, F. F. Wallraf, and H. Lindner).

# DOLLS AND PUPPETS

"Das Marionettentheater Münchener Künstler" (*Deutsche Kunst und Dekoration*, xix, pp. 89–93).

*Das Puppentheater* (organ of the puppet-theatre section of the society zur Förderung der deutschen Theaterkultur).

*Der Puppenspieler* (organ of the Deutscher Bund für Puppenspiel).

*Le Séraphin de l'enfance* (texts, Nancy, n.d.).

*Loutkar* (organ of the Union Internationale des Marionnettes, Prague. This society has also published a number of pamphlets relating to puppets and puppet-showmen).

*Petit Répertoire de Guignol* (Nice, n.d.).

*Punch and Puppets* ("The British Standard Hand Books," No. 38, n.d.).

Illustrations of various puppets in *The Theatre Arts Monthly*, June 1925, September 1925, November 1925, December 1925, June 1926.

# INDEX

507

# DOLLS AND PUPPETS

# INDEX

# INDEX

bran-stuffed, 128; character, German, 180; child, 170 *sqq.*, 204; clay, magical, of the Akikuyu, 64; clockwork, 262; cloth, 170; collectors of, 191–192, 198–201; cone-shaped, 26, 30, 130, 217; considered as spirits, 36; cork, 247; costume, 190 *sqq.*; dedication of, to divinities, 107–108, 109; drawing-room, 218 *sqq.*; dress-, used by tailors, 95–96; dressed, French, 160–162, German, 162 *sqq.*; edible, 247–249; educational value of, 171 *sqq.*, 185; exhibitions of, 178, 183, 184, 187–190, 192, 194, 198, 219, 223, 247; of exotic peoples, 202–217, psychological interest of, 202; fashion, 143 *sqq.*, French, of 1914–18, 196–198; female, 105–106, 114 *sqq.*, 123, 125, 134 *sqq.*, 160, 175, 192 *sqq.*, 218 *sqq.*, predominance of, 106, 202, 287; gingerbread, 248; Greek, earliest known, mostly female, 105–108; grotesque, of U.S.A., 217, 218; heads of, 127, 128, 155–156, 164, 183–184; of Hopi Indians, 48–49, 213; illustrating costumes of women war-workers, 196–198; indestructible German, 184; love of adults for, 55–56; male, 114, 125–126, 160, 214; materials used for, in the nineteenth century, 247; mechanical, 263; of misfortune, 64; with movable heads and eyes, 127; museum collections of, 188; paper, 208, 210, 224; *papier mâché*, 154, 155; prehistoric, 35 *sqq.*; in propaganda work, 198; rag, 110, 202, 211, 213; rattle, 105–106, 112, 214; sawdust-stuffed, 128; Siberian Tschuktchi, 45, 212; sin-bearing Japanese, 208; of South American nations and tribes, 213 *sqq.*; speaking and walking, 156; and spiritualism, 246; substitution of, for human victims, 70; *tapa*, of the Santa Cruz islands, 65; tea-cosy, 218, 247; teddy-bear, 218; toy, 24, in ancient times, 103, early, in Europe, 110, German, 105, 110, in the nineteenth century, 154 *sqq.*, in the modern period, 171 *sqq.*, American, modern, 216 (*see also* Nürnberg *and* Sonneberg); tumbling, Chinese, 204 *sqq.*; used for decorative purposes, 218–225; used in magic and magical rites, 57 *sqq.*, 204, 208; utensils in the form of, 235–244; of various lands and peoples—*see under names*; warrior, of the Winnebagos, 49 (*see also* Tin soldiers *and* Warriors); wax, English, 155, German,

115, Greek, 106, Haussa, 217, Mexican Indian, 213; wooden, 128, 180; worn as pendants, 218
Dolls' guillotine, a, 217
Dolls' houses, seventeenth-century, 118 *sqq.*
Dolls' marriage, a, in India, 203
Dolls' riding match, Prignitz, 246
Dolls' utensils in Swiss lake-dwellings, 103
Doré, Gustave, puppets by, 346
Dory, Mme Myrthas, war-worker, dolls by, 196–198
Drawing-room dolls, 218 *sqq.*
Dresden artists, dolls designed by, 180–183
Dress-figures, or -dolls, 95–96. *See also* Mannequin
Dressmakers, dolls used by, 134 *sqq.*
Droz, Pierre and Henri, automata of, 263
Druid images, 253
Dubois, J. E., tin soldiers produced by, 295–296
Duprez, G. L., private puppet theatre of, 346
Duranty, —, puppet theatre of, 346
Dürer, Albrecht, crib made after, 285; lay figures ascribed to, 96, 98–99
Duse, Eleonora, on the marionette, 424–426; on the puppet theatre, 395
Dutch East Indies (Sumatra, etc.), ancestor images of, 42; dolls illustrating native costumes of, 190; image magic in, 64–65; the Javanese shadow-play in, 360
*Dziady*, the, 50

École Medgyès, the, in Paris, puppet-plays of, 430
Edible dolls, 247–249
Education, the doll as medium of, 171, 173, Kasperle as medium of, 398–400
Effigies, burning of, 87–88. *See also* 'Ragged regiment' *and* Waxworks
Eggingk, Theo, puppets by, 440
Egypt, automata and movable images in, 252, 255–256; dolls of, 104–105; dress figures in, 96; edible figures in, 247; funeral images in, 78 *sqq.*; image magic of, 59; obese female idols in, 29; portrait-masks of mummies in, 89; prehistoric 'stake figures' in, 34; shadow-plays in, 360 *sqq.*; 'stick figures' of, 235; talismans and amulets in, 53–54; toy figures in, 104
Ehlert, Ernst, puppets by, 412; on the proper aspect of the marionette, 412;

# INDEX

tria, warrior dolls of, 290
:alian Kasperle theatre, development of, 341–342
talian painters, lay figures used by, 96 *sqq.*
taly, doll-burning in, after Carnival, 246; dress figures in, 96 *sqq.*; edible dolls in, 248; *fantoccini* of, 306; funeral images in, 92; home of the Christmas crib, 269 *sqq.*, 284; image magic in, 60; the marionette theatre in, 340 *sqq.*, that of Podrecca, 424 *sqq.*; marionettes in, attempts to improve, 309–310; *schardana* figures in, 34; wax *ex voto* figures in, 72; wax figures in, 101
Ito-Ayatsuri puppet theatre, Japan, 389
Iwowski, Carl, and his hand puppets, 404–406

Jacob, Max, and his puppets, 440
Jacques, 343
Japan, doll festivals in, 204–211; doll-making in, 166; funeral sacrifices in, images substituted for, 87; image magic for revenge in, 61; puppet theatres in, 386 *sqq.*, influence of, on live actors, 430; rag-doll amulets of, 54; shadow theatre of, 351
Jaufental family, the, Christmas crib of, 280
Java, marionettes in, 390–392; the shadow-play in, 352 *sqq.*, influence of, in the West, 382, 415
Jester—*see* Buffoon
*Jolie catin, la,* 262
Josserand, Louis, and the Guignol of Lyons, 343
Judas dolls, 246
Judy, introduction of, 324
Jugglers, puppets shown by, 300–301, 302
Jumeau and Son, movable necks for dolls invented by, 155
Jupiter Ammon, statue of, with movable head, 252

Kadiueo dolls, 214
Käferlin, Anna, doll's house of, 120
Kager, Mathias, 117
Kaiserberg, Geiler von, 110, 111
Kändler, Johann, modeller of Meissen figures, and his followers, 228–229; a porcelain table set by, 267
*Karagödschi,* the, 363, 364
Karagöz, the Turkish, 303, history of, 362–363, 364
Karaya dolls, 214

Karberg, Bruno, Javanese-style shadow theatre of, 382
Kaspar, 442
Kasperl Larifari, of Pocci, 339
Kasperle, 316, 321, 334; books on, by Bonus and Böcklin, 404; derivation of, 304; remodelled by Küper, 333–334
Kasperle theatre, the, 312, 316, 318; on the Dvina during the War, 444 *sqq.*; value of, to children, 397–398, 404
Kaulitz, Marion, doll artist, 183–184
Kempelen, Wolfgang von, automata of, 263
*Kerutjil,* the, type of Javanese marionette-play, 390
Khodinskoie Plain, giant figures in a procession on, 255
Kieninger, Johann, mountain crib made by, 283–284
Kings and notables in waxwork shows, 93–94
Klamrot, Anton, tin-soldier museum of, 297
*Klaubauf,* the, 249
Kleinhempel, Fritz and Erich, character dolls of, 180
*Kletzenkrampus,* the, 249
*Kletzenmännlein,* the, 249
Knights Templars, the, and the alleged idol Baphomet, 67
*Kobold* (puppet), the, 300
Koch, Rüttmann, and Bartosch, shadow-play film of, 383
Koenig, Marie, ethnographical dolls collected by, 201
*Komödienbüchlein* (Pocci), 338
Konewka, —, silhouette artist, 370
Kopeckj, Matthias, 325
Koran, the, on idol-making, 36, 211
*Koroplastoi,* the, 106
*Korwars,* Papuan, 41–42
*Krampus,* the, 249
Krieger, Betty, costume dolls by, 219
Kruse, Käthe, dolls by, 184–186, 224
*Kui-lui,* Chinese marionettes, 384
Kunstwart, the, patron of the puppet-play, 397–398
Küper, —, and his puppets, 333–334

La Grille, —, marionette-operas produced by, 312
La Tène period, metal warrior figurines of, 34; votive images of, 68
Lafleur, 343
*Lares* and *penates,* the, 38–39, 109
Lay figures, 96 *sqq.*
Lazarski, Mme, 198

# INDEX

Steatopygy in idols, 28–29
Steiff, Margarethe, and her cloth dolls, 170
Stick figures and dolls, 29, 34, 235, 244, 249
Stone Age centres of idol statuary, 30–33
Strasbourg Cathedral, clock automata of, 259
Strettwag, the bronze chariot of, warrior dolls in, 291
Styria, Christmas cribs in, 276
Sudan, the, dolls in, 29, 217
Sumatra, ancestor images of, 42; guardian dolls of, 63; the Perminak in, 54
Sutradhara, the, 299–300
Switzerland, folk pastimes of, dolls in 245–246; image magic in, 58, 88; lake dwellings of, dolls' utensils in, 103; the marionette theatre in, 418–421; prehistoric figurines in, 28
Syrian form of shadow-figures, 361

TABLE sets, porcelain, famous examples of, 267–268
Tableaux given with puppets, 266
Tableaux vivants and puppet-shows, 266
Tadema (scarecrows), derivation of the term, 243
Takemoto Chikuyo Gidayu, marionette theatre founded by, 388
Tale of Nauplius, The, the automatic play produced by Philo of Byzantium, 256–257
Tale of a Tub (Jonson), a shadow-play in, 365
Talismans, 43, 53 sqq.; the idea involved in, 56
Tallsack, the, and its fair, 249
Tanagra figures, 81 sqq.; considered as grave images, 81 sqq.; German figures compared with, 231–232
Tangarva, image of, 47
Tankards, trick, in doll form, 238–239
Tapa doll, the, 65
Taschner, Ignatius, 408; puppet-heads by, 406
Tatermann, the, 300, 309
Tea-cosy dolls, 218, 247
Teatro dei Piccoli, Rome, 424 sqq.
Teddy-bear dolls, 218
Teschner, Richard, puppet theatre of, Oriental influence on, 415–418
Théâtre d'Art, the, 370
Théâtre Érotique de la Rue de la Santé, 346
Theatres, use of dolls in, 245
Theatrum mundi, the, 261, 266
Thirteenth-century writers on the puppet-play, 300

Thoma, Hans, 414
Thorwaldsen, B., and his dough-cake figure, 248
Thüringer ware, dolls of, 234
Tietz, Hermann, 183
Tiki images, Maori, 44
Tilting toys, 288–289
Tin soldiers, 287–297; ancestry and evolution of, 27, 290, 293; in Andersen's fairy-tales, 250; exhibitions of, 297; makers and vendors of, 261, 292 sqq.; in museums and collections, 297; Prussian models of, 296–297
Tippoo Sahib, tiger automaton of, 263
Tirol, the, Christmas cribs in, 276, 280, 282 sqq.
Titero, the, mentioned in Don Quixote, 311
Toby, the dog, 312, 317
Tocha, Tocke, or Docke, early German for 'doll,' 110–111; identified with mima, 300
Togo, clay dolls in, 217
Torriani, Giovanni, male automaton of, 260; marionettes of, 309–310
Toy armies, made for French kings, 292; makers of, 292 sqq.
Toy dolls, ancient Egyptian, 104–105; English, 128, 155, 156, 158–160; exhibitions and collections of, 187–201; French, 122–127, 130–132, 155, 160–162, 166–170, 176; German, 105, 110 sqq., 128, 132–133, 154, 162–166, 178, 180, 182–186; Greek and Trojan, 105, 106–108; historical development of, 24; of Hopi Indians, 103; Indian, 104; modern American, 216; Roman, 108–109
Toy soldiers, materials used for, 288, 289, 290, 291, 292, 293, 294. See also Tin soldiers
Toys, wooden, designers of, 180, 182
Tragant, 267
Transylvania, the doll in festivals of, 246
Travaglia, Pietro, puppets by, 319
Treu, Michael Daniel, puppet theatre of, repertoire of, 314
Trinkets, in human form, 240–242
Troy, dolls, idols, and figurines found at, 26, 30, 33, 39, 105, 112, 287
Tumbling doll, Chinese, 204
Turkish shadow-play, the, 361, 362–364
Tussaud, Mme, and her waxworks, 94–95
Tut-ench-Amun, death image of, 96; dress figure of, ibid.

521

# DOLLS AND PUPPETS

Printed in the USA
CPSIA information can be obtained
at www.ICGtesting.com
LVHW091542260124
769820LV00001B/3